Instructor's Resource Manual

Marketing:

Concepts and Strategies

William M. Pride

Texas A & M University

O. C. Ferrell

Colorado State University

HOUGHTON MIFFLIN COMPANY   BOSTON   NEW YORK

V.P., Editor-in-Chief: **George T. Hoffman**
Associate Sponsoring Editor/Development Manager: **Susan M. Kahn**
Editorial Assistant: **Amy Galvin**
Manufacturing Coordinator: **Chuck Dutton**
Executive Marketing Manager: **Steven W. Mikels**

Printed in the U.S.A.

ISBN: 0-618-47448-X

123456789-EB-09 08 07 06 05

CONTENTS

Transition Guide

A GUIDE FOR INSTRUCTORS WHO ARE SWITCHING TO PRIDE/FERRELL *MARKETING: CONCEPTS AND STRATEGIES* 13/E

To help with your course preparation, we have compiled the following list of major text changes and a list of chapter-by-chapter changes.

MAJOR CHANGES FOR THIS EDITION

Marketing: Concepts and Strategies is a comprehensive exploration of the concepts, theories, and practices on which the field of marketing is based. This edition is revised and updated to address the dynamic issues emerging in the current technology-driven environment, and to still stress the importance of traditional marketing issues. These revisions assist students in gaining a full understanding of marketing practices pertinent today and helping them anticipate increasing future changes.

- *Consolidation of strategic planning and implementation.* The chapter on implementing and controlling marketing strategies has moved to the front of the text and consolidated with Chapter 2 on planning marketing strategy. This should help students recognize that strategic planning is a comprehensive process that requires implementation and control in order to be successful.

- *Changes in the treatment of E-marketing and customer relationship management.* The chapter about marketing on the Internet has been moved forward in the text and combined with our discussion of customer relationship management. This chapter has also been updated to reflect new trends in the constantly changing environment of the Internet. This allows for greater integration of technology into the discussion of marketing mix elements throughout the remainder of the text.

- *New illustrations and examples.* All new advertisements from well-known firms are employed to illustrate chapter topics. Experiences of real-world companies are used to exemplify marketing concepts and strategies throughout the text. Most of these examples are new. Others have been updated or expanded.

CHANGES IN EVERY CHAPTER

- *Opening vignettes.* All of the chapter opening vignettes are new. They are written to introduce the theme of each chapter by focusing on actual companies and how they deal with real-world situations.

- *Boxed features.* Each chapter includes two of the four types of boxed features that highlight important themes: "Building Customer Relationships," "Ethics and Social Responsibility," "Tech Know," and "Global Marketing." All of the boxed features are new in this edition.

- *New Snapshot features.* All 22 Snapshot features are new and engage students by highlighting interesting, up-to-date statistics that link marketing theory to the real world.

- *End-of-chapter cases.* Each chapter contains two cases, including a video case. A number of video cases are new to this edition, profiling a firm to illustrate concrete application of marketing strategies and concepts. Each case has three or four questions to test students' comprehension of the major issues.

- *End-of-part Strategic Cases.* There are eight end-of-part strategic cases, three of them new and the others updated, that incorporate issues found throughout all the chapters in each part. Students are required to integrate the content of these multiple chapters to answer the questions at the end of each case. Companies profiled in these cases include *USA Today*, Mattel, FedEx, Reebok, XM Satellite Radio, Home Depot, Bass Pro Shops, and Napster.

CHAPTER-BY-CHAPTER CHANGES

Part One: Marketing Strategy and Customer Relationships

Chapter 1: An Overview of Strategic Marketing

Revisions

- Opening Vignette about King's Saddlery and King Ropes replaces vignette about competition in the video game industry

- Snapshot "Wireless dialing in U.S." replaces "Average U.S. family earned $63,410"

- Video Case 1.1 "Finagle A Bagel" replaces "Harte-Hanks Provides Customer Relationship Management Services"

- Case 1.2 "Indy Racing League vs. Open Wheel Racing Series: Who Will Win the Race?" replaces "Montgomery Ward: The Rise and Fall of an American Retailing Icon"

Additions

- Building Customer Relationships box "The Perils of Using Celebrities in Advertising"

- Global Marketing box "Gruma Tortillas Folds up U.S. Market"

Deletions

- Global Marketing box "Chupa Chups: Sweetening the World, One Country at a Time"

- Building Customer Relationships box "Home Depot Develops Relationships with Its Customers"

Chapter 2: Planning, Implementing, and Controlling Marketing Strategies

This chapter consolidates Chapters 2 and 22 from the 12th edition.

Revisions

- Opening Vignette about Fiji Natural Artisan Bottled Water replaces vignette about Kimberly-Clark's marketing strategy to promote paper towels

- Subsection on SWOT analysis moves into section on assessing organizational resources and opportunities

- Snapshot "Buying downloads instead of CDs" replaces "Executives note hot business topics"

- Key term *marketing objectives* moves into section on establishing an organizational mission and goals

- Section on implementing marketing strategies moves from old Chapter 22

- Subsection on approaches to marketing implementation (including internal marketing and total quality management) moves from old Chapter 22

- Subsection on organizing marketing activities (including organizing by functions, products, regions, and types of customers) moves from old Chapter 22

- Subsection on controlling marketing activities (including establishing performance standards, evaluating actual performance, taking corrective action, and problems in controlling marketing activities) moves from old Chapter 22

- Numerous key terms move from old Chapter 22

- Figure 2.5 "The Marketing Control Process" moves from old Chapter 22

- Video Case 2.1 "The Global Expansion of Subway Sandwich Shops" (previously Video Case 5.1) is updated and replaces "Buzzsaw.com: Building Strategically on the Web"

- Case 2.2 "Saturn: A Different Kind of Company. A Different Kind of Car," is updated

Additions
- Ethics and Social Responsibility box "Recycling Disposable Cameras"

- Building Customer Relationships box "Red Bull Energizes Sales with Stimulating Marketing Strategy"

Deletions
- Subsection on growth strategies for business units, including old Figure 2.4 "Competitive Growth Strategies"

- Table 2.1 "Matching the Marketing Mix to Intensive Growth Strategies"

- Subsection on components of the marketing plan

- Figure 2.5 "The Marketing Planning Cycle"

- Building Customer Relationships box "Renaissance Pen Company: Developing the Write Marketing Strategy"

- Building Customer Relationships box "Pro Bowling Goes High-Tech"

Strategic Case 1
"*USA Today*: The Nation's Newspaper" is updated

Part Two: The Global Environment and Social and Ethical Responsibilities

Chapter 3: The Marketing Environment

Revisions

- Opening Vignette about Porsche replaces vignette about FedEx

- Snapshot "Most frequent consumer fraud complaints" replaces "Cost of federal regulations"

- Video Case 3.1 "Netscape Navigates a Changing Environment" is updated

- Case 3.2 "Frito-Lay Adapts to Changes in the Environment" replaces "Microsoft Versus the U.S. Government"

Additions

- Ethics and Social Responsibility box "Is Sharing Music and Movie Files Ethical?"

- Tech Know box "Cellphones: Technology Fuels Competition"

Deletions

- Global Marketing box "India 3.0"

- Marketing Citizenship box "Legal Issues at Wal-Mart"

Chapter 4: Social Responsibility and Ethics in Marketing

Revisions

- Opening Vignette about the Better Business Bureau replaces vignette about Tomra's rePlanet recycling program

- Snapshot "Fueling up with hydrogen technology" replaces "How often we help the environment"

- Video Case 4.1 "New Belgium Brewing Company" is updated

- Case 4.2 "Scandal at Martha Stewart Living Omnimedia Inc." replaces "Danger on the Highway: Bridgestone/Firestone's Tire Recall"

Additions

- Table 4.1 "Best Corporate Citizens"

- Ethics and Social Responsibility box "Has Wal-Mart Become Too Powerful?"

- Ethics and Social Responsibility box "Qwest Struggles with Legal Issues"

Deletions

- Table 4.1 "A Sampling of Socially Responsible Marketers"

- Marketing Citizenship box "Worldwise, Inc., Turns Green into Green"

- Marketing Citizenship box "Royal Caribbean Cleans Up"

Chapter 5: Global Markets and International Marketing

Revisions

- Opening Vignette about Starbucks replaces vignette about recording artist Shakira

- Trade and economic statistics are updated

- Table 5.2 "A Comparative Economic Analysis of Canada, Switzerland, and the United States" is updated

- Statistics in section "Regional Trade Alliances, Markets, and Agreements" are updated

- Subsection on the North American Free Trade Agreement is expanded and updated

- Snapshot "Where's the beef going?" replaces "Top U.S. cigarette importers"

- Table 5.4 "The Ten Largest Global Corporations" (previously Table 5.3) is updated

- Video Case 5.1 "BMW International" replaces "The Global Expansion of Subway Restaurants"

- Case 5.2 "Gillette Company" replaces "Dat'l Do-It Cooks Up Hot Exports"

Additions

- Global Marketing box "Supersizing Europeans"

- Table 5.3 "The Ten Largest Global Franchisers"

- Global Marketing box "Chupa Chups: Sweetening the World, One Country at a Time" (previously in Chapter 1)

Deletions

- Global Marketing box "Heinz's Global Success"

- Global Marketing box "Universal Studios Goes to Japan"

Strategic Case 2

"Mattel Takes on Global Challenges" is new

Part Three: Using Technology and Information to Build Customer Relationships

Chapter 6: E-Marketing and Customer Relationship Management

This chapter was previously Chapter 23 in the 12th edition and has been significantly revised to accommodate its new location.

Revisions

- Opening Vignette about Google replaces vignette about eBay

- Entire chapter is reorganized and updated
- Key term *database* is moved from Chapter 7
- Section on E-marketing strategies is streamlined due to earlier location in text
- Snapshot "Millions logging onto dating sites" replaces "West Coast Cities Most Wired"
- Section on legal and ethical issues in e-marketing is updated to reflect new statistics and legislation
- Video Case 6.1 "4SURE.com Targets Business Customers" is updated
- Case 6.2 "eBay Auctions Everything" replaces "Napster: Copyright Infringement or Technological Breakthrough"

Additions

- Building Customer Relationships box "Harris Poll Uses Internet to Survey Customers"
- Table 6.1 "Internet Use Around the World, by Selected Country"
- Table 6.2 "Types of Advertising on Websites" (previously was text in Chapter 23)
- Section on customer relationship management
- Ethics and Social Responsibility box "Europe Takes the Lead in Privacy Protection"
- Table 6.3 "Common Reactions to Spam"

Deletions

- Figure 23.1 "The Projected Growth of e-Commerce Worldwide"
- Table 23.1 "A Dot-Com Graveyard"
- Key terms *hypertext, Uniform Resource Locator (URL), banner ads, click-through rate, keyword ads, button ads, pop-up ads, pop-under ads,* and *sponsorship ads*
- Global Marketing box "Mexico's PRI Party Woos Younger Voters"
- Marketing Citizenship box "TRUSTe: 'Building a Web You Can Believe In'"

Chapter 7: Marketing Research and Information Systems

This chapter was previously Chapter 6 in the 12th edition.

Revisions

- Opening Vignette about VNU replaces vignette about Procter & Gamble's marketing research
- Snapshot "Popularity of sport drinks" replaces "Minority buying power"
- Table 7.1 "Internal Sources of Secondary Data" is revised
- Table 7.2 "External Sources of Secondary Data" is revised
- Table 7.4 "Resources for Marketing Information" is updated
- Table 7.6 "Top Marketing Research Firms" is updated

- Internet Exercise "World Association of Opinion and Marketing Research Professionals" replaces "American Demographics' Marketing Tools Directory"

- Video Case 7.1 "IRI Provides Marketing Research Data from Multiple Sources" is updated

- Case 7.2 "A Look-Look at Youth Trends" is updated

Additions

- Ethics and Social Responsibility box "Burger King's Relationship with Coke Fizzles After Marketing Research Debacle"

- Building Customer Relationships box "Reality TV or Marketing Research"

Deletions

- Key term *database* is moved to Chapter 6

- Building Customer Relationships box "Anthropologists Unearth Marketing Secrets"

- Tech*Know box "Mining Data"

Strategic Case 3

"FedEx Corporation" is new

Part Four: Target Markets and Customer Behavior

Chapter 8: Target Markets: Segmentation and Evaluation

This chapter was previously Chapter 7 in the 12th edition.

Revisions

- Opening Vignette about the Disney Channel replaces vignette about Nokia

- Snapshot "More are choosing to live alone" replaces "Marital status of women"

- Video Case 8.1 "BuyandHold.com Is Bullish on Smaller Investors" is updated

- Case 8.2 "IKEA Targets Do-It-Yourselfers" replaces "LifeSprint Targets Seniors with a Taste for Nutrition"

Additions

- Building Customer Relationships box "The New American Household"

- Building Customer Relationships box "Understanding Mature Customers"

- Figure 8.4 "Spending Levels of Three Age Groups or Selected Product Categories"

- Figure 8.6 "VALS™ Types and Sports Preferences"

Deletions

- Global Marketing box "Harlem Globetrotters Target Families Around the World"

- Building Customer Relationships box "Who Is the NASCAR Customer?"
- Figure 7.4 "Spending Levels of Two Age Groups of Selected Product Categories"

Chapter 9: Consumer Buying Behavior

This chapter was previously Chapter 8 in the 12th edition.

Revisions

- Opening Vignette about Marketing addressing the issue of "Cool" replaces the vignette about McDonald's new food tastes
- Snapshot "When do Americans shop?" replaces "Frugality begins at home"
- Discussion of *subcultures* under the subsection "Culture and Subcultures" is modified
- Subsection "African-American Subculture" is updated
- Subsection "Hispanic Subculture" is updated
- Video Case 9.1 "Building Customer Experiences at Build-A-Bear" is updated
- Case 9.2 "AutoTrader.com Fuels Online Buying of Used Cars" replaces "Marketing to Women: A Lucrative Direction for Automakers"

Additions

- Building Customer Relationships box "Observing Customers in Their Native Habitats"
- Building Customer Relationships box "One Nation, Many Subcultures"

Deletions

- Tech*Know box "Makeover for Online Beauty Sites"
- Marketing Citizenship box "Battling Unethical Consumer Behavior"

Chapter 10: Business Markets and Buying Behavior

This chapter was previously Chapter 9 in the 12th edition.

Revisions

- Opening Vignette about Brighton replaces vignette about Sodexho Marriott
- Snapshot "What do buyers earn?" replaces "Executives rate customer service"
- The data in Table 10.1 "Number of Establishments and Industry Growth" are updated
- Table 10.2 "Spending by Various Types of Governments" is updated
- Video Case 10.1 "VIPdesk Brings Concierge Services to Business Markets" replaces "Oracle Meets the Challenges of Serving Business Customers"
- Case 10.2 "WebMD Delivers Online Services to Health Care Providers" replaces the case entitled "Resellers Sweet on Jo's Candies"

Additions

- Ethics and Social Responsibility box "Is It Ethical to Buy Business from Your Customers?"
- Tech Know box "Online Auctions Click with Businesses"

Deletions

- Tech*Know box "Digging Deeper into Buying Behavior"
- Global Marketing box "Developing Business in Developing Countries"

Strategic Case 4

"Reebok Races into the Urban Market" is new

Part Five: Product Decisions

Chapter 11: Product Concepts

This chapter was previously Chapter 10 in the 12th edition.

Revisions

- Opening Vignette about McDonald's McGriddle replaces vignette about Windy Conditions Kite Systems
- Snapshot "Is photographic film in the decline stage?" replaces "Making cars faster, smoother, exotic"
- New examples are included in Table 11.3 "Product Successes and Failures"
- Video Case 11.1 "Sony's PlayStation Plays On and On" is updated
- Case 11.2 "Dell Mixes It Up with Computers, Electronics, and More" replaces "Schwinn: Reviving a Classic American Brand"

Additions

- Tech Know box "Nokia: Phone Fun and Games"
- Building Customer Relationships box "Kodak Pictures a Digital Future"

Deletions

- Building Customer Relationships box "Revitalizing a Maturing Brand"
- Marketing Citizenship box "From a Joke to a Successful Product"

Chapter 12: Developing and Managing Products

This chapter was previously Chapter 11 in the 12th edition.

Revisions

- Opening Vignette about Segway replaces vignette about Campbell Soup Company

- Snapshot "Generating product ideas" replaces "More workers involved in virtual work"
- Table 12.1 has been revised to reflect changes in the most popular test markets
- Video Case 12.1 "Cali Cosmetics Positions Products with Olive Oil" is revised
- Case 12.2 "Using the 3Rs to Drive Product Innovation at 3M" replaces "Can Pepsi Make Pepsi One the One?"

Additions

- Ethics and Social Responsibility box "Lying to Customers"
- Building Customer Relationships box "General Motors Takes Slow-Selling Products Off the Road"

Deletions

- Building Customer Relationships box "Modifying Trucks with a Woman's Touch"
- Building Customer Relationships box "Weaving Product Quality: Longaberger Company"

Chapter 13: Branding and Packaging

This chapter was previously chapter 12 in the 12th edition.

Revisions

- Opening Vignette about Brand Mascots replaces vignette about the Nike trademark
- Snapshot "Consumers often choose the store brand" replaces "Kids' top brand picks"
- Table 13.1 "The World's Most Valuable Brands" is updated
- The discussion about Labeling is updated to include coverage of the new nutritional labeling requirements regarding trans fatty acids
- Video Case 13.1 "PlumpJack Winery Pours Out Cork Controversy" is revised
- Case 13.2 "Harley Davidson Brand Roars into Its Second Century" replaces "Hearts on Fire: Branding the Symbol of Commitment"

Additions

- Building Customer Relationships box "The Power of Private Distributor Brands"
- Tech Know box "Technology Brings Eye-Catching Colors to Packaging "

Deletions

- Building Customer Relationships box "3Com Reboots Its Brand"
- Tech*Know box "The Tricky Art of Online Co-Branding"

Chapter 14: Services Marketing

This chapter was previously Chapter 13 in the 12th edition.

Revisions

- Opening Vignette about Nickelodeon replaces vignette about Royal Caribbean's customer service

- Snapshot "Internet + personal contact = financial services" replaces "Services that adults use most"

- Video Case 14.1 "The New Wave of Marketing at New England Aquarium" replaces "Merrill Lynch Direct Logs On to Online Trading"

- Case 14.2 "AARP Strengthens Its Brand and Services" is updated

Additions

- Building Customer Relationships box "Segmentation Blurred by Combining Marketing Efforts in Car Rental Services"

- Ethics and Social Responsibility box "Nonprofits Benefit from Savvy"

Deletions

- Building Customer Relationships box "USAA's Personalized Service Keeps Customers Loyal"

- Marketing Citizenship box "Is It Ethnical to Market Sex-Selection Services?"

Strategic Case 5

"Radio Goes Sky-High at XM Satellite Radio" is new

Part Six: Distribution Decisions

Chapter 15: Marketing Channels and Supply Chain Management

This chapter was previously Chapter 14 in the 12th edition.

Revisions

- Opening Vignette about Hard Rock Café replaces vignette about Polo Ralph Lauren's website

- Snapshot "Intensive distribution of sports drinks" replaces "Where books were purchased in 2000"

- Video Case 15.1 "Smarter Channel Management at SmarterKids" replaces "CommercialWare Powers Multiple Channels for Retailers"

- Case 15.2 "Grainger Wires the Channel for Business Products" is revised

Additions

- Tech Know box "U.S. Armed Forces Revamp Their Supply-Chain Management Strategies"

- Building Customer Relationships box "Partnering with Channel Members"

Deletions

- Building Customer Relationships box " Using Supply Chain Management at Barnes & Noble"

- Tech*Know box "Office Depot Links Multiple Channels"

Chapter 16: Wholesaling and Physical Distribution

This chapter was previously Chapter 15 in the 12th edition.

Revisions

- Opening Vignette about Skechers replaces vignette about Homestore.com's real estate website

- Snapshot "Consolidation among beer wholesalers" replaces "Reach out and touch someone"

- The proportional costs of the physical distribution function shown in Figure 16.3 are updated

- Figure 16.4 "The Portion of Intercity Freight Paid By Various Transportation Modes" is revised

- Video Case 16.1 "Quick International Courier Delivers Time-Sensitive Shipments" is updated

- Case 16.2 "Wal-Mart Competes Using Efficient, Low-Cost Physical Distribution" is updated

Additions

- Tech Know box "TAL Manages JCPenney Shirt Inventory"

- Global Marketing box "How OshKosh B'Gosh Brings Bib Overalls from Abroad"

Deletions

- Global Marketing box "Selecting Distributors for Global Markets"

- Building Customer Relationships box "FedEx Custom Critical Coddles Customers"

Chapter 17: Retailing and Direct Marketing

This chapter was previously Chapter 16 in the 12th edition.

Revisions

- Opening Vignette about Krispy Kreme replaces vignette about JCPenney's focus on online retailing

- Snapshot "It's in the mail" replaces "How often and where do we shop?"

- The section on Non-store Retailing and Direct Marketing is reorganized and revised

- The telemarketing section is revised to include coverage of the do-not-call registry

- Table 17.2 "Top 20 Franchises and Their Startup Costs" is expanded and updated

- Video Case 17.1 "REI Scales New Heights in Retailing" replaces "1-800-Flowers Keeps Its Business in Bloom"

- Case 17.2 "Costco Offers Low Prices and a Unique Product Mix" replaces "Whole Foods Grows Up"

Additions

- Tech Know box "Dell Builds PCs and Profits Through Direct Marketing"

- Global Marketing box "Fueling Customers in Thailand with Gas, Coffee, and Convenience"

Deletions

- Tech*Know box "How Stores Are Battling Online Rivals"
- Global Marketing box "Country-by-Country Differences in Online Shopping"

Strategic Case 6

"The Home Depot Reinforces Its Strong Channel Strategy" is new

Part Seven: Promotion Decisions

Chapter 18: Integrated Marketing Communications

This chapter was previously Chapter 17 in the 12th edition.

Revisions

- Opening Vignette about Jones Soda Company's Turkey & Gravy Soda replaces vignette about sports marketing
- Snapshot "Consumers prefer custom messages" replaces "Online advertising in the United States"
- Video Case 18.1 "Jordan's Furniture" replaces "Brainshark Enhances Promotional Messages"
- Case 18.2 "Carb Wars: New Diets Turn the Food Industry Upside Down" replaces "PETsMART: Reinforcing the Bond Between Humans and Their Pets"

Additions

- Building Customer Relationships box "Rivals Team Up to Advertise Cereal"
- Table 18.2 "Product Categories with Greatest Distribution of Coupons"
- Key term *buzz marketing*
- Ethics and Social Responsibility box "Truth in Advertising"

Deletions

- Marketing Citizenship box "Cause Branding at Timberland"
- Tech*Know box "Guerilla Marketing with Buddy Lee"
- Table 17.2 "Characteristics of Coupons and Coupon Redemption"

Chapter 19: Advertising and Public Relations

This chapter was previously Chapter 18 in the 12th edition.

Revisions

- Opening Vignette about Apple's iPod and iTunes replaces vignette about how large companies are embracing the Internet for advertising

- Snapshot "Categories of biggest Internet advertisers" replaces "Who watches Super Bowl ads?"

- Table 19.1 "Twenty Leading National Advertisers" is updated

- Table 19.2 "Total Advertising Expenditures" is updated

- Table 19.3 "Characteristics, Advantages, and Disadvantages of Major Advertising Media" is updated

- The ad used to illustrate the components of a print advertisement is new

- Internet Exercise "LEGO Company" replaces "Turbonium.com"

- Video Case 19.1 "Vail Resorts Uses Public Relations to Put Out a Fire" replaces "The Ups and Downs of Dot-Com Advertising"

- Case 19.2 "Microsoft: Crafting Image Through Public Relations" is updated

Additions

- Building Customer Relationships box "Remodeling Advertising Messages"

- Building Customer Relationships box "PR Battles"

Deletions

- Tech*Know box "New Takes on Television Advertising"

- Building Customer Relationships box "Is Sex Effective in Advertising?"

Chapter 20: Personal Selling and Sales Promotion

This chapter was previously Chapter 19 in the 12th edition.

Revisions

- Opening Vignette about McDonald's sales promotion replaces vignette about Whirlpool

- Building Customer Relationships box "Whirlpool Puts Salespeople in the 'Real Whirled'" is updated and was previously the chapter's opening vignette

- Snapshot "What's in it for me?" replaces "Why good workers leave"

- Subsection "Motivating Salespeople" is revised

- The sales promotion sections are significantly reorganized

- Section "Consumer Sales Promotion Methods" is revised

- Section "Trade Sales Promotion Methods" is revised

- Video Case 20.1 "Selling Bicycles and More at Wheelworks" is updated

- Case 20.2 "IBM Reorganizes to Improve Selling Solutions" replaces "Sales Promotion Puts the Fizz into Dr Pepper"

Additions

- Ethics and Social Responsibility box "Responsible Selling Improves Customer Relationships"
- Table 20.1 "Average Salaries for Sales Representatives and Executives"
- Figure 20.2 "Effect of Income on Coupon Usage"
- Figure 20.3 "Effect of Age on Coupon Usage"

Deletions

- Building Customer Relationships box "Sales Promotion Builds Share for McDonald's"
- Global Marketing box "Global Marketers Put Sampling to Work"
- Key term *count-and-recount*

Strategic Case 7

"Bass Pro Shops Reels Them In with Sales Promotion" is revised, updated, and moved from Part 4 in the 12th edition

Part Eight: Pricing Decisions

Chapter 21: Pricing Concepts

This chapter was previously Chapter 20 in the 12th edition.

Revisions

- Opening Vignette about CD prices replaces vignette about personal computer price wars
- Snapshot "How much is that book?" replaces "Few drivers yielding to gas costs"
- Video Case 21.1 "JetBlue's Flight Plan for Profitability" is updated
- Case 20.1 "Priceline.com Lets Customers Set Prices" is updated

Additions

- Building Customer Relationships box "The Ups and Downs of Beef Prices"
- Building Customer Relationships box "Inside the PC Price War"

Deletions

- Building Customer Relationships box "Do Low Prices Build e-Loyalty?"
- Marketing Citizenship box "Protecting Brand Name Drug Prices"

Chapter 22: Setting Prices

This chapter was previously Chapter 21 in the 12th edition.

Revisions

- Opening Vignette about toy prices replaces vignette about Family Dollar Stores

- Snapshot "Would you pay top dollar?" replaces "Every penny counts at the pump"

- Internet Exercise about T-Mobile replaces exercise about VoiceStream

- Video Case 22.1 "Pricing for New Balance" replaces "VIPdesk.com: At Your Service at a Reasonable Price" (now Case 10.1)

- Case 22.2 "General Motors Tries to Reduce Reliance on Rebates" replaces "Apple iMac: Byting into Pricing"

Additions

- Building Customer Relationships box "Wireless Companies Ring Up Competitive Pricing Strategies"

- Building Customer Relationships box "Family Dollar Stores' Strategy Is Driven by Everyday Low Prices"

Deletions

- Global Marketing box "De Beers Polishes Prestige Pricing"

- Tech*Know box "Using Software to Set Prices"

Strategic Case 8

"Napster 2.0: The Cat Is Back" replaces "Blockbuster Puts the Spotlight on Pricing"

To the Instructor

The *Instructor's Resource Manual* contains a variety of teaching aids for *Marketing: Concepts and Strategies*, by William M. Pride and O. C. Ferrell. We designed this manual to assist instructors as much as possible in teaching basic marketing courses.

Chapter Teaching Aids

For each chapter there is a teaching resources quick reference guide, a purpose and perspective section, a guide for using color transparencies, a lecture outline, teaching transparency masters, suggested answers to text discussion and review questions, and comments on the cases.

The **quick reference guide** that opens each set of chapter materials in the *Instructor's Resource Manual* will help you easily identify and locate the resources available to aid you in presenting the chapter material to your class.

The **purpose and perspective** section gives an overview of the major topics covered in this chapter. We state why the chapter is included and how it fits into the total framework. This section is an introduction, not a summary.

The **guide for using color transparencies** gives suggestions for appropriate ways to use the transparencies while presenting chapter materials in class. The transparencies are identified to show whether they appear within the textbook or are additional illustrations. For example, transparencies that repeat illustrations from the text are identified according to the double-number label provided in the textbook (such as Figure 2.1). Illustrations that are not directly from the text are labeled with a chapter number reference and alphabet label (such as Figure 2A).

For each chapter, we also include a **lecture outline** that can be used in a variety of ways. Besides basing lectures on the outlines, you may want to supplement or correlate the outlined topics with your own lecture materials. The lecture outlines also can be used for a quick review of the topics covered in the chapter. Cross references to the boxed features in the text and to the color transparencies are provided within the outline for your convenience.

Several teaching **transparency masters** (two class exercises, a debate issue, and a chapter quiz) are included for every chapter. The primary intent of the class exercises is to encourage students to apply key terms from the text in actual business settings. A secondary intent is to provide students with opportunities to participate in classroom discussion, which will enhance their communication skills. Instructors who grade participation in the classroom may find these particularly useful. This manual contains the exercise objectives and possible answers. You may approach these exercises in at least the following three ways or some combination thereof:

1. **Small groups**. The class may be separated into groups of three to five students to discuss questions among themselves. After allowing time for small group discussion, call for representatives from the small groups for their conclusions. Debate or differences of opinion will facilitate students' learning the material. Requiring students to generate responses forces them to internalize the concepts. This method may be used with small or large classes and may be a useful way of creating involvement in larger classes where you cannot personally interact with all students.

2. **Class discussion.** When classes are small enough, or time is limited, these exercises can lead individual students to respond in class discussion. Depending on the makeup of the class and your instructional preferences, some questions may be geared for more individual responses.

3. **Class lectures.** Enough background material and suggestions are provided in the instructor's manual for these exercises to constitute full lectures. The discussion questions may be used to provoke thought and do not necessarily require verbal responses from students.

The key benefits of using these exercises are (1) variety in classroom experiences, (2) better learning and internalization of marketing concepts, and (3) enhancement of communication and social skills of students.

The suggested **answers to discussion and review questions** are not intended to be the *only* acceptable answers. We tried to develop the questions to encourage creative thinking, so some of the answers should be based on students' judgments and personal insights. Because many of our suggested answers are short and concise, you may want to examine additional dimensions in class.

Comments on the cases present additional information and suggestions that could be helpful when discussing the cases in class. We did not attempt to provide singular, optimal solutions to these cases. In fact, at times we discuss incorrect marketing decisions to help clarify the concepts covered in the text. In some instances it is easier to point out what went wrong than to formulate a strategy that guarantees success. The purpose of the questions at the end of the cases is to direct class discussions to relevant areas. For the video cases, information about the videos is provided.

The need for students to develop creativity and critical thinking is discussed, but seldom are there devices to encourage the development of decision skills. The **application questions** at the end of each text chapter are designed to help students develop critical thinking, creativity, and decision-making skills. They are structured to give students an appreciation of how the concepts and frameworks presented in the text are used in marketing decision making. The application questions require students to consider business situations in their community as well as nationally known businesses. Each question is developed from concepts or frameworks from the chapter in the text. They are general in nature but are specific in application to the specific location. Some of the questions involve problem solving in that they ask the student to "help" a manager make a marketing decision using the information available or using a "real world" business. This may require some analysis and observation of local business, or it may require that the student research a business or type of organization at the library or online. Other questions can be answered through group discussion or brainstorming exercises.

The process of answering these questions provides the opportunity for application of the text content. There are no specific "right" answers, but you can determine the degree to which the student has "correctly" applied the concepts and frameworks from the text. The answer should include an explanation of the marketing concept or framework, a brief description of the problem, alternative solutions, and a discussion of what "should be done." Students should be allowed to explore conventional solutions as well as unconventional methods so long as they support their reasoning. Remember that this is an exercise that encourages the students to think and be creative. Avoid looking for only one correct answer. You may remind them before assigning the questions that the methods developed in the text have been tested and proven to be effective, but that there may be better solutions or answers to the problems or questions presented.

The application questions may be assigned to be turned in at the beginning of the following class, in which case you can take the opportunity to evaluate the answers and provide written feedback. Provide more time as you deem necessary for these questions.

The questions could be assigned so that students present the answers in class. Presentation or discussion at the beginning of the class provides the students an opportunity to participate in class and promotes discussion in general. The more involved students are in the class, the more they will probably learn.

This is also another opportunity for other students to be exposed to different approaches to solving a problem. Discussion at the beginning of class may also allow the students to talk more freely about different answers. The student should be encouraged to become involved without the threat of being wrong. Focus on the logic and use of concepts in the text to reach a solution.

Another possible use of the application questions is to assign a question to different groups of students, instructing each to approach the question from a different perspective and support the approach. This allows you to set up a class debate on different marketing concepts or methods of solving problems. An in-class debate promotes participation by all and encourages critical evaluation of answers.

These are several possible uses of the application questions, and we encourage you to consider other uses as well. If a unique and effective use is discovered, please let us know, and we will share the ideas in future editions of the text.

Other Teaching Aids

This manual also includes a number of other teaching aids. In the beginning of the manual, we provide a transition guide to help instructors who are switching from the previous edition. There is a sample quarter syllabus, listing the chapters we recommend assigning on a quarter or shortened time-frame basis. We have also included a Video Easy-Reference Table providing key information about the videos that are available for each chapter.

In addition, there is a brief guide to using the Pride/Ferrell Marketing Learning Center on the Web. Each element in the Learning Center is described. Tips for getting started and special teaching suggestions for using the Web site are also provided.

At the end of this manual, we have provided three Appendices. Appendix A presents comments on the end-of-part strategic cases. Appendix B provides answers to the discussion and review questions that follow the financial analysis appendix in the text. Appendix C presents three role-play/simulation exercises to facilitate teamwork and critical thinking. Detailed notes on how these role-play exercises might be used in class are provided.

This manual is provided to help you teach from *Marketing: Concepts and Strategies*. Because we realize that instructors use many different approaches to teach basic marketing, we provide a comprehensive package of materials that satisfies a wide variety of instructional needs. Although you may not use all these materials, we hope this manual is of value to you. Your comments and suggestions are always welcome; they can help us significantly in developing a better set of instructional materials.

William M. Pride

O. C. Ferrell

Quarter Syllabus

As authors who teach the basic marketing course on a regular basis, we recognize that it is difficult for some professors to cover every chapter in the text. We view the 22 chapters as a menu for you to select from, based on your personal teaching philosophy for this course. For example, we customarily assign between 18 and 20 chapters for in-house lecture and discussion. Chapters not assigned as part of regular class meetings can be used as outside reading or reference. Because many professors have asked us what chapters we would assign on a quarter or shortened time-frame basis, we provide the following selection. These chapters are considered the most fundamental to understanding the basics of marketing if there is time for only 18 chapters to be covered in a term.

Chapter 1   An Overview of Strategic Marketing

Chapter 2   Planning, Implementing, and Controlling Marketing Strategies

Chapter 3   The Marketing Environment

Chapter 4   Social Responsibility and Ethics in Marketing

Chapter 6   E-Marketing and Customer Relationship Management

Chapter 7   Marketing Research and Information Systems

Chapter 8   Target Markets: Segmentation and Evaluation

Chapter 9   Consumer Buying Behavior

Chapter 10   Product Concepts

Chapter 12   Developing and Managing Products

Chapter 13   Branding and Packaging

Chapter 15   Marketing Channels and Supply Chain Management

Chapter 17   Retailing and Direct Marketing

Chapter 18   Integrated Marketing Communications

Chapter 19   Advertising and Public Relations

Chapter 20   Personal Selling and Sales Promotion

Chapter 21   Pricing Concepts

Chapter 22   Setting Prices

Video Easy-Reference Table

Chapter		Case and Video Titles	Length	Tape/ DVD Number	Segment Number
1	Case Title:	Finagle A Bagel			
	Company:	Finagle A Bagel	14:59	1	1
2	Case Title:	The Global Expansion of Subway Sandwich Shops			
	Company:	Subway	10:19	1	2
3	Case Title:	Netscape Navigates a Changing Environment			
	Company:	Netscape	5:58	1	3
4	Case Title:	New Belgium Brewing Company			
	Company:	New Belgium Brewing Company	10:00	1	4
5	Case Title:	BMW International			
	Company:	BMW International	12:38	1	5
6	Case Title:	4SURE.com Targets Business Customers			
	Company:	4SURE.com	1:59	1	6
7	Case Title:	IRI Provides Marketing Research Data from Multiple Sources			
	Company:	IRI	5:09	1	7
8	Case Title:	BuyandHold.com Is Bullish on Smaller Investors			
	Company:	BuyandHold.com	4:04	1	8
9	Case Title:	Building Customer Experiences at Build-A-Bear			
	Company:	Build-A-Bear	3:19	1	9
10	Case Title:	VIPdesk Brings Concierge Services to Business Markets			
	Company:	VIPdesk	5:24	1	10
11	Case Title:	Sony's PlayStation Plays On and On			
	Company:	Sony	1:45	2	11
12	Case Title:	Cali Cosmetics Positions Products with Olive Oil			
	Company:	Cali Cosmetics	2:29	2	12
13	Case Title:	PlumpJack Winery Pours Out Cork Controversy			
	Company:	PlumpJack Winery	2:20	2	13
14	Case Title:	The New Wave of Marketing at New England Aquarium			
	Company:	The New England Aquarium	11:09	2	14
15	Case Title:	Smarter Channel Management at SmarterKids			
	Company:	SmarterKids	4:29	2	15

16	*Case Title:*	Quick International Courier Delivers Time-Sensitive Shipments			
	Company:	Quick International Courier	4:13	2	16
17	*Case Title:*	REI Scales New Heights in Retailing			
	Company:	REI	12:45	2	17
18	*Case Title:*	Jordan's Furniture			
	Company:	Jordan's Furniture	15:30	2	18
19	*Case Title:*	Vail Resorts Uses Public Relations to Put Out a Fire			
	Company:	Vail Resorts	18:00	2	19
20	*Case Title:*	Selling Bicycles and More at Wheelworks			
	Company:	Wheelworks	9:53	2	20
21	*Case Title:*	JetBlue's Flight Plan for Profitability			
	Company:	JetBlue	6:10	2	21
22	*Case Title:*	Pricing for New Balance			
	Company:	New Balance	10:56	2	22

Guide to Using the Pride/Ferrell Marketing Learning Center

With this edition of Pride/Ferrell *Marketing: Concepts and Strategies*, we offer an enhanced edition of the successful Pride/Ferrell Marketing Learning Center, a one-stop guide to the world of online marketing. The objective of this material is twofold: (1) to get students to use the Internet for research and (2) to give students an opportunity to see how marketing can be conducted online. The Learning Center provides dynamic materials about marketing on the Internet; Internet Exercises for Chapters 1–22; links to marketing organizations, publications, and other information resources; interactive study materials; online key term and chapter review materials; Marketing Plan worksheets; and career information. The content of this webpage will be updated regularly to ensure that it keeps pace with the rapidly evolving Internet and continues to provide strong examples of the Internet as a marketing medium. As such, the Marketing Learning Center represents a unique opportunity to give students hands-on insight into this exciting medium.

GETTING STARTED

The Pride/Ferrell Marketing Learning Center is available on the Web at http://www.prideferrell.com./ Accessing this site requires a computer with a modem, web-browsing software (such as Netscape or Internet Explorer), and access to the Internet. Most university computer labs can satisfy the first two requirements, and faculty and student computer accounts fulfill the third. Your college or university's computer systems administrator can provide the specifics about logging on to your system and navigating the World Wide Web with the software available. The Marketing Learning Center can also be accessed through accounts on America Online, CompuServe, and other national computer information services, as well as local Internet service providers. Systems administrators for those services can provide specific information about logging on to their services and getting to the Marketing Learning Center webpage.

THE MARKETING LEARNING CENTER

http://www.prideferrell.com

The Marketing Learning Center consists of several elements:

Internet Exercises. This section of the Marketing Learning Center provides Internet-related exercises for each of the twenty-two chapters of the text. These exercises reinforce chapter concepts by guiding students to specific World Wide Web sites and asking them to evaluate the sites and their information from a marketing perspective. For example, students may be invited to go online with the American Marketing Association, read recent articles in *Business Ethics* magazine, observe online retailers, use *American Demographics* Power Tools, and learn about the goods and services of specific firms all while expanding their knowledge of marketing. The website will be updated regularly, so the exercises will change as dictated by the content of the webpages chosen. A guide to the answers of current exercises can be found in the instructor-related section of the website.

ACE Online Self-tests. These questions allow students to practice taking tests and get immediate scoring results.

e-Center Resources. This section contains links to a variety of marketing information resources, including marketing organizations, publications, and other information sources. This section will be continually updated.

Company links. Hot links to companies featured in the text are provided so that students can further their research and understanding of the marketing practices of these companies.

Online glossary and *chapter summary.* These sections help students review key concepts and definitions.

Marketing Plan worksheets. These worksheets take students step-by-step through the process of creating their own marketing plans. Along with the text discussion and sample marketing plan, this project helps students apply their knowledge of marketing theories.

Career Center. A downloadable Personal Career Plan Guide and links to various marketing careers websites will help students explore their options and plan their job searches.

Additionally, as mentioned, the Learning Center offers an instructor's section with resources for instructors, teaching suggestions, and more specific answers for the student exercises; these will change regularly to match updated exercises.

SUGGESTIONS FOR USING THE MARKETING LEARNING CENTER

Instructors can use the Pride/Ferrell Marketing Learning Center in a variety of ways. Many instructors have indicated that they devote class time to the topic of marketing on the Internet. Students can be assigned to complete Internet Exercises for each chapter you cover over the course of the semester. The exercises may be completed individually, with students handing in their answers on paper or emailing them to your university email box. Classes can also be divided into groups, with each group assigned an Internet Exercise as a group project to be presented to the rest of the class or prepared as a written or email report. In lieu of assigning the exercises, students may be required to write a paper evaluating one or more websites as to how they illustrate the marketing concepts described in the assigned chapter. Students should also be directed to use the e-Center Resources for class work and research.

CHAPTER 1

An Overview of Strategic Marketing

TEACHING RESOURCES QUICK REFERENCE GUIDE

Resource	Location
Purpose and Perspective	IRM, p. 1
Guide for Using Color Transparencies	IRM, p. 2
Lecture Outline	IRM, p. 2
Notes for Class Exercises, Debate Issue, and Chapter Quiz	IRM, p. 7
Class Exercise 1	IRM, p. 9
Class Exercise 2	IRM, p. 10
Debate Issue	IRM, p. 11
Chapter Quiz	IRM, p. 12
Answers to Discussion and Review Questions	IRM, p. 13
Comments on the Cases	IRM, p. 14
Case 1.1	IRM, p. 14
Video	Tape 1/DVD 1, Segment 1
Video Information	IRM, p. 15
Multiple-Choice Questions About the Video	IRM, p. 15
Case 1.2	IRM, p. 16
Transparency Acetates	Transparency package
Examination Questions: Essay	TB, p. 1
Examination Questions: Multiple-Choice	TB, p. 1
Examination Questions: True-False	TB, p. 23
Author-Selected Multiple-Choice Test Items	TB, p. 670
HMClassPrep Presentation Resources	CD-ROM
PowerPoint Slides	Instructor's website and ClassPrep CD

Note: Additional resources are updated periodically and may be found on the accompanying student and instructor websites at http://www.prideferrell.com/.

PURPOSE AND PERSPECTIVE

The purpose of this chapter is to give students an overview of strategic marketing and provide a general framework for studying the field of marketing. First, we present a definition of marketing and explore each element of the definition in detail. This exploration defines key marketing concepts including customers, target market, the marketing mix, the exchange process, relationship marketing, and the marketing environment. Because we believe that an understanding of the marketing concept is fundamental, we devote several pages to this area, including its basic components, development, and implementation. We also take a brief look at the concept of value, which customers are demanding more than ever. We then explore the process of marketing management, which includes planning, organizing, implementing, and controlling marketing activities to encourage marketing exchanges. Finally, we examine the importance of marketing in our global society.

GUIDE FOR USING COLOR TRANSPARENCIES

There are two groups of color transparencies. The transparencies identified by a double number are the same as the figures in the text. The transparencies labeled with a number and a letter are illustrations that do not appear in the text, but they can be used as additional examples of concepts discussed.

Part 1 Opener	Marketing Strategy and Customer Relationships
Figure 1.1	Components of Strategic Marketing
Figure 1.2	Exchange Between Buyer and Seller
Figure 1A	Chapter 1 Outline
Figure 1B	Key Definitions: Marketing, Marketing Concept
Figure 1C	College Student Travel Market
Figure 1D	Key Definition: Customer Relationship Management (CRM)
Figure 1E	Marketing Costs and Profits for Selected Products
Figure 1F	Managing Customer Relationships
Figure 1G	Marketing Is Used in Nonprofit Organizations
Figure 1H	Top Internet Album Sales, Week of November 20, 2004
Figure 1I	Starting Salaries for College Graduates

LECTURE OUTLINE

(Transparency Part 1 Opener)

(Transparency Figure 1A: Chapter Outline)

I.   **Defining Marketing**
We define *marketing* as the process of creating, distributing, promoting, and pricing goods, services, and ideas to facilitate satisfying exchange relationships with customers in a dynamic environment.

(Transparency Figure 1B)

A.   **Marketing Focuses on Customers**

(Transparency Figure 1.1)

1.   As the purchasers of the products that organizations develop, promote, distribute, and price, *customers* are the focal point of all marketing activities.
2.   The essence of marketing is to develop satisfying exchanges from which both customers and marketers benefit.
3.   Organizations generally focus their marketing efforts on a specific group of customers, or *target market*.

B.   **Marketing Deals with Products, Distribution, Promotion, and Price**
Marketing involves developing and managing a product, making the product available in the right place and at a price acceptable to buyers, and communicating information to help customers determine if the product will satisfy their needs. These activities—product, distribution, promotion, and pricing—are known as the *marketing mix* because marketers decide what type of each element to use and in what amounts.

1.   **The Product Variable**
The product variable of the marketing mix deals with researching customers' needs and wants and designing a product that satisfies them.

a)   A *product* can be a good, a service, or an idea.
(1)   Good—a physical entity you can touch

           (2) Service—the application of human and mechanical efforts to people or objects to provide intangible benefits to customers

           (3) Idea—concept, philosophy, image, or issue

      b)   The product variable also involves creating or modifying brand names and packaging and may include decisions regarding warranty and repair services.

      c)   Product variable decisions and related activities are important because they are directly involved with creating products that meet customers' needs and wants.

  2. **The Distribution Variable**

In dealing with the distribution variable, a marketing manager makes products available in the quantities desired to as many target market customers as possible, keeping total inventory, transportation, and storage costs as low as possible.

  3. **The Promotion Variable**

The promotion variable relates to activities used to inform individuals or groups about an organization and its products.

      a)   Promotion can be aimed at increasing public awareness of an organization and of new or existing products.

      b)   Promotional activities can also educate customers about product features or urge people to take a particular stance on a political or social issue.

(Building Customer Relationships: *The Perils of Using Celebrities in Advertising*)

  4. **The Price Variable**

The price variable relates to decisions and actions associated with establishing pricing objectives and policies and determining product prices. Price is a critical component of the marketing mix because customers are concerned about the value obtained in an exchange.

  5. Marketing mix variables are often viewed as controllable because they can be modified; however, economic conditions, competitive structure, or government regulations may limit how much marketing managers can alter them.

C. **Marketing Builds Satisfying Exchange Relationships**

  1. Individuals and organizations engage in marketing to facilitate *exchanges*—that is, the provision or transfer of goods, services, or ideas in return for something of value.

  2. Four conditions must exist for an exchange to occur:

      a)   Two or more individuals, groups, or organizations must participate, and each must possess something of value desired by the other party.

      b)   The exchange should provide a benefit or satisfaction to both parties involved in the transaction.

      c)   Each party must have confidence in the promise of the "something of value" held by the other.

      d)   To build trust, the parties to the exchange must meet expectations.

  3. An exchange will not necessarily take place just because these conditions exist; marketing activities can occur even without an actual transaction or sale. Figure 1.2 depicts the exchange process.

(Transparency Figure 1.2)

  4. Marketing activities should attempt to create and maintain satisfying exchange relationships.

    D.   **Marketing Occurs in a Dynamic Environment**
1. The *marketing environment*, which includes competitive, economic, legal and regulatory, technological, and socio-cultural forces, surrounds the customer and affects the marketing mix as shown in Figure 1.1.
2. The forces of the marketing environment affect a marketer's ability to facilitate exchanges in three ways:
   a) They affect customers' lifestyles, standards of living, and preferences and needs for products.
   b) They help determine whether and how a marketing manager can perform certain marketing activities.
   c) They may affect a marketing manager's decisions and actions by influencing buyers' reactions to the firm's marketing mix.
3. Marketing environment forces can fluctuate quickly and dramatically.
4. Changes in the marketing environment produce uncertainty for marketers and at times hurt marketing efforts, but they also create opportunities.
5. Marketing mix elements—product, distribution, promotion, and price—are factors over which an organization has control; the forces of the environment, however, are subject to far less control.

II.   **Understanding the Marketing Concept**

(Transparency Figure 1B)

According to the *marketing concept,* an organization should try to provide products that satisfy customers' needs through a coordinated set of activities that also allows the organization to achieve its goals.

    A.   **Basic Elements of the Marketing Concept**
1. Customer satisfaction is the major focus of the marketing concept.
   a) To implement the marketing concept, an organization focuses on customer analysis, competitor analysis, and integration of the firm's resources to provide customer value and satisfaction, as well as long-term profits.
   b) The firm must also continue to alter, adapt, and develop products to keep pace with customers' changing desires and preferences.
2. The marketing concept is not a second definition of marketing. It is a management philosophy guiding an organization's overall activities.
3. It is important for marketers to consider not only current buyers' needs, but also the long-term needs of society.

    B.   **Evolution of the Marketing Concept**
1. **The Production Orientation**
   a) During the second half of the nineteenth century, the Industrial Revolution was in full swing in the United States.
   b) As a result of new technology and new ways of using labor, products poured into the marketplace, where consumer demand for the new manufactured goods was strong.
2. **The Sales Orientation**
   a) Between the mid-1920s and the early 1950s, business-people viewed sales as the major means of increasing profits.
   b) During this era, businesspeople believed that the major marketing activities were personal selling, advertising, and distribution.

3. **The Marketing Orientation**
   a) By the early 1950s, some businesspeople recognized that they must first determine what customers want and then produce it, rather than make products and try to persuade customers that what they need is what was produced.
   b) A *marketing orientation* requires the "organizationwide generation of market intelligence pertaining to current and future customer needs, dissemination of the intelligence across departments, and organizationwide responsiveness to it."
   c) Today, businesses want to satisfy customers and build meaningful, long-term buyer-seller relationships.

C. **Implementing the Marketing Concept**
   1. To implement the marketing concept, a marketing-oriented organization must accept some general conditions and recognize and deal with several problems.
      a) Management must first establish an information system to discover customers' real needs and then use the information to create satisfying products.

(Transparency Figure 1C)

   b) To satisfy customers' objectives as well as its own, a company must also coordinate all its activities.

III. **Managing Customer Relationships**
   A. Achieving the full profit potential of each customer relationship should be the fundamental goal of every marketing strategy.
      1. At the most basic level, profits can be obtained through relationships in the following ways:
         a) By acquiring new customers
         b) By enhancing the profitability of existing customers
         c) By extending the duration of customer relationships
      2. Implementing the marketing concept means optimizing the exchange relationship—the relationship between a company's financial investment in customer relationships and the return generated by customers responding to that investment.
   B. The term *relationship marketing* refers to "long-term, mutually beneficial arrangements in which both the buyer and seller focus on value enhancement through the creation of more satisfying exchanges."
      1. Relationship marketing continually deepens the buyer's trust in the company, and, as the customer's confidence grows, this in turn increases the firm's understanding of the customer's needs.
      2. Eventually this interaction becomes a solid relationship that allows for cooperation and mutual dependency.
   C. *Customer relationship management (CRM)* focuses on using information about customers to create marketing strategies that develop and sustain desirable customer relationships.

(Transparency Figure 1D)

   1. By increasing customer value over time, organizations try to retain and increase long-term profitability through customer loyalty.
   2. Managing customer relationships requires identifying patterns of buying behavior and using that information to focus on the most promising and profitable customers.

(Transparency Figure 1F)

IV. **Value-Driven Marketing**
   A.   To manage customer relationships, organizations must develop marketing mixes that create value for customers. We view *value* as a customer's subjective assessment of benefits relative to costs in determining the worth of a product (customer value = customer benefits – customer costs).

(Transparency Figure 1E)

   1.   Customer benefits include anything a buyer receives in an exchange.
   2.   Customer costs include anything a buyer must give up to obtain the benefits provided by the product. Costs include the monetary price of the product as well as less obvious nonmonetary costs such as time and effort.
   B.   The process people use to determine the value of a product is not highly scientific.
   C.   In developing marketing activities, it is important to recognize that customers receive benefits based on their experiences.
   D.   The marketing mix can be used to enhance perceptions of value.

V.   **Marketing Management**
   A.   *Marketing management* is the process of planning, organizing, implementing, and controlling marketing activities to facilitate exchanges effectively and efficiently.
   1.   "Effectiveness" is the degree to which an exchange helps achieve an organization's objectives.
   2.   "Efficiency" refers to minimizing the resources an organization must spend to achieve a specific level of desired exchanges.
   B.   Planning is a systematic process of assessing opportunities and resources, determining marketing objectives, and developing a marketing strategy and plans for implementation and control.
   C.   Organizing marketing activities involves developing the internal structure of the marketing unit.
   D.   Proper implementation of marketing plans hinges on coordination of marketing activities, motivation of marketing personnel, and effective communication within the unit.
   E.   The marketing control process consists of establishing performance standards, comparing actual performance with established standards, and reducing the difference between desired and actual performance.

VI. **The Importance of Marketing in Our Global Economy**
   A.   **Marketing Costs Consume a Sizable Portion of Buyers' Dollars**
   1.   About one-half of a buyer's dollar goes to pay the costs of marketing.
   2.   Because marketing expenses consume such a significant portion of our dollars, you should know how this money is used.
   B.   **Marketing Is Used in Nonprofit Organizations**
   1.   Marketing is also important in organizations working to achieve goals other than ordinary business objectives such as profit.
   2.   Government agencies engage in marketing activities to fulfill their mission and goals.
   3.   In the private sector, nonprofit organizations also employ marketing activities to create, distribute, promote, and even price programs that benefit particular segments of society.

(Transparency Figure 1G)

   C.   **Marketing Is Important to Business and the Economy**
   1.   Businesses must sell products to survive and grow, and marketing activities help sell their products.

2. Marketing activities help produce the profits that are essential not only to the survival of individual businesses but also to the health and ultimate survival of the global economy.

D. **Marketing Fuels Our Global Economy**
1. Profits from marketing products contribute to the development of new products and technologies.
2. Advances in technology, along with falling political and economic barriers and the universal desire for a higher standard of living, have made marketing across national borders commonplace while stimulating global economic growth.

(Global Marketing: *Gruma Tortillas Folds up U.S. Market*)

E. **Marketing Knowledge Enhances Consumer Awareness**
1. Studying marketing allows us to assess a product's value and flaws more effectively.
2. Understanding marketing enables us to evaluate corrective measures (such as laws, regulations, and industry guidelines) that could stop unfair, damaging, or unethical marketing practices.

F. **Marketing Connects People Through Technology**
1. New technology, especially technology related to computers and telecommunications, helps marketers understand and satisfy more customers than ever before.
2. The Internet has also become a vital tool for marketing to consumers and other businesses.

(Transparency Figure 1H)

G. **Socially Responsible Marketing Can Promote the Welfare of Customers and Society**
1. The success of our economic system depends on marketers whose values promote trust and cooperative relationships in which customers are treated with respect.
2. By managing concern about the impact of marketing on society, a firm can protect the interests of the general public and the natural environment.

H. **Marketing Offers Many Exciting Career Prospects**
1. From 25 to 33 percent of all civilian workers in the United States perform marketing activities.
2. Whether a person earns a living through marketing activities or performs them voluntarily in nonbusiness projects, marketing knowledge and skills are valuable assets.

(Transparency Figure 1I)

NOTES FOR CLASS EXERCISES, DEBATE ISSUE, AND CHAPTER QUIZ

On the following pages, you will find two class exercises, a debate issue, and a chapter quiz. These are formatted in large-size type so that you can use them as class handouts or for making transparencies. Below are the authors' comments on the class exercises, the debate topic for this chapter, and the answers to the chapter quiz.

Comments on Class Exercise 1

The objective of this class exercise is to help students understand how the marketing concept works and to be able to apply the marketing concept to the implementation of marketing strategy.

Question 1. To generate interest, you might ask, "Why are some local firms doing poorly or going out of business?" or "What bad experiences have you had with local companies?" The causes for business failure or bad experiences can then be traced back to weak need satisfaction and poor coordination (e.g., lack of marketing orientation). You may also want to cover the implementation of the marketing concept (acceptance by top management, need for information systems, and reorganization).

Question 2. Customer satisfaction/seller satisfaction: An exchange must be satisfying to both the buyer and the seller. Some firms offer products that few people want and thus do not satisfy customers. Other firms offer what people want, but not at a price that will allow the firms to stay in business. Cover the four conditions required for an exchange to take place when explaining this point.

Maintaining long-term, positive relationships: Students will likely have examples of car dealers or others who are more concerned with making the immediate sale than they are with building customer relationships. Mercedes dealerships and salespeople, on the other hand, make it a point to know their customers and maintain contact after the sale.

Recognizing and responding to environmental forces: Marketing occurs in a dynamic environment— including laws, regulations, political activities, societal pressures, changing economic and competitive conditions, and technological advances.

Selecting and clearly defining target markets: Organizations that try to be all things to all people typically end up not satisfying the needs of any customer group very well.

The marketing mix: product, distribution, promotion, price: Examples of problems with the marketing mix might include poorly prepared food or small portion sizes at restaurants; banks or campus offices that have inconvenient hours; overpricing PCs in undifferentiated segments; or new stores with low customer awareness levels.

Question 3. Most students can distinguish between goods and services. In addition to political and religious organizations, you as an instructor are marketing ideas to your students.

Question 4. Some firms are still operating as if they were in the production or sales orientations, when businesspeople emphasized technology, personal selling, or advertising rather than customers.

Comments on Class Exercise 2

The objective of this class exercise is to help students understand the meaning of a "product" and differentiate between a good, a service, and an idea. Answers:

1. Overnight stay in a hotel   **service**
2. DVD player   **good**
3. This marketing course   **service**
4. Dry cleaning   **service**
5. Political party platform   **idea**
6. Advice from a marriage counselor   **idea/service**
7. Utilities, such as electricity   **service**
8. Meal at Red Lobster   **good/service**
9. Pair of jeans   **good**
10. A movie at a theater   **service**
11. Candy bar   **good**
12. Airplane flight   **service**

DEBATE ISSUE

Is the marketing concept short-term oriented?

CHAPTER QUIZ

Answers to Chapter Quiz 1. c; 2. a; 3. c; 4. d.

Class Exercise 1

1. Of all the organizations and companies in your area, which ones do not appear to be implementing the marketing concept?

   - Are they trying to satisfy their customers' needs or their own needs?

   - Are their efforts coordinated?

   - Are all employees working together to satisfy customers?

2. With what areas of marketing are these organizations or companies having difficulty? Why are they failing in these areas?

   - Customer satisfaction/seller satisfaction

   - Maintaining long-term, positive relationships

   - Recognizing and responding to environmental forces

   - Selecting and clearly defining target markets

   - The marketing mix: product, distribution, promotion, price

3. Which of these organizations' or companies' "products" are primarily goods? Services? Ideas?

4. Would you characterize these organizations or companies as having a marketing orientation? Why or why not?

Class Exercise 2

A PRODUCT CAN BE A GOOD, A SERVICE, OR AN IDEA. HOW WOULD YOU CLASSIFY THE FOLLOWING PRODUCTS?

1. Overnight stay in a hotel
2. DVD player
3. This marketing course
4. Dry cleaning
5. Political party platform
6. Advice from a marriage counselor
7. Utilities, such as electricity
8. Meal at Red Lobster
9. Pair of jeans
10. A movie at a theater
11. Candy bar
12. Airplane flight

Debate Issue

IS THE MARKETING CONCEPT SHORT-TERM ORIENTED?

YES	NO
• Marketers learn the immediate wants of customers and develop products to satisfy those wants.	• No component of the marketing concept requires that it be used on a short-term basis.
• Studying the long-term needs of customers entails considerable time and expense.	• If managers focus on short-term objectives and performance, it is not the fault of the marketing concept.
• Companies are producing products with minor modifications rather than assessing latent or unseen needs.	• Japanese marketers have a reputation for having a long-term focus, yet they are very successful at embracing the marketing concept.
• Marketers are merely responding to the marketplace rather than striving for revolutionary or innovative products.	• Being long-term oriented does not mean that a marketer cannot follow the marketing concept.

Chapter Quiz

1. Marketing is best defined as
   a. developing a product and matching it with its market.
   b. advertising and selling products.
   c. creating marketing mixes to facilitate satisfying exchange relationships with customers.
   d. transferring goods to stores to make them available.
   e. a process of bringing buyers and sellers together.

2. A marketing manager decides what combination of variables is needed to satisfy customers' needs for a general type of product. What are the essential variables that the marketing manager combines?
   a. Product variables, price variables, distribution variables, and promotion variables
   b. Marketing environment variables
   c. Product variables and promotion variables
   d. Product variables, price variables, and customer variables
   e. Product variables, price variables, customer variables, and promotion variables

3. A Panasonic DVD player has average marketing costs and sells for $100. Approximately how many of the buyer's dollars go to marketing costs?
   a. $25   d. $75
   b. $35   e. $85
   c. $50

4. The focal point of all marketing activities is
   a. profits.   d. customers.
   b. promotion and selling. e. competitors.
   c. the marketing concept.

ANSWERS TO DISCUSSION AND REVIEW QUESTIONS

1. **What is marketing? How did you define the term before you read this chapter?**

   The text defines *marketing* as the process of creating, distributing, promoting, and pricing goods, services, and ideas to facilitate satisfying exchange relationships with customers in a dynamic environment. The second part of this question can be used to stimulate class discussion about how the average person views marketing.

2. **What is the focus of all marketing activities? Why?**

   Customers are the focal point of all marketing activities because they are the purchasers of the products that organizations develop, promote, distribute, and price.

3. **What are the four variables of the marketing mix? Why are these elements known as variables?**

   The marketing mix is the combination of activities that are planned, organized, implemented, and controlled to meet the needs of customers within the target market. These activities are product, distribution, promotion, and price. They are called *variables* because marketing managers decide what type of each element to use and in what amounts.

4. **What conditions must exist before a marketing exchange can occur? Describe a recent exchange in which you participated.**

   For an exchange to take place, four conditions must exist. First, two or more individuals, groups, or organizations must participate, and each must possess something of value that the other party desires. Second, the exchange should provide a benefit or satisfaction to both parties involved in the transaction. Third, each party must have confidence in the promise of the "something of value" held by the other. Finally, both parties to the exchange must meet expectations. The second part of this exercise can be used to stimulate class discussion about exchanges based on students' experiences.

5. **What are the forces in the marketing environment? How much control does a marketing manager have over these forces?**

   The marketing environment, which surrounds both customers and the marketing mix, includes competitive, economic, political, legal and regulatory, technological, and sociocultural forces. Marketers have little control over these environmental forces, but they must be aware of them, adapt to them, and capitalize on the opportunities they provide.

6. **Discuss the basic elements of the marketing concept. Which businesses in your area use this philosophy? Explain why.**

   The marketing concept is an organizational philosophy that states that an organization should try to provide products that satisfy customers' needs through a coordinated set of activities that also allows the organization to achieve its goals. The major focus is customer satisfaction. The answers to the other parts of this question are based on local examples.

7. **How can an organization implement the marketing concept?**

   To implement the marketing concept, a marketing organization must first establish an information system to discover customers' real needs and then use the information to create satisfying products. The organization must also coordinate all its activities.

8.   **What is customer relationship management? Why is it so important to "manage" this relationship?**

Customer relationship management focuses on using information about customers to create marketing strategies that develop and sustain desirable customer relationships. "Managing" customer relationships is important to marketers because it can foster customer loyalty and thereby increase long-term profitability. A loyal lifelong customer can be worth a considerable sum of money, so the loss of such customers could result in lower profits.

9.   **What is value? How can marketers use the marketing mix to enhance customers' perception of value?**

The text defines value as a customer's subjective assessment of benefits relative to costs in determining the worth of a product. Examples of ways marketers can modify their marketing mixes to enhance perceptions of value include offering product features or enhancements that provide benefits desired by customers, using promotion to create an image and prestige characteristics that customers consider in their assessment of value, pricing products according to how customers use them, and offering convenient distribution outlets.

10.   **What types of activities are involved in the marketing management process?**

Marketing management is the process of planning, organizing, implementing, and controlling marketing activities to facilitate exchanges effectively and efficiently. Planning is a systematic process of assessing opportunities and resources, deter-mining marketing objectives, and developing a marketing strategy and plans for implementation and control. Organizing marketing activities involves developing the internal structure of marketing units. Implementation entails coordinating marketing activities, motivating marketing personnel, and effectively communicating within the marketing unit. The marketing control process consists of establishing performance standards, comparing actual performance with established standards, and reducing the difference between desired and actual performance.

11.   **Why is marketing important in our society? Why should you study marketing?**

Marketing is important in our society because it provides employment for many people and helps sell products, which in turn generate the profits that are essential not only to the survival of individual businesses, but also to the health and ultimate survival of the global economy. Many organizations other than businesses use marketing activities, and approximately 25 to 33 percent of all U.S. civilian workers perform marketing activities. The study of marketing is important because marketing costs consume a sizable portion of buyers' dollars, and a knowledge of how that money is used helps consumers understand why products cost as much as they do. Studying marketing activities also enables consumers to weigh the costs, benefits, and flaws associated with marketing activities and to evaluate laws, regulations, and industry guidelines intended to stop unfair, misleading, and unethical marketing practices.

COMMENTS ON THE CASES

CASE 1.1 FINAGLE A BAGEL

This case introduces students to a small business as an opportunity to see how a real-world organization employs marketing activities.

The first question asks students to define Finagle A Bagel's marketing mix. The case indicates that Finagle A Bagel's primary products are bagels and bagel-related products. The products are distributed through retail stores. The only promotion mix elements described in the case are customer interaction and the company's loyalty program, the Finagle A Bagel card, which rewards customers for their purchases. The company's products are priced to provide a good value, regardless of store location.

Question 2 asks about the forces from the marketing environment that provide opportunities or threats for Finagle A Bagel. Most students will cite sociocultural forces as a major environmental force that Finagle A Bagel has already exploited to provide products that satisfy its target market. However, changes in eating habits, such as the growth in popularity of low-carbohydrate diets that limit bread intake, may affect the company's success. A competitor could also threaten Finagle a Bagel by targeting its customers with less expensive products. Economic conditions could affect customers' willingness to patronize Finagle a Bagel. Changes in regulations could also constrain the company.

The third question asks whether Finagle a Bagel appears to be implementing the marketing concept. Responses to this question will be subjective, but most students will cite the company's focus on the customer as evidence that it is implementing the marketing concept.

Video Information

Company:	Finagle A Bagel
Location:	Tape 1/DVD 1, Segment 1
Length:	14:59

Video Overview: This video examines Finagle A Bagel's approach to customer service and marketing. Finagle A Bagel focuses on providing fresh food made to each individual customer's preference, and rewards customers using a frequent buyer program that can be tracked online. The company also strives to produce uncommon and innovative new bagel products by conducting informal research with customers and employees. Social responsibility is also an important component of the Finagle A Bagel operation, with many bagels being donated to schools and nonprofit organizations each year.

MULTIPLE-CHOICE QUESTIONS ABOUT THE VIDEO

1. Finagle A Bagel is based in which of the following cities?
    a.   New York City
    b.   Toledo
    c.   Santa Fe
    d.   Boston
    e.   San Francisco

2. To reinforce its brand and reward customer loyalty, Finagle A Bagel uses which of the following strategies?
    a.   Frequent buyer card
    b.   Coupons
    c.   Website
    d.   Direct mail advertising
    e.   Both a and c

3. What term does Finagle A Bagel use to refer to its customers?
    a.   Clients
    b.   Guests
    c.   Patrons
    d.   Diners
    e.   Bagelers

ANSWERS TO MULTIPLE-CHOICE QUESTIONS ABOUT THE VIDEO

1.   d
2.   e
3.   b

CASE 1.2 INDY RACING LEAGUE VS. OPEN WHEEL RACING SERIES: WHO WILL WIN THE RACE?

To introduce this case, you may want to ask students if any of them ever watch auto racing on television or have attended an actual CART or IRL racing event.

The first question asks students to identify CART's product. Students should be able to identify the firm's product as organizing and providing auto racing services.

The second question asks what CART could do to better promote its products. Students' answers will vary but should suggest promotional tactics that will help CART convey the excitement of street racing and distinguish it from other racing leagues like IRL and NASCAR. This case also asks how sponsorships should fit into CART's promotional plans. Given CART's current financial state, most students will agree that gaining additional sponsorships will be crucial in helping the organization turn around.

The third question asks how CART can use the strengths of its international driver and race events to its advantage and to relate the selection of racecourse to the distribution variable. Responses will vary, but students should recognize that CART may be able to draw on its international appeal to help sustain it while it rebuilds in the U.S.; it may also be able to capitalize on its international strengths in promoting Indy-car racing in the U.S. As to the second part of the question, student answers should demonstrate recognition of the "place" element represented by the racetrack in CART's marketing mix.

CHAPTER 2

Planning, Implementing, and Controlling Marketing Strategies

TEACHING RESOURCES QUICK REFERENCE GUIDE

Resource	Location
Purpose and Perspective	IRM, p. 17
Guide for Using Color Transparencies	IRM, p. 18
Lecture Outline	IRM, p. 18
Notes for Class Exercises, Debate Issue, and Chapter Quiz	IRM, p. 25
Class Exercise 1	IRM, p. 27
Class Exercise 2	IRM, p. 28
Debate Issue	IRM, p. 29
Chapter Quiz	IRM, p. 30
Answers to Discussion and Review Questions	IRM, p. 31
Comments on the Video Case	IRM, p. 32
Video	Tape 1/DVD 1, Segment 2
Video Information	IRM, p. 33
Multiple-Choice Questions About the Video	IRM, p. 33
Transparency Acetates	Transparency package
Examination Questions: Essay	TB, p. 29
Examination Questions: Multiple-Choice	TB, p. 29
Examination Questions: True-False	TB, p. 45
Author-Selected Multiple-Choice Test Items	TB, p. 670
HMClassPrep Presentation Resources	CD-ROM
PowerPoint Slides	Instructor's website

Note: Additional resources are updated periodically and may found on the accompanying student and instructor websites at http://www.prideferrell.com/.

PURPOSE AND PERSPECTIVE

This chapter focuses on strategic planning. To help students understand how marketing activities fit into the "big picture," we begin this chapter with an overview of the strategic planning process. Next, we examine how organizational resources and opportunities affect strategic planning and the role played by the organization's mission statement. After discussing the development of both corporate and business-unit strategy, we explore the nature of marketing strategy and the creation of the marketing plan. Finally, we examine the implementation of marketing strategies, the organization of the marketing unit, and the marketing control process.

GUIDE FOR USING COLOR TRANSPARENCIES

There are two groups of color transparencies. The transparencies identified by a double number are the same as the figures and tables in the text. The transparencies labeled with a number and a letter are illustrations that do not appear in the text, but they can be used as additional examples of concepts discussed.

LECTURE OUTLINE

(Transparency Figure 2A: Chapter Outline)

I. **Understanding the Strategic Planning Process**

(Transparency Figure 2.1)

Through the process of *strategic planning*, a firm establishes an organizational mission and goals, corporate strategy, marketing objectives, marketing strategy, and, finally, a marketing plan.

   A.   The process begins with a detailed analysis of the organization's strengths and weaknesses and identification of opportunities and threats within the marketing environment.

   B.   Based on this analysis, the firm can establish or revise its mission and goals, and then develop corporate strategies to achieve these goals.

   C.   Next, each functional area of the organization (marketing, production, finance, human resources, etc.) establishes its own objectives and develops strategies to achieve them.

   D.   In the marketing area, marketing objectives should be designed so that their achievement will contribute to the corporate strategy and so that they can be accomplished through efficient use of the firm's resources.

   E.   To achieve its marketing objectives, an organization must develop a *marketing strategy*, which includes identifying and analyzing a target market and developing a marketing mix to satisfy individuals in that market.

(Transparency Figure 2B)

   F.   The strategic planning process ultimately yields a marketing strategy that is the framework for a *marketing plan*, which is a written document that specifies the activities to be performed to implement and control an organization's marketing activities.

II. **Assessing Organizational Resources and Opportunities**

   A.   The strategic planning process begins with an analysis of the marketing environment. Economic, competitive, political, legal and regulatory, technological, and sociocultural forces can constrain an organization and influence its overall goals; they can also create favorable opportunities.

B.   Any strategic planning effort must assess an organization's available financial and human resources and capabilities, as well as how the level of these is likely to change in the future.
1.   Resources can also include goodwill, reputation, and brand names.
2.   Resources also include *core competencies*—things a firm does extremely well— sometimes so well that they give the company an advantage over its competition.
C.   Analysis of the marketing environment also involves identification of opportunities in the marketplace.
1.   When the right combination of circumstances and timing permits an organization to take action to reach a particular target market, a *market opportunity* exists.

(Transparency Figure 2C)

2.   *Strategic windows* are temporary periods of optimum fit between the key requirements of a market and the particular capabilities of a firm competing in that market.
D.   When a company matches a core competency to opportunities it has discovered in the marketplace, it is said to have a *competitive advantage*.

(Transparency Figure 2D)

E.   **SWOT Analysis**
One tool marketers use to assess an organization's strengths, weaknesses, opportunities, and threats is the *SWOT analysis*.

(Transparency Figure 2B)

1.   Strengths and weaknesses are internal factors that can influence an organization's ability to satisfy its target markets.
a)   "Strengths" refer to competitive advantages or core competencies that give the firm an advantage in meeting the needs of its target markets.
b)   "Weaknesses" refer to any limitations that a company faces in developing or implementing a marketing strategy.
c)   Both strengths and weaknesses should be examined from a customer perspective because they are meaningful only when they help or hinder the firm in meeting customer needs.
2.   Opportunities and threats exist independently of the firm and therefore represent issues to be considered by all organizations, even those that are not competitors.
a)   "Opportunities" refer to favorable conditions in the environment that could produce rewards for the organization if acted upon properly.
b)   "Threats" refer to conditions or barriers that may prevent the firm from reaching its objectives.

(Transparency Figure 2.2)

(Ethics and Social Responsibility: Recycling Disposable Cameras)

3.   When an organization matches internal strengths to external opportunities, it creates competitive advantages in meeting the needs of its customers.
4.   Companies should also act to convert internal weaknesses into strengths and external threats into opportunities.

III.   **Establishing an Organizational Mission and Goals**
A.   The goals of any organization should be derived from its *mission statement*, which is a long-term view, or vision, of what the organization wants to become. An organization's mission really answers two questions:
1.   Who are our customers?
2.   What is our core competency?

B. An organization's goals and objectives, derived from its mission statement, guide the remainder of its planning efforts.

1. Goals focus on the end results sought by the organization.

2. A *marketing objective* states what is to be accomplished through marketing activities.

    a) Marketing objectives should be based on a careful study of the SWOT analysis and should relate to matching strengths to opportunities and/or the conversion of weaknesses or threats.

    b) Marketing objectives should

        (1) be expressed in clear, simple terms so that all marketing personnel understand exactly what they are trying to achieve.

        (2) be written so that they can be measured accurately.

        (3) specify a time frame for accomplishment.

        (4) be consistent with both business-unit and corporate strategy.

IV. **Developing Corporate, Business-Unit, and Marketing Strategies**

In any organization, strategic planning begins at the corporate level and proceeds from there to the business-unit and marketing levels.

(Transparency Figure 2.3)

A. **Corporate Strategy**

(Transparency Figure 2B)

1. *Corporate strategy* determines the means for utilizing resources in the functional areas of marketing, production, finance, research and development, and human resources to reach the organization's goals.

    a) Corporate strategy determines not only the scope of the business, but also its resource deployment, competitive advantages, and overall coordination of functional areas.

    b) Corporate strategy is used by all organizations, not just corporations.

2. Corporate strategy planners are concerned with broad issues such as corporate culture, competition, differentiation, diversification, interrelationships between business units, and environmental and social issues.

    a) They attempt to match the resources of the organization with the opportunities and threats in the environment.

    b) They are also concerned with defining the scope and role of the firm's business units so that they are coordinated to reach the ends desired.

A. **Business-Unit Strategy**

The next step in strategic planning is to determine future business directions and develop strategies for individual business units.

1. A *strategic business unit (SBU)* is a division, product line, or other profit center within the parent company. Strategic planners should recognize the strategic performance capabilities of each SBU and carefully allocate resources among the divisions.

2. Several tools allow a firm's portfolio of strategic business units, or even individual products, to be classified and visually displayed according to the attractiveness of various markets and the business's relative market share within those markets.

    a) A *market* is a group of individuals and/or organizations that have needs for products in a product class and have the ability, willingness, and authority to purchase these products.

    b) The percentage of a market that actually buys a specific product from a specific company is referred to as that product's (or business unit's) *market share.*

3. The *market-growth/market-share matrix*, the Boston Consulting Group (BCG) approach, is based on the philosophy that a product's market growth rate and its market share are important considerations in determining its marketing strategy.
   a) All the firm's SBUs and products should be integrated into a single, overall matrix and evaluated to determine appropriate strategies for individual products and overall portfolio strategies.
   b) Managers can use this model to determine and classify each product's expected future cash contributions and future cash requirements.
   c) Figure 2.4, based on work by the BCG, classifies a firm's products into four basic types:

(Transparency Figure 2.4)

   (1) "Stars" have a dominant share of the market and good prospects for growth; they use more cash than they generate to finance growth, add capacity, and increase market share.
   (2) "Cash cows" have a dominant share of the market but low prospects for growth; typically they generate more cash than is required to maintain market share.
   (3) "Dogs" have a subordinate share of the market and low prospects for growth; these products are often found in established markets.
   (4) "Question marks," sometimes called "problem children," have a small share of a growing market and generally require a large amount of cash to build market share.
   d) The long-term health of an organization depends on having some products that generate cash (and provide acceptable profits) and others that use cash to support growth.

B. **Marketing Strategy**
The next phase in strategic planning is the development of strategies for each functional area of the organization.

1. Within the marketing area, a strategy is typically designed around two components: (1) the selection of a target market and (2) the creation of a marketing mix that will satisfy the needs of the chosen target market.
2. **Target Market Selection**

(Transparency Figure 2E)

   a) The target market has to be chosen before the organization can adapt its marketing mix to meet this market's needs and preferences.
      (1) Should a company select the wrong target market, all other marketing decisions will be a waste of time.
      (2) Identification and analysis of a target market provide a foundation on which a marketing mix can be developed.
   b) When exploring possible target markets, marketing managers try to evaluate how entering them would affect the company's sales, costs, and profits.
   c) Marketers should also assess whether the company has the resources to develop the right mix of product, price, promotion, and distribution to meet the needs of a particular target market.

(Building Customer Relationships: Red Bull Energizes Sales with Stimulating Marketing Strategy)

3. **Creating the Marketing Mix**
   a) The decisions made in creating a marketing mix are only as good as the organization's understanding of the target market.
      (1) This understanding typically comes from careful, in-depth research into the characteristics of the target market.
      (2) While demographic information is important, the organization should also analyze customer needs, preferences, and behavior with respect to product design, pricing, distribution, and promotion.
   b) Marketing mix decisions should also have two other characteristics:
      (1) All marketing mix decisions should be consistent with the business-unit and corporate strategies; this allows the organization to achieve its objectives on all three planning levels.
      (2) All marketing mix decisions should be flexible to permit the organization to alter its marketing mix in response to changes in market conditions, competition, and customer needs
   c) It is at the marketing mix level that a firm details how it will achieve a competitive advantage.
   d) It is important that the firm attempt to make this advantage sustainable. A *sustainable competitive advantage* is one that cannot be copied by the competition.

V. **Creating the Marketing Plan**
   A major concern in the strategic planning process is *marketing planning*, the systematic process of assessing marketing opportunities and resources, determining marketing objectives, defining marketing strategies, and establishing guidelines for implementation and control of the marketing program.

   A. The outcome of this process is the development of a marketing plan, a written document that outlines and explains all the activities necessary to implement marketing strategies. It describes the firm's current position or situation, establishes marketing objectives for the product or product group, and specifies how the organization will attempt to achieve these objectives.
   B. Developing a clear, well-written plan, though time consuming, is important.
      1. It is the basis for internal communication among employees.
      2. It covers the assignment of responsibilities and tasks, as well as schedules for implementation.
      3. It presents objectives and specifies how resources are to be allocated to achieve these objectives.
      4. It helps marketing managers monitor and evaluate the performance of a marketing strategy.
   C. Organizations use many different formats when devising marketing plans, which may be written for strategic business units, product lines, individual products or brands, or specific markets. Most plans share some common components, as shown in Table 2.2.

VI. **Implementing Marketing Strategies**
   A. *Marketing implementation* is the process of putting marketing strategies into action.
      1. Although implementation is often neglected in favor of strategic planning, the implementation process itself can determine whether a marketing strategy succeeds.
      2. Marketing strategies almost always turn out differently than expected. In essence, organizations have two types of strategy.
         a) *Intended strategy* is the strategy the organization decided on during the planning phase and wants to use.

        b)   *Realized strategy* is the strategy that actually takes place. It comes about during the process of implementing the intended strategy.

B.   **Approaches to Marketing Implementation**

   1.   **Internal Marketing**

      a)   Organizations effectively have two sets of customers:

         (1)   *External customers* are the individuals who patronize a business.

         (2)   *Internal customers* are the employees who work for a company.

         (3)   The needs of both sets of customers must be satisfied through marketing activities if implementation is to be successful.

      b)   *Internal marketing* is a management philosophy that coordinates internal exchanges between the organization and its employees to achieve successful external exchanges between the organization and its customers.

      c)   Internal marketing refers to the managerial actions necessary to make all members of the marketing organization understand and accept their roles in implementing the marketing strategy.

      d)   Internal marketing may involve market segmentation, product development, research, distribution, and public relations and sales promotion.

   2.   **Total Quality Management**

   Total quality management (TQM) is a philosophy that uniform commitment to quality in all areas of the organization will promote a culture that meets customers' perceptions of quality.

      a)   TQM involves coordinating efforts at improving customer satisfaction, increasing employee participation and empowerment, forming and strengthening supplier partnerships, and facilitating an organizational culture of continuous quality improvement.

      b)   TQM requires continuous quality improvement and employee empowerment.

         (1)   Continuous quality improvement is built around the notion that quality is free and involves building in quality from the very beginning. An important tool is *benchmarking*, the measuring and evaluating of the quality of an organization's goods, services, or processes as compared with the best-performing companies in the industry.

         (2)   *Empowerment* gives customer-contact employees the authority and responsibility to make marketing decisions without seeking the approval of their supervisors.

C.   **Organizing Marketing Activities**

   1.   Firms that truly adopt the marketing concept develop a distinct organizational culture—a culture based on a shared set of beliefs that makes the customer's needs the pivotal point of a firm's decisions about strategy and operations.

(Transparency Figure 2F)

   2.   If the marketing concept serves as a guiding philosophy, the marketing unit will be closely coordinated with other functional areas such as production, finance, and human resources.

   3.   The organizational structure of a marketing department establishes the authority relationships among marketing personnel and specifies who is responsible for making certain decisions and performing particular activities.

      a)   A *centralized organization* is one in which the top-level managers delegate very little authority to lower levels of the organization.

      b)   A *decentralized organization* delegates authority as far down the chain of command as possible.

4.   There is no single best approach to organizing the marketing unit; the best approach(es) depends on the number and diversity of the firm's products, the characteristics and needs of the people in the target market, and many other factors.

5.   A marketing unit can be organized according to functions, products, regions, or types of customers; it can also be organized using a combination of these approaches.

    a)   **Organizing by Functions**
- (1)   Some marketing departments are organized by general marketing functions, such as marketing research, product developments, distribution, sales, advertising, and customer relations.
- (2)   The functional structure is fairly common because it works well for some businesses with centralized marketing operations; however, it can cause serious coordination problems in more decentralized firms.

    b)   **Organizing by Products**
- (1)   Organizing by product is appropriate for firms that produce and market diverse products.
- (2)   This structure gives a firm the flexibility to develop special marketing mixes for different products.
- (3)   Although this approach can be flexible, it can be also rather expensive unless efficient categories of products are grouped together to reduce duplication and improve coordination of product management.

    c)   **Organizing by Regions**
- (1)   Organizing by region is appropriate for large firms that market products nationally or internationally.
- (2)   This structure is effective for firms whose customers' characteristics and needs vary greatly from one region to another.

    d)   **Organizing by Types of Customers**
Organizing by types of customers is appropriate for a firm that has several groups of customers whose needs and problems differ significantly.

D.   **Controlling Marketing Activities**
The formal *marketing control process* consists of establishing performance standards, evaluating actual performance by comparing it with established standards, and reducing the differences between desired and actual performance.

(Transparency Figure 2.5)

1.   **Establishing Performance Standards**
    a)   Planning and controlling are closely linked because plans include statements about what is to be accomplished.
    b)   A *performance standard* is an expected level of performance against which actual performance can be compared.
    c)   Performance standards should be tied to organizational goals.

2.   **Evaluating Actual Performance**
    a)   Marketing managers must know what employees are doing and have information about the activities of external organizations that provide the firm with marketing assistance.
    b)   Records of actual performance are compared with performance standards to determine whether and how much of a discrepancy exists.

3.   **Taking Corrective Action**
    a)   Marketing managers have several options for reducing a discrepancy between performance standards and actual performance:
- (1)   Improve actual performance

          (2)   Reduce or totally change the performance standard

          (3)   Do both

    b)   Improving performance may require better methods of motivating marketing personnel or more effective techniques for coordinating marketing efforts.

4.   **Problems in Controlling Marketing Activities**

    a)   The information required to control marketing activities may be unavailable or available only at a high cost.

    b)   The frequency, intensity, and unpredictability of environmental changes may hamper control.

    c)   The time lag between marketing activities and their results limits a marketer's ability to measure the effectiveness of specific marketing activities.

    d)   Because marketing and other business activities overlap, marketing managers cannot determine the precise cost of marketing activities, which makes it difficult to know if the outcome of marketing activities is worth the expense.

    e)   It is very hard to develop exact performance standards for marketing personnel.

NOTES FOR CLASS EXERCISES, DEBATE ISSUE, AND CHAPTER QUIZ

On the following pages, you will find two class exercises, a debate issue, and a chapter quiz. These are formatted in large-size type so that you can use them as class handouts or for making transparencies. Below are the authors' comments on the class exercises, the debate topic for this chapter, and the answers to the chapter quiz.

Comments on Class Exercise 1

The purpose of this exercise is to apply organizational structure principles to multinational corporations marketing in the European Union.

Question 1. A centralized organization avoids confusion among the marketing staff, vagueness in marketing strategy, and autonomous decision makers who are out of control. The down side is that they may be too dependent on a few top managers and too slow to respond to market changes. Decentralized organizations may foster innovation and greater responsiveness to customers but may be inefficient and have blurred strategies (as seen in the next question). You might ask if any students have visited EU countries and ask them if there seem to be many differences or similarities among the countries. Most will indicate some significant differences exist, which would suggest a need for a more decentralized organization. You might then ask if they saw some products (McDonald's, Coke, or Pepsi) almost everywhere in Europe, which might indicate some similarity of needs.

There is really no correct answer for the second part of the question, since research (Samiee and Roth 1992) has so far found that no differences exist in performance between centralized/standardized and decentralized/adaptation organizations.

Question 2. A marketing-oriented organization is one that concentrates on discovering what buyers want and providing it in a way that lets it achieve its objectives. Just as U.S. consumers have different preferences (and thus different segments), Europeans do as well: Germans want a product that's gentle on lakes and rivers and will pay more for it. Spaniards want cheaper products that get shirts white and soft. Greeks want smaller packages that allow them to hold down the cost of each store visit. Trying to find a product that meets everyone's needs or preferences has been difficult for Lever.

Question 3. Decentralized organizations with different target markets and products might be more likely to organize by regions that have similar needs. Centralized organizations (as P&G has become in the EU) may be more prone to organize by functions. However, even though they are attempting to market pan-European products, the breadth of Procter & Gamble product lines may require organizing according to product.

Question 4. Formal controls involve performance standards, evaluation of actual performance, and corrective action to remedy shortfalls (see *Figure 2.5*). Informal controls include self-control, social or group control, and cultural control through acceptance of a firm's value system. Centralized control systems, seeking to achieve unified strategic performance, would likely emphasize formal controls. Autonomous units in decentralized organizations may depend on more informal controls.

Additional information: Mars renamed its big-selling Marathon chocolate bar in Britain Snickers; renamed Europe's most successful candy bar, Raider chocolate biscuit, Twix; changed the name of Bonitos in France to M&Ms and changed color, coatings, and formula. However, difficulties arose in changing Milky Way and Mars bars. In the EU, a Mars bar is caramel and chocolate, which is the Milky Way in the United States. Milky Way bars exist in Europe, but they don't have any caramel. Mars bars in the United States contain almonds. Product changes such as these (and in Lever's situation) may result in loss in market share.

Sources for company information: E. S. Browning, "In Pursuit of the Elusive Euroconsumer," *Wall Street Journal*, April 23, 1992, B1; Saeed Samiee and Kendall Roth, "The Influence of Global Marketing Standardization on Performance," *Journal of Marketing*, April 1992, 1–17.

Comments on Class Exercise 2

Because market shares and market growth potential are constantly changing, the products listed in this exercise could be classified very differently today than they might have been when this edition was in production.

1.	Chrysler/Dodge minivans	**cash cow**
2.	LP records	**dog**
3.	Levi's blue jeans	**cash cow**
4.	AirTran	**question mark**
5.	Windows XP	**star/cash cow**
6.	Pizza Hut Pan Pizza	**cash cow**
7.	Miller Light	**cash cow**
8.	Tampa Bay Buccaneers	**problem child**
9.	Digital video discs	**star**
10.	Black and white televisions	**dog**

DEBATE ISSUE

Is the Boston Consulting Group's market-growth/market-share matrix a good strategic planning tool?

CHAPTER QUIZ

Answers to Chapter Quiz 1. a; 2. e; 3. b; 4. c.

Class Exercise 1

MULTINATIONAL CORPORATIONS (MNCS) COMPETING ON A GLOBAL BASIS HAVE APPROACHED ORGANIZATIONAL STRUCTURE AND STRATEGIC CONTROL WITH TWO BASIC METHODS. SOME FIRMS, SUCH AS MARS, INC., AND PROCTER & GAMBLE, HAVE BECOME HIGHLY CENTRALIZED AND ATTEMPT TO PRODUCE STANDARDIZED PRODUCTS WORLDWIDE. OTHERS, SUCH AS UNILEVER AND NESTLÉ SA, HAVE TRADITIONALLY BEEN MORE DECENTRALIZED BUT ARE NOW MOVING TOWARD GREATER CENTRALIZATION. THESE COMPANIES ARE ALL TRYING TO MARKET THEIR PRODUCTS TO EUROPE IN SEARCH OF COMMON NEEDS AND PERCEPTIONS SHARED BY ALL EUROPEANS.

1. What are the advantages of a centralized organization and of a decentralized organization? Which do you think would better suit organizations marketing to the European Union (EU)?

2. Lever, the EU subsidiary of Unilever, has sold Snuggle fabric softener in ten EU countries under seven names, with different bottles, different strategies and sometimes different formulas. Lever is slowly trying to change to a single brand name. What problems might a marketing-oriented organization encounter in doing so?

3. Considering the number and diversity of the firm's products and the characteristics and needs of the target market(s), should a firm such as Lever be organized by function, products, regions, or types of customers in Europe? What about a firm such as Procter & Gamble, which is introducing standardized products with standardized names across Europe?

4. The type of marketing control process that is employed by these MNCs is dependent on the internal and external environment. If a MNC is highly centralized, would you expect the control process to be primarily formal or informal?

Class Exercise 2

USING BCG'S MARKET GROWTH/MARKET SHARE MATRIX, HOW WOULD YOU CLASSIFY THE FOLLOWING PRODUCTS?

1. **Chrysler/Dodge minivans**
2. **LP records**
3. **Levi's blue jeans**
4. **AirTran**
5. **Windows XP**
6. **Pizza Hut Pan Pizza**
7. **Miller Light**
8. **Tampa Bay Buccaneers**
9. **Digital video discs**
10. **Black and white televisions**

Debate Issue

IS THE BOSTON CONSULTING GROUP'S MARKET GROWTH/MARKET SHARE MATRIX A GOOD STRATEGIC PLANNING TOOL?

YES

- Allows a firm to examine its existing products to determine the overall configuration of its offering

- Uncovers strengths and weaknesses of firm's product offering

- Suggests areas where examination of the product should take place

NO

- Reporting tool that highlights past business practice

- Detrimental when used alone

- Improper philosophy can be tagged to a given category within the matrix

- Provides a general overview but no specific directions for strategy

Chapter Quiz

1. Kate is upset because the bank did not credit her account with a deposit, which resulted in a returned check to Kate's mortgage company. When she was told the branch manager was on vacation, she expected to have to wait two weeks to have the matter resolved. Kate was surprised when the receptionist apologized for the error, and drafted a letter to the mortgage company while Kate waited. The bank was engaging in which type of decision-making strategy?

   a. Employee empowerment
   b. Centralized management
   c. Structured
   d. Immediate-focused
   e. Product-focused

2. Sam's employer is currently developing a new marketing strategy. The top managers have developed the marketing strategy and have given it to Sam so that he can now develop an implementation plan. Sam's company will *most likely* end up with which type of strategy?

   a. Decentralized
   b. Rigid
   c. Intended
   d. Centralized
   e. Realized

3. Stratford Manufacturing is interested in total quality management and wants to learn more about its principles. Which of the following elements will Stratford *not* address in its investigation of TQM?

   a. Improving customer satisfaction
   b. Purchasing lowest-cost materials
   c. Increasing employee participation
   d. Strengthening supplier partnerships
   e. Continuous product improvements

4. The Berkdorf Shoe Company is currently writing its marketing plan. Berkdorf is aware of possible new legislation that will limit the amount of glue that can be used in shoes that are marketed as "genuine leather" and considers this in its marketing plan. Which component of the marketing plan does this information *most likely* fit into?

   a. Executive summary
   b. Marketing strategies
   c. Opportunities and threats
   d. Strengths and weaknesses
   e. Marketing objectives

ANSWERS TO DISCUSSION AND REVIEW QUESTIONS

1. **Identify the major components of strategic planning, and explain how they are interrelated.**

   The major components of strategic planning include analysis of the organization's strengths and weaknesses and identification of its threats and opportunities, establishment of an organizational mission and goals, and development of corporate and business-unit strategies. Within the marketing area, the process continues with the establishment of marketing objectives, development of a marketing strategy and, ultimately, the creation of a marketing plan.

2. **What are the two major parts of a marketing strategy?**

   The two major parts of a marketing strategy are identifying and analyzing a target market and developing a marketing mix to satisfy individuals in that market.

3. **What are some issues to consider in analyzing a firm's resources and opportunities? How do these issues affect marketing objectives and marketing strategy?**

   The strategic planning process begins with an analysis of the marketing environment—including economic, competitive, political, legal and regulatory, technological, and sociocultural forces. The process must also include an assessment of an organization's available financial and human resources and capabilities, as well as how the level of these is likely to change. These analyses help the firm pinpoint its core competencies and identify any market opportunities that may be available in the marketplace that the firm can craft marketing strategies to exploit.

4. **How important is the SWOT analysis to the marketing planning process?**

   A SWOT analysis outlines the internal strengths and weaknesses of a firm and the external opportunities and threats. This information can be used to develop appropriate strategies for converting weaknesses into strengths, threats into opportunities, and to match strengths to opportunities.

5. **How should organizations set marketing objectives?**

   Marketing objectives must be consistent with the organization's goals. They should be written so that they are clear and measurable, and should state what is to be accomplished in what time frame.

6. **Explain how an organization can create a competitive advantage at the corporate, business-unit, and marketing strategy levels.**

   A competitive advantage exists when a firm matches its core competency to opportunities it has discovered in the marketplace. One way a firm can achieve a competitive advantage at the corporate level is through corporate mergers. The talents and abilities that one corporation possesses can be combined with different competencies of another organization, to be matched to opportunities in the marketplace. At the business-unit level, a competitive advantage can be developed by intensifying growth in those products or services that a company has mastered and that also have great potential customer markets. A competitive advantage would also be created when a company has the foresight to diversify into other markets and/or products that capitalize on its current skills and knowledge. At the marketing strategy level, a competitive advantage can be created by careful analysis of customers and their needs and then selecting the appropriate target market. The selection of the target market should not only meet an anticipated customer need, but should also be appropriate for the core competencies that an organization holds.

7. **Refer to question 6. How can an organization make its competitive advantages sustainable over time? How difficult is it to create sustainable competitive advantages?**

   A sustainable competitive advantage is one that cannot be copied by competitors. A sustainable advantage is developed by capitalizing on a firm's strengths and developing an expertise in an area that cannot be copied by the competition. Rather than attempting to be all things to all customers, a firm might choose a specific area of concentration and focus on becoming the best in that area. The degree of difficulty in maintaining a sustainable competitive advantage would depend on the specific area of expertise and the ease of entry by the competitor. For example, store location is one sustainable competitive advantage that would present some degree of difficulty for the competitor to challenge. However, a sustainable competitive advantage of lowest price would be more easily copied by the competition.

8. **What benefits do marketing managers gain from planning? Is planning necessary for long-run survival? Why or why not?**

   Planning helps marketing managers define their strategy in light of resources and opportunities. Planning forces the marketing manager to determine the difference between objectives and current performance. Specifying expected results, identifying the resources needed, describing the activities, and monitoring the activities allow the firm to achieve its long-term goals and survive.

9. **Why does an organization's intended strategy often differ from its realized strategy?**

   There are several possibilities for explaining why the intended strategy, developed in the planning phase, often does not get implemented exactly as planned. Since the environment is constantly changing, the intended strategy must also change. Therefore, it becomes the realized strategy— that which actually gets implemented. Another reason that the intended strategy differs from the realized strategy is that the managers often develop the intended strategy separately from the plans for its implementation; therefore, it may not work the way they envisioned, due to changes required for actual operation.

10. **Why might an organization use multiple bases for organizing its marketing unit?**

    Product features may dictate that the marketing unit be structured by product, and customer characteristics may require that the unit be organized by region or customer type. The use of multiple bases allows the firm to acquire the benefits from several approaches. The primary benefit is flexibility.

11. **What are the major steps of the marketing control process?**

    The major steps in the marketing control process are a) establishing performance standards, b) evaluating actual performance by comparing it with performance standards, and c) reducing the differences between desired and actual performance.

COMMENTS ON THE VIDEO CASE

CASE 2.1 THE GLOBAL EXPANSION OF SUBWAY SANDWICH SHOPS

This case explores how Subway expanded into foreign markets by overcoming several communication and cultural barriers. Subway's approach to opening international restaurants has been to keep its basic menu items and ingredients the same throughout the world, and allow for the addition of a few "local" items on the menu, making more exceptions only to meet strict cultural or religious requirements.

The first question asks what market opportunities and strategic windows Subway has been able to capitalize on. Students' responses will vary but should indicate an understanding of the concepts of market opportunities and strategic windows. Most responses will relate to the company's capitalizing on a growing health-consciousness by promoting the low-fat content of some of its sandwiches and the development of new low-fat or low-carb products. The weight-loss story of Jared Fogle represents a strategic window which Subway was quick to exploit to promote its low-fat offerings.

Question 2 asks students to conduct a brief SWOT analysis of Subway based on the facts presented in the case. Responses will vary but should express a basic understanding of the firm's strengths and weaknesses and the opportunities and threats it faces. For example, many students will cite the firm's well-known name and low-fat menu as strengths and the growing trend of low-carbohydrate diets as an opportunity it can capitalize on.

The third question asks students to describe Subway's apparent marketing mix and target markets. Responses will vary but should demonstrate a basic understanding of the marketing mix and target markets. Most students should be able to recognize that Subway's products are made-to-order sandwiches distributed through franchised retail stores around the world and promoted for their weight-loss benefits. The case does not specifically address price, but it would appear that Subway's products are priced to provide a good value for its target market, which would seem to include all consumers looking for an alternative to traditional fast-food fare.

Video Information

Company: Subway

Location: Tape 1/DVD 1, Segment 2

Length: 10:19

Video Overview: The video provides a brief introduction to Subway and the growth of the company before exploring how the company expanded into a large number of foreign markets by overcoming communication and cultural barriers. Subway's approach to opening international restaurants is to keep the basic menu items and ingredients the same throughout the world, but allow for the addition of local items to satisfy local cultural or religious requirements.

MULTIPLE-CHOICE QUESTIONS ABOUT THE VIDEO

1.   Subway opened its very first international store in
   a.   Afghanistan.
   b.   Oman.
   c.   Bahrain.
   d.   Croatia.
   e.   France.
2.   When Subway enters a new market, the first issues it faces are
   a.   building brand awareness.
   b.   learning about potential customers' customs.
   c.   adapting the menu to local tastes and finding quality local suppliers.
   d.   translating commercials into the local language and adapting the menu to local tastes.
   e.   building brand awareness and learning about potential customers' customs.

3.   In the United States and abroad, Subway has positioned its menu as

     a.   a health-conscious alternative.
     b.   tastier than local restaurants.
     c.   faster than local restaurants.
     d.   quieter than local restaurants.
     e.   the quintessential American fast-food joint.

ANSWERS TO MULTIPLE-CHOICE QUESTIONS ABOUT THE VIDEO

1.   c

2.   e

3.   a

CASE 2.2 SATURN: "A DIFFERENT KIND OF COMPANY. A DIFFERENT KIND OF CAR."

To introduce this case, you may want to ask students if any of them own a Saturn and if so, if they have had a good ownership experience. Ask those who have an opinion about Saturn to compare their experiences with the company as described in the case.

The first question asks students to assess whether Saturn's marketing planning efforts have been successful. Based on strong initial demand and satisfaction ratings for Saturn vehicles as cited in the case, most students will agree that Saturn's efforts were quite successful for the first few years. By the mid 1990s, however, Saturn's sales stagnated as consumers turned to larger vehicles, especially minivans, pickup trucks, and sport-utility vehicles, during a booming economy. Many students will cite Saturn's failure to respond to this change in the marketplace as evidence that its planning efforts floundered in the second half of the 1990s. To further stimulate classroom discussion, you might also ask students whether the strategic window for sport-utility vehicles had already closed by the time Saturn introduced the Vue SUV, not too long before gas prices began rising. You might also ask them to update the case as to the status of the Ion, a vehicle targeted at Generation Ys, and then relate the vehicle's success or failure to this question.

Question 2 asks what Saturn should do as competitors attempt to copy its unique brand image and pricing and dealer service policies. Students' responses will vary, but this question should prompt a lively discussion as to various strategies Saturn could pursue in an effort to further differentiate its product from those of competitors. Many students will see that deviating from the company's long-time pricing strategy could affect its reputation with Saturn devotees, so the company's options may be limited to changes in the product and promotion variables.

The third question asks students to describe the target market and marketing mix used by Saturn. Responses will vary, but students should generally recognize that Saturn focuses on people who want a high-quality vehicle and are not likely to buy a General Motors vehicle. This market primarily comprises college-educated men and women between the ages of 25 and 49. Saturn's product includes smaller, high-quality sedans, coupes, wagons, and an SUV and minivan, along with service, ease of buying, and the idea that it is a different buying experience. Distribution is through exclusive Saturn dealerships, and the prices are competitive. Promotion involves low-pressure selling in the dealerships and a straight-talk, people-oriented philosophy in advertising.

CHAPTER 3

The Marketing Environment

TEACHING RESOURCES QUICK REFERENCE GUIDE

Resource	Location
Purpose and Perspective	IRM, p. 35
Guide for Using Color Transparencies	IRM, p. 36
Lecture Outline	IRM, p. 36
Notes for Class Exercises, Debate Issue, and Chapter Quiz	IRM, p. 42
Class Exercise 1	IRM, p. 45
Class Exercise 2	IRM, p. 46
Debate Issue	IRM, p. 47
Chapter Quiz	IRM, p. 48
Answers to Discussion and Review Questions	IRM, p. 49
Comments on the Cases	IRM, p. 52
Case 3.1	IRM, p. 52
Video	Tape 1/DVD 1, Segment 3
Video Information	IRM, p. 53
Multiple-Choice Questions About the Video	IRM, p. 53
Case 3.2	IRM, p. 53
Transparency Acetates	Transparency package
Examination Questions: Essay	TB, p. 57
Examination Questions: Multiple-Choice	TB, p. 57
Examination Questions: True-False	TB, p. 82
Author-Selected Multiple-Choice Test Items	TB, p. 670
HMClassPrep Presentation Resources	CD-ROM
PowerPoint Slides	Instructor's website

Note: Additional resources are updated periodically and may be found on the accompanying student and instructor websites at http://www.prideferrell.com/.

PURPOSE AND PERSPECTIVE

In this chapter we examine competitive, economic, political, legal and regulatory, technological, and sociocultural forces in the marketing environment. First we discuss environmental scanning, environmental analysis, and two general approaches firms use to respond to environmental forces: a passive approach and an aggressive approach. Next we discuss competitive forces, focusing on the types of competition and competitive structures. Then we consider the effect of general economic conditions, consumer demand, and spending behavior. Next we define political forces—how they influence business decisions and how businesses may react to them. In our presentation of legal forces, we cover two broad categories: procompetitive laws and consumer protection laws. Then we consider the effect of compliance programs. In dealing with regulatory forces, we describe the potential effects of federal, state, and local government and nongovernment regulatory units on marketing decisions and discuss specific ways legal and regulatory forces affect marketers' decisions. We then describe technology and consider the impact of technology on society and on marketing decisions. Finally, we define sociocultural forces and discuss diversity, demographic factors, cultural values, and consumer movements.

GUIDE FOR USING COLOR TRANSPARENCIES

There are two groups of color transparencies. The transparencies identified by a double number are the same as the tables in the text. The transparencies labeled with a number and a letter are illustrations that do not appear in the text, but they can be used as additional examples of concepts discussed.

Part 2 Opener	The Global Environment and Social and Ethical Responsibilities
Table 3.1	Selected Characteristics
Figure 3.1	American Customer Satisfaction Index
Table 3.2a	Major Federal Laws Affecting Marketing Decisions
Table 3.2b	Major Federal Laws Affecting Marketing Decisions (continued)
Table 3.2c	Major Federal Laws Affecting Marketing Decisions (continued)
Table 3.3	Major Federal Regulatory Agencies
Figure 3.2	Top Ten Activities for Wireless Web Device Users
Figure 3A	Chapter 3 Outline
Figure 3B	Key Definitions: Marketing Environment
Figure 3C	Types of Competition
Figure 3D	Ranking Products Consumers Would Cut Back on if Spending Decreased
Figure 3E	Changes in Cultural Values About Health Affect Meat Consumption Patterns
Figure 3F	Go to My Room? Gladly! Kids' Adoption of Technology
Figure 3G	The Proportion of Households in America with Married Couples Has Declined Over the Last Four Decades
Figure 3H	How We Exercise Our Buying Power Is Changing
Figure 3I	Adoption and Use of Technology: Cars
Figure 3J	Adoption and Use of Technology: Banking

LECTURE OUTLINE

(Transparency: Part 2 Opener)

(Transparency Figure 3A: Chapter Outline)

I. **Examining and Responding to the Marketing Environment**

(Transparency Figure 3B)

The marketing environment consists of external forces that directly or indirectly influence an organization's acquisition of inputs (human, financial, and natural resources and raw materials, and information) and creation of outputs (goods, services, or ideas). These influences can create opportunities and threats for marketers.

A. **Environmental Scanning and Analysis**
1. *Environmental scanning* is the process of collecting information about forces in the marketing environment.
    a) Scanning involves observation, secondary sources such as business, trade, government, and general-interest publications, and marketing research.
    b) Environmental scanning can give marketers an edge over competitors in taking advantage of current trends.
2. *Environmental analysis* is the process of assessing and interpreting the information gathered through scanning.

a) Marketers evaluate the information for accuracy, try to resolve inconsistencies in the data, and assign significance to the findings.
b) Environmental analysis enables marketers to identify potential threats and opportunities linked to environmental changes.

B. **Responding to Environmental Forces**
1. Some marketers view environmental forces as uncontrollable and remain passive and reactive to the environment.
2. Other marketers believe that environmental forces can be shaped (through economic, psychological, political, or promotional skills), and these marketers are, to a certain extent, proactive.
3. Which approach is most appropriate for a particular firm depends on its managerial philosophies, objectives, financial resources, customers, human skills, and other environmental forces.

II. **Competitive Forces**
A. **Types of Competition**
1. A marketer generally defines *competition* as other firms that market products similar to or that can be substituted for its products in the same geographic area.
2. These competitors can be classified into one of four types:

(Transparency Figure 3C)

a) *Brand competitors* market products with similar features and benefits to the same customers at similar prices.
b) *Product competitors* compete in the same product class, but their products have different features, benefits, and prices.
c) *Generic competitors* provide very different products that solve the same problem or satisfy the same basic customer need.
d) *Total budget competitors* compete for the limited financial resources of the same customers.
3. All four types of competition can affect a firm's marketing performance, but brand competitors are the most significant because buyers typically see the different products of these firms as direct substitutes.

B. **Types of Competitive Structures**
The number of firms that supply a product may affect the strength of competition.

1. A *monopoly* exists when a firm offers a product that has no close substitute, making it the sole source of supply.

(Transparency Table 3.1)

2. An *oligopoly* exists when a few sellers control the supply of a large proportion of a product.
3. *Monopolistic competition* exists when a firm with many potential competitors attempts to develop a marketing strategy to differentiate its product.
4. *Pure competition*, if it existed, would entail a large number of sellers, no one of which could significantly influence price or supply.

C. **Monitoring Competition**
1. Marketers need to monitor the actions of major competitors to determine what specific strategies competitors are using and how those strategies affect their own.
2. It is not enough to analyze available information; the firm must develop a system for gathering ongoing information about competitors.

III. **Economic Forces**
Economic forces in the marketing environment influence both marketers' and customers' decisions and activities.

A. **Economic Conditions**
Changes in general economic conditions affect (and are affected by) supply and demand, buying power, willingness to spend, consumer expenditure levels, and the intensity of competitive behavior. Fluctuations in the economy follow a general pattern often referred to as the *business cycle*, which traditionally consists of four stages:

1. *Prosperity* is a stage of the business cycle characterized by low unemployment and relatively high total income, which together cause buying power to be high. Marketers often expand their product offerings to take advantage of increased buying power.
2. *Recession* is a stage of the business cycle during which unemployment rises and total buying power declines, stifling both consumer and business spending.

(Transparency Figure 3D)

a) Marketers should focus on marketing research during a recession to determine precisely what functions buyers want and integrate these functions into their product.
b) Promotion efforts should emphasize value and utility.
3. *Depression* is a business cycle stage in which unemployment is extremely high, wages are very low, total disposable income is at a minimum, and consumers lack confidence in the economy.
4. *Recovery* is a stage of the business cycle in which the economy moves from depression or recession to prosperity. Marketers should be as flexible as possible to be able to adjust their strategies as economic gloom subsides and buying power increases.

B. **Buying Power**
1. The strength of a person's *buying power* depends on economic conditions and the size of the resources—money, goods, and services that can be traded in an exchange—that enable the individual to make purchases.

(Transparency Figure 3H)

2. Major sources of buying power are income, credit, and wealth.
a) *Income* is money received through wages, rents, investments, pensions, and subsidy payments for a given period.
(1) *Disposable income*, or after-tax income, is used for spending or saving. It is affected by wage levels, rate of unemployment, interest rates, dividend rates, and tax rates.
(2) *Discretionary income* is disposable income available for spending and saving after an individual has purchased the basic necessities of food, clothing, and shelter.
b) Credit enables people to spend future income now or in the near future, but it increases current buying power at the expense of future buying power.
c) *Wealth* is the accumulation of past income, natural resources, and financial resources.
3. Marketers need to be aware of current levels of and expected changes in buying power because they directly affect the types and quantities of goods and services that consumers purchase.

C. **Willingness to Spend**
    1. People's *willingness to spend* (their inclination to buy because of expected satisfaction from a product) is, to some degree, related to their ability to buy.

    (Transparency Figure 3.1)

    2. Willingness to spend is affected by several factors:
        a) Buying power
        b) A product's price and its value
        c) The amount of satisfaction received from a product already owned
        d) Expectations about future employment, income levels, prices, family size, and general economic conditions

IV. **Political Forces**
Political, legal, and regulatory forces of the marketing environment are closely interrelated.

A. Marketing organizations must maintain good relations with elected political officials because
    1. Political officials well disposed toward particular firms or industries are less likely to create or enforce laws and regulations unfavorable to these companies.
    2. Political officials can influence how much a government agency purchases and from whom.
    3. Political officials can play key roles in helping organizations secure access to foreign markets.

B. Although some marketers view political forces as beyond their control and simply adjust to conditions arising from those forces, other firms seek to influence political forces through public protests or campaign contributions.
    1. Although laws limit corporate contributions to campaign funds for specific candidates, it is legal for businesses and other organizations to contribute to political parties.
    2. Marketers can also influence the political process through political action committees (PACs) that solicit donations from individuals and then contribute these funds to candidates running for political office.
    3. Companies can also participate in the political process through lobbying to persuade public and/or government officials to favor a particular position in decision making.

V. **Legal and regulatory forces**
A number of federal laws influence marketing decisions and activities.

(Transparencies Table 3.2a, Table 3.2b, Table 3.2c)

A. **Procompetitive Legislation**
Procompetitive legislation refers to laws designed to preserve competition.

B. **Consumer Protection Legislation**
Federal and state consumer protection laws deal with consumer safety, hazardous materials, information disclosure, and specific marketing practices.

C. **Encouraging Compliance with Laws and Regulations**
    1. Legal violations usually occur when marketers develop programs that unknowingly or unwittingly overstep legal bounds.

    (Ethics and Social Responsibility: Is Sharing Music and Film Files Ethical?)

    2. To ensure that marketers comply with the law, the federal government is increasing organizational accountability for misconduct through detailed guidelines that regulate the sentencing of companies convicted of breaking the law.

         a)   The basic philosophy of the Federal Sentencing Guidelines for Organizations is that companies are responsible for crimes committed by their employees.

         b)   These guidelines hold companies accountable for the illegal actions of their employees (previously, laws punished only those employees directly responsible for an offense, not the company).

         c)   The guidelines focus on crime prevention and detection by mitigating penalties for firms that have chosen to develop compliance programs should one of their employees be involved in misconduct.

D.   **Regulatory Agencies**

(Transparency Table 3.3)

   1.   Federal regulatory agencies influence many marketing activities, including product development, pricing, packaging, advertising, personal selling, and distribution, and they often have the power to enforce specific laws.

         a)   The *Federal Trade Commission (FTC)* influences marketing activities the most.

            (1)   It regulates a variety of business practices and focuses in particular on curbing false advertising, misleading pricing, and deceptive packaging and labeling.

            (2)   It can issue complaints and cease-and-desist orders, and can require companies to run corrective advertising.

            (3)   It also assists businesses in complying with laws.

         b)   Other regulatory units are limited to dealing with specific products, services, or business activities.

   2.   All states, as well as many cities and towns, have regulatory agencies that enforce laws and regulations regarding marketing practices within their states or municipalities.

E.   **Self-Regulatory Forces**

   1.   In an attempt to be good corporate citizens and to prevent government intervention, some businesses try to regulate themselves. A number of trade associations have developed self-regulatory programs.

   2.   The best-known nongovernmental regulatory group is the *Better Business Bureau*, a local agency supported by local businesses that aids in settling problems between specific business firms and customers.

         a)   The Council of Better Business Bureaus is a national organization composed of all local Better Business Bureaus.

         b)   The National Advertising Division of the Council of Better Business Bureaus operates a self-regulatory program that investigates claims of alleged deceptive advertising.

   3.   The *National Advertising Review Board (NARB)* is a self-regulatory entity that considers cases in which an advertiser challenges issues raised by the National Advertising Division about an advertisement. Though it has no official enforcement powers, the NARB can publicize questionable practices and file complaints with the FTC.

   4.   Self-regulatory programs have both advantages and disadvantages over laws and regulatory agencies.

         a)   Self-regulatory programs have the advantage of being less expensive to establish and implement, having more realistic and operational guidelines, and reducing the need to expand government bureaucracy.

         b)   Self-regulatory programs are limited because they are not mandatory for nonmembers, may lack the tools or authority to enforce guidelines, and may be less strict than those established by government agencies.

VI. **Technological Forces**
Technology is the application of knowledge and tools to solve problems and perform tasks more efficiently.

A. **Impact of Technology**
   1. Technology determines how society satisfies its physiological needs, such as improving communication.
   2. Technology can help marketers and consumers become more productive, but it also raises controversial issues.
   3. The effects of technology relate to such characteristics as dynamics, reach, and the self-sustaining nature of technological progress.
      a) The dynamics of technology involve the constant change that often challenges the structures of social institutions.
      b) Reach refers to the broad nature of technology as it moves through society.
      c) The self-sustaining nature of technology relates to the fact that technology acts as a catalyst to spur even faster development.
   4. The expanding opportunities for e-commerce—the sharing of business information and the ability to maintain business relationships and conduct marketing transactions via telecommunications networks—are changing the relationship between marketers and consumers.

(Tech Know: Cellphones: Technology Fuels Competition)

B. **Adoption and Use of Technology**
   1. It is important for firms to determine when a technology is changing an industry and to define the strategic influence of the new technology.

(Transparency Figure 3.2)

   2. The extent to which a firm can protect inventions stemming from research also influences its use of technology.
   3. Through "technology assessment," managers try to foresee the effects of new products and processes on the firm's operations, on other business organizations, and on society in general.

(Transparency Figure 3F)

(Transparency Figure 3I)

(Transparency Figure 3J)

VII. **Sociocultural Forces**
Sociocultural forces are the influences in a society and its culture(s) that bring about changes in attitudes, beliefs, norms, customs, and lifestyles.

A. **Demographic and Diversity Characteristics**
Changes in a population's demographic characteristics—age, gender, race, ethnicity, marital and parental status, income, and education—have a significant bearing on relationships and individual behavior because they lead to changes in how people live and consume products.

   1. One demographic change affecting the U.S. marketplace is the increasing proportion of older consumers.
   2. The number of singles is also on the rise, and they have different spending patterns than couples and families with children.

(Transparency Figure 3G)

3. The United States is about to enter another baby boom, and these children are more diverse than previous generations.
4. Immigration is increasing the multicultural nature of U.S. society.
5. These and other changes bring unique problems and opportunities for marketers.

B. **Cultural Values**

Changes in values have dramatically influenced people's needs and desires for products; these values change at varying speeds.

1. Issues of health, nutrition, and exercise have increased in importance, affecting behavior, lifestyles, and product choices.

(Transparency Figure 3E)

2. The concept of family is changing, though children remain important.
3. Today's consumers are more concerned about the natural environment.

C. **Consumerism**
1. *Consumerism* is a varied array of independent individuals, groups, and organizations seeking to protect consumers' rights.
2. They achieve their objectives by writing letters to companies, lobbying government agencies, broadcasting public service announcements, and boycotting companies whose activities they deem irresponsible.

NOTES FOR CLASS EXERCISES, DEBATE ISSUE, AND CHAPTER QUIZ

On the following pages, you will find two class exercises, a debate issue, and a chapter quiz. These are formatted in large-size type so that you can use them as class handouts or for making transparencies. Below are the authors' comments on the class exercises, the debate topic for this chapter, and the answers to the chapter quiz.

Comments on Class Exercise 1

The objective of this class exercise is to identify environmental forces that may affect a firm's marketing strategy and spark class discussion about the role marketers play within their communities. Wal-Mart's 950 Supercenter stores average between 100,000 and 200,000 square feet and offer one-stop shopping for discounted general merchandise and groceries. As indicated in the exercise, these stores have been controversial in some communities where residents fear the stores will profoundly affect their economy and quality of life. As indicated in the exercise, their concerns relate to urban sprawl, the continuing viability of local "mom and pop" stores, the destruction of historic sites (some sites have been destroyed to make way for Wal-Mart Supercenters), the ability of local tax dollars to support infrastructure to handle increased traffic associated with the stores, and the impact on local culture, especially downtown areas. As a result of these concerns, more than 150 communities in the United States and Canada have rejected developments featuring "big box" retailers like Wal-Mart or pressured developers to withdraw their plans.

In this exercise, students should attempt to classify these concerns as well as other issues they may think of according to the environmental forces introduced in the book. Below are some potential responses students may offer, from the perspective of both Wal-Mart and affected community residents. As an additional exercise, you might ask students what Wal-Mart could do to address the concerns of these communities.

Competitive Issues

- Residents may fear that Wal-Mart's low prices and product selection will make it difficult for small local firms to compete, forcing some of these firms out of business.

- Residents may fear that neighbors who once patronized downtown merchants may abandon those businesses in favor of traveling to a Wal-Mart Supercenter in a nearby city, again harming local firms.

Economic Forces:

- Residents may fear that Wal-Mart's entry into their community will hurt the local economy by putting local firms out of business.

- Residents may fear that Wal-Mart's entry into their community will be harmful because the community likely will have to build new infrastructure to support the store.

- Wal-Mart Supercenters may bring as many as 450 new jobs to a community.

- Wal-Mart Supercenters will generate significant tax revenues that remain within the community.

Political Forces:

- Communitites that fear the development of a new Wal-Mart Supercenter may lobby their elected or appointed local officials to reject zoning for the development or otherwise make it difficult to open a new store.

Legal and Regulatory Forces:

- Communities that fear the entrance of a Wal-Mart store may enact ordinances that make it difficult or impossible to develop "big box" retailers like Wal-Mart and Home Depot.

Sociocultural Forces:

- Residents may fear the impact a Wal-Mart Supercenter may have on their community's quality of life and sense of identity.

Comments on Class Exercise 2

The goal of this exercise is to help students realize the differences among the six marketing environmental forces. Answers:

1. Prosperity — **economic**
2. Federal Trade Commission — **regulatory**
3. Personal computers that understand human speech — **technological**
4. Development and widespread use of cellular phones — **technological**
5. People's willingness to spend — **economic**
6. Contributions to campaign funds — **political**
7. A society's high material standard of living — **sociocultural**
8. Sherman Antitrust Act — **legal**
9. Better Business Bureau — **regulatory**
10. Consumerism — **sociocultural**
11. Discretionary income — **economic**
12. Food and Drug Administration — **regulatory**
13. A monopoly — **competitive**
14. Government purchases of goods and services — **political**
15. Group of people threatening to boycott the sponsors of a television program that they believe contains too much sex and violence — **sociocultural**

DEBATE ISSUE

Is self-regulation an effective way to control and maintain good marketing practices?

CHAPTER QUIZ

Answers to Chapter Quiz 1. a; 2. b; 3. b; 4. a.

Class Exercise 1

ALTHOUGH WAL-MART SUPERCENTERS HAVE GEN-ERATED GREAT CUSTOMER SATISFACTION, THEY HAVE ALSO PROMPTED QUESTIONS ABOUT THEIR IMPACT ON COMMUNITIES. THESE ISSUES RELATE TO URBAN SPRAWL, THE VIABILITY OF LOCAL "MOM AND POP" STORES, THE DESTRUCTION OF HISTORIC SITES, THE ABILITY OF LOCAL TAX DOLLARS TO SUPPORT INFRASTRUCTURE TO HANDLE INCREASED TRAFFIC, AND THE IMPACT ON LOCAL CULTURE. SOME COMMUNITIES HAVE SUCCESSFULLY FOUGHT TO KEEP THEIR HOMETOWN IDENTITIES WAL-MART FREE. ON THE OTHER HAND, ONE NEW WAL-MART SUPERCENTER CAN CREATE 450 JOBS AND GEN-ERATE MILLIONS OF DOLLARS IN LOCAL TAXES. WHAT IMPACT ARE THESE SUPERCENTERS LIKELY TO HAVE ON THE FOLLOWING?

- **Competitive forces**

- **Economic forces**

- **Political forces**

- **Legal and regulatory forces**

- **Technological forces**

- **Sociocultural forces**

Class Exercise 2

THE SIX ENVIRONMENTAL FORCES ARE COMPETITIVE, ECONOMIC, POLITICAL, LEGAL AND REGULATORY, TECHNOLOGICAL, AND SOCIOCULTURAL. WITH WHICH FORCE IS EACH OF THE FOLLOWING MOST DIRECTLY ASSOCIATED?

1. Prosperity
2. Federal Trade Commission
3. Personal computers that understand human speech
4. Development and widespread use of cellular phones
5. People's willingness to spend
6. Contributions to campaign funds
7. A society's high material standard of living
8. Sherman Antitrust Act
9. Better Business Bureau
10. Consumerism
11. Discretionary income
12. Food and Drug Administration
13. A monopoly
14. Government purchases of goods and services
15. Group of people threatening to boycott the sponsors of a television program that they believe contains too much sex and violence

Debate Issue

IS SELF-REGULATION AN EFFECTIVE WAY TO CONTROL AND MAINTAIN GOOD MARKETING PRACTICES?

YES

- Self-regulation is less expensive and less restrictive than governmental regulation.

- Failure to implement self-regulation may lead to government intervention.

- Self-regulation leads to fewer complications within an industry.

- Self-regulation is a means of encouraging socially responsible behavior that enhances consumer goodwill.

NO

- Participation in self-regulation programs is voluntary in most industries.

- The industry trade associations that establish self-regulation guidelines have no authority to enforce the regulations.

- Companies that follow self-regulation guidelines are often at a competitive disadvantage relative to companies that do not.

- Industry-established regulations may not be as stringent as those established by the government.

Chapter Quiz

1. If M&M Mars Candies found a magazine article that provided key information on the television viewing habits of major candy consumer groups, this would be an example of information obtained through environmental

   a. scanning.

   b. forces.

   c. analysis.

   d. strategizing.

   e. management.

2. Which of the following would represent a brand competitor for Ford's Expedition sport utility vehicle?

   a. Dodge Caravan

   b. Chevrolet Suburban

   c. Ford Ranger

   d. Taxi ride

   e. Chevrolet Blazer rented from Avis

3. To move toward greater organizational accountability, the United States Sentencing Commission introduced guidelines that mitigate penalties for developing compliance programs called the

   a. Organizational Compliance Guidelines.

   b. Federal Sentencing Guidelines for Organizations.

   c. Federal Trade Guidelines.

   d. Antitrust Guidelines.

   e. Consumer Protection Guidelines.

4. Mixed concrete cannot be shipped farther than twenty-five miles because the concrete might harden in the truck. Citrus County Concrete Company is the only supplier of mixed concrete to customers within a thirty-mile radius. Citrus County Concrete is an example of which one of the following competitive structures?

   a. Monopoly

   b. Oligopoly

   c. Monopolistic competition

   d. Pure competition

   e. Monopsony

ANSWERS TO DISCUSSION AND REVIEW QUESTIONS

1.   **Why are environmental scanning and analysis important to marketers?**

Understanding the current state of the marketing environment and recognizing the threats and opportunities arising from changes within it help marketing managers assess the performance of current marketing efforts and develop marketing strategies for the future.

2.   **What are the four types of competition? Which is most important to marketers?**

Four types of competition include *brand competitors*, which market products with similar features, benefits, and prices to the same customers; *product competitors*, which compete in the same product class but their products have different features, benefits, and prices; *generic competitors*, which provide very different products that satisfy the same basic customer need; and *total budget competitors*, which compete for the limited financial resources of the same customers. Although all four types of competition can affect a firm's marketing performance, brand competitors are the most significant because buyers typically see the different products of these firms as direct substitutes for each other.

3.   **In what ways can each of the business cycle stages affect consumers' reactions to marketing strategies?**

Prosperity. Assuming a low level of inflation, total buying power is high because unemployment is low and aggregate income is high. Thus customers have the ability to purchase.

Recession. Total buying power declines because unemployment rises. The lack of buying power coupled with the general pessimism that often accompanies recession causes consumer spending to decline. Buyers become more conscious of price and value, desiring products that are basic and fundamental.

Depression. Total disposable income is at a minimum because wages are very low and unemployment is extremely high. Because of low disposable income and a total lack of confidence in the economy, consumers cut their spending to a minimum.

Recovery. Disposable income increases as the high unemployment rate declines. Customers become more optimistic about the state of the economy. Consumer spending levels increase.

4.   **What business cycle stage are we experiencing currently? How is this stage affecting business firms in your area?**

This question is designed to prompt students to analyze the current state of our economy and to evaluate the effects of these economic conditions on local businesses. One major issue to consider is the degree to which the state of the national economy affects local businesses.

5.   **Define *income, disposable income*, and *discretionary income*. How does each type of income affect consumer buying power?**

Income is the amount of money an individual receives through wages, rents, investments, pensions, and subsidy payments for a given time period. Disposable income is income remaining after paying taxes and is used for spending and/or saving. Discretionary income is disposable income that is available for spending and/or saving after an individual has purchased the basic necessities of food, clothing, and shelter. Each income measure relates to consumers' buying power because the size of each may affect the degree of buying power.

6. **How is consumer buying power affected by wealth and consumer credit?**

   As current credit use increases, so does current buying power. By allowing persons to spend future income now, credit increases current buying power but reduces future buying power. Wealth also increases buying power. Wealthy persons can use their wealth not only for current purchases but also to generate additional income and to acquire large amounts of credit.

7. **What factors influence a buyer's willingness to spend?**

   Factors that influence a buyer's willingness to spend are the product's price and value, the individual's level of satisfaction obtained from currently used products, family size, and the consumer's expectations about future employment, income, prices, and general economic conditions.

8. **Describe marketers' attempts to influence political forces.**

   Firms attempt to influence the political structure by helping to elect officials who are or will be favorable toward business interests. The help sometimes takes the form of campaign contributions, both legal and illegal. Such support may be simply to protect against unfavorable legislation rather than to prompt favorable legislation. Elected officials are expected to respond by supporting the business during their terms of office. Companies may also form political action committees (PACs), or they may lobby elected officials to favor a particular position.

9. **What types of problems do marketers experience as they interpret legislation?**

   Many laws and regulations that affect marketers are written in vague terms, and marketers must resort to legal counsel rather than rely on their own interpretations. Because the laws are sometimes ambiguous, a marketer may choose to operate in a legally questionable way to determine the extent to which it can function before being prosecuted under the law. Or, to ensure compliance with a law that is vaguely worded, a marketer may take a very conservative stand. New sentencing guidelines, which hold both companies and employees accountable in the event of a violation, have encouraged more firms to establish legal compliance programs.

10. **What are the goals of the Federal Trade Commission? List the ways in which the FTC affects marketing activities. Do you think a single regulatory agency should have such broad jurisdiction over so many marketing practices? Why or why not?**

    The FTC enforces laws and establishes guidelines and operating procedures. A major goal is to assist and inform businesses so that they may comply with the laws. The FTC explains to businesses what is considered unfair, deceptive, or illegal and considers each case on its own merits rather than strictly applying a single set of guidelines for all firms. The agency may encourage firms in an industry to establish their own trade practices voluntarily, but it also has the power to set guidelines. The FTC's actions affect marketing decisions and activities such as pricing, advertising, labeling, packaging, product development, and distribution.

    Because marketing involves continuous change, new marketing practices must be evaluated by the FTC each year. As new commissioners are appointed, FTC rulings regarding what is illegal or unfair also change. To do their job effectively, marketers must constantly review FTC decisions to discern the agency's current attitudes and positions.

11. **Name several nongovernmental regulatory forces. Do you believe self-regulation is more or less effective than governmental regulatory agencies? Why?**

One well-known nongovernmental agency is the Better Business Bureau (BBB), a local unit supported by local businesses. The BBB is concerned primarily with providing aid in settling problems that arise between consumers and businesses. The second part of this exercise can be used to stimulate class discussion about self-regulation. Businesspeople generally view self-regulation as a preferable alternative to further governmental intervention, but self-regulation may be unenforceable or less strict.

12. **What does the term *technology* mean to you? Do the benefits of technology outweigh its costs and potential dangers? Defend your answer.**

As the chapter states, spacecraft, computers, and the Internet are applications or outgrowths of technology, but none of them *is* technology. As defined in this chapter, technology is the application of knowledge and tools to accomplish tasks and solve problems. Students should be aware of this distinction.

Students should discuss aspects of their lives affected by technology, such as working, playing, learning, eating, drinking, sleeping, and other areas. In discussing the favorable and unfavorable aspects of technology, factors such as improved productivity, improved goods and services, increased leisure time, and improvements in education, communication, transportation, and entertainment should be weighed against the unfavorable technological effects of polluted air and water, health hazards, unemployment, and any other factors that students view as unwanted effects of technological applications.

13. **Discuss the impact of technology on marketing activities.**

Because technology affects people's desires for goods and services, it affects marketing activities. Technology influences the types of products that marketers can offer for sale; the production process, which affects the quality and price of products; the ways marketers reach consumers to communicate about products; and the way products are transported and stored.

14. **What factors determine whether a business organization adopts and uses technology?**

A business organization's use of technology is determined by the firm's ability to use it, consumers' ability and willingness to buy technologically improved products, the perceived long-run effects of applying technology, the extent to which the firm is technologically based, the degree to which technology is used as a competitive tool, and the extent to which the business can protect resulting technological applications through patents or other means.

15. **What is the evidence that cultural diversity is increasing in the United States?**

Statistics indicate immigration has increased, resulting in a greater population of minorities in the United States. These statistics suggest that blacks and Hispanics will comprise 13 percent and 17.6 percent, respectively, of the U.S. population by the year 2025. Additionally, the percentage of older Americans is increasing, as is the number of people under age 18. Such changes may have a profound effect on marketing activities.

16. **In what ways are cultural values changing? How are marketers responding to these changes?**

Among the cultural changes occurring are an increased emphasis on health, nutrition, fitness, the family, the environment, and a shift away from conspicuous consumption. Marketers are responding by researching these changing values and developing new products to address them.

17. **Describe consumerism. Analyze some active consumer forces in your area.**

Consumerism is a social movement that offers consumers means for expressing dissatisfaction and correcting some of the conditions that have caused it. Examples of forces in the students' area might include the Better Business Bureau, government agencies, independent consumer groups, or individual consumer activists.

COMMENTS ON THE CASES

[◉🔲◉] *CASE 3.1 NETSCAPE NAVIGATES A CHANGING ENVIRONMENT*

This case focuses on Netscape Communications and how it both exploited and responded to forces in the marketing environment. To introduce the case, you might ask if any students are using a Netscape web browser, subscribing to AOL's Netscape-branded dial-up Internet service, or regularly visiting the Netscape web site to use its free e-mail services or to check news stories. Ask whether these students have positive associations with the Netscape name and why. The purpose is to focus discussion on the factors that influence consumer attitudes and choices.

The first question asks about the factors in the marketing environment that helped Netscape achieve success and what factors later harmed the company. Students' responses will vary, but most should recognize that Netscape was founded because of a technological advance developed by one of its founders. The company's web browser had no significant competition in its early years, which allowed the company to grow. Also, sociocultural forces were a factor, with media hype over the Internet prompting more people to seek out products for web browsing. However, Microsoft's introduction of Internet Explorer and its decision to bundle this into Windows operating system software created intense competition that stifled Netscape's growth. Political, legal, and regulatory issues played an important role in the antitrust case against Microsoft. Before that case was resolved, AOL acquired Netscape and adopted Microsoft's browser rather than Netscape's browser. Finally, AOL identified customer interest in low-priced, basic Internet access and extended the Netscape brand to that type of service.

The second question asks about the advantages and disadvantages of AOL's decision to apply the Netscape brand to a basic dial-up Internet service. One advantage is that the brand is familiar to consumers and maintains a positive image. A second advantage is that the brand allows AOL to differentiate the basic Internet service from its broadband service and other offerings. One disadvantage is that customers may be confused because the Netscape brand has been associated with a web browser, not dial-up Internet service. A second disadvantage is that positioning Netscape as a brand of basic dial-up service may limit AOL's ability to use the brand on the Netscape Learning Center and other offerings.

The third question asks students to describe the current competitive structure of the web browser industry and assess the implications for Netscape's future in web browsers. Students probably know that Microsoft's Internet Explorer has maintained its market leader position, although smaller competitors such as Mozilla and Opera continue to operate. However, no strong challenger is currently battling Microsoft the way Netscape did at its peak. In the near term, because AOL is using the brand on dial-up Internet service, Netscape is unlikely to regain strength as a major player in web browsers.

Video Information

Company:	Netscape
Location:	Tape 1/DVD 1, Segment 3
Length:	5:58

Video Overview: This video examines how Netscape Communications has responded to forces in the marketing environment, particularly competitive and technological forces. After an intense fight with rival Microsoft, Netscape had to reinvent itself in an attempt to regain a part of its market position.

MULTIPLE-CHOICE QUESTIONS ABOUT THE VIDEO

1. According to the Netscape video, an extranet is a(n) _____ network.

    a.   public corporate
    b.   external public
    c.   internal corporate
    d.   private virtual
    e.   enterprise software

2. According to the Netscape video, the company's strategy is to become a(n)

    a.   enterprise software company.
    b.   extranet software company.
    c.   intranet software company.
    d.   Department of Defense contractor.
    e.   quick and nimble company.

3. In the Netscape video, Netscape CEO James Barksdale accused rival Microsoft of being a(n)

    a.   oligopoly.
    b.   monopoly.
    c.   monopolistic competitor.
    d.   brand competitor.
    e.   pure competitor.

ANSWERS TO MULTIPLE-CHOICE QUESTIONS ABOUT THE VIDEO

1. d

2. a

3. b

CASE 3.2 FRITO-LAY ADAPTS TO CHANGES IN THE ENVIRONMENT

The purpose of this case is to help students grasp the influence of complex environmental factors and changes on major marketing decisions. Frito-Lay snacks are available nationally, so this case should appeal to students because of their familiarity with the brand.

The first question asks students how competition affected Frito-Lay's responses to changes in the marketing environment. The case mentions that in anticipation of new FDA rules requiring food labels to disclose trans fats, Kraft (among other competitors) were getting ready to label foods and, where possible, reformulate recipes to reduce or replace trans fats. Frito-Lay took the spotlight and showed its commitment to customers by becoming the first in the industry to disclose trans fats and reduce or replace them. Frito-Lay also developed Stax potato crisps, packaged in a resealable container, as a response to Procter & Gamble's popular Pringles crisps.

Question 2 asks students to consider how cultural values affected the decisions made by food manufacturers in the snack-food industry. In recent years, consumers have become more aware of the risks of trans fats and more interested in healthy food and lifestyles. This prompted snack-food manufacturers to make current products healthier and develop new products with low or no trans fat content.

Question 3 asks why Frito-Lay would make a point of being the first food manufacturer to eliminate trans fats from its best-selling snack products, even years before the new labeling requirement took effect. Frito-Lay believed that it would gain an important competitive advantage by taking a leadership role in taking trans fats out of its most popular snack products. Because consumers were taking more interest in the issue of trans fats, Frito-Lay wanted to be seen as marketing healthier snack-food products.

CHAPTER 4

Social Responsibility and Ethics in Marketing

TEACHING RESOURCES QUICK REFERENCE GUIDE

Resource	Location
Purpose and Perspective	IRM, p. 55
Guide for Using Color Transparencies	IRM, p. 56
Lecture Outline	IRM, p. 56
Notes for Class Exercises, Debate Issue, and Chapter Quiz	IRM, p. 61
Class Exercise 1	IRM, p. 63
Class Exercise 2	IRM, p. 64
Debate Issue	IRM, p. 65
Chapter Quiz	IRM, p. 66
Answers to Discussion and Review Questions	IRM, p. 67
Comments on the Cases	IRM, p. 70
Case 4.1	IRM, p. 70
Video	Tape 1/DVD 1, Segment 4
Video Information	IRM, p. 71
Multiple-Choice Questions About the Video	IRM, p. 71
Case 4.2	IRM, p. 72
Transparency Acetates	Transparency package
Examination Questions: Essay	TB, p. 89
Examination Questions: Multiple-Choice	TB, p. 89
Examination Questions: True-False	TB, p. 114
Author-Selected Multiple-Choice Test Items	TB, p. 670
HMClassPrep Presentation Resources	CD-ROM
PowerPoint Slides	Instructor's website

Note: Additional resources are updated periodically and may be found on the accompanying student and instructor websites at http://www.prideferrell.com/.

PURPOSE AND PERSPECTIVE

This chapter surveys the role of social responsibility and ethics in marketing decision making. We begin by defining social responsibility and exploring its economic, legal, ethical, and philanthropic dimensions. We also discuss social responsibility issues, such as the natural environment, consumerism, and the marketer's role as a member of the community. Next we take a more detailed look at the role of ethics in marketing decisions. We consider ethical issues in marketing, the ethical decision-making process, and ways to improve ethical conduct in marketing. Finally, we focus on incorporating social responsibility and ethics into strategic planning.

GUIDE FOR USING COLOR TRANSPARENCIES

There are two groups of color transparencies. The transparencies identified by a double number are the same as the figures and tables in the text. The transparencies labeled with a number and a letter are illustrations that do not appear in the text, but they can be used as additional examples of concepts discussed.

LECTURE OUTLINE

(Transparency Figure 4A: Chapter Outline)

I. **The Nature of Social Responsibility**
   A. *Social responsibility* refers to an organization's obligation to maximize its positive impact and minimize its negative impact on society. It deals with the total effect of all marketing decisions on society.

(Transparency Figure 4B)

   1. There is ample evidence to demonstrate that ignoring society's demands for responsible marketing can destroy customers' trust and even prompt government regulations.
   2. Socially responsible activities can generate positive publicity and boost sales. Socially responsible efforts have a positive effect on local communities and indirectly help the sponsoring organization by attracting goodwill, publicity, and potential customers and employees.

(Transparency Figure 4C)

   3. While social responsibility is a positive concept in itself, most organizations embrace it in the expectation of indirect long-term benefits.
   B. **The Dimensions of Social Responsibility**
   1. Socially responsible organizations strive for *marketing citizenship* by adopting a strategic focus for fulfilling the economic, legal, ethical, and philanthropic social responsibilities that their stakeholders expect of them.
   2. *Stakeholders* include those constituents who have a "stake" or claim in some aspect of a company's products, operations, markets, industry, and outcomes; these include customers, employees, investors and shareholders, suppliers, governments, communities, and many others.

(Transparency Figure 4D)

3.   The economic, legal, ethical, and philanthropic dimensions of social responsibility can be viewed as a pyramid, as shown in Figure 4.1.

(Transparency Figure 4.1)

a)   At the most basic level, all companies have an economic responsibility to be profitable so they can provide a return on investment to their owners and investors, create jobs for the community, and contribute goods and services to the economy.

(Ethics and Social Responsibility: Has Wal-Mart Become Too Powerful?)

b)   Marketers are expected to obey all laws and regulations.

c)   *Marketing ethics* refers to principles and standards that define acceptable conduct in marketing as determined by various stakeholders, including the public, government regulators, private interest groups, consumers, industry, and the organization itself.

(Transparency Figure 4B)

(1)   The most basic of these principles have been codified as laws and regulations to encourage marketers to conform to society's expectations of conduct.

(2)   Ethical marketing decisions foster trust, which helps to build long-term marketing relationships.

d)   Philanthropic responsibilities are not required of a company, but they promote human welfare or goodwill, as do the economic, legal, and ethical dimensions of social responsibility.

(1)   Many firms use *cause-related marketing* by linking their products to a particular social cause on an ongoing or short-term basis.

(Transparency Figure 4E)

(2)   Some companies are going beyond financial contributions and adopting a *strategic philanthropy* approach, which is the synergistic use of organizational core competencies and resources to address key stakeholders' interests and achieve both organizational and social benefits.

C.   **Social Responsibility Issues**
Managers make decisions related to social responsibility every day. To be successful, a business must determine what customers, government regulators, and competitors, as well as society in general, want or expect in terms of social responsibility. There are three major categories of social responsibility issues.

1.   **The Natural Environment**
One of the more common ways marketers demonstrate social responsibility is through programs designed to protect and preserve the natural environment.

a)   Many companies are making contributions to environmental protection organizations, sponsoring and participating in clean-up events, promoting recycling, retooling manufacturing processes to minimize waste and pollution, and generally reevaluating the effects of their products on the natural environment.

b)   *Green marketing* refers to the specific development, pricing, promotion, and distribution of products that do not harm the natural environment.

c)   Although demand for economic, legal, and ethical solutions to environmental problems is widespread, the environmental movement in marketing includes many different groups, whose values and goals often conflict.

d)   Some environmentalists and marketers believe that companies should work to protect and preserve the natural environment by implementing the following goals:

(1)   Eliminate the concept of waste
(2)   Reinvent the concept of a product
(3)   Make prices reflect products' true cost
(4)   Make environmentalism profitable

2.   **Consumerism**
Consumerism refers to the efforts of independent individuals, groups, and organizations working to protect the rights of consumers.

a)   A number of interest groups and individuals have taken action against companies they consider irresponsible by lobbying government officials and agencies, engaging in letter-writing campaigns and boycotts, and making public service announcements.

b)   Of great importance to the consumer movement are four basic rights spelled out by President John F. Kennedy. These rights include the following:

(1)   The right to safety means that marketers have an obligation not to market a product that they know could harm consumers.

(2)   The right to be informed means that consumers should have access to and the opportunity to review all relevant information about a product before buying it.

(3)   The right to choose means that consumers should have access to a variety of products and services at competitive prices; they should also be assured of satisfactory quality and service at a fair price.

(4)   The right to be heard ensures that consumers' interests will receive full and sympathetic consideration in the formulation of government policy.

3.   **Community Relations**
Social responsibility also extends to marketers' roles as community members.

a)   Individual communities expect marketers to make philanthropic contributions to civic projects and institutions and to be "good corporate citizens."

b)   From a positive perspective, a marketer can significantly improve its community's quality of life through employment opportunities, economic development, and financial contributions to educational, health, cultural, and recreational causes.

II.   **The Nature of Ethics**

A.   Marketers should be aware of ethical standards for acceptable conduct from several viewpoints—company, industry, government, customers, special interest groups, and society at large.

(Ethics and Social Responsibility: Qwest Struggles with Legal Issues)

1.   When marketing activities deviate from accepted standards, the exchange process can break down, resulting in customer dissatisfaction, lack of trust, and lawsuits.

2.   Marketing ethics goes beyond legal issues.

a)   Although we often try to draw a boundary between legal and ethical issues, the distinction between the two is often blurred in decision making.

b)   The legal system provides a formal venue for marketers to resolve ethical disputes as well as legal ones.

B.   **Ethical Issues in Marketing**

An *ethical issue* is an identifiable problem, situation, or opportunity requiring an individual or organization to choose from among several actions that must be evaluated as right or wrong, ethical or unethical. Marketers must be able to identify these issues and decide how to resolve them.

(Transparency Figure 4F)

1.   Product-related ethical issues generally arise when marketers fail to disclose risks associated with a product or information regarding the function, value, or use of a product. Ethical issues also arise when marketers fail to inform customers about existing conditions or changes in product quality.

2.   Promotion can create ethical issues in a variety of ways, among them false or misleading advertising and manipulative or deceptive sales promotions, tactics, and publicity. Other ethical issues are linked to promotion, including the use of bribery in personal selling situations.

3.   In pricing, common ethical issues are price fixing, predatory pricing, and failure to disclose the full price of a purchase.

4.   Ethical issues in distribution involve relationships among producers and marketing middlemen. Other serious issues include manipulating a product's availability for purposes of exploitation and using coercion to force intermediaries to behave in a specific manner.

C.   **The Ethical Decision-Making Process**

(Transparency Figure 4.3)

1.   **Individual Factors**

a)   When people need to resolve ethical conflicts in their daily lives, they often base their decisions on their own values and principles of right or wrong.

(Transparency Figure 4G)

b)   However, research has established that an organization's values often have more influence on marketing decisions than a person's own values.

2.   **Organizational Factors**

a)   Marketers resolve ethical issues not only on the basis of what they learned from their backgrounds, but also on the basis of what they learn from others in the organization. The outcome of this learning process depends on the strength of each individual's personal values, opportunity for unethical behavior, and exposure to others who behave ethically or unethically.

b)   *Organizational*, or *corporate, culture* can be defined as a set of values, beliefs, goals, norms, and rituals that members of an organization share. An organization's culture gives its members meaning and suggests rules for how to behave and deal with problems within the organization.

c)   Top management, especially the chief executive officer or vice president of marketing, sets the ethical tone for the entire organization.

d)   Coworkers' influence on ethical choices depends on a person's exposure to unethical behavior. Especially in gray areas, the more a person is exposed to unethical activity by others in the organizational environment, the more likely it is that he or she will behave unethically.

e)   Organizational pressure plays a key role in creating ethical issues.

3.   **Opportunity**

a)   Opportunity—conditions that limit barriers or provide rewards—may also shape ethical decisions in marketing.

b)   If a marketer takes advantage of an opportunity to act unethically and is rewarded or suffers no penalty, he or she may repeat such acts as other opportunities arise.

c)   Opportunity to engage in unethical conduct is often a better predictor of unethical activities than personal values.

d)   Professional codes of conduct and ethics-related policies influence opportunity by prescribing what behaviors are acceptable.

e)   Individual factors as well as organizational culture may influence whether an individual becomes opportunistic and tries to take advantage of situations unethically.

D.   **Improving Ethical Conduct in Marketing**

(Transparency Figure 4H)

1.   It is possible to improve ethical conduct in an organization by hiring ethical employees and eliminating unethical ones.

a)   An organization must rid itself of "bad apples" through screening techniques and enforcement of the firm's ethics standards.

b)   The problem of the "bad barrel" can be resolved by redesigning the organization's image and culture so that it conforms to industry and societal norms of ethical conduct.

2.   If top management develops and enforces ethics and legal compliance programs to encourage ethical decision making, then it becomes a force to help individuals make better decisions.

3.   **Codes of Conduct**

a)   To improve ethics, many organizations have developed *codes of conduct* (also called codes of ethics), which consist of formalized rules and standards that describe what the company expects of its employees.

b)   Codes of conduct promote ethical behavior by reducing opportunities for unethical behavior; employees know both what is expected of them and what kind of punishment they face if they violate the rules.

c)   Codes of conduct do not have to be so detailed that they take into account every situation, but they should provide guidelines that enable employees to achieve organizational objectives in an ethical, acceptable manner.

4.   **Ethics Officers**

a)   Organizational compliance programs must have oversight by high-ranking persons in the organization known to abide by legal and common ethical standards.

b)   Ethics officers usually are responsible for creating and distributing the code of conduct, enforcing the code, and meeting with organizational members to discuss or provide advice about ethical issues. They may also set up toll-free "hotlines" to provide advice.

5.   **Implementing Ethics and Legal Compliance Programs**

a)   To nurture ethical conduct in marketing, open communication and coaching on ethical issues are essential. This requires providing employees with ethics training, clear channels of communication, and follow-up support throughout the organization.

b)   It is important that companies consistently enforce standards and impose penalties or punishment on those who violate codes of conduct. The company must also take reasonable steps in response to violations of standards and, as appropriate, revise the compliance program to diminish the likelihood of future misconduct.

        c)   The identification of ethical issues and implementation of compliance programs and codes of conduct that incorporate both legal and ethical concerns constitute the best approach to preventing violations and avoiding litigation.

III.   **Incorporating Social Responsibility and Ethics into Strategic Planning**

     A.   Although the concepts of ethics and social responsibility are used interchangeably, it is important to distinguish between the two concepts.

        1.   Ethics relates to individual and group decisions—judgments about what is right or wrong in a particular decision-making situation.

        2.   Social responsibility deals with the total effect of marketing decisions on society.

     B.   If other persons in an organization approve of an activity, and it is legal and customary within the industry, chances are that the activity is acceptable from both an ethical and a social responsibility perspective.

(Transparency Figure 4I)

(Transparency Figure 4J)

     C.   **Being Socially Responsible and Ethical Is Not Easy**

(Transparencies Figure 4K (1), Figure 4K (2))

        1.   To promote socially responsible and ethical behavior while achieving organizational goals, marketers must monitor changes and trends in society's values.

        2.   After determining what society wants, marketers must then attempt to predict the long-term effects of decisions pertaining to those wants.

        3.   There are costs associated with many of society's demands.

        4.   In trying to satisfy the desires of one group, marketers may dissatisfy others.

        5.   Balancing society's demands to satisfy all members of society is difficult, if not impossible. Marketers must evaluate the extent to which members of society are willing to pay for what they want.

     D.   **Social Responsibility and Ethics Improve Marketing Performance**

        1.   There is increasing evidence that being socially responsible and ethical pays.

        2.   Recognition is growing that the long-term value of conducting business in a socially responsible manner far outweighs short-term costs.

        3.   While it is true that the concepts of ethics and social responsibility are controversial, it is possible—and desirable—to incorporate ethics and social responsibility into the planning process.

NOTES FOR CLASS EXERCISES, DEBATE ISSUE, AND CHAPTER QUIZ

On the following pages, you will find two class exercises, a debate issue, and a chapter quiz. These are formatted in large-size type so that you can use them as class handouts or for making transparencies. Below are the authors' comments on the class exercises, the debate topic for this chapter, and the answers to the chapter quiz.

Class Exercise 1

The objective of this class exercise is to help students identify ethical issues and understand the importance of codes of ethics.

Question 1. You might ask students which of the listed gifts "crosses the line" with regard to their own perception of what is ethical. Students might change their minds about acceptable gifts if asked, "What if everyone did it?" A distribution manager who accepts a gift of any magnitude may make a decision that is not necessarily in the best interest of the company (e.g., selecting a higher-cost trucking company because it provides box seats to ball games).

Question 2. You might ask students if they know of instances in their own jobs where organizational relationships have had a negative or positive effect on ethical decision making. For instance, how does seeing a boss file inaccurate expense reports (to cover unauthorized expenditures) affect others in the firm? How might people react when peers take supplies or merchandise home?

Question 3. The role of opportunity may determine whether a person will behave ethically. You might also want to ask, "What if I gave an exam and left the classroom for the hour—would you be more likely to cheat?" Opportunity may be a better predictor of unethical activities than personal values.

Question 4. An effective code of ethics should let employees know both what is expected of them and the punishment for violating the rules. For instance, a firm may have a policy against accepting any gifts valued over $25. The penalty for accepting anything over that amount may be dismissal. However, simply having a policy or code will be ineffective if top management and superiors do not support and enforce it.

Class Exercise 2

The main objective of this exercise is to discuss the complex issues in defining ethical behaviors. Have the class discuss the ethical issues in each situation and determine whether the action described is ethical or unethical. You could also have the students discuss what it means to be ethical or unethical. Can a manager be truly ethical across all situations? What is the role of understanding the circumstances in ethical decision making? Try not to moralize by telling the students the right answer (if there is one). Encourage the students to reach a group consensus.

DEBATE ISSUE

Can ethics be taught?

CHAPTER QUIZ

Answers to Chapter Quiz 1. b; 2. a; 3. e; 4. c.

Class Exercise 1

YOU ARE THE DISTRIBUTION MANAGER FOR A LARGE CONSUMER PRODUCTS FIRM. YOUR COMPANY IS ABOUT TO RELEASE A VERY LARGE SHIPMENT OF PRODUCTS. AS MANAGER, YOU MUST CHOOSE AMONG SEVERAL TRANSPORTATION COMPANIES THAT ARE COMPETING FOR YOUR BUSINESS. SALES REPRESENTATIVES FROM RAILROAD AND TRUCKING COMPANIES OFTEN MAKE CALLS TO YOUR OFFICE. YOUR DECISION WILL MEAN THE LOSS OR GAIN OF MILLIONS OF DOLLARS OF REV-ENUE FOR THESE COMPANIES.

1. Which of the following gifts would you be willing to accept from sales representatives of the transportation companies?

   - Pen and pencil set (with the company's logo)
   - Five-year supply of scratch pads (with logo)
   - Dinner for four at an exclusive restaurant
   - Season tickets to a professional football team
   - Fruits and nuts delivered to you each Christmas
   - Three-day, all-expense-paid golfing vacation
   - $500 in cash
   - Bag of groceries delivered to your home each week
   - Lavish trip to the Cayman Islands

2. What role would top management, superiors, and peers play in your decision on accepting these gifts?

3. If you had the chance to take some of the gifts on the list without anyone knowing, would you?

4. Would a code of ethics or an ethical corporate culture help you in making your decision?

Class Exercise 2

HOW ETHICAL ARE THE FOLLOWING BEHAVIORS?

1. The manufacturer of a leading insect spray changes the formulation of its product to eliminate problems with some people being allergic to one of its ingredients. The manufacturer does not inform consumers. The change in the formula will make the product less effective.

2. A bribe is paid to a company official in the island country of Kocomo to facilitate the movement of a product in that country. Bribes are a normal and expected business practice in Kocomo.

3. A beer company engages in an advertising campaign that targets undergraduate college students, many of whom are under the legal drinking age.

4. A rental car company strongly advises customers to purchase insurance when renting a car. Although most personal car insurance policies cover insured motorists when driving a rental car, most rental car customers are not aware of it.

5. *Consumer Reports* publishes the results of a study on shampoos that provides strong evidence that all shampoos are basically the same. In fact, the results suggest that a mild dishwashing liquid will do the same job for a lot less money. After the study is published, a leading shampoo marketer claims that its latest product will remove oil, add body, condition, and replenish hair better than any competing shampoo and do it all in one step.

Debate Issue

CAN ETHICS BE TAUGHT?

YES

- Courses on business ethics can teach students how to analyze ethical dilemmas.

- By focusing on those factors that influence marketing decisions (individual factors, organizational factors, and opportunity), students can understand why decision makers behave as they do.

- Many companies and colleges are instituting ethical training programs to teach the principles of ethical decision making.

- Once the training is complete, students can apply what they have learned to the ethical dilemmas they face.

NO

- An individual's beliefs, values, and morals are developed long before he or she enters school or begins a career.

- Every person's morality is shaped by his or her social experiences with family, friends, school, and church.

- No course or training session in marketing ethics can change a person's deep-rooted and long-held beliefs and values.

- Learning ethical principles does not guarantee that they will be used.

Chapter Quiz

1. Marketing ethics
   a. refers to laws and regulations that govern marketing.
   b. refers to principles and standards that define acceptable conduct in marketing.
   c. maximizes an organization's positive impact and minimizes its negative impact on society.
   d. is most important for advertising agencies.
   e. applies well-defined rules for appropriate marketing behavior.

2. Which of the following is *not* one of the four dimensions of social responsibility as presented in your text?
   a. Green marketing
   b. Philanthropic
   c. Ethical
   d. Economic
   e. Legal

3. Based on the text, which of the following is *not* a factor that influences the ethical decision-making process?
   a. Opportunity
   b. Individual factors
   c. Organizational culture
   d. Organizational pressure
   e. Salary or wages

4. Which of the following is *not* a goal of green marketing?
   a. Eliminate the concept of waste
   b. Reinvent the concept of a product
   c. Make the work force match the population in terms of diversity
   d. Make prices reflect the cost
   e. Make environmentalism profitable

ANSWERS TO DISCUSSION AND REVIEW QUESTIONS

1. **What is social responsibility, and why is it important?**

    Social responsibility refers to an organization's obligation to maximize its positive impact and minimize its negative impact on society. Ignoring society's demands for responsible marketing can destroy customers' trust, prompt government regulation or litigation, and jeopardize a marketer's financial standing. On the other hand, socially responsible activities can generate positive publicity and boost sales. Most organizations embrace the concept of social responsibility with the expectation of indirect long-term benefits.

2. **What are stakeholders? What role do they play in strategic marketing decisions?**

    Stakeholders include those constituents who have a "stake" or claim in some aspect of a company's products, operations, markets, industry, and outcomes; these include customers, employees, investors and shareholders, suppliers, governments, communities, and many others. Because stakeholders interact with marketers, they affect and are affected by marketing strategy decisions. Their expectations also determine the economic, legal, ethical, and social responsibilities marketers should fulfill.

3. **What are four dimensions of social responsibility? What impact do they have on marketing decisions?**

    Social responsibility includes economic, legal, ethical, and philanthropic dimensions. Economic and legal responsibilities are the most basic levels of social responsibility; failure to consider them may mean that a marketer is not around long enough to engage in ethical or philanthropic activities. The most basic of marketing ethics principles have been codified as laws and regulations to encourage marketers to conform to society's expectations of conduct. Philanthropic efforts are not required of a company, but they promote human welfare and goodwill.

4. **What is strategic philanthropy? How does it differ from more traditional philanthropic efforts?**

    Strategic philanthropy refers to the synergistic use of organizational core competencies and resources to address key stakeholders' interests and to achieve both organizational and social benefits. This approach differs from more traditional philanthropic efforts through its strategic linkage of employees and organizational resources and expertise to address key stakeholders' concerns.

5. **What are some major social responsibility issues? Give an example of each.**

    Among major social responsibility issues are the natural environment, consumerism, and community relations. Students' responses to the second part of the exercise will vary, but they should be able to cite appropriate examples for each issue.

    The Natural Environment: Examples might include specific companies that are making contributions to environmental protection organizations, sponsoring and participating in clean-up events, promoting recycling, and retooling manufacturing processes to minimize waste and pollution.

    Consumerism: Examples might include specific companies that have responded positively to consumer issues, such as StarKist's dolphin-safe tuna.

    Community Relations: Examples might include specific companies that have made significant financial or resource contributions to social causes or companies that engage in strategic philanthropy by tying their social programs to their own goals.

6. **What is the difference between ethics and social responsibility?**

   Marketing ethics is a dimension of social responsibility that refers to principles and standards that define acceptable conduct in marketing. Social responsibility is a broader concept that refers to an organization's obligation to maximize its positive impact and minimize its negative impact on society. Ethics relates to doing the "right thing" in making individual and group decisions, whereas social responsibility deals with the total effect of marketing decisions on society.

7. **Why is ethics an important consideration in marketing decisions?**

   It is important for marketers to go beyond legal issues and work to foster mutual trust among individuals and in marketing relationships. Consumers generally regard unethical marketing activities, such as deceptive advertising, misleading selling tactics, price collusion, and marketing of harmful products, as unacceptable and often refuse to do business with marketers who engage in such practices. Additionally, engaging in questionable activities may prompt government regulation or litigation and jeopardize a marketer's financial standing.

8. **How do the factors that influence ethical or unethical decisions interact?**

   Individual factors, organizational factors (e.g., organizational culture, organizational relationships, organizational pressure), and opportunity are the three factors that interact to determine ethical decisions in marketing. People often base their decisions on their own values and principles of right or wrong, but ethical choices in marketing are most often made jointly, in work groups and committees, or in conversations with coworkers. Within the organization, superiors (especially top management), peers, subordinates, organizational culture, and organizational pressure play key roles in the ethical decision-making process. When opportunities are available, individuals can act according to their own best interests if the organization has provided limited direction. In the absence of strong leadership or organizational policies on ethics, marketers may base their decisions on their own values or the observed behavior of coworkers and take advantage of opportunities to act improperly.

9. **What ethical conflicts could exist if business employees fly on certain airlines just to receive benefits for their personal "frequent-flyer" programs?**

   The potential for ethical conflicts would depend on the company's policy. If the company has a policy that specifies that frequent-flyer mileage belongs to the company, then no ethical conflict would exist. However, if the company allows its employees to keep all frequent-flyer mileage, then it would depend on whether the employee chose the better value for the company. If the employee chooses a higher-priced airline just to get the frequent-flyer miles, then the company is being injured and the employee's action would be unethical. If the employee's airline happens to be the best value, then both parties benefit. A company could eliminate the potential for ethical conflicts by making airline reservations for all employees.

10. **Give an example of how each component of the marketing mix can be affected by ethical issues.**

   Answers for these will vary, but students should be able to cite appropriate examples.

   Product: The brand name can be misleading. Citrus Hill Fresh Orange Juice was changed due to the controversy over its being made from concentrate—not fresh orange juice. The product can be dangerous—General Motors mounted fuel tanks of some pickup trucks outside the frame, even though they were found to be involved in fiery crashes twice as often as other trucks.

   Promotion: False or misleading advertising claims. Mobil agreed to stop making claims of biodegradability of its trash bags. Aggressive telemarketing of questionable products (worthless securities, vacations with strings attached, and so on) over the phone.

   Pricing: Inflating prices during peak sales periods and/or manipulating the supply of the product. Nintendo allegedly raised its prices by 20 to 30 percent during the Christmas season and then limited the supply of the games.

   Distribution: Distributing counterfeit products. Some record stores distribute bootleg recordings, and some computer software retailers are making unauthorized copies of software.

11. **How can the ethical decisions involved in marketing be improved?**

   Ethical decisions in marketing organizations can be improved by eliminating unethical persons through screening techniques, by enforcing the firm's ethical standards, and by improving the organization's ethical standards. Establishing and enforcing codes of conduct and other corporate policies on ethics help eliminate the opportunity to act unethically. Appointment of an ethics officer can help a firm establish a code of conduct, train employees to deal with ethical issues, and take action on possible violations of the code of conduct. Establishing and enforcing codes of ethics and effective ethical compliance programs can also help minimize penalties to an organization should one of its employees break the law.

12. **How can people with different personal values work together to make ethical decisions in organizations?**

   While individuals may define ethics differently and not agree on personal ethical standards, they should be able to join together and agree on standards of acceptable behavior to guide all marketing decisions within the organization. Providing employees with clear codes of conduct, ethics training, clear channels of communication, and follow-up support throughout the organization can help them understand the company's position on specific ethical issues as well as the punishment should they violate the company's policies.

13. **What tradeoffs might a company have to make to be socially responsible and responsive to society's demands?**

   There are costs associated with many of society's demands and satisfying these demands often involves tradeoffs. For example, society has expressed a demand for a cleaner environment and the preservation of wildlife habitats, but it also wants low-priced products. Moreover, in trying to satisfy the desires of one group, marketers may dissatisfy others. Thus, marketers must carefully evaluate the extent to which members of society are willing to pay for what they want, and it must assess the impact of any social responsibility program on its specified target markets.

14. **What evidence exists that being socially responsible and ethical is worthwhile?**

Research has shown that companies that do not develop strategies and programs to incorporate ethics and social responsibility into their organizational cultures may suffer poor marketing performance and the potential costs of legal violations, civil litigation, and damaging publicity when questionable activities are publicized. Companies that do incorporate ethics and social responsibility into their strategic plans experience improved marketing performance as a result of a more positive reputation among consumers, which may lead to increased sales.

COMMENTS ON THE CASES

CASE 4.1 NEW BELGIUM BREWING COMPANY

This case should help students recognize that even small businesses can be socially responsible and their initiatives can help them gain a competitive advantage. The founders of New Belgium Brewing Company have attempted to address social concerns about the natural environment throughout the process of brewing and marketing its craft beers. The firm's environmental efforts have won the firm numerous awards and devoted customers.

The first question asks students to describe the steps the company has taken to be socially responsible. According to the case, New Belgium looks for cost-efficient, energy-saving alternatives to conducting business and reducing its impact on the environment. Examples of these alternatives include the firm's investment in wind power, reuse of brewing resources, recycling of supplies, use of natural lighting in the brew house, and encouraging employees to ride bicycles to work. Additionally, the firm contributes $1/barrel of beer sold to various cultural, social, environmental, and drug and alcohol awareness programs.

Question 2 asks students how New Belgium can justify donating $1/barrel of beer sold to environmental and community causes. Responses will vary, but students should recognize that New Belgium's philanthropic efforts have helped the firm gain a reputation for being a socially responsible marketer, which may give the firm a competitive advantage in the increasingly competitive market for microbrewed beers. As long as the firm has satisfied its economic and legal social responsibilities, its managers are free to pursue whatever level of philanthropic responsibility they feel appropriate and desired by stakeholders.

The third question asks whether New Belgium Brewing Company's actions and initiatives exemplify a socially responsible business given that its primary product, beer, is considered inherently harmful by some members of society. This question should prompt a spirited discussion as to whether and how the inherent nature of a company's products relate to stakeholder perceptions of its social responsibility. To fuel this discussion, you might remind students that larger brewing companies, including Anheuser-Busch and Miller Brewing, also donate funds and resources to charitable causes and run advertisements that encourage consumers to drink responsibly. As a devil's advocate, you might also ask students whether they think that New Belgium is more socially responsible than a hypothetical pharmaceutical firm which markets a life-saving drug yet does not make charitable donations or otherwise go beyond fulfilling its basic economic and legal responsibilities. Students' responses to the primary question will vary, but the discussion should help them recognize that the idea of social responsibility remains some-what subjective and depends on the perceptions of diverse stakeholder groups.

Video Information

Company:	New Belgium Brewing Company
Location:	Tape 1/DVD 1, Segment 4
Length:	10:00

Video Overview: This video profiles a small business that has made environmental responsibility a core operating principle. The New Belgium Brewing Company has won numerous awards for addressing the founders' social concerns about the natural environment throughout the process of brewing and marketing the firm's "microbrews." The small brewery also engages in corporate philanthropy to benefit the communities it serves.

MULTIPLE-CHOICE QUESTIONS ABOUT THE VIDEO

1. New Belgium believes it is essential to expand its technological capabilities. To accomplish this, _____ percent of all its technology purchases are new technology, with _____ percent of that being unproven technology with a high risk of failure.
   a. 20; 20
   b. 20; 50
   c. 50; 20
   d. 50; 50
   e. 80; 20

2. New Belgium Brewing Company uses which type of power to reduce waste?
   a. Wind power
   b. Steam power
   c. Solar power
   d. Hydroelectricity
   e. Pedal power

3. New Belgium Brewing Company uses all of the following to reduce waste *except:*
   a. evaporative cooling.
   b. sun tubes.
   c. methane gas from waste water.
   d. air conditioning.
   e. paper recycling.

ANSWERS TO MULTIPLE-CHOICE QUESTIONS ABOUT THE VIDEO

1. b

2. a

3. d

CASE 4.2 SCANDAL AT MARTHA STEWART LIVING OMNIMEDIA INC.

When assigning this case, you may want to have students research a brief update, as some or all of the issues described in the case may have been resolved by this time. To begin the class discussion of the case, you might want to ask students how many have watched Martha Stewart's TV shows or read one of her magazines. To spark a marketing-oriented discussion of the issues, you might also ask students who have strong opinions about Martha Stewart if the scandal has affected their opinion of her and her branded products.

The first question asks how Martha Stewart's involvement in the insider-trading scandal affected her company and branded products. According to the case, the scandal harmed the company, as evidenced by declining television ratings and magazine advertising revenues. Additionally, the scandal jeopardized the company's continued viability without Martha Stewart at the helm.

Question 2 asks students whether Stewart's full-page newspaper ad proclaiming her innocence was ethical, and what level of responsibility Stewart has to her company and its stakeholders. Students' responses will vary according to their own ethical standards and views. Some, especially those with positive feelings toward Martha Stewart, will argue that she has the right to defend herself and to attempt to protect her name and her company. They may even argue that a failure to defend her name could be considered irresponsible toward some stakeholder groups, especially investors, employees, and customers. Others, particularly those with negative feelings toward Martha Stewart, may argue that few scandal subjects can afford to take out such an expensive ad and that the ad may have unfairly appealed to the firm's customers. In any case, most students will agree that Stewart, as founder and then-chairman and CEO, had full responsibility for her actions.

The third question asks students to consider whether Martha Stewart Living Omnimedia can survive her conviction. This question is designed to help students look beyond the issues in the case to the consequences companies face for the actions of individuals within them. Responses will vary, but students should be able to cite examples and concepts from the case and text to support their answers.

CHAPTER 5

Global Markets and International Marketing

TEACHING RESOURCES QUICK REFERENCE GUIDE

Resource	Location
Purpose and Perspective	IRM, p. 73
Guide for Using Color Transparencies	IRM, p. 73
Lecture Outline	IRM, p. 74
Notes for Class Exercises, Debate Issue, and Chapter Quiz	IRM, p. 79
Class Exercise 1	IRM, p. 82
Class Exercise 2	IRM, p. 83
Debate Issue	IRM, p. 84
Chapter Quiz	IRM, p. 85
Answers to Discussion and Review Questions	IRM, p. 86
Comments on the Cases	IRM, p. 88
Case 5.1	IRM, p. 88
Video	Tape 1/DVD 1, Segment 5
Video Information	IRM, p. 88
Multiple-Choice Questions About the Video	IRM, p. 89
Case 5.2	IRM, p. 89
Transparency Acetates	Transparency package
Examination Questions: Essay	TB, p. 121
Examination Questions: Multiple-Choice	TB, p. 121
Examination Questions: True-False	TB, p. 143
Author-Selected Multiple-Choice Test Items	TB, p. 670
HMClassPrep Presentation Resources	CD-ROM
PowerPoint Slides	Instructor's website

Note: Additional resources are updated periodically and may be found on the accompanying student and instructor websites at http://www.prideferrell.com/.

PURPOSE AND PERSPECTIVE

This chapter examines the increasing importance and unique features of global markets and international marketing. We show how target market selection in foreign countries is structured by the environment by covering the basic environmental variables. Several regional and global trade agreements, alliances, and markets are considered. We examine the levels of commitment American firms have to international marketing. Finally, we look at customization versus globalization of international marketing strategies.

GUIDE FOR USING COLOR TRANSPARENCIES

There are two groups of color transparencies. The transparencies identified by a double number are the same as the figures and tables in the text. The transparencies labeled with a number and a letter are illustrations that do not appear in the text, but they can be used as additional examples of concepts discussed.

LECTURE OUTLINE

(Transparency Figure 5A: Chapter Outline)

I. **The Nature of International Marketing**
    A. Technological advances and rapidly changing political and economic conditions are making it easier for more companies to market their products overseas as well as at home.
    B. *International marketing* involves developing and performing marketing activities across national boundaries.

(Transparency Figure 5B)

(Transparency Figure 5C)

    C. Many U.S. firms are finding that international markets provide tremendous opportunities for growth.

II. **Environmental Forces in International Markets**
    A successful international marketing strategy requires a careful environmental analysis to understand the needs and desires of foreign customers. Differences in sociocultural, economic, political, legal, and technological forces can profoundly affect marketing strategies.

    A. **Cultural, Social, and Ethical Forces**
        1. Cultural, social, and ethical differences among nations can have significant effects on marketing activities.
        2. Because marketing activities are primarily social in purpose, they are influenced by beliefs and values regarding family, religion, education, health, and recreation.
        3. It can be difficult to transfer marketing symbols, trademarks, logos, and even products to international markets.
        4. Cultural differences may also affect marketing negotiations and decision-making behavior.
        5. Buyers' perceptions of other countries can influence product adoption and use.
        6. When products are introduced from one nation into another, acceptance is far more likely if there are similarities between the two cultures.

(Transparency Figure 5D)

(Global Marketing: Supersizing Europeans)

        7. Differences in ethical standards can also affect marketing efforts.

(Transparency Figure 5E)

B. **Economic Forces**
Global marketers need to understand the international trade system, particularly the economic stability of individual nations as well as trade barriers that may stifle marketing efforts.

1. Economic differences among nations dictate many of the adjustments that must be made in marketing abroad.
2. Marketers should consider whether a nation imposes trade restrictions.
    a) An *import tariff* is any duty levied by a nation on goods bought outside its borders and brought in.
    b) A *quota* is a limit on the amount of goods an importing country will accept for certain product categories in a specific time period.
    c) An *embargo* is a government's suspension of trade in a particular product or with a given country.
    d) *Exchange controls* are government restrictions on the amount of a particular currency that can be bought or sold.
3. Countries may limit imports to maintain a favorable *balance of trade*, which is the difference in value between a nation's exports and imports.
4. Knowledge about per capita income, credit, and the distribution of income provides general insights into market potential.
    a) *Gross domestic product (GDP)* is an overall measure of a nation's economic standing; it is the market value of a nation's total output of goods and services for a given period.
    b) Per capita income is gross domestic product in relation to population.
5. Opportunities for international trade are not limited to countries with the highest incomes.

(Transparency Figure 5F)

C. **Political and Legal Forces**
1. A nation's political system, laws, regulatory bodies, special interest groups, and courts all have great impact on international marketing.
2. A government's policies toward public and private enterprise, consumers, and foreign firms influence marketing across national boundaries through tariff and nontariff barriers.
3. Differences in national standards are illustrated by the use of payoffs and bribes, which are deeply entrenched practices in some governments.

D. **Technological Forces**
1. Advances in technology (i.e., e-mail, voice mail, fax, cellular phones, and the Internet) have made international marketing more affordable and convenient.
2. In many developing countries that lack the level of technological infrastructure found in the United States, marketers are beginning to capitalize on opportunities to "leapfrog" existing technology.

III. **Regional Trade Alliances, Markets, and Agreements**
Although more firms are beginning to view the world as one huge marketplace, various regional trade alliances and specific markets affect companies engaging in international marketing; some create opportunities, others impose restraints.

(Transparency Figure 5G)

A.   **The North American Free Trade Agreement (NAFTA)**
1.   *The North American Free Trade Agreement (NAFTA)*, which went into effect in 1994, effectively merged Canada, Mexico, and the United States into one market of more than 421 million consumers.
    a)   NAFTA will eliminate virtually all tariffs on goods produced in and traded between Canada, Mexico, and the United States to create a totally free trade area by 2009.
    b)   NAFTA makes it easier for U.S. businesses to invest in Mexico and Canada, provides protection for intellectual property, expands trade by requiring equal treatment of U.S. firms in both countries, and simplifies country-of-origin rules.
    c)   Canada's consumers are relatively affluent and represent a significant market for U.S. firms.
    d)   The growth of Mexico's economy represents a significant opportunity for U.S. firms and, despite some economic instability, provides an opportunity to reach other Latin American countries while strengthening NAFTA.
2.   Efforts to create a Free Trade Area of the Americas (FTAA), a free trade agreement among the 34 nations of North and South America, were expected to be completed in 2005.
3.   Although NAFTA has been controversial, it has become a positive factor for U.S. firms wishing to engage in international marketing.

B.   **The European Union (EU)**
1.   The *European Union (EU)*—which today includes Austria, Belgium, Cyprus, the Czech Republic, Denmark, Estonia, Finland, France, Hungary, Germany, Greece, Ireland, Italy, Latvia, Lithuania, Luxembourg, Malta, the Netherlands, Poland, Portugal, Slovakia, Slovenia, Spain, Sweden, and the United Kingdom—was officially formed in 1958 to promote trade among its members.
2.   To facilitate free trade among members, the EU is working toward the standardization of business regulations and requirements, import duties, and value-added taxes; the elimination of customs checks; and the creation of a standardized currency for use by all members. (Austria, Belgium, Finland, France, Germany, Ireland, Italy, Luxembourg, the Netherlands, Portugal, and Spain have begun using a common currency, the "euro.") These changes have not been without controversy, however.
3.   As the EU nations attempt to function as one large market, consumers in the EU may become more homogeneous in their needs and wants. Marketers should be aware, however, that cultural differences among the nations may require modifications in the marketing mix for customers in each nation.

C.   **The Common Market of the Southern Cone (MERCOSUR)**
1.   The *Common Market of the Southern Cone (MERCOSUR)* was established in 1991 to unite Argentina, Brazil, Paraguay, and Uruguay as a free trade alliance.
2.   The alliance promotes the free circulation of goods, services, and production factors among member nations.

D.   **Asia-Pacific Economic Cooperation (APEC)**
1.   The *Asia-Pacific Economic Cooperation (APEC)*, established in 1989, promotes open trade and economic and technical cooperation among member nations, which today include Australia, Brunei Darussalam, Canada, Chile, China, Chinese Taipei, Indonesia, Hong Kong, Japan, Korea, Malaysia, Mexico, New Zealand, Papua New Guinea, Peru, the Philippines, Russia, Singapore, Thailand, the United States, and Vietnam.

2.   APEC differs from other international trade alliances in its commitment to facilitating business and its practice of allowing the business/private sector to participate in a wide range of alliance activities.

3.   Despite economic turmoil and a recession in Asia in recent years, companies of the APEC have become increasingly competitive and sophisticated in global business.

    a)   Despite the high volume of trade between the United States and Japan, the two nations continue to struggle with cultural and political differences and are, in general, at odds over how to do business with each other.

    b)   The People's Republic of China represents a huge potential market opportunity with its 1.3 billion people, but there are many risks associated with doing business in China.

    c)   Pacific Rim regions, such as South Korea, Thailand, Singapore, Taiwan, Vietnam, and Hong Kong, have become major manufacturing and financial centers.

E.   **General Agreement on Tariffs and Trade (GATT) and World Trade Organization (WTO)**

1.   The *General Agreement on Tariffs and Trade (GATT)* is based on negotiations between member countries to reduce worldwide tariffs and increase international trade; it provides a forum for tariff negotiations and a place where international trade problems can be discussed and resolved.

2.   The most recent round of negotiations, the Uruguay Round, reduced trade barriers for most products and provided new rules to prevent *dumping*, the selling of products at unfairly low prices.

3.   The Uruguay Round also created the *World Trade Organization (WTO)* to promote free trade among member nations.

IV.   **International Involvement**

(Transparency Figure 5H)

Marketers engage in international marketing activities at several levels of involvement that cover a wide spectrum.

(Transparency Figure 5.1)

A.   **Importing and Exporting**

1.   Importing and exporting require the least amount of effort and commitment of resources.

    a)   *Importing* is the purchase of products from a foreign source.

    b)   *Exporting* is the sale of products to foreign markets. Finding an exporting intermediary to take over most marketing functions associated with selling to other countries entails minimal effort and cost.

(Transparency Figure 5I)

2.   Export agents bring together buyers and sellers from different countries; they collect a commission for arranging sales.

3.   Buyers from foreign companies and governments provide a direct method of exporting and eliminate the need for an intermediary.

B.   **Trading Companies**

1.   Marketers sometimes employ a *trading company*, which links buyers and sellers in different countries but is not involved in manufacturing and does not own assets related to manufacturing.

2.   An important function of trading companies is taking title to products and performing all the activities necessary to move the products from the domestic country to a foreign country.

3.   Trading companies reduce risk for firms interested in getting involved in international marketing.

C.   **Licensing and Franchising**

1.   *Licensing* is an alternative to direct investment requiring a licensee to pay commissions or royalties on sales or supplies used in manufacturing.

a)   Exchanges of management techniques or technical assistance are primary reasons for licensing arrangements.

b)   Licensing is an attractive alternative to direct investment when the political stability of a foreign country is in doubt or when resources are unavailable for direct investment.

2.   *Franchising* is a form of licensing in which a company (the franchiser) grants a franchisee the right to market its product, using its name, logo, methods of operation, advertising, products, and other elements associated with the franchiser's business, in return for a financial commitment and an agreement to conduct business in accordance with the franchiser's standard of operations. This arrangement allows franchisers to minimize the risks of international involvement in four ways:

a)   The franchiser does not have to put up a large capital investment.

b)   The franchiser's revenue stream is fairly consistent because franchisees pay a fixed fee and royalties.

c)   The franchiser retains control of its name and increases global penetration of its product.

d)   The franchise agreements ensure a certain standard of behavior from franchisees, which protects the franchise name.

D.   **Contract Manufacturing**

Contract manufacturing occurs when a company hires a foreign firm to produce a designated volume of the firm's product to specifications, and the final product carries the domestic firm's name.

E.   **Joint Ventures**

1.   A *joint venture* is a partnership between a domestic firm and a foreign firm or government.

a)   Control of the joint venture may be split equally, or one partner may control decision making.

b)   Joint ventures often are a political necessity because of nationalism and government restrictions on foreign ownership; they also provide legitimacy in the eyes of the host country's citizens.

c)   Joint ventures are assuming greater global importance because of cost advantages and the number of inexperienced firms entering foreign markets.

2.   *Strategic alliances*, the newest form of international business structure, are partnerships formed to create competitive advantage on a worldwide basis.

a)   Strategic alliances differ from joint ventures in that the alliance partners may have been traditional rivals competing for market share in the same product class.

b)   The success rate of international alliances could be higher if there were a better fit between the companies.

c)   A strategic alliance should focus on a joint market opportunity from which all partners can benefit.

   F.   **Direct Ownership**
       1.   Once a company makes a long-term commitment to marketing in a foreign nation that has a promising political and economic environment, *direct ownership* of a foreign subsidiary or division is a possibility.
       2.   The term *multinational enterprise* refers to firms that have operations or subsidiaries in many countries.

(Transparency Figure 5J)

(Transparency 5K)

       1.   A wholly owned foreign subsidiary may be allowed to operate independently of the parent company so that its management can have more freedom to adjust to the local environment.

V.   **Customization Versus Globalization of International Marketing Strategies**

(Transparency Figure 5L)

   A.   Traditionally, international marketing strategies have customized marketing mixes according to cultural, regional, and national differences.

(Global Marketing: Chupa Chups: Sweetening the World, One Country at a Time)

   B.   At the other end of the spectrum, *globalization* of marketing involves developing marketing strategies as though the entire world (or its major regions) were a single entity; a globalized firm markets standardized products in the same way everywhere.

(Transparency Figure 5B)

   C.   For many years, marketers have attempted to globalize their marketing mixes as much as possible by employing standardized products, promotional campaigns, prices, and distribution channels for all markets.
   D.   International marketing demands some strategic planning if a firm is to incorporate sales into its overall marketing strategy.

NOTES FOR CLASS EXERCISES, DEBATE ISSUE, AND CHAPTER QUIZ

On the following pages, you will find two class exercises, a debate issue, and a chapter quiz. These are formatted in large-size type so that you can use them as class handouts or for making transparencies. Below are the authors' comments on the class exercises, the debate topic for this chapter, and the answers to the chapter quiz.

Comments on Class Exercise 1

The objective of this class exercise is to point out how various environmental forces may influence a company's marketing strategy. The information contained in the examples came from an actual in-class discussion among students, many of whom were from European countries. The text offers numerous other examples that students can use if they have not been to Europe.

1.   In the EuroDisney situation, students may point out that Disney's advertising would definitely be affected. Not only would the language in an ad have to be changed, but the availability of media would also affect Disney's strategy. In addition, the increased use of public transportation in Europe might change how Disney builds the facility (i.e., parking lots, shuttle buses).

2. In the McDonald's situation, some students may question whether a fast-food restaurant makes sense in Europe. Fast food is popular in America because we greatly value our time. Likewise, the conversion to a metric system would require changes in all of McDonald's portion sizes (i.e., a 20-ounce soft drink equals .59 liters).

3. When the NFL expands into Spain, it must obviously convert all measurements to the metric system. In addition, the new team should be concerned over the actions of excited sports fans and plan accordingly.

4. Federal Express would be concerned about the availability of transportation and communication networks in Hungary. Additional concerns might include changes in weights and measurements, pricing, and advertising.

5. If Procter & Gamble begins to sell Safeguard soap in France, the company has a unique challenge: How do you convince people who are less concerned about body odor to buy deodorant soap? This problem will force many changes in the company's advertising.

In addition to these specific changes, students should recognize other changes. Will bribes or payoffs be required to establish businesses in these foreign countries? How will inflation rates affect the prices these companies must charge for their products and services? Can the people of these countries even afford to buy the products and services? McDonald's is having this problem in Moscow, where a Big Mac costs as much or more than many Muscovites make in an entire month.

Comments on Class Exercise 2

This exercise asks students to match each factor with its corresponding environmental force, but it should not end there. Ask your students to explain their own customs, such as handshaking, the use of color, or behavior at sporting events. Chances are they take these things for granted in their lives and will have some difficulty explaining them to the class. Then correlate this difficulty to the challenge of understanding the environmental forces affecting international marketing activities. Most likely answers are the following:

	Characteristic	**Environmental Force**
1.	Handshaking	**Cultural**
2.	Religion	**Cultural**
3.	Transportation networks	**Economic**
4.	Computer literacy	**Social/technological**
5.	Sporting events	**Social**
6.	Color preferences	**Cultural**
7.	Standard of living	**Economic**
8.	Role of children in the family	**Social/cultural**
9.	Communications equipment	**Technological**
10.	Touching	**Cultural**
11.	Import restrictions	**Political/legal**
12.	Government stability	**Political/legal**
13.	Climate	**Economic**
14.	Language	**Cultural/social**
15.	Payoffs and bribes	**Cultural/political/legal**

DEBATE ISSUE

Are the criticisms leveled against Japanese businesses justified?

CHAPTER QUIZ

Answers to Chapter Quiz 1. b; 2. b; 3. a; 4. d.

Class Exercise 1

THERE ARE MANY DIFFERENCES BETWEEN EUROPEAN COUNTRIES AND THE UNITED STATES. THE FOLLOWING ARE JUST SAMPLES:

CULTURAL: Advertising in many European countries often contains nudity. Some Europeans are not as concerned with body odor and cleanliness as are people in the United States.

SOCIAL: People in the United States are often more serious and aggressive about religion than people in some European countries. Sports fans (particularly those of soccer) in Europe are much more fanatic and violent; in some cases, large fences are needed to separate the fans of different teams.

ECONOMIC: European countries in general place a greater emphasis on public transportation (train and bus) than does the United States. Many European countries face much higher inflation rates than does the United States.

POLITICAL/LEGAL: In some European countries, bribes and payoffs are common business practices. Other countries allow the sale of addictive drugs without prosecution. Prostitution is legal in some countries.

TECHNOLOGICAL: Most countries outside the United States use the metric system. Television and radio are often not as widespread as they are in the United States.

BASED ON YOUR UNDERSTANDING OF DIFFERENCES BETWEEN EUROPEAN COUNTRIES AND THE UNITED STATES, HOW MIGHT A U.S. COMPANY'S MARKETING STRATEGY BE AFFECTED IN EACH OF THE FOLLOWING SITUATIONS?

a. **The Walt Disney Company opens EuroDisney in Paris, France.**

b. **McDonald's opens a fast-food restaurant in Berlin, Germany.**

c. **The National Football League forms a team in Barcelona, Spain.**

d. **Federal Express begins overnight package delivery to Hungary.**

e. **Procter & Gamble begins to sell Safeguard soap in France.**

Class Exercise 2

THE FOLLOWING ENVIRONMENTAL FORCES AFFECT INTERNATIONAL MARKETS: CULTURAL AND SOCIAL, ECONOMIC, TECHNOLOGICAL, AND POLITICAL/LEGAL. WITH WHICH FORCE IS EACH OF THE FOLLOWING MOST CLOSELY ASSOCIATED?

1. Handshaking
2. Religion
3. Transportation networks
4. Computer literacy
5. Sporting events
6. Color preferences
7. Standard of living
8. Role of children in the family
9. Communications equipment
10. Touching
11. Import restrictions
12. Government stability
13. Climate
14. Language
15. Payoffs and bribes

Debate Issue

ARE THE CRITICISMS LEVELED AGAINST JAPANESE BUSINESSES JUSTIFIED?

YES

- The United States carries an extremely large trade imbalance with Japan.

- Japanese direct investment in the United States continues to escalate.

- Japanese firms are increasing capacity, reducing costs, and developing new technologies faster than U.S. firms.

- The Japanese unfairly restrict U.S. imports.

- American consumers are becoming increasingly dependent on Japanese products.

- The entire world economy is becoming dominated by the Japanese.

NO

- The total of all foreign investment in the U.S. economy (including Japanese) is only about 4 percent.

- The British and Canadians have more investment in the United States than do the Japanese.

- Foreign investment in other countries is becoming a typical business practice as globalization becomes a reality.

- Many U.S. companies, like Ford and Chrysler, own substantial portions of some Japanese companies, like Mitsubishi and Mazda.

- Foreign investment in the United States is beneficial because it is being directed at permanent assets like plant and equipment—this stimulates American industry by providing jobs and stabilizing the economy.

Chapter Quiz

1. The Shelby Company plans to export expensive consumer gift items to Germany. The *best* overall economic measure of market potential would be Germany's
   a. gross domestic product.
   b. gross domestic product per capita.
   c. gross national product.
   d. balance of trade.
   e. unemployment rate.

2. Japan's Sony Corporation is a prime example of a multinational enterprise. With this in mind, which of the following would *most* accurately characterize Sony's operations?
   a. Sony follows a strategy of market globalization.
   b. Sony has operations or subsidiaries in many different countries.
   c. Sony places most of its emphasis on profits generated in foreign countries.
   d. Sony would not expect its foreign operations to share the same goals as the parent firm.
   e. Sony does not concern itself with differences in markets around the world.

3. Which of the following is true about NAFTA?
   a. It remains politically controversial.
   b. It will increase the total output of goods and services in foreign markets.
   c. It will decrease the total number of jobs in the United States.
   d. It eliminated all tariffs on goods traded between the United States, Canada, and Mexico.
   e. It will reduce the number of illegal aliens in the United States.

4. The IBC Corporation—a U.S.-based watch maker—recently entered into a partnership agreement with the Australian government to make watches. What type of partnership agreement does this situation *most likely* represent?
   a. Trading company
   b. Licensing arrangement
   c. Direct ownership arrangement
   d. Joint venture
   e. Combination in restraint of trade

ANSWERS TO DISCUSSION AND REVIEW QUESTIONS

1. **How does international marketing differ from domestic marketing?**

   International marketing differs from domestic marketing in that exchanges occur across national boundaries. When marketing occurs across national boundaries, decisions should take into account differences in the marketing environment and the unique needs of customers in other countries.

2. **What factors must marketers consider as they decide whether to engage in international marketing?**

   International marketing involvement relates to the firm's goals and the perceived opportunity from serving foreign markets. To develop desired profits and growth, marketers sometimes consider it necessary to cross national boundaries.

3. **Why are the largest industrial corporations in the United States so committed to international marketing?**

   The largest industrial corporations in the United States are committed to international marketing because their resources and market opportunities can be optimized in serving foreign markets. The profit bases of such companies as ExxonMobil and the Cola-Cola Company have been increased tremendously by increasing the size of the world markets these companies serve.

4. **Why do you think this chapter focuses on an analysis of the international marketing environment?**

   The environment is a major consideration in analyzing international marketing. If a marketing strategy is to be effective across national boundaries, the complexities of all environments must be understood. The cultural, social, ethical, economic, political/ legal, and technological environments of many foreign countries differ considerably from those in the United States.

5. **A manufacturer recently exported peanut butter with a green label to a nation in the Far East. The product failed because it was associated with jungle sickness. How could this mistake have been avoided?**

   If the manufacturer had used a marketing intelligence system or conducted marketing research, it would have better understood the culture, taboos, and attitudes of the nation. Had the green label been tested in the foreign country, the results would have indicated that green had inappropriate connotations for a food label.

6. **If you were asked to provide a small tip (or bribe) to have a document approved in a foreign nation where this practice is customary, what would you do?**

   This question relates to the values and ethical standards of the individual involved. There is no right or wrong answer in this situation, but such tips should be avoided if possible. In the United States, this type of payment is considered a bribe and therefore is unethical and probably illegal.

7. **How will NAFTA affect marketing opportunities for U.S. products in North America (the United States, Mexico, and Canada)?**

   NAFTA makes it easier for U.S. businesses to invest in Mexico and Canada, provides protection for intellectual property, expands trade by requiring equal treatment of U.S. firms in both countries, and simplifies country-of-origin rules, hindering Japan's use of Mexico as a staging ground for further penetration into U.S. markets. It gives U.S. firms greater access to desirable Mexican and Canadian markets. Relaxation of licensing requirements gives smaller firms that previously could not afford to invest in Mexico and Canada the opportunity to do business there without actually having to locate there. NAFTA also should lead to more efficient markets, due to increased competition, and the long-term prospects of including most Western Hemisphere countries in the alliance offer the promise of additional opportunities for U.S. marketers.

8. **In marketing dog food to Latin America, what aspects of the marketing mix would a U.S. firm need to alter?**

   Extensive research should be conducted to determine how the marketing strategy should be altered. The target market should be defined properly. The product, price, promotion, and distribution will have to be developed to match the needs of dog owners in the country to be served.

9. **What should marketers consider as they decide whether to license or enter into a joint venture in a foreign nation?**

   A decision to license or to enter into a joint venture in a foreign country depends on the nature of the product and the political and economic stability of the nation being served. Licensing is not as risky as a joint venture because the licensee pays commissions or royalties on the sales of supplies used in manufacturing in a foreign country. This technique is an alternative to direct investment. The joint venture is a partnership between a domestic and a foreign firm and/or government. In a joint venture, there is always the possibility that the domestic and foreign firms will disagree, and the foreign firm can be at a disadvantage. There is always the possibility of expropriation—the foreign country may take over all control of a joint venture. On the other hand, a joint venture often guarantees that a firm will gain a foreign market, and it may help develop local support for the firm's products.

10. **Discuss the impact of strategic alliances on marketing strategies.**

    Strategic alliances, partnerships formed to create competitive advantage on a world-wide basis, are the newest form of international business structure. In some areas they are becoming the predominant means of competing. For example, Chrysler and Mitsubishi have formed Diamond Star Motors in Normal, Illinois, to produce Plymouth and Mitsubishi nameplates. Both cars are basically the same except for minor steel metal and nameplate changes. This plant is owned 50 percent by Chrysler and 50 percent by Mitsubishi and helps to strengthen each company's product mix. Through the efficiency of joint manufacturing, each company is able to share in the lower costs of production. The impact of strategic alliances such as this on marketing strategies is that the companies can offer high-quality products at the lowest competitive price available and focus on their unique approaches to promotion and distribution.

11. **Contrast globalization with customization of marketing strategies. Is one practice better than the other? Explain.**

Marketers have traditionally customized marketing strategies according to cultural, regional, and national differences. Increasingly, more firms are attempting to globalize marketing strategies by treating the entire world (or significant major regions) as a single entity; they market standardized products in the same way everywhere. Although there are economic and competitive advantages to globalizing strategies, some aspects of the marketing mix (media allocation, retail outlets, price) are difficult to globalize. Even global advertising campaigns may have to be translated into different languages to succeed, and some products may require significant modifications for different countries. Thus, it is difficult to say that one strategy is "better" than the other.

COMMENTS ON THE CASES

CASE 5.1 BMW INTERNATIONAL

This case examines the "mass customization" strategy employed by BMW. BMW's approach to increasing sales seems to involve expanding the number of premium models it offers in order to target more luxury-seeking customers at a greater range of prices.

The first question asks how BMW developed such a successful international marketing strategy. Based on the facts presented in the case, it appears that BMW has spent considerable resources researching the needs and desires of automobile buyers in order to more precisely target new models to appeal to buyers seeking luxury and a prestigious image. The company has gained some new models through acquisition (e.g. Rolls Royce) and developed others based on its understanding of consumers' desire to own and drive a BMW. In addition, the company has maintained its focus on distinction and quality.

Question 2 asks students to compare BMW's worldwide marketing strategy with that of American car manufacturers such as Ford and GM. Students should recognize that Ford and GM have attempted to target every market segment with specific models and brands (e.g., Chevrolet for entry-level buyers and Cadillac for upscale buyers), whereas BMW focuses solely on high-end customers with premium vehicles. However, BMW's current strategy of offering more "trade-up" models at lower prices suggests that it is moving closer to the U.S. firms' strategies.

The third question asks students to ponder whether BMW's global marketing strategy satisfies the requirements of the concept of globalization as described in the chapter. The text defines globalization as developing marketing strategies as though the entire world (or major regions of it) were a single entity; a globalized firm markets standardized products in the same way everywhere. Based on the facts presented in the case, it would appear that BMW is not following a pure strategy of globalization but more of a "mass customization" strategy that involves tailoring products, prices, and distribution for specific demographic- and lifestyle-based segments rather than for customers in specific geographic areas.

Video Information

Company:	BMW International
Location:	Tape 1/DVD 1, Segment 5
Length:	12:38

Video Overview: T his video provides an overview of the BMW Group's global marketing strategy. While the BMW brand has always been focused on maintaining an image of high value and status, the company is also attempting to appeal to a larger range of customers by attracting new market segments. This strategy includes the development of new products in the luxury brand accessible category, like the Mini and the 318i. BMW has also achieved success through product diversification within its various lines, which are designed to appeal to different target markets.

MULTIPLE-CHOICE QUESTIONS ABOUT THE VIDEO

1.   The BMW Group includes which of the following brands?

    a.   Mini
    b.   Mercedes
    c.   Rolls Royce
    d.   Both a and b
    e.   Both a and c

2.   The phenomenon of _____ describes people's willingness to pay more for quality products that matter to them, even if they have to make sacrifices in other areas.

    a.   overspending
    b.   financial planning
    c.   trading up
    d.   budgeting
    e.   status building

3.   BMW's global strategy is best described as

    a.   mass customization.
    b.   selling more vehicles at lower margins.
    c.   customization for elite markets.
    d.   appeal to mass markets.
    e.   luxury vehicles at discount prices.

ANSWERS TO MULTIPLE-CHOICE QUESTIONS ABOUT THE VIDEO

1.   e

2.   c

3.   a

CASE 5.2 GILLETTE COMPANY

This case explores the history of marketing strategies of a well-known firm. You might begin the discussion by asking students how many have one or more Gillette products in their homes or how many students have encountered Gillette products when traveling outside the U.S. If you have foreign nationals in your class, ask them what Gillette brands mentioned in the case they may have used in their homes.

The first question asks students to consider the environmental factors that have contributed to Gillette's success and challenges in global markets. Students answers may vary, but most should recognize that that social and cultural factors have been key to Gillette's success in markets around the world. Technological forces have also benefited the company through new advances and products like the Mach 3 shaving system and long-life batteries. Like any company doing business across national borders, Gillette faces challenges related to changes in these forces as well as issues related to economic, political, and legal forces associated with doing business in foreign countries.

Question 2 asks about the strategy Gillette appears to have adopted for international marketing. Although not specifically addressed in the case, it would appear that Gillette essentially markets the same products everywhere. However, students should recognize that Gillette must adapt some aspects of its marketing mix to accommodate language and measurement differences, as well as differences in cultural, legal, and regulatory forces in each country in which it markets.

The third question asks students to consider how Gillette can continue to compete effectively in the battery and grooming markets. Responses will vary but should reflect strategic thinking about the company's continued viability in the highly competitive grooming and battery markets. Answers may range from increased research and development to keep abreast of changing social and cultural trends that may lead to new product developments or adaptations to divesting some subsidiaries that operate in industries where the company may not be able to keep pace.

CHAPTER 6

E-Marketing and Customer Relationship Management

TEACHING RESOURCES QUICK REFERENCE GUIDE

Resource	Location
Purpose and Perspective	IRM, p. 91
Guide for Using Color Transparencies	IRM, p. 92
Lecture Outline	IRM, p. 92
Notes for Class Exercises, Debate Issue, and Chapter Quiz	IRM, p. 98
Class Exercise 1	IRM, p. 101
Class Exercise 2	IRM, p. 102
Debate Issue	IRM, p. 103
Chapter Quiz	IRM, p. 104
Answers to Discussion and Review Questions	IRM, p. 105
Comments on the Video Case	IRM, p. 107
Video	Tape 1/DVD 1, Segment 6
Video Information	IRM, p. 107
Multiple-Choice Questions About the Video	IRM, p. 108
Transparency Acetates	Transparency package
Examination Questions: Essay	TB, p. 149
Examination Questions: Multiple-Choice	TB, p. 150
Examination Questions: True-False	TB, p. 170
Author-Selected Multiple-Choice Test Items	TB, p. 670
HMClassPrep Presentation Resources	CD-ROM
PowerPoint Slides	Instructor's website

Note: Additional resources are updated periodically and may be found on the accompanying student and instructor websites at http://www.prideferrell.com/.

PURPOSE AND PERSPECTIVE

This chapter explores marketing on the fastest growing medium to date: the Internet. The phenomenal growth of this medium presents opportunities for marketers to forge relationships with consumers and business customers on an interactive basis. We begin with a definition of the concepts of electronic commerce and electronic marketing. Then we examine the characteristics that differentiate electronic marketing from traditional marketing activities. Next, we explore how marketers are using the Internet to build competitive advantage. Then we revisit the concept of customer relationship management, introduced in Chapter 1, by examining how the Internet and information technology help marketers facilitate customer relationship management. Finally, we consider some of the ethical and legal issues that affect Internet marketing.

GUIDE FOR USING COLOR TRANSPARENCIES

There are two groups of color transparencies. The transparencies identified by a double number are the same as the figures and tables in the text. The transparencies labeled with a number and a letter are illustrations that do not appear in the text, but they can be used as additional examples of concepts discussed.

Part 3 Opener	Using Technology and Information to Build Customer Relationships
Table 6.2	Types of Advertising on Websites
Figure 6A	Chapter 6 Outline
Figure 6B	Key Definitions: E-Commerce vs. E-Marketing
Figure 6C	Basic Characteristics of E-Marketing
Figure 6D	Uses for Digital Marketing
Figure 6E	E-Commerce by Ethnicity
Figure 6F	Accessibility
Figure 6G	Reasons Shoppers Cite for Buying Online
Figure 6H	Technology Drives CRM
Figure 6I	Financial Costs of Cyber Attacks
Figure 6J	Legal and Ethical Issues

LECTURE OUTLINE

(Transparency Part 3 Opener)

(Transparency Figure 6A: Chapter Outline)

I. **Marketing on the Internet**
   A. A number of terms have been used to describe marketing activities and commercial transactions on the Internet.
      1. One of the most popular terms is *electronic commerce* (or *e-commerce*), which has been defined as "the sharing of business information, maintaining business relationships, and conducting business transactions by means of telecommunications networks."

(Transparency Figure 6B)

      2. Since the text focuses on how the Internet relates to all aspects of marketing, we use the term *electronic marketing* (or *e-marketing*) to refer to the strategic process of creating, distributing, promoting, and pricing products for targeted customers in the virtual environment of the Internet.
   B. One of the most important benefits of e-marketing is the ability of marketers and customers to share information.
      1. Through company websites, consumers can learn about a firm and its products and ask questions, voice complaints, indicate preferences, and otherwise communicate about their needs and desires.
      2. The Internet has also changed the way marketers communicate and develop relationships with their employees and suppliers.

(Transparency Figure 6D)

      3. Telecommunications technology offers additional benefits to marketers, including rapid response, expanded customer service capability, decreased costs of operation, and reduced geographic barriers.
   C. Many Internet-based "dot.com" companies failed because they thought the only thing that mattered was brand awareness.

1. The reality is that Internet markets are more similar to traditional markets than they are different.
2. Like traditional marketing strategies, successful e-marketing strategies depend on creating, distributing, promoting, and pricing products that customers need or want, not merely developing a brand name or reducing the costs associated with online transactions.
3. Electronic marketing has not changed all industries, although it has had a significant impact in some industries where the costs of business and consumers transactions are very high.

D. **Basic Characteristics of Electronic Marketing**

(Transparency Figure 6C)

1. **Addressability**
   a) *Addressability* refers to a marketer's ability to identify customers before they make a purchase.
      (1) The technology of the Internet makes it possible for visitors to a website to identify themselves and to provide information about their product needs and wants before making a purchase.
      (2) Many websites encourage visitors to register in order to maximize their use of a site or to gain access to premium areas.
   b) Addressability represents the ultimate expression of the marketing concept.
      (1) With knowledge they garner about individual customers through their websites, marketers can tailor marketing mixes more precisely to target customers with narrow interests.
      (2) Addressability also facilitates tracking website visits and online buying activity, which makes it easier for marketers to accumulate data about individual customers to enhance future marketing efforts.
   c) Some website software can store a *cookie*, or identifying string of text, on a visitor's computer.
      (1) Marketers use cookies to track how often a particular user visits the website, what he or she may look at while there, and in what sequence.
      (2) Cookies permit website visitors to customize services, such as virtual shopping carts, as well as the particular content they see when they log onto a webpage.
      (3) The use of cookies can be an ethical issue: If a website owner can use cookies to link a visitor's interests to a name and address, that information could be sold to advertisers and other parties without the visitor's consent or knowledge.

2. **Interactivity**
   Interactivity allows customers to express their needs and wants directly to the firm in response to the firm's marketing communications.

   a) Interactivity helps marketers maintain high-quality relationships with existing customers by shaping their expectations and perceptions.
   b) One implication of interactivity is that a firm's customers can also communicate with other customers (and noncustomers). For this reason, differences in the amount and type of information possessed by marketers and their customers are not as pronounced as in the past.
   c) Interactivity enables marketers to capitalize on the concept of community to help customers derive value from the firm's products and website.

(1) *Community* refers to a sense of group membership or feeling of belonging by individual members of a group.

(2) Because such communities have well-defined demographics and common interests, they represent a valuable audience for advertisers.

3. **Memory**

Memory refers to a firm's ability to access databases or data warehouses containing individual customer profiles and past purchase histories and to use these data in real time to customize its marketing offer to a specific customer.

a) A *database* is a collection of information arranged for easy access and retrieval.

b) Current software technology allows marketers to identify a visitor to a website instantaneously, locate that customer's profile in their database, and then display the customer's past purchases or suggest new products based on past purchases while the customer is still visiting the site.

c) Applying memory to large numbers of customers represents a significant advantage when a firm uses it to learn more about individual customers each time they visit the firm's website.

4. **Control**

a) In the context of e-marketing, *control* refers to customers' ability to regulate the information they view, as well as the rate and sequence of their exposure to that information.

(1) The Web is sometimes referred to as a "pull" medium because users determine what they view at websites; website operators' ability to control the content users look at and in what sequence is limited.

(2) In contrast, television can be characterized as a "push" medium because the broadcaster determines what the viewer sees once he or she has selected a particular channel.

b) For e-marketers, the primary implication of control is that attracting and retaining customers' attention is more difficult.

(1) Marketers have to work harder and more creatively to communicate the value of the website clearly and quickly, or the viewers will lose interest and click to another site.

(2) Innovative promotional activities may be required to publicize a website. Some marketers advertise their websites on other firms' sites and on *portals*, which are multiservice websites that serve as gateways to other websites.

5. **Accessibility**

The ability to obtain the extraordinary amount of information available on the Internet is referred to as *accessibility*.

(Transparency Figure 6F)

a) Because customers can access in-depth information about competing products, they are much better informed about a firm's products and their relative value than ever before.

b) Accessibility also dramatically increases the competition for the Internet users' attention.

c) Accessibility also relates to making information available for employees to service customers.

6. **Digitalization**

Digitalization is the ability to represent a product, or at least some of its benefits, as digital bits of information.

a)   This ability means the Internet can be used to distribute, promote, and sell those features apart from the physical item itself.

b)   In addition to creating distribution efficiencies, digitizing part of a product's features allows new combinations of features and services to be created quickly and inexpensively.

E.   **E-Marketing Strategies**

There are significant differences in how marketing mix components are developed and combined into a marketing strategy in the electronic environment of the Web.

(Building Customer Relationships: Harris Poll Uses Internet to Survey Consumers)

1.   **Target Markets**

The Internet has become an important medium for reaching consumers in the United States and abroad.

(Transparency Figure 6E)

a)   Although men dominate Internet usage statistics, Internet use by women, children, teenagers, and seniors is growing.

b)   More people are using the Internet to make purchases and conduct banking transactions.

2.   **Product Considerations**

Through e-marketing, companies can provide products, including goods, services, and ideas, that offer unique benefits and improve customer satisfaction.

a)   The online marketing of goods is accelerating rapidly.

b)   Services may have the greatest potential for marketing success.

c)   The proliferation of information on the World Wide Web has itself spawned new services, including web search engines and directories and portals.

d)   Even ideas, such as distance learning and corporate training, have the potential to be successful on the Internet.

3.   **Distribution Considerations**

The Internet can be viewed as a new distribution channel.

a)   Physical distribution is especially compatible with e-marketing.

b)   The ability to process orders electronically and increase the speed of communications via the Internet reduces inefficiencies, costs, and redundancies throughout the entire marketing channel.

c)   More firms are exploiting advances in information technology to synchronize the relationships between their manufacturing or product assembly and their customer contact operations.

d)   One of the most visible members of any marketing channel is the retailer, and the Internet is increasingly becoming a retail venue.

(Transparency Figure 6G)

4.   **Promotion Considerations**

a)   The Internet is an interactive medium that can be used to inform, entertain, and persuade target markets to accept an organization's products.

(Transparency Table 6.2)

b)   The accessibility and interactivity of the Internet allow marketers to complement their traditional media usage for promotional efforts.

        c)   Many companies augment their traditional advertising campaigns with web-based promotions; many are also offering buying incentives and adding value to products online through the use of sales promotions, such as coupons.

        d)   The characteristics of e-marketing make promotional efforts on the Internet significantly different from those that use more traditional media.

            (1)   Because Internet users can control what they see, customers who visit a firm's website are there because they chose to be, which implies they are interested in the firm's products and therefore may be more involved in the message and dialog provided by the firm.

            (2)   The interactive nature of the Internet allows marketers to enter into dialogs with customers to learn more about their interests and needs, and then to tailor promotional messages to the individual customer based on that dialog.

            (3)   Addressability can make marketing efforts directed at specific customers more effective.

    5.   **Pricing Considerations**

        a)   E-marketing facilitates both price and nonprice competition because the accessibility characteristic of e-marketing gives consumers access to more information about the costs and prices of products than has ever been available to them before.

        b)   Some organizations are implementing low-price policies through the Internet.

II.   **Customer Relationship Management**

    A.   One characteristic of companies engaged in e-marketing is a renewed focus on relationship marketing by building customer loyalty and retaining customers—that is, customer relationship management (CRM). (Chapter 1 defined customer relationship marketing as using information about customers to create marketing strategies that develop and sustain desirable long-term customer relationships.)

        1.   A focus on customer relationship management is possible in e-marketing because of marketers' ability to target individual customers.

            a)   This effort is enhanced over time as customers invest time and effort into "teaching" the firm what they want.

            b)   This investment in the firm also increases the costs that a customer would incur by switching to another company.

        2.   The addressability, interactivity, and memory characteristics of e-marketing allow marketers to identify specific customers, establish interactive dialogs with them to learn about their needs, and combine this information with their purchase histories to customize products to meet those needs.

        3.   The ability to identify individual customers allows marketers to shift their focus from targeting groups of similar customers to increasing their share of an individual customer's purchases—i.e., from "share of the market" to "share of customer."

            a)   Focusing on share of customer requires recognizing that all customers have different needs and that all customers do not have equal value to a firm. The 80/20 rule suggests that 80 percent of profits come from 20 percent of customers.

            b)   Advances in technology and data collection techniques now permit firms to profile customers in real time, which allows them to assess the lifetime value of individual customers.

               (1)   Some customers may be too expensive to retain giving the low level of profits they generate.

               (2)   Companies can discourage these unprofitable customers by requiring them to pay higher fees for additional services.

B. **Technology Drives CRM**
    CRM focuses on building satisfying exchange relationships between buyers and sellers by gathering data at all customer-contact points—telephone, fax, online, and personal—and analyzing those data to understand customers' needs and desires.

(Transparency Figure 6H)

1. Companies are increasingly automating and managing customer relationships through technology.
2. Using technology, marketers can analyze interactions with customers to identify performance issues and even build a library of "best practices" for customer interaction.
3. Sales automation can link a firm's sales force to e-marketing applications that facilitate selling and providing service to customers.

C. **Customer Satisfaction Is the End Result of CRM**
    1. Although technology drives CRM and can help companies build relationships with desirable customers, too often it is used as a cost-reduction tactic or a selling tool, with little thought toward developing and sustaining long-term relationships.
        a) Customer relationship management is effective only when it is developed as a relationship-building tool.
        b) Some critics view CRM as a form of manipulation, perhaps because of the software and information technology associated with collecting information from customers and responding to their desires.
        c) However, using CRM does not require collecting every conceivable piece of data from consumers or trying to sell customers products they don't want.
        d) Instead of trying to control customers, marketers should try to develop relationships that derive from the trust gained over many transactions and are sustained by customers' belief that the company genuinely desires their continued patronage.
    2. What marketers can do with CRM technology is identify their most valuable customers so that they can make an investment in building long-term relationships with those customers.
    3. To be successful, marketers must measure the effectiveness of CRM systems in terms of their progress toward developing satisfactory customer relationships.
    4. The most important component of CRM is remembering that it is not about technology, but about relationships with customers.

III. **Legal and Ethical Issues in E-marketing**
    How marketers use technology to gather information—both online and off—to foster long-term relationships with customers has raised numerous legal and ethical issues.

(Transparency Figure 6I)

(Transparency Figure 6J)

A. One of the most controversial issues has to do with the personal information that companies collect from website visitors.
    1. Some people fear that collecting personal information from website users may violate their privacy, especially if it is done without their knowledge.
    2. Many in the industry are urging self-policing on this issue to head off potential regulation. One such effort toward self-policing is the online privacy program developed by the BBBOnLine subsidiary of the Council of Better Business Bureaus.

3.   Few laws specifically address personal privacy in the context of e-marketing, but the standards for acceptable marketing conduct implicit in other laws and regulations can generally be applied to e-marketing.

4.   The most serious strides toward regulating privacy issues associated with e-marketing are emerging in Europe.

(Ethics and Social Responsibility: Europe Takes the Lead in Privacy Protection)

B.   *Spam*, or unsolicited commercial e-mail (UCE), is likely to be the next target of government regulation in the United States.

1.   Many Internet users feel that spam violates their privacy, steals their resources, and is rather like receiving a direct-mail promotional piece with postage due.

2.   Others, however, appreciate the opportunity to learn about new products.

3.   The debate over spam is far from over, and legislation to regulate it has been enacted on both the state and federal level. The Controlling the Assault of Non-Solicited Pornography and Marketing (CAN-SPAM) law, which bans fraudulent or deceptive unsolicited commercial e-mail and requires senders to provide information on how recipients can opt out of receiving additional messages, went into effect in 2004.

C.   The Internet has also created issues associated with intellectual property, the copyrighted or trademarked ideas and creative materials developed to solve problems, carry out applications, educate, and entertain others.

1.   Intellectual property losses have become a global concern because of disparities in the enforcement of laws throughout the world.

2.   The Digital Millennium Copyright Act (DCMA) was passed to protect copyrighted materials on the Internet in the U.S.

3.   Protecting trademarks can be difficult.

a)   Some companies have discovered that another firm has registered a URL that duplicates or is very similar to their own trademarks. The "cybersquatter" then attempts to sell the right to use the URL to the legal trademark owner.

b)   The Federal Trademark Dilution Act of 1995 gives trademark owners the right to protect their trademarks, prevents the use of trademark-protected entities, and requires the relinquishment of names that duplicate or closely parallel registered trademarks.

D.   As the Internet continues to evolve, more legal and ethical issues will arise.

1.   Recognizing this, the American Marketing Association has developed a Code of Ethics for Marketing on the Internet.

2.   Marketers and all other Internet users should make an effort to learn and abide by basic "netiquette" (Internet etiquette) to ensure they get the most out of the resources available on this growing medium.

NOTES FOR CLASS EXERCISES, DEBATE ISSUE, AND CHAPTER QUIZ

On the following pages, you will find two class exercises, a debate issue, and a chapter quiz. These are formatted in large-size type so that you can use them as class handouts or for making transparencies. Below are the authors' comments on the class exercises, the debate topic for this chapter, and the answers to the chapter quiz.

Class Exercise 1

The objective of this exercise is to improve students' recognition of the characteristics of e-marketing. Answers:

1. Memory

2. Digitalization

3. Addressability

4. Control

5. Interactivity

6. Accessibility

Class Exercise 2

The objective of this class exercise is to help students see that all kinds of firms can include a virtual component in their marketing strategies, but also that some types of businesses are better suited for e-commerce than others. There are no "correct" answers, but students should attempt to rank each company as to the degree to which it might be suited for e-commerce.

1. *Home Depot*. Possible rating: 2-4. Customers may need personal advice and instruction, and it would be inefficient to ship many of the items directly to a customer's home.

2. *Toys 'R' Us*. Possible rating: 4-6. There will always be a need for traditional store atmospherics and opportunities to see how products work and how children respond to specific products.

3. *Barnes & Noble*. Possible rating: 5-7. Books have been sold quite successfully online by this company and its competitor Amazon.com.

4. *McIlhenny Company*. Possible rating: 4-6. For many people, traditional store outlets will be adequate for most consumer grocery products, but the Internet lends itself well for specialty food products like McIlhenny's Tabasco Sauce. McIlhenny is even offering some products exclusively on its website.

5. *Hallmark*. Possible rating: 6-8. As more consumers gain access to the Internet, online greeting cards become more efficient; through the Internet, greeting cards can also include sound and visual effects.

6. *The Gap*. Possible rating: 3-5. Although much apparel may be sold online, many people still want to see the clothes and try them on before buying.

7. *Blockbuster Video*. Possible rating: 5-8. Although many people prefer going to a a store to view product availability in an interesting and helpful atmosphere, the development and growth of online DVD services such as NetFlix indicates that movie rentals can be facilitated through the Internet.

8. *Ford*. Possible rating: 4-6. While many customer relationships can be maintained online, the need for traditional service and contact with the physical product may still be desired and needed by some customers.

9. *University of Phoenix*. Possible rating: 5-8. It is becoming easier for universities to provide courses on the Internet because of improvements in technology. The University of Phoenix, the largest private university in the United States, is rapidly expanding its online distance learning program.

10. *Batteries Plus*. Possible rating: 3-5. Batteries (especially car and camera batteries) are often emergency purchases, and consumers may not have time to wait for an online seller to ship the battery to them. Additionally, some consumers may need or want installation services, especially for car batteries and watch batteries.

DEBATE ISSUE

Is traditional marketing losing its position to e-marketing?

CHAPTER QUIZ

Answers to Chapter Quiz 1. b; 2. a; 3. e; 4. d.

Class Exercise 1

IDENTIFY THE E-MARKETING CHARACTERISTICS THAT RELATE TO THE FOLLOWING EXAMPLES

_____ 1. Bluefly.com asks visitors to provide their e-mail address, clothing preferences, brand preferences, and sizes so it can create a customized online catalog matching the customer's specified preferences.

_____ 2. FedEx's web-based software allows customers to track their own packages from starting point to destination.

_____ 3. CDNow asks music lovers to supply information about their listening tastes so that the company can recommend new releases.

_____ 4. Visitors to Yahoo! can search the site for topics of interest and click to those sites the search service finds.

_____ 5. Amazon.com recognizes visitors by name if they have purchased from the site before and then offers suggestions about products they might be interested in based on their previous purchases.

_____ 6. MasterCard International grants a Shop Smart seal to e-commerce sites that use advanced security systems for credit card purchases.

Class Exercise 2

IN THE FUTURE, MOST MARKETING STRATEGIES WILL CONTAIN A VIRTUAL AS WELL AS TRADITIONAL COMPONENT. RATE EACH OF THE FOLLOWING COMPANIES ON A SCALE OF 1 (TRADITIONAL) TO 10 (VIRTUAL) AS TO THEIR STRATEGY FOR CUSTOMER RELATIONSHIPS.

1. **Home Depot (home improvement)**

   1 2 3 4 5 6 7 8 9 10

2. **Toys 'R' Us (toys)**

   1 2 3 4 5 6 7 8 9 10

3. **Barnes & Noble (books)**

   1 2 3 4 5 6 7 8 9 10

4. **McIlhenny Company (Tabasco and hot sauce)**

   1 2 3 4 5 6 7 8 9 10

5. **Hallmark (greeting cards)**

   1 2 3 4 5 6 7 8 9 10

6. **The Gap (apparel)**

   1 2 3 4 5 6 7 8 9 10

7. **Blockbuster Video (video rental and video/CD sales)**

   1 2 3 4 5 6 7 8 9 10

8. **Ford (automobiles)**

   1 2 3 4 5 6 7 8 9 10

9. **University of Phoenix (education)**

   1 2 3 4 5 6 7 8 9 10

10. **Batteries Plus (batteries)**

    1 2 3 4 5 6 7 8 9 10

Debate Issue

IS TRADITIONAL MARKETING LOSING ITS POSITION TO E-MARKETING?

YES	NO
• Brand name web-sites are becoming the dominant source for many products (e.g., Amazon.com).	• Traditional stores will continue to dominate as the major providers of most products (e.g., BookPeople).
• Customers prefer to shop online for many products.	• Online shopping cannot replace the fun and enjoyment of store shopping.
• Many products are cheaper through e-marketing because of efficiencies in performing marketing functions.	• Traditional marketing channels are usually the most efficient way to make products available.
• Assessing target market potential to buy is easier through e-marketing.	• Many products require creative personal selling and personal communication to establish the best prospects.

Chapter Quiz

1. Which of the following services is *not* one of the basic characteristics of electronic marketing?

   a. Control
   b. Cookies
   c. Addressability
   d. Accessibility
   e. Memory

2. The e-marketing characteristic that relates to the ability to identify customers before they make a purchase is

   a. addressability.
   b. interactivity.
   c. control.
   d. memory.
   e. digitalization.

3. Visitors to the Living Online website have established a sense of group membership or feeling of belonging by individual members; they have become a

   a. market segment.
   b. target public.
   c. target market.
   d. commune.
   e. community.

4. Kraft's website offers recipes and tips on entertaining to help consumers get the most out of their products. This is an example of Internet

   a. product.
   b. distribution.
   c. price.
   d. promotion.
   e. digitalization.

ANSWERS TO DISCUSSION AND REVIEW QUESTIONS

1. **How does addressability differentiate e-marketing from the traditional marketing environment? How do marketers use cookies to achieve addressability?**

   Addressability refers to a marketer's ability to identify customers before they make a purchase. Marketers have always had the ability to identify potential customers, but this ability was limited to relatively homogeneous groups of customers of high-priced products because of the expense of maintaining a sales force and building and/or acquiring extensive databases. The technology of the Internet makes it possible for visitors to a website to identify themselves and to provide information about their product needs and wants before making a purchase.

   Cookies are identifying strings of text placed on a website visitor's computer. With cookies, marketers can track how often a particular user visits the website, what he or she may look at while there, and in what sequence. This information can then be used to customize services, such as virtual shopping carts, for individual visitors.

2. **Define *interactivity* and explain its significance. How can marketers exploit this characteristic to improve relations with customers?**

   Interactivity allows customers to express their needs and wants directly to the firm in response to its marketing communications. This characteristic allows customers to interact with marketers (and other customers) in real time. Marketers can exploit this characteristic by building online communities to help customers derive greater value from their products and websites. They can also utilize communications technology to bring together representatives of the firm and their customers over the Internet.

3. **Memory gives marketers quick access to customers' purchase histories. How can a firm use this capability to customize its product offerings?**

   Memory refers to a firm's ability to access databases or data warehouses containing individual customer profiles and past purchase histories and to use these data to customize its marketing offer to a specific customer. Many firms have taken advantage of this capability to provide customized content for each customer. Bluefly.com, for example, asks visitors to provide their e-mail addresses, clothing and brand preferences, and sizes so that it can create a customized "My Catalog" that matches each customer's preferences.

4. **Explain the distinction between *push* and *pull* media. What is the significance of control in terms of using websites to market products?**

   With a "push" media, like television, the content broadcaster determines what the viewer (or listener) sees once he or she has selected a particular channel. In contrast, with a "pull" media, like the Web, operators have less control over the content users look at and in what sequence. The user can choose the path he or she takes through the content. The significance of control with regard to websites is that users have more control over how they view a particular website, and marketers have to work harder and more creatively to communicate the value of their website clearly and quickly, or the viewer will lose interest and go elsewhere.

5. **What is the significance of digitalization?**

   Digitalization is the ability to represent a product, or at least some of its benefits, as digital bits of information. The significance of this ability is that the Internet can be used to distribute, promote, and sell those features apart from the physical product itself. It can also allow a company to add value to existing products as FedEx has done by giving customers the ability to track their packages online.

6. **How can marketers exploit the characteristics of the Internet to improve the product element of the marketing mix?**

Through their websites, companies can add value to their products by offering distinct benefits and improve customer satisfaction. Services, such as home buying and stock trading, especially benefit from online marketing activities because Internet technology allows customers to specify and search for specific attributes and often saves them time and money. Additionally, companies can create unique products to target specific customers, as GolfWeb has done with its website.

7. **How do the characteristics of e-marketing affect the promotion element of the marketing mix?**

The interactivity of the Internet enables marketers to inform, entertain, and persuade target markets to accept their products. The accessibility presents marketers with an opportunity to expand and complement their traditional promotional efforts with promotions that add value to their products.

8. **How does e-marketing facilitate customer relationship management?**

E-marketing facilitates customer relationship management because it makes it possible to target individual customers, often with more precision and accuracy than ever before. The addressability, interactivity, and memory characteristics of e-marketing permit marketers to identify specific customers, establish interactive dialogs with them to learn about their needs, and combine this information with their purchase histories to customize products to meet those needs.

9. **How can technology help marketers improve their relationships with customers?**

Information technology, particularly customer relationship management software, can help companies capture data about customers from all customer-contact points and analyze this information to improve performance and understanding of customers' needs and desires. This information can then help firms build trust and ultimately long-term relationships with desirable customers.

10. **Electronic marketing has raised a number of ethical questions related to consumer privacy. How can cookies be misused? Should the government regulate the use of cookies by marketers?**

Cookies, which are strings of identifying text placed on a website visitor's computer, have been rather controversial. Although they help e-marketers learn more about their visitors and to customize their websites to individual customers, there are some concerns about how cookies can be used. If a website owner can use cookies to link a visitor's interests to a name and address, that information could be sold to advertisers and other parties without the visitor's consent or knowledge. Consequently, many people are nervous about cookie technology, and some even turn off the cookie capability of their web browser software.

The second part of this exercise should stimulate lively class discussion as students' feelings on this issue may vary widely. Some will argue for government intervention, but others will argue that the Internet should police itself. Students may need to be reminded that if consumers are fearful of privacy issues associated with cookie technology, marketers should tread carefully. Responsible e-marketers will disclose to website visitors what information they are collecting and how they are using it.

COMMENTS ON THE VIDEO CASE

4SURE.COM TARGETS BUSINESS CUSTOMERS

This case profiles 4SURE.com, an Internet-based company that engages primarily in marketing to businesses online. Unlike many "dot.coms," 4SURE.com has found success by staying close to its customers.

The first question asks how 4SURE.com exploits the characteristics of e-marketing to serve its customers and which of these characteristics are most important to the firm's success. Although not explicitly expressed in the case, all of the characteristics of e-marketing described in the text can be exploited by 4SURE.com, but addressability, interactivity, and memory seem to be most important. The addressability characteristic allows the firm to store data about customers' purchases and to use that information to customize its product assortment more precisely to match the needs of its customers. The interactivity characteristic allows customers to express their needs and wants directly to the firm. The memory characteristic refers to a firm's ability to access databases containing individual customer profiles and past purchase histories. This capability allows 4SURE.com to store customers' shipping and credit-card information so that the next time they order, they can do so with a single mouse click. These characteristics add value to the products 4SURE.com stocks.

Question 2 asks students to describe 4SURE.com's marketing mix and explain how it differs from a more traditional retailer. The product component of 4SURE.com's marketing mix includes goods such as computers, hardware, software, and related supplies. As an online retailer, the firm's product component also includes its easy-to-navigate websites, powerful search engine, fast checkout, convenient payment policies, and product guarantees. The company fills customers' orders directly through distributors or manufacturers, although it has built its own warehouse to ensure that it can fill orders quickly, even overnight. The firm's prices are very competitive. With regard to the promotion element, the case is not explicit, but 4SURE.com has benefited from positive publicity generated from receiving several prestigious awards for its product selection, ease of use, privacy policy, and strong customer support. In many respects, 4SURE.com's marketing mix is quite similar to that offered by more traditional "brick-and-mortar" category killers like Office Depot or Staples. For its business customers, being able to transact business online may be more convenient than having an employee drive to a nearby office-supply store to restock.

The third question asks students to assess 4SURE.com's strategy of focusing primarily on business markets. This question requires students to integrate the material they have learned from the previous chapters to evaluate a company's strategy and performance. Responses will vary, but most will assess the firm's strategy positively in that the company is focusing on a lucrative market segment that is likely to have few objections to shopping for largely standardized products online. By building strong relationships with its customers, 4SURE.com can better satisfy their needs and ensure their loyalty, even while other "dot.coms" that are less focused are failing.

Video Information

Company:	4SURE.com
Location:	Tape 1/DVD 1, Segment 6
Length:	1:59

Video Overview: This video profiles 4SURE.com, which markets office and computer supplies to large and small businesses (and some consumers) through two websites: solutions4sure.com and computers4sure.com. The video focuses on the firm's strong customer service and the decisions and activities required to maintain that level of customer service.

MULTIPLE-CHOICE QUESTIONS ABOUT THE VIDEO

1.   According to the video, the thing that sets 4SURE.com apart is the fact that it is

    a.   sales-driven.
    b.   computer-driven.
    c.   marketing-driven.
    d.   people-driven.
    e.   highly automated.

2.   According to the video, an essential part of 4SURE.com's business philosophy is

    a.   understanding customers.
    b.   understanding computers.
    c.   competitive prices.
    d.   huge product selection.
    e.   a powerful search engine.

3.   In the 4SURE.com video, an executive describes the firm's decision to keep its sales and support staff inhouse as a

    a.   market opportunity.
    b.   strategic advantage.
    c.   competitive advantage.
    d.   competitive weapon.
    e.   core competency.

ANSWERS TO MULTIPLE-CHOICE QUESTIONS ABOUT THE VIDEO

1.   d

2.   a

3.   e

CASE 6.2 EBAY AUCTIONS EVERYTHING

To introduce this case, you may want to ask students if any of them have ever visited the eBay website or purchased anything through the site. Ask those who have experience to describe the process and assess its ease of use.

The first question asks students to identify the basic characteristics of e-marketing that are most important to eBay. Students responses may vary but most should recognize that control (which refers to customers' ability to regulate the information they view and the rate and sequence of their exposure) and accessibility (which refers to customers' ability to obtain the vast amount of information available on the Internet) seem to be most important to eBay, although other characteristics also facilitate eBay's role as an intermediary.

The second question asks students to describe eBay's marketing mix and how it differs from a more traditional retailer. Students should recognize first that eBay is essentially a retailer that operates as an intermediary between buyers and sellers. Its product is the service and infrastructure that it provides to facilitate these transactions. It has also developed new services that target specific groups of customers, such as small businesses. Although not explicit in the case, it would seem that its pricing is competitive given its high rate of growth worldwide. Although not explicit in the case, most students will have encountered promotions for the website and/or experienced word-of-mouth communications about it. In many respects, eBay's marketing mix is quite similar to that offered by more traditional "brick-and-mortar" flea market or consignment store, but the product choices available to customers is far, far greater.

The third question asks whether eBay has done enough to prevent fraud on its site. Responses will vary, but this question should prompt a debate about how much responsibility website operators bear for fraud perpetrated by customers and what can realistically be done to prevent it.

CHAPTER 7

Marketing Research and Information Systems

TEACHING RESOURCES QUICK REFERENCE GUIDE

Resource	Location
Purpose and Perspective	IRM, p. 111
Guide for Using Color Transparencies	IRM, p. 112
Lecture Outline	IRM, p. 112
Notes for Class Exercises, Debate Issue, and Chapter Quiz	IRM, p. 119
Class Exercise 1	IRM, p. 121
Class Exercise 2	IRM, p. 122
Debate Issue	IRM, p. 123
Chapter Quiz	IRM, p. 124
Answers to Discussion and Review Questions	IRM, p. 125
Comments on the Cases	IRM, p. 127
Case 7.1	IRM, p. 127
Video	Tape 1/DVD 1, Segment 7
Video Information	IRM, p. 127
Multiple-Choice Questions About the Video	IRM, p. 128
Case 7.2	IRM, p. 128
Transparency Acetates	Transparency package
Examination Questions: Essay	TB, p. 175
Examination Questions: Multiple-Choice	TB, p. 175
Examination Questions: True-False	TB, p. 201
Author-Selected Multiple-Choice Test Items	TB, p. 670
HMClassPrep Presentation Resources	CD-ROM
PowerPoint Slides	Instructor's website

Note: Additional resources are updated periodically and may be found on the accompanying student and instructor websites at http://www.prideferrell.com/.

PURPOSE AND PERSPECTIVE

This chapter focuses on the ways of gathering information needed for marketing decisions. First, we discuss the role of marketing research in decision making and problem solving. We also identify a set of steps to follow in conducting a marketing research project: 1) locating and defining problems or research issues, 2) designing the research project, 3) collecting data, 4) interpreting research findings, and 5) reporting research findings. Then we turn to the methods of gathering marketing research data. We describe various sources of secondary data. We explore primary data collection methods in detail, focusing on sampling, survey methods, observation methods, and experimentation. We discuss how new technologies, such as the Internet, aid marketers in collecting, organizing, and interpreting marketing research data. Finally, we consider ethical and international issues in marketing research.

GUIDE FOR USING COLOR TRANSPARENCIES

There are two groups of color transparencies. The transparencies identified by a double number are the same as the figures and tables in the text. The transparencies labeled with a number and a letter are illustrations that do not appear in the text, but they can be used as additional examples of concepts discussed.

Figure 7.1	The Five Steps of the Marketing Research Process
Table 7.3	Comparison of the Four Basic Survey Methods
Figure 7A	Chapter 7 Outline
Figure 7B	Key Definitions: Marketing Research, Marketing Information System (MIS)
Figure 7C	U.S. Hot Dog Consumption
Figure 7D	Sources of Secondary Data
Figure 7E	Top 5 "Brain Gain" and "Brain Drain" Markets
Figure 7F	Types of Marketing Research
Figure 7G	Top 10 Metro Markets for Married and Unmarried Gay and Lesbian Households
Figure 7H	How to Collect Primary Data
Figure 7I	Global Marketing Research

LECTURE OUTLINE

(Transparency Figure 7A: Chapter Outline)

I. **The Importance of Marketing Research**
A. *Marketing research* is the systematic design, collection, interpretation, and reporting of information to help marketers solve specific marketing problems or take advantage of market opportunities.

(Transparency Figure 7B)

1. It is a process for gathering information not currently available to decision makers.
2. The purpose of marketing research is to inform an organization about customers' needs and desires, marketing opportunities for particular goods and services, and changing attitudes and purchase patterns of customers.

(Transparency Figure 7C)

B. Marketing research can help a firm better understand market opportunities, ascertain the potential for success for new products, and determine the feasibility of a particular marketing strategy.
C. Marketing research is used by all sorts of organizations to help develop marketing mixes to match the needs of customers.
D. The real value of marketing research is measured by improvements in a marketer's ability to make decisions.
1. Marketers should treat information in the same manner as other resources utilized by the firm, and they must weigh the costs of obtaining information against the benefits derived.
2. Information should be judged worthwhile if it results in marketing activities that better satisfies the firm's target customers, leads to increased sales and profits, or helps the firm achieve some other goal.

II. **The Marketing Research Process**
To maintain the control needed to obtain accurate information, marketers approach marketing research as a process with logical steps. These steps should be viewed as an overall approach to conducting research rather than as a rigid set of rules to be followed in each project.

(Transparency Figure 7.1)

A. **Locating and Defining Problems or Research Issues**
1. The first step in launching a research study is problem or issue definition, which focuses on uncovering the nature and boundaries of a situation or question related to marketing strategy or implementation. The first sign of a problem is typically a departure from some normal function, such as conflicts between or failures in attaining objectives.
2. Marketing research often focuses on identifying and defining market opportunities or changes in the environment. When a firm discovers a market opportunity, it may need to conduct research to understand the situation more precisely so it can craft an appropriate marketing strategy.

(Transparency Figure 7E)

3. To pin down the specific boundaries of a problem or an issue through research, marketers must define the nature and scope of the situation in a way that requires probing beneath the superficial symptoms.

B. **Designing the Research Project**
Once the problem or issue has been defined, the next step is *research design*, an overall plan for obtaining the information needed to address it. This step requires formulating a hypothesis and determining what type of research is most appropriate for testing the hypothesis.

1. **Developing a Hypothesis**
    a) A *hypothesis* is an informed guess or assumption about a certain problem or set of circumstances.
    b) It is based on all the insight and knowledge available about the problem or circumstances from previous research studies and other sources.
    c) Sometimes several hypotheses are developed during an actual research project; the hypotheses that are accepted or rejected become the study's chief conclusions.
2. **Types of Research**
    The hypothesis being tested determines whether an exploratory, descriptive, or causal approach will be used for gathering data.

(Transparency Figure 7F)

    a) When marketers need more information about a problem or want to make a tentative hypothesis more specific, they may conduct *exploratory research*. They may review information in the firm's own records, examine publicly available data, or question knowledgeable people inside or outside the organization to gain insights into the problem.
    b) If marketers need to understand the characteristics of certain phenomena to solve a particular problem, *descriptive research* can aid them.
        (1) Descriptive studies can range from general surveys of customers' education, occupation, or age to specifics on how they use products or how often they purchase them.
        (2) Descriptive studies generally demand much prior knowledge and assume the problem or issue is clearly defined.
    c) In *causal research*, it is assumed that a particular variable X causes a variable Y. Marketers must plan the research so that the data collected prove or disprove that X causes Y.

3. **Research Reliability and Validity**
In designing research, marketing researchers must ensure that research techniques are both reliable and valid.

    a)   A research technique has *reliability* if it produces almost identical results in repeated trials.

    b)   To have *validity*, the method must measure what it is supposed to measure, not something else.

C. **Collecting Data**
The next step in the marketing research process is collecting data to help prove (or disprove) the research hypothesis. The research design must specify what types of data to collect and how they will be collected.

1. **Types of Data**

    a)   *Primary data* are observed and recorded or collected directly from respondents. This type of data must be gathered by observing phenomena or surveying people of interest.

    b)   *Secondary data* are compiled both inside and outside the organization for some purpose other than the current investigation.

2. **Sources of Secondary Data**

(Transparency Figure 7D)

Marketers often begin the data collection phase of the marketing research process by gathering secondary data.

    a)   Internal sources of secondary data can include the organization's own database, which may contain information about past marketing activities, as well as accounting records.

    b)   External sources of data include periodicals, government publications, unpublished sources, online databases, or outside services.

(Transparency Figure 7G)

3. **Methods of Collecting Primary Data**
The collection of primary data is a more lengthy, expensive, and complex process than the collection of secondary data.

(Transparency Figure 7H)

    a)   **Sampling**

        (1)   Because the time and resources available for research are limited, it is almost impossible to investigate all members of a target market or other population.

            (a)   A *population*, or "universe," includes all the elements, units, or individuals of interest to researchers for a specific study.

            (b)   By systematically choosing a limited number of units—a *sample*—to represent the characteristics of a total population, researchers can project the reactions of a total market or market segment.

        (2)   *Sampling* in marketing research is the process of selecting representative units from a total population. Most types of marketing research employ sampling techniques. There are two basic types of sampling: probability sampling and nonprobability sampling.

        (3)   With *probability sampling*, every element in the population being studied has a known chance of being selected for study.

(a)   When marketers employ *random sampling*, all the units in a population have an equal chance of appearing in the sample.

(b)   Another kind of probability sampling is *stratified sampling*, which divides the population of interest into groups according to a common attribute, and then a random sample is chosen within each group.

(4)   *Nonprobability sampling* is more subjective than probability sampling because there is no way to calculate the likelihood that a specific element of the population will be chosen. One type of nonprobability sampling is *quota sampling*, in which researchers divide the population into groups and then arbitrarily choose participants from each group.

b)   **Survey Methods**

(1)   Marketing researchers often employ sampling to collect primary data through mail, telephone, online, or personal interview surveys.

(a)   Selection of a survey method depends on the nature of the problem or issue, the data needed to test the hypothesis, and the resources, such as funding and personnel, available to the researcher.

(b)   Gathering information through surveys is becoming increasingly difficult because fewer people are willing to participate.

(Transparency Table 7.3)

(2)   In a *mail survey*, questionnaires are sent to respondents, who are encouraged to complete and return them.

(a)   Mail surveys are used most often when the individuals in the sample are spread over a wide area and funds for the survey are limited.

(b)   A mail survey is the least expensive survey method as long as the response rate is high enough to produce reliable results.

(c)   The main disadvantages of this method are the possibility of a low response rate and of misleading results if respondents differ significantly from the population being sampled.

(d)   Premiums or incentives that encourage respondents to return questionnaires have been effective in developing panels of respondents who are interviewed regularly by mail.

(3)   In a *telephone survey*, an interviewer records respondents' answers to a questionnaire over a phone line.

(a)   Telephone surveys have some advantages over mail surveys, including higher rate of response, speed, and the ability to gain rapport with respondents and ask probing questions.

(b)   Telephone surveys have several disadvantages.

Few people like to participate in telephone surveys, which can limit participation and distort representation.

Telephone surveys are limited to oral communication; visual aids or observation cannot be included.

Interpreters of results must make adjustments for subjects who are not at home, do not have telephones, have unlisted numbers, or screen or block calls.

(4)   In an *online survey*, questionnaires can be transmitted to respondents who have agreed to be contacted and have provided their e-mail addresses.

(a)   The potential advantages of e-mail surveys are quick response and lower cost than traditional mail, telephone, and personal interview surveys if the response rate is adequate.

(b)   More firms are also using websites to conduct surveys.

(5) In a *personal interview survey*, participants respond to questions face to face.

  (a) One such research technique is the *in-home (door-to-door) interview*, which takes place in the respondent's home.

  (b) The object of a *focus-group interview* is to observe group interaction when members are exposed to an idea or concept. These interviews are often conducted informally in small groups of eight to twelve people and allow customer attitudes, behavior, lifestyles, needs, and desires to be explored.

  (c) Another option is the *telephone depth interview*, which combines the traditional focus group's ability to probe with the confidentiality provided by telephone surveys.

  (d) *Shopping mall intercept interviews* involve interviewing a percentage of individuals passing by certain "intercept" points in a mall. An *on-site computer interview* is a variation of the mall intercept interview, in which respondents complete a self-administered questionnaire displayed on a computer monitor.

c) **Questionnaire Construction**

  (1) Questions must be clear, easy to understand, and directed toward a specific objective.

  (2) A common mistake in constructing questionnaires is to ask questions that interest the researchers but do not yield information useful in deciding whether to accept or reject a hypothesis.

  (3) Questions are usually of three kinds: open-ended, dichotomous, and multiple-choice (as shown in the text).

  (4) Researchers must be careful about questions that a respondent might consider too personal or that might require an admission of activities that other people are likely to condemn.

d) **Observation Methods**

In using observation methods, researchers record individuals' overt behavior, taking note of physical conditions and events. Direct contact with subjects is avoided.

  (1) Observation may include the use of ethnographic techniques, such as watching customers interact with a product in a real-world environment.

(Building Customer Relationships: Reality TV or Marketing Research?)

  (2) Observation may also be combined with interviews.

  (3) Data gathered through observation can sometimes be biased if the person is aware of the observation process.

  (a) An observer can be placed in a natural market environment, such as a grocery store, without biasing or influencing shoppers' actions.

  (b) If the presence of a human observer is likely to bias the outcome or if human sensory abilities are inadequate, mechanical means may be used to record behavior.

  (4) Observation is straightforward and avoids a central problem of survey methods: motivating respondents to state their true feelings or opinions. However, it tends to be descriptive.

e) **Experimentation**

In an *experiment*, marketing researchers attempt to maintain certain variables while measuring the effects of experimental variables.

(1) Experimentation requires that an independent variable (one not influenced by or dependent on other variables) be manipulated and the resulting changes in a dependent variable (one contingent on, or restricted to, one value or set of values assumed by the independent variable) be measured.

(2) Experimentation is used in marketing research to improve hypothesis testing.

D. **Interpreting Research Findings**

After collecting data to test their hypotheses, marketers need to interpret the research findings.

1. The first step in drawing conclusions from most research is displaying the data in table format.

2. Next, the data must be analyzed. *Statistical interpretation* focuses on what is typical or what deviates from the average.

3. Data require careful interpretation by the marketer.

4. Managers must understand the research results and relate them to a context that permits effective decision making.

E. **Reporting Research Findings**

1. The final step in marketing research is to report the research findings. The marketer must take a clear, objective look at the findings to see how well the gathered facts answer the research question or support or negate the initial hypotheses.

2. The report of the research results is usually a formal, written document.

3. Bias and distortion can be a major problem if the researcher is intent upon obtaining favorable results.

III. **Using Technology to Improve Marketing Information Gathering and Analysis**

Technology is making information for marketing decisions increasingly accessible.

A. **Marketing Information Systems**

1. A *marketing information system (MIS)* is a framework for the day-to-day management and structuring of information gathered regularly from sources both inside and outside an organization. It provides a continuous flow of information about prices, advertising, expenditures, sales, competition, and distribution expenses.

(Transparency Figure 7B)

2. The main focus of the marketing information system is on data storage and retrieval, as well as on computer capabilities and management's information requirements.

3. An effective marketing information system starts by determining the objective of the information—that is, by identifying decision needs that require certain information. The firm can then specify an information system for continuous monitoring to provide regular, pertinent information on both the external and internal environment.

B. **Databases**

1. A database is a collection of information arranged for easy access and retrieval.

2. Databases allow marketers to tap into an abundance of information useful in making marketing decisions: internal sales reports, newspaper articles, company news releases, government economic reports, bibliographies, and more, often accessed through a computer system.

3. Marketing researchers can also use commercial databases developed by information research firms to obtain useful information for marketing decisions.

4. Information provided by a single firm on household demographics, purchases, television viewing behavior, and responses to promotions such as coupons and free samples is called *single-source data*.

C. **Marketing Decision Support Systems**

A *marketing decision support system (MDSS)* is customized computer software that aids marketing managers in decision making by helping them anticipate the effects of certain decisions.

D. **The Internet and Online Information Services**

1. The Internet has evolved as a most powerful communication medium, linking customers and companies around the world via computer networks with e-mail, forums, webpages, and more.
2. There are many useful sources of information online, and companies can also mine their own websites for useful information.
3. Marketing researchers can also subscribe to online services, which typically offer subscribers such specialized services as databases, news services, and forums, as well as access to the Internet itself.
4. While most webpages are open to anyone with Internet access, many big companies also maintain internal webpages, called "intranets," that allow employees to access such internal data as customer profiles and product inventory.

IV. **Issues in Marketing Research**

A. **The Importance of Ethical Marketing Research**

1. Because marketing managers and other professionals are relying more on marketing research, marketing information systems, and new technologies to make better decisions, it is essential that professional standards be established by which such research may be judged reliable.
2. Such standards are necessary because of the ethical and legal issues that develop in gathering marketing research data.
3. Organizations like the Marketing Research Association have developed codes of conduct and guidelines to promote ethical marketing research. (See *Table 7.5* in text)

(Ethics and Social Responsibility: Burger King's Relationship with Coke Fizzles After Marketing Research Debacle)

B. **International Issues in Marketing Research**

1. The marketing research process described in this chapter is used globally, but to ensure that the research is valid and reliable, data-gathering methods may have to be modified to allow for differences in sociocultural, economic, political, legal, and technological forces in different regions of the world.

(Transparency Figure 7I)

2. Experts recommend a two-pronged approach to international marketing research.
   a) The first phase involves a detailed search for and analysis of secondary data to gain greater understanding of a particular marketing environment and to pinpoint issues that must be taken into account in gathering primary research data.
   b) The second phase involves field research using many of the methods described in the chapter, including focus groups and telephone surveys, to refine a firm's under-standing of specific customer needs and preferences.
      (1) Specific differences among countries can have a profound influence on data gathering.
      (2) Primary data gathering may have a greater chance of success if the firm employs local researchers who better understand how to approach potential respondents and can do so in their own language.

NOTES FOR CLASS EXERCISES, DEBATE ISSUE, AND CHAPTER QUIZ

On the following pages, you will find two class exercises, a debate issue, and a chapter quiz. These are formatted in large-size type so that you can use them as class handouts or for making transparencies. Below are the authors' comments on the class exercises, the debate topic for this chapter, and the answers to the chapter quiz.

Comments on Class Exercise 1

The objective of this class exercise is to apply the marketing research process to solving a marketing problem.

Question 1. The answers to this question will depend on how the students view the opportunity on your campus. Typical problem statements might include "We don't know if a sizable, profitable market exists for Fluff-and-Fold," or "We don't know which dorms at what times offer good opportunities for our service." You might suggest that *focus groups* could help define the problem more clearly.

Question 2. Most students will take the example and adapt it. However, you might push them further by asking, "Can you be any more specific about the target market? For instance, do you expect more underclassmen will use the service? More males or females?" Other typical hypotheses might involve service expectations (one-day pick up and delivery) and daily operation issues (primary demand on weekends versus weekdays).

Question 3. This may be a good time to explain how a focus group can help resolve or clarify research problems. You may even want to set up a focus group discussion in class. After students have developed a few open-ended questions (for example, "How much would you be willing to pay for Fluff-and-Fold service?"), you might want to allow time for students to gather from one another information related to the questions. You might also point out that inexpensive data collection such as focus groups or polling customers can ensure better marketing decisions.

Question 4. Observation, combined with interviews, may be an efficient way to deter-mine what times students will need the service. However, observation alone will not assess true feelings or opinions.

In part a), perhaps the best way to select a sample is through the use of stratified sampling, especially if demand is likely to vary by classification (freshmen, etc.). The student directory should provide this information. However, quota sampling, which is nonprobabilistic, may suffice for exploratory research.

In part b), mail surveys may be the cheapest (because of campus mail) and may be suitable to the short surveys most students will develop. However, response rate may be low. Phone surveys might increase the response rate, but finding students at home may be problematic. Personal interviews conducted at central meeting points on campus might help overcome refusals but might also introduce interviewer and sample bias.

In part c), you may want to illustrate the problems associated with double-barreled, leading, nonmutually exclusive, and exhaustive questions, among others. You might even have students collect data by using these questions.

Comments on Class Exercise 2

This exercise is designed to prompt students to think about how to solve data collection problems. Students should discuss the merits of alternative data collection methods as they solve each problem. Obviously, each problem can be solved by more than one collection method. The students should decide which data collection procedure is best for each situation and be able to defend their choices.

Possible answers:

1. Telephone interviews or possibly focus-group interviews

2. Mall intercept interviews

3. Telephone interviews

4. This information can be obtained most easily in a census report. However, if census information is too dated to be useful, the next best source might be the U.S. Department of Housing. Overall, this type of data is usually available in secondary form from government or industry sources.

5. A mail survey of Sears' charge customers

DEBATE ISSUE

Does marketing research (surveys, telephone interviewing) invade a respondent's privacy?

CHAPTER QUIZ

Answers to Chapter Quiz 1. b; 2. c; 3. b; 4. c.

Class Exercise 1

YOU ARE CONSIDERING OPENING A NEW "FLUFF-AND-FOLD" LAUNDRY PICK-UP, CLEANING, AND DELIVERY SERVICE FOR STUDENTS. YOU ARE UNCERTAIN WHETHER SUFFICIENT DEMAND EXISTS, AND YOU HAVE QUESTIONS ABOUT WHEN STUDENTS WILL NEED YOUR SERVICE MOST AND WHAT LEVEL OF SERVICE THEY WILL REQUIRE. YOU REALIZE THAT MAR-KETING RESEARCH CAN HELP SOLVE YOUR INFORMATION NEEDS. YOU MUST NOW DECIDE HOW TO BEST ANSWER THESE QUESTIONS.

1. Define the problem.

2. Design the research project.

3. After consulting any secondary data available, you decide to conduct an exploratory study with students in your classes. Develop open-ended questions to ask other students that will provide information regarding your hypotheses.

4. Having gained some insight into the problem, you are now ready to conduct a descriptive study. You decide to conduct a survey to further test your refined hy-potheses. However, you have several decisions to make regarding this study.

   a. What type of sampling approach (random, stratified, area, quota) will you use and why?

   b. What survey method (mail, telephone, personal interview) will you use and why?

   c. How will you construct the questionnaire? Develop open-ended, dichotomous, or multiple- choice questions that will test your hypotheses. Remember to remain impartial and inoffensive.

Class Exercise 2

WHAT IS THE MOST APPROPRIATE DATA COLLECTION METHOD FOR EACH OF THE FOLLOWING RESEARCH QUESTIONS?

1. How do consumers in South Dakota feel about Christmas shopping?

2. How do JC Penney customers feel about Penney's customer service?

3. What is the opinion of U.S. consumers toward a Chrysler advertisement that questions the quality of Japanese cars?

4. How many people nationwide currently live in apartments?

5. How do Sears' charge customers view that company's new pricing policy?

Debate Issue

DOES MARKETING RESEARCH (SURVEYS, TELEPHONE INTERVIEWING) INVADE A RESPONDENT'S PRIVACY?

YES

- A great deal of marketing research asks questions that are too personal.

- Some marketing research, especially telephone and personal interviews, is nothing more than a disguise for sales presentations.

- The information obtained from marketing research is often used to develop mailing lists that are used to sell consumers products that they may not want.

- Sometimes the true nature of the research is disguised to get consumers to respond.

NO

- The right to privacy deals with an individual's ability to restrict personal information.

- Individual respondents must decide for themselves how much of their personal lives they will share with others.

- What constitutes private information and public information is ultimately up to the individual respondent.

- As long as the researcher obtains the consent of the respondent, the research does not invade the respondent's privacy.

Chapter Quiz

1. Marketing information systems and marketing research have changed rapidly because customers and companies around the world have been linked by
   a. the computer.
   b. the Internet.
   c. the Interactive Network.
   d. electronic online services.
   e. telecommunications.

2. Dan was given the task of conducting a research project for his firm and proceeds with the following steps. He asks questions to determine the research topic, conducts a telephone survey, writes a report describing the survey results, and gives that report to his boss. Which step of the marketing research process has Dan omitted?
   a. Collecting data
   b. Defining and locating problems
   c. Interpreting research
   d. Designing the research project
   e. Reporting research findings

3. A study that is valid and reliable
   a. is called a marketing research study.
   b. measures what it is supposed to measure and produces almost identical results every time.
   c. is expensive to implement and complete.
   d. measures subtle differences in the population being studied.
   e. is difficult to produce without expert researchers.

4. Chelsea, Ltd., a retail clothing store chain, wants to use observation methods to gather information about shopping behavior. Which of the following should Chelsea know about observation methods of data collection?
   a. Observation uses secondary sources of data.
   b. Observation depends on mall interviews.
   c. Observation can tell Chelsea what is being done, but not why.
   d. Observation focuses on open-ended questions.
   e. Observation works best for telephone surveys.

ANSWERS TO DISCUSSION AND REVIEW QUESTIONS

1. **What is marketing research? Why is it important?**

    Marketing research is the systematic design, collection, interpretation, and reporting of information to help marketers solve specific marketing problems or take advantage of market opportunities. It is important because it can help a firm better understand market opportunities, ascertain the potential for success for new products, and determine the feasibility of a particular marketing strategy.

2. **Describe the five steps in the marketing research process.**

    Students should be able to describe each of the following steps:

    a. Locating and defining the problem or research issue

    b. Designing the research project

    c. Collecting data

    d. Interpreting research findings

    e. Reporting research findings

3. **What is the difference between defining a research problem and developing a hypothesis?**

    A research problem is the question that is to be answered, whereas a hypothesis is an assumption or supposition about the solution to be explored.

4. **Describe the different types of approaches to marketing research and indicate when each should be used.**

    Exploratory research is conducted to gather more information about a problem or to make a tentative hypothesis more specific. Descriptive research is conducted to clarify the characteristics of certain phenomena to solve a particular problem. Causal research assumes that a particular variable X causes a variable Y. It is used when information is needed on causal relationships and more complex hypotheses are required.

5. **Where are data for marketing research obtained? Give examples of internal and external data.**

    Data for marketing research can come from internal sources or external sources. Internal sources might include the company's financial and operational records or customer contacts. Examples of internal data would be advertising expenses, sales figures, and customer complaints. External sources might include government publications, trade associations, marketing research companies, and business magazines. Examples of external data would be census information, consumer trends, or competitors' prices.

6. **What is the difference between probability sampling and nonprobability sampling? In what situation would it be best to use random sampling? Stratified sampling? Quota sampling?**

    In probability sampling, every element in the population being studied has a known chance of being selected for study. In nonprobability sampling, there is no way to calculate the likelihood that a specific element of the population being studied will be chosen. Random sampling works best when it is easy to number or identify all units in a population and give each unit a known or equal opportunity of appearing in the sample. Stratified sampling is useful when units such as individuals are not available on a list but geographic areas such as blocks or census tracts can be used. Then researchers use a random selection process to pick out units or individuals to be sampled. Quota sampling differs from the other sampling techniques because it is judgmental. Quota samples are often used in exploratory research that is not projected to the total population.

7. **Suggest some ways of encouraging respondents to cooperate in mail surveys.**

    An incentive such as a premium can be offered to those who participate. A well-written letter stating the importance of the survey can be helpful. Sampling from a population that is interested in the topic under investigation will increase response. Using a short, easy-to-fill-out questionnaire is also helpful.

8. **If a survey of all homes with listed telephone numbers is conducted, what sampling design should be used?**

    A simple random probability sample of phone numbers should be acceptable in this case.

9. **Describe some marketing problems that could be solved through information gained from observation.**

    Personal observation can be used to solve problems such as shoplifting, spoilage, and breakage. Also, demographic characteristics can be observed and classified. One could observe and plot license plates on a map to obtain a geographic market profile. Other examples in which observation is important are television ratings (such as Nielsen's) and traffic flow.

10. **What is a marketing information system, and what should it provide?**

    A marketing information system is a framework for the day-to-day management and structuring of information gathered regularly from sources both inside and outside an organization. A marketing information system should provide information about prices, advertising expenditures, sales, competition, consumer behavior, and distribution expenses. The value of a marketing information system is measured by the improvements it makes in the marketer's ability to make decisions.

11. **Define a database. What is its purpose, and what does it include?**

    A database is a collection of information arranged for easy access and retrieval, usually stored in a computer. A database allows a marketer to retrieve information to be used in making marketing decisions. The database might include information from newspaper articles, company news releases, government reports, and economic data.

12. **How can marketers use online services and the Internet to obtain information for decision making?**

    Through online services and the Internet, marketers can access databases, send e-mail, and create and peruse webpages. They can communicate with other marketers and customers as well.

13. **What role does ethics play in marketing research? Why is it important for marketing researchers to be ethical?**

    Because of the ethical and legal issues that develop in gathering marketing research data, it is essential that professional standards be established by which such research may be judged. Without clear understanding and agreement among all parties, including mutual adoption of standards, ethical conflict can lead to mistrust and questionable research results.

14. **How does marketing research in other countries differ from marketing research in the United States?**

    Marketing research in other countries uses the same five-step process described in this chapter. However, modifications may be necessary to allow for differences in sociocultural, economic, political, legal, and technological forces of the marketing environment in other countries.

COMMENTS ON THE CASES

[◉I◉] *CASE 7.1 IRI PROVIDES MARKETING RESEARCH DATA FROM MULTIPLE SOURCES*

This case examines how Information Resources Inc. (IRI) refines the data generated from checkout scanners to help its clients track what products are selling and at what price at different locations throughout the nation. With this information, IRI's manufacturing and retailing customers can make better marketing strategy decisions and thereby improve their competitive position.

The first question asks how the data gathered by IRI is useful in customer relationship marketing. According to the case, IRI's services facilitate customer relationship management by using marketing research and information technology to provide profiles of consumers, including behaviors and attitudes. By helping marketers make better decisions, IRI's information can help these manufacturers and retailers provide greater value for their customers, which should improve their relationship with these customers.

Question 2 asks about the advantage of integrating scanner data with television viewing behavior. Students should be able to recognize that integrating these two sets of data should help marketers make better marketing strategy decisions, especially with regard to promotion. By understanding what television shows are watched by the target customers of a particular product, marketers can allocate their promotional dollars more effectively (and efficiently).

The third question asks students to compare the usefulness of behavioral scanner data with data conducted through marketing surveys. Students responses here will vary, but the question should prompt a discussion about the appropriateness of various types of marketing research methods in different situations. Behavioral data obtained through checkout scanners can help marketers track what products are selling and at what price at different locations throughout the nation. Survey data can help marketers understand why products are selling and the factors that lead customers to make purchasing decisions. The reality is that both types of data may be necessary to develop marketing strategies that satisfy customer needs and desires.

Video Information

Company: IRI

Location: Tape 1/DVD 1, Segment 7

Length: 5:09

Video Overview: The video illustrates how Chicago-based Information Resources, Inc. (IRI) uses the data provided by checkout scanners to help track what products are selling and at what price at different locations throughout the nation. The raw data can be manipulated in many ways to provide information useful for evaluating the success of new products, validating pricing decisions, and monitoring new marketing programs. This information can also help IRI's manufacturing and retailing customers remain competitive which, in turn, provides better quality, greater value, and lower prices for consumers.

MULTIPLE-CHOICE QUESTIONS ABOUT THE VIDEO

1.   According to the video, Information Resources Inc. can help its manufacturing and retailing customers do all of the following except

    a.   assess their pricing strategies.
    b.   assess their promotion strategies.
    c.   determine the ideal formulation for their product.
    d.   determine how well their product is selling in one region compared to another region.
    e.   assess the effects of their competitors' strategies.

2.   According to the video, Information Resources Inc.'s checkout scanner service is called

    a.   BehaviorScan.
    b.   InfoScan.
    c.   DataScan.
    d.   MarketScan.
    e.   ScanCam.

3.   According to the video, Information Resources Inc. analyzes the data from checkout scanners in _____ supermarkets, drugstores, and mass merchandisers every week.

    a.   5,000
    b.   20
    c.   200
    d.   2,000
    e.   20,000

ANSWERS TO MULTIPLE-CHOICE QUESTIONS ABOUT THE VIDEO

1.   c

2.   b

3.   e

CASE 7.2 A LOOK-LOOK AT YOUTH TRENDS

This case examines a firm that may be of some interest to students because it explores trends among teenagers and young adults for its corporate customers. Look-Look.com is an online research firm that conducts surveys and uses other research techniques to help companies better understand the youth market.

The first question asks how the information Look-Look.com supplies helps marketers appeal to teenagers and young adults. Keeping up with the dynamic tastes, interests, and desires of today's youth has become very challenging for marketers, and few research firms have been able to meet this challenge. By regularly surveying and interacting with a hand-picked, prescreened panel of 20,000 young people from around the world, Look-Look can gain insight into youth trends in nearly real time. This insight can help the firm's customers better understand their market and respond more quickly to changes in this market.

Question 2 asks about the advantages the methods Look-Look.com employs have over traditional marketing research methods. Look-Look's use of online surveys should offer the same benefits of traditional marketing research surveys, but the fact that they are conducted online should allow Look-Look to analyze the resulting data more quickly. Look-Look's use of nontraditional methods, such as "e-dialogs" with youth correspondents and photographers, should help the company gain even greater insight into what young people are thinking and interested in, which can help the company pinpoint youth trends and fads for the benefit of its corporate clients.

The third question asks students to consider criticisms that Look-Look.com's core trendsetting respondents are too "hip" to reflect the tastes of mainstream teens and young adults and whether this might be a problem for a company relying on Look-Look data to develop a marketing strategy. Responses to this question will vary, but the question should help students recognize the importance of obtaining a representative sample for any type of marketing research.

CHAPTER 8

Target Markets: Segmentation and Evaluation

TEACHING RESOURCES QUICK REFERENCE GUIDE

Resource	Location
Purpose and Perspective	IRM, p. 131
Guide for Using Color Transparencies	IRM, p. 132
Lecture Outline	IRM, p. 132
Notes for Class Exercises, Debate Issue, and Chapter Quiz	IRM, p. 139
Class Exercise 1	IRM, p. 141
Class Exercise 2	IRM, p. 142
Debate Issue	IRM, p. 143
Chapter Quiz	IRM, p. 144
Answers to Discussion and Review Questions	IRM, p. 145
Comments on the Cases	IRM, p. 149
Case 8.1	IRM, p. 149
Video	Tape 1/DVD 1, Segment 8
Video Information	IRM, p. 150
Multiple-Choice Questions About the Video	IRM, p. 150
Case 8.2	IRM, p. 151
Transparency Acetates	Transparency package
Examination Questions: Essay	TB, p. 207
Examination Questions: Multiple-Choice	TB, p. 208
Examination Questions: True-False	TB, p. 234
Author-Selected Multiple-Choice Test Items	TB, p. 670
HMClassPrep Presentation Resources	CD-ROM
PowerPoint Slides	Instructor's website

Note: Additional resources are updated periodically and may be found on the accompanying student and instructor websites at http://www.prideferrell.com./

PURPOSE AND PERSPECTIVE

This chapter covers 1) the definition of a market, 2) how organizations identify target markets, and 3) how to estimate market potential and forecast sales. First, we define a market and discuss the characteristics that groups must possess to be considered a market. Then, we describe in detail the five steps in the target market selection process. In discussing the process, we describe three targeting strategies: undifferentiated, concentrated, and differentiated. We examine in some detail the process of choosing segmentation variables and the types of variables that marketers use. Finally, we consider how to evaluate market potential and how to forecast sales.

GUIDE FOR USING COLOR TRANSPARENCIES

There are two groups of color transparencies. The transparencies identified by a double number are the same as the figures in the text. The transparencies labeled with a number and a letter are illustrations that do not appear in the text, but they can be used as additional examples of concepts discussed.

Part 4 Opener	Target Markets and Customer Behavior
Figure 8.1	Target Market Selection Process
Figure 8.2a	Targeting Strategies: Undifferentiated
Figure 8.2b	Targeting Strategies: Concentrated
Figure 8.2c	Targeting Strategies: Differentiated
Figure 8.3	Segmentation Variables for Consumer Markets
Figure 8.4	Spending Levels of Three Age Groups for Selected Product Categories
Figure 8.5	Family Life Cycle Stages as a Percentage of All Households
Figure 8.6	VALS™ Types and Sports Preferences
Figure 8A	Chapter 8 Outline
Figure 8B	Key Definitions: Consumer Market, Market Segmentation
Figure 8C	The Three Types of Targeting Strategies
Figure 8D	Who Are Not the Big Spenders?
Figure 8E	Which Marketers Are Interested in Growth Rates of College Age People?
Figure 8F	Who Uses Cell Phones?
Figure 8G	Changes in Median Age of First Marriages for Men and Women
Figure 8H	Which Age Groups Are the Most Important to the U.S. Economy?
Figure 8I	Lifestyle Dimensions
Figure 8J	Variables for Segmenting Business Markets
Figure 8K	Types of Sales Forecasts
Figure 8L	What Type of Targeting Strategy Does Nabisco Use for Its Cookie Product Line?

LECTURE OUTLINE

(Transparency Part 4 Opener)

(Transparency Figure 8A: Chapter Outline)

I.   **What Are Markets?**
    A.   **Requirements of a Market**
        1.   They must exhibit a need for a particular product.
        2.   They must possess the ability to purchase the product.
        3.   They must be willing to buy the product.
        4.   They must have the authority to buy the product.
    B.   **Types of Markets**

(Transparency Figure 8B)

        1.   *Consumer market*—individuals who purchase with the intent to consume or directly benefit from the purchased good. They do not intend to profit from the purchase through resale.
        2.   *Business market*—individuals or groups that buy a specific kind of product for resale, direct use in producing other products, or use in general, daily operations.

II. **Target Market Selection Process**

(Transparency Figure 8.1)

Marketers generally employ a five-step process for target market selection: identifying the appropriate targeting strategy, determining which segmentation variables to use, developing market segment profiles, evaluating relevant market segments, and selecting specific target markets.

III. **Step 1: Identify the Appropriate Targeting Strategy**

(Transparency Figure 8C)

The targeting strategy used is affected by target market characteristics, product attributes, and the organization's objectives and resources.

A. **Undifferentiated Strategy**

(Transparency Figure 8.2a)

1. The *undifferentiated targeting strategy* is one in which an organization defines an entire market for a particular product as its target market, designs a single marketing mix, and directs it at the entire market.
2. The underlying assumption is that the needs of the target market for specific kinds of product are very similar; thus the business can satisfy most customers with a single marketing mix.
3. There are two requirements for effective use of this approach.
   a) A *homogeneous market* is one in which a large proportion of customers have similar needs for a product.
   b) The organization must be able to develop and maintain a single marketing mix that satisfies customers' needs.

B. **Concentrated Strategy Through Market Segmentation**
1. *Heterogeneous markets* are markets made up of individuals or organizations with diverse product needs.
2. *Market segmentation* is the process of dividing the total market into groups or segments that have relatively similar product needs for the purpose of designing a marketing mix that will more precisely match the needs of individuals in a selected segment.

(Transparency Figure 8B)

3. A *market segment* consists of individuals, groups, or organizations with one or more similar characteristics that cause them to have relatively similar product needs.
4. There are five conditions for effective segmentation.
   a) Consumers' needs for the product must be heterogeneous.
   b) The segments must be identifiable and divisible.
   c) The total market should be divided so that segments can be compared with respect to estimated sales potential, costs, and profits.
   d) At least one segment must have enough profit potential to justify the development and maintenance of a special marketing mix for that segment.
   e) The organization must be able to reach the chosen segment with a particular marketing mix.
5. *Concentrated targeting strategy* is a strategy in which an organization targets a single market segment using one marketing mix.

(Transparency Figure 8.2b)

a) Advantages
(1) Specialization gives the firm an opportunity to analyze the characteristics and needs of a distinct customer group carefully and then focus all marketing efforts into satisfying that group's needs.
(2) A firm can generate large sales volume by reaching a single segment.
(3) A firm with rather restricted resources is able to compete with much larger organizations.
b) Disadvantages
(1) If the segment's demand for the product declines, the company's financial strength also declines.
(2) Success in one segment may preclude entry into another segment.

C. **Differentiated Strategy Through Market Segmentation**

(Transparency Figure 8.2c)

Differentiated targeting strategy is a strategy in which an organization targets two or more segments by developing a marketing mix for each segment.

(Transparency Figure 8L)

1. Advantages
   a) A business can increase its sales in a total market by focusing on more than one segment.
   b) Sales to additional market segments may absorb excess production capacity.
2. Disadvantages
   a) A greater number of production processes, materials, and skills means higher production costs.
   b) Several distinct promotion plans and distribution methods are required, resulting in higher marketing costs.

IV. **Step 2: Determine Which Segmentation Variables to Use**
A. *Segmentation variables* are characteristics of individuals, groups, or organizations that are used to divide a market into segments. Marketers consider the following factors when choosing segmentation variables.
   1. The segmentation variable should be related to customers' needs for, uses of, or behavior toward the product.
   2. The variable must be measurable.
   3. The company's resources and capabilities determine the number and size of segment variables used.
   4. Choice of segmentation variables is a critical step because an inappropriate variable limits the chances of developing a successful marketing strategy.
B. **Variables for Segmenting Consumer Markets**

(Transparency Figure 8.3)

1. **Demographic Variables**

(Transparency Figure 8.4)

a) Those commonly used by marketers include age, gender, race, ethnicity, income, education, occupation, family size, family life cycle, religion, and social class.

(Transparency Figure 8.5)

(Transparency Figure 8D)

(Transparency Figure 8E)

(Transparency Figure 8F)

(Transparency Figure 8G)

(Transparency Figure 8H)

b)   They are often closely related to customers' product needs and purchasing behavior.
c)   They can be readily measured through observation or survey methods.

(Building Customer Relationships: The New American Household)

2.   **Geographic Variables**
a)   Geographic variables include climate, terrain, city size, and urban/rural values.
b)   *Market density* refers to the number of potential customers within a unit of land area, such as a square mile.
c)   *Geodemographic segmentation* clusters people in zip code areas and even smaller neighborhood units based on lifestyle and demographic information.
d)   *Micromarketing* is an approach to market segmentation in which organizations focus precise marketing efforts on very small geographic markets, such as community, and even neighborhood markets.

3.   **Psychographic Variables**
A psychographic variable can be used by itself to segment a market or combined with other types of segmentation variables. The following are the types most commonly used to segment markets.

a)   Personality characteristics
(1)   These can be useful for segmentation when a product resembles many competing products and consumers' needs are not greatly affected by other segmentation variables.
(2)   Marketers almost always select personality characteristics that many people view positively.
b)   Motives
(1)   A market is divided according to consumers' reasons for making a purchase.
(2)   Personal appearance, affiliation, status, safety, and health are examples of motives affecting the types of products purchased and the choice of stores in which they are bought.
c)   Lifestyle segmentation

(Transparency Figure 8I)

(1)   Lifestyle segmentation groups individuals according to how they spend their time, importance of things in their surroundings, beliefs about themselves and broad issues, and some demographic characteristics.
(2)   This variable encompasses numerous characteristics related to people's activities, interests, and opinions.

(Transparency Figure 8.6)

(3)   One of the more popular programs that studies lifestyle is conducted by the Stanford Research Institute's Value and Lifestyle Program (VALS); its research has identified the following.

(a)   Three broad consumer groups: Outer-Directed, Inner-Directed, and Need-Driven consumers
(b)   Five basic lifestyle groups: Strugglers, Action-Oriented, Status-Oriented, Principle-Oriented, and Actualizers

(Building Customer Relationships: Understanding Mature Customers)

4.   **Behavioristic Variables**
a)   These variables commonly involve consumers' product use.
(1)   Users and nonusers
(2)   Heavy, moderate, and light users
b)   How consumers use or apply the products may also determine segmentation.
c)   *Benefit segmentation* is the division of a market according to benefits that consumers want from the product.
C.   **Variables for Segmenting Business Markets**

(Transparency Figure 8J)

1.   **Geographic Location.** Variations in organizations' demands result from differences in climate, terrain, consumer preferences, or similar factors.
2.   **Type of Organization.** Required product features, distribution systems, price structures, and selling strategies may vary among different types of organizations.
3.   **Customer Size.** An organization's size may affect the purchasing procedures and types and quantities of products desired.
4.   **Product Use.** How a firm uses products affects the types and amounts of products purchased and the manner in which they are purchased.

V.   **Step 3: Develop Market Segment Profiles**
A.   Market segment profiles describe the similarities among potential customers within a segment and explain the differences among people and organizations in different market segments.
B.   A profile can deal with demographic characteristics, geographic factors, product benefits sought, lifestyles, brand preferences, or usage rates.
C.   Market segment profiles provide marketers with an understanding of how a business can use its capabilities to serve potential customer groups.

VI.   **Step 4: Evaluate Relevant Market Segments**
A.   **Sales Estimates**
1.   Potential sales for a segment can be measured along several dimensions, including product, geographic area, time, and level of competition.
2.   *Market potential* is the total amount of a product for all firms in an industry that customers will purchase within a specified period at a specific level of industrywide marketing activity.
a)   It can be stated in terms of dollars or units and can refer to a total market or to a market segment.
b)   When analyzing market potential, it is important to indicate the time frame and the level of industry marketing activities.
3.   *Company sales potential* is the maximum percentage of market potential that an individual firm within an industry can expect to obtain for a specific product.
a)   Factors that influence a company's sales potential are the size of the market sales potential, the magnitude of industrywide marketing activities, and the intensity and effectiveness of the firm's marketing activities relative to those of its competitors.
b)   There are two general approaches to measuring company sales potential: breakdown and buildup.

(1)   The *breakdown approach* measures company sales potential based on a general economic forecast for a specific time period and the sales potential derived from it. The marketing manager starts with broad comprehensive forecasts of general economic activity, estimates market potential, and then estimates the company's sales potential.

(2)   The *buildup approach* measures company sales potential by estimating how much of a product a potential buyer in a specific geographic area will purchase in a given time period, multiplying the estimate by the total number of potential buyers in that area, and adding the totals for each area to calculate market potential.

B.   **Competitive Assessment**
1.   Sales estimates may be misleading without competitive information.
2.   Several questions must be asked about competitors in the segments being considered.
   a)   How many competitors exist?
   b)   What are their strengths and weaknesses?
   c)   Do several competitors have major market shares and together dominate the segment?
   d)   Can our company create a marketing mix to compete effectively against competitors' marketing mixes?
   e)   Is it likely that new competitors will enter this segment?
   f)   If so, how will they affect our firm's ability to compete successfully?

C.   **Cost Estimates**
1.   Meeting the needs of a target segment can be expensive.
2.   If costs are too high, marketers may treat the segment as being inaccessible.

VII.   **Step 5: Select specific target markets**
A.   Marketers first decide whether there are enough differences in customers' needs to warrant the use of market segmentation.
1.   If customer needs are homogeneous, the undifferentiated approach may be the best choice.
2.   If customer needs are heterogeneous, then one or more target markets must be selected.
B.   The firm's management must consider whether the organization has the financial resources, managerial skills, employee expertise, and facilities to enter and compete effectively in selected segments.

VIII.   **Developing sales forecasts**
A.   A *sales forecast* is the amount of a product the firm actually expects to sell during a specific period at a specified level of marketing activities.

(Transparency Figure 8K)

1.   Businesses use the sales forecast for planning, organizing, implementing, and controlling their activities.
2.   Common problems in companies that fail are improper planning and lack of realistic sales forecasts.
3.   Sales forecasting techniques fall into five categories.
B.   **Executive Judgment**
1.   *Executive judgment* is based on the intuition of one or more executives.
2.   It is inexpensive and expedient.
3.   It works reasonably well when product demand is relatively stable and the forecaster has years of market-related experience.
4.   It is unscientific.

C. **Surveys**
1. A *customer forecasting survey* is a survey of customers regarding what types and quantities of products they intend to buy during a specific period.
   a) Customers must be willing and able to make accurate estimates of future product requirements.
   b) Surveys reflect buying intentions, not actual purchases.
   c) Surveys consume much time and money.
2. A *sales force forecasting survey* consists of estimates by a firm's salespeople of their anticipated sales in their territories for a specified period.
   a) The sales staff is closer to customers on a daily basis than other company personnel and, therefore, should know more about customers' future product needs.
   b) Forecasts can be prepared for single territories, divisions consisting of several territories, regions made up of multiple divisions, or the total geographic market.
   c) For the survey to be effective, salespeople as a group must be accurate—or at least consistent estimators.
   d) Assuming that the survey is well administered, the sales force can have the satisfaction of helping to establish reasonable sales goals.
   e) Salespeople should be assured that their forecasts are not used to set their sales quotas.
   f) The *expert forecasting survey* is a sales forecast prepared by professionals such as economists, management consultants, advertising executives, college professors, or other persons outside the firm with solid experience in a specific market.
   g) The *Delphi technique* is a procedure in which experts create initial forecasts, submit them to the company for averaging, and have the results returned to them so that they can make individual refined forecasts. The ultimate goal is to develop a highly accurate sales forecast.

D. **Time Series Analysis**
1. With *time series analysis*, a forecaster uses the firm's historical sales data to discover a pattern, or patterns, in the firm's sales over time and generally involves trend, cycle, seasonal, and random factor analyses.
2. *Trend analysis* focuses on aggregate sales data from a period of many years to determine whether annual sales are generally rising, falling, or staying about the same.
3. *Cycle analysis* is examination of sales figures over a period of three to five years to ascertain whether sales fluctuate in a consistent, periodic manner.
4. *Seasonal analysis* is an analysis of daily, weekly, or monthly sales figures to evaluate the degree to which seasonal factors influence sales.
5. *Random factor analysis* attempts to attribute erratic sales variations to random, nonrecurrent events.

E. **Regression Analysis**
1. *Regression analysis* is a method of predicting sales based on finding a relationship between past sales and one or more variables such as population, per capita income, or gross domestic product.
2. Simple regression analysis uses one independent variable, whereas multiple regression analysis includes two or more independent variables.
3. These methods are useful only when a precise relationship can be established and are therefore futile when no historical data exists, as with new products.

F.   **Market Tests**
1.   A *market test* involves making a product available to buyers in one or more test areas and measuring purchases and consumer responses to distribution, promotion, and price.
2.   Market tests provide information about consumers' actual rather than intended purchases.
3.   They are effective in estimating sales of new products or of existing products in new geographic areas.
4.   The chief disadvantages of market tests are that they are time-consuming and expensive.
G.   **Using Multiple Forecasting Methods**
1.   Although some businesses rely on a single sales forecasting method, most use several techniques to attempt to validate the results from one technique.
2.   Methods used for short-range forecasts are often inappropriate for long-range forecasting.

NOTES FOR CLASS EXERCISES, DEBATE ISSUE, AND CHAPTER QUIZ

Comments on Class Exercise 1

The objective of this class exercise is to gain a thorough understanding of segmentation variables by designing a target market for a new retail operation.

Question 1. Other ways of asking this question are "What kinds of retail stores do you wish were available here?" and "What kinds of restaurants or retail outlets have you seen in other places that might work here?" Students can usually think of successful operations in their hometowns that are not available locally. It is important to stress the necessity of the market being large enough or the segment being profitable enough to support their choice of retail operations.

Question 2. Students could spend the entire class period on this question, so encourage them to be brief. An example might be this: Open an upscale restaurant and bar that serves dinners ($7–$12) and drinks, located on the corner of University Avenue and First Street.

Question 3. The answer to this question will depend on the type of product or service being offered, but students often assume a concentrated strategy is best when a differentiated targeting strategy is more appropriate. For instance, most restaurants have breakfast, lunch, dinner, and perhaps late night segments, each having different needs.

Question 4. This question should take up the majority of the exercise time. Ask students to look carefully at *each* variable to determine if it will help develop a better marketing mix to meet customer needs. Most students will define their target markets by demographic or geographic variables because psychographic and behavioristic variables are harder to understand. Push them by asking, "Why would people go to your store?" (motives) and "What are they really buying at your store besides the product?" (benefits).

Comments on Class Exercise 2

This exercise is designed to get students to think in terms of segmentation variables discussed in the chapter. For example, what demographic, geographic, psychographic, or lifestyle variables could have been used to segment the market for baby food (variable 2)? Lifestyle segmentation variables could include:

1.   Consumers who want nothing but all-natural ingredients

2.   Upscale consumers who want gourmet baby food

3.   Time-conscious consumers who need instant or quick meals for their babies

Many other combinations are possible. Encourage students to be creative and imaginative. As with most exercises, there are no right or wrong answers. The following list includes variables or characteristics that could be used to segment markets for specific products.

	Characteristic	**Environmental Force**
1.	Recreational vehicles (RVs)	**age, income**
2.	Baby food	**family life cycle, age**
3.	Rolls Royce automobiles	**income, social class**
4.	Snow tires	**climate**
5.	Hotel rooms	**income, business vs. tourism**
6.	Magazines	**age, job, education, ethnicity, gender**
7.	Soft drinks	**age, gender**
8.	Movies	**age, family life cycle**
9.	Shoes	**age, income, lifestyle**
10.	Bicycles	**income, age, lifestyle**
11.	Air passenger service	**income, business vs. tourism**
12.	Cameras	**lifestyle, occupation, income**
13.	Swimsuits	**age, climate, gender**
14.	Restaurants	**income, age, city size, lifestyle**
15.	Snowboards	**age, climate**

DEBATE ISSUE

Makers of athletic shoes use benefit segmentation. For the average shoe buyer, are the performance benefits real?

CHAPTER QUIZ

Answers to Chapter Quiz 1. b; 2. a; 3. e; 4. a.

Class Exercise 1

YOU HAVE JUST RECEIVED A SIZABLE INHERI-TANCE AND AFTER GIVING PART OF IT TO CHARITY, YOU NOW HAVE $500,000 TO BEGIN A NEW RETAIL OPERATION IN YOUR LOCAL AREA. WHAT KIND OF OPERATION WILL YOU OPEN?

1. **What market or segment of a market exists in your area with unfulfilled needs or wants?**

2. **Briefly describe the nature of the operation you would open to meet the needs of a specific market segment(s).**

   a. **Product or service?**

   b. **Price range?**

   c. **Location?**

3. **Will you use a concentrated or a differentiated targeting strategy? Why?**

4. **What segmentation variables will be useful in describing your target market(s)? Why?**

Class Exercise 2

IDENTIFY ONE OR SEVERAL CHARACTERISTICS OR VARIABLES THAT COULD BE USED TO SEGMENT THE MARKETS FOR EACH OF THE FOLLOWING PRODUCTS.

1. Recreational vehicles (RVs)
2. Baby food
3. Rolls Royce automobiles
4. Snow tires
5. Hotel rooms
6. Magazines
7. Soft drinks
8. Movies
9. Shoes
10. Bicycles
11. Air passenger service
12. Cameras
13. Swimsuits
14. Restaurants
15. Snowboards

<u>Debate Issue</u>

MAKERS OF ATHLETIC SHOES USE BENEFIT SEGMENTATION. FOR THE AVERAGE SHOE BUYER, ARE THE PERFORMANCE BENEFITS REAL?

<u>YES</u>

- The shoes are designed for specific uses, which justifies the purchases of specific types of shoes for specific activities, like basketball shoes for basketball and running shoes for running.

- The use of a specific shoe for a different activity will reduce performance.

- Specially designed shoes provide the benefit of maximized comfort for the wearer when performing the activity for which the shoes were designed, even if there is no real improvement on that person's performance.

- Specially designed shoes are often designed to reduce the risk of injury for the wearer, which is another benefit.

<u>NO</u>

- The average person's performance in a specific activity will not be significantly reduced if a shoe for a different activity is used.

- The existence of cross-trainer shoes suggests that the average person can use one pair of shoes for multiple activities.

- The total cost of purchasing multiple pairs of shoes is too high relative to the slightly enhanced performance received, if any.

Chapter Quiz

1. Which of the following is *not* a requirement or characteristic of a market?

    a. The ability to purchase a product
    b. A large number of people or organizations
    c. The authority to buy a product
    d. The willingness to use buying power
    e. The need for a specific product in a specific product category

2. A disadvantage of the concentrated targeting strategy is that

    a. the firm's financial condition is tied to a single and specialized marketing mix.
    b. large sales volumes cannot be generated.
    c. production costs may be higher than with other strategies.
    d. marketing personnel may become dissatisfied with the limited opportunities provided by this approach.
    e. marketing costs are often higher than for other strategies.

3. The psychographic variable that includes numerous characteristics related to people's activities, interests, and opinions is

    a. motive.   d. stage in family life cycle.
    b. social class.   e. lifestyle.
    c. personality.

4. In an effort to forecast his firm's sales for the coming year, Henry Thompson takes sales for the last three years and calculates a growth trend. Henry is employing which forecasting method?

    a. Time series analysis   d. Regression analysis
    b. Executive judgment   e. Market tests
    c. Surveys

ANSWERS TO DISCUSSION AND REVIEW QUESTIONS

1. **What is a market? What are the requirements for a market?**

A market is an aggregate of people who, as individuals and/or organizations, have needs for products in a product class and have the ability, willingness, and authority to purchase such products. For an aggregate of people to be a market, they must need the product, have the ability to purchase it, be willing to purchase it, and have the authority to purchase it.

2. **In your local area, identify a group of people with unsatisfied product needs who represent a market. Could this market be reached by a business organization? Why or why not?**

In answering this question, students should demonstrate that their suggested markets meet the requirements of a market as discussed in Question 1.

3. **Outline the five major steps in the target market selection process.**

Although marketers may use various methods for selecting a target market, they commonly use a five-step process. Step 1 is to identify the appropriate targeting strategy. The three basic strategies are undifferentiated strategy, concentrated strategy, and differentiated strategy. After determining which targeting strategy to use, marketers move to Step 2, determining which segmentation variables to use. There are specific variables for both consumer and business markets. Step 3 is to develop market segment profiles so that marketers better understand how their business can use its capabilities to serve potential customer groups. In Step 4, marketers evaluate relevant market segments, analyzing sales estimates, competition, and estimated costs for each segment. The fifth and final step is to select specific target markets. Marketers must decide whether there are enough differences in customers' needs to recommend segmentation and, if so, in which of these segments to participate.

4. **What is an undifferentiated strategy? Under what conditions is it most useful? Describe a present market situation in which a company is using an undifferentiated strategy. Is the business successful? Why or why not?**

When an organization designs a single marketing mix and directs it at the entire market for a particular product, it is employing an undifferentiated targeting strategy. This strategy is effective under two conditions. First, the market must be homogeneous. A large proportion of customers in a total market must have similar needs for the product. If customers have a variety of needs, the company will not be able to satisfy them with one product. Second, the company must be able to develop and maintain a single marketing mix that satisfies customers' needs. It must identify common needs among most customers in the total market and possess the means to reach a sizable portion of that market.

5. **What is market segmentation? Describe the basic conditions required for effective segmentation. Identify several firms that use market segmentation.**

In market segmentation, a) the total market is divided into groups consisting of people with relatively similar product needs and b) a marketing mix (or mixes) is (are) designed to fit precisely the needs of the people in a segment (or segments).

For this process to be effective, consumers' needs must be heterogeneous; the segments must be identifiable and divisible; the segments must be comparable in terms of sales potential, costs, and profit; and one segment must have enough profit potential to justify the development and maintenance of a marketing mix for that segment. In addition, the firm must be able to reach the chosen segment with a particular marketing mix.

6. **List the differences between concentrated and differentiated strategies, and describe the advantages and disadvantages of each.**

    The main difference between the concentrated strategy and the differentiated strategy of market segmentation is that the concentrated strategy directs marketing efforts toward a single market segment using one marketing mix, whereas the differentiated strategy directs marketing efforts at two or more market segments using a different marketing mix for each segment.

    The concentrated strategy enables a firm to specialize in one market segment and penetrate it effectively, thereby creating larger sales volume. Also, it allows a firm with limited resources to compete with larger firms. The concentrated strategy can be risky, however, because the firm relies solely on one segment; if the strategy fails, the firm has nothing to offset the decline. Also, if the firm becomes well entrenched in one segment, it may have difficulty expanding into other segments because of its image.

    The differentiated strategy enables a firm to increase total sales by focusing on more than one segment. This is especially useful if a firm has excess production capacity, because it allows the firm to use this capacity. However, the cost of production usually increases with increased production runs; the firm typically must increase its marketing activities to implement several distinct distribution and promotion plans for different segments.

7. **Identify and describe four major categories of variables that can be used to segment consumer markets. Give examples of product markets that are segmented by variables in each category.**

    The four major categories of market segmentation variables are demographic, geographic, psychographic, and behavioristic.

    Demographic variables include such items as gender, age, income, marital status, and the like. These types of variables are used frequently because they are measurable and closely related to customers' product needs.

    Geographic variables include climate, terrain, natural resources, population density, and subcultural values.

    Psychographic variables include personality, motives, and lifestyles. Psychographic variables can be used alone to segment markets or be combined with other segmentation variables. However, psychographic variables are difficult to measure accurately.

    Behavioristic variables are customer characteristics directly related to consumers' relationships to the product, such as product usage rate.

    When discussing examples, students should be encouraged to use local and regional as well as national examples.

8. **What dimensions are used to segment business markets?**

    Business markets are segmented according to geography, type of organization, customer size, and product use.

9. **Define geodemographic segmentation. Identify several types of firms that might employ this type of market segmentation, and explain why.**

    A type of demographic segmentation, geodemographic segmentation groups people in ZIP codes or smaller neighborhood units based on income, education, occupation, type of housing, ethnicity, family life cycle, and level of urbanization. In this way, marketers are able to isolate precise demographic units where demand for a specific product is concentrated and design special advertising campaigns, promotions, pricing, and other features of micromarketing.

    Students' answers to this part of the question will vary. Example: Financial and health care service providers might want to use geodemographic segmentation. A neighborhood composed mostly of senior citizens on fixed incomes, for example, would require particular health care services. Another composed of upper-income professionals might be an appropriate target for certain financial services.

10. **What is a market segment profile? Why is it an important step in the target market selection process?**

    A market segment profile describes similarities among potential customers within a segment and explains the differences among people and organizations in different market segments. Profiles are composed of a variety of elements such as geographic or demographic factors, lifestyles, product benefits sought, brand preferences, and usage rates. Developing profiles is necessary in order to more accurately assess the degree to which the organization's products fit potential product needs and to better understand how its capabilities will serve potential customer segments.

11. **Describe the important factors that marketers should analyze to evaluate market segments.**

    After identifying several appropriate potential market segments, marketers evaluate them further to eliminate some from continued attention. Three factors that marketers analyze for each segment are sales estimates, competition, and estimated costs. Potential sales can be estimated with respect to product level, geographic area, time, and level of competition. Market potential, expressed as dollars or units, is the total amount of a product that customers will purchase within a specified period from all firms in an industry. Company sales potential is the maximum percentage of market potential that an individual company within an industry can expect to gain for a specific product. In addition to obtaining sales estimates, firms must consider their competitors. Unless firms evaluate other organizations that operate in segments under consideration, sales estimates can be deceptive. For example, if a number of competitors already operate within a potential segment, marketers may decide that despite excellent sales estimates, that segment doesn't provide adequate marketing opportunities. Finally, marketers must estimate the costs of developing unique product features, attractive package design, generous product warranties, extensive advertising, and other marketing mix requirements. The costs of reaching particular segments may simply be too high.

12. **Why is a marketer concerned about sales potential when trying to select a target market?**

    Sales potential is important to a marketer because the firm incurs a certain cost in developing and maintaining a marketing mix. To achieve long-term survival, the firm must be able to recover these costs and make at least a reasonable profit. By estimating the sales potential of possible target markets, a marketer is in a better position to achieve long-term survival. Estimates of sales potential are necessary to determine which market segments are substantial enough to justify the development of marketing mixes.

13. **Why is selecting appropriate target markets important to an organization that wants to adopt the marketing concept philosophy?**

    According to the marketing concept philosophy, an organization should attempt to provide products that satisfy customers' needs through a coordinated set of activities that also allows the organization to achieve its goals. Customer satisfaction is the major aim of the marketing concept. To successfully adopt the marketing concept, therefore, identifying the right target market is critical. For example, if an organization chooses a market that doesn't need or want a product or can't afford it, customers will not be satisfied and sales will be poor. However, companies that analyze target markets carefully and choose appropriately have more likelihood of serving customers' needs and achieving their own objectives.

14. **What is a sales forecast? Why is it important?**

    The sales forecast is the amount of a product that a company expects to sell over a period at a specified level of marketing activity. The development of a sales forecast is important because many operating units within the company use the forecast in planning, organizing, implementing, and controlling their activities, and their success depends on its accuracy.

15. **What are the two primary types of surveys a company might use to forecast sales? Why would a company use an outside expert forecasting survey?**

    The two primary types of surveys a company might use to forecast sales are the customer forecasting survey and the sales force forecasting survey. In the first type, marketers ask customers what types and quantities of products they plan to purchase during a specific period. In the second type, the sales force estimates anticipated sales in their territories for a specified period of time.

    Sometimes companies decide to use an outside expert forecasting survey instead of conducting their own. Economists, management consultants, college professors, and other experts have knowledge about specific markets, and because they, as outsiders, can remain more objective. In addition, outside expert surveys avoid some of the potential drawbacks of sales force surveys such as biases based on recent sales experience, intentional underestimation of sales potential because of the belief that sales goals will be determined by the forecast, or dislike of paperwork. Therefore, an outside survey is apt to be more objective than those conducted by inside personnel and possibly more accurate.

16. **Under what conditions are market tests useful for sales forecasting? Discuss the advantages and disadvantages of market tests.**

    Market tests are especially useful for testing new products because no previous sales history is available for those products. In addition, market tests are useful if the test areas represent the entire market because testing the product in a few cities is considerably cheaper than introducing it to the entire market.

    The primary advantages of market tests are that they measure actual purchasing behavior rather than buying intentions and the volume of purchases can be measured against various levels of marketing activities. However, market tests are time-consuming and expensive. Also, consumers' responses may vary after the test, making the test a poor indicator of market response.

17. **Discuss the benefits of using multiple forecasting methods.**

Most firms use multiple sales forecasting methods. While all forecasting methods have value, none are without drawbacks. Executive judgment is not necessarily objective. Customer surveys are time-consuming and expensive. Sales force surveys and market tests each have several drawbacks. Time series analysis is not always dependable. Regression analysis is not useful for predicting new product sales. A benefit of using multiple forecasting methods is that one method can make up for the shortcomings of another. In addition, marketers can use one or more methods to validate the results of another.

Multiple forecasting methods are also useful when a company markets a variety of product lines or when a single product is sold in different segments. Because different forecasting methods are more accurate for different length forecasts, organizations may find it effective to use one forecast method to predict short-range sales and another to predict long-range sales.

COMMENTS ON THE CASES

CASE 8.1 BUYANDHOLD.COM IS BULLISH ON SMALLER INVESTORS

The purpose of this case is to show how a company can effectively target a market segment that mainstream firms in an industry choose not to serve. You may want to start by asking students about recent stock market news and how economic fluctuations typically affect people who invest in stocks. Also, ask why people might want to buy and hold stocks for long periods, regardless of day-to-day changes in stock market conditions. Then contrast this long-term approach to investing with the way day traders quickly buy and sell stock to grab more immediate profits. With this foundation, students will be able to understand who BuyandHold.com is targeting and why.

In the first question, students are asked to identify the type of general targeting strategy that BuyandHold.com is using. This is a concentrated targeting strategy, in which BuyandHold.com created one marketing mix to serve a single market segment.

The second question asks students to identify the segmentation variables that BuyandHold.com is using. One main variable is behavior, primarily how often customers buy or sell stocks. BuyandHold.com is targeting the segment of customers who buy regularly and hold onto stocks for the long term. The company also uses the behavioristic variable of benefit segmentation. Another main variable is the demographic variable of income.

In the third question, students are asked to consider whether BuyandHold.com should change its targeting strategy as more competitors start marketing to the cost-conscious segment. Those who believe the company should change its targeting strategy may point to the need to avoid profit-sapping price wars and higher marketing costs as competition increases. However, a stronger case can be made by those who believe the company should not make changes, because this would undermine its positioning and could drive away current customers. Instead, the company may want to find ways of differentiating itself by adding value at a modest cost, such as offering webcast seminars on investing to educate its customers.

Video Information

Company:	BuyandHold.com
Location:	Tape 1/DVD 1, Segment 8
Length:	4:04

Video Overview: BuyandHold.com caters to a segment of the market that the mainstream brokerage giants generally ignore. This is a low-income segment of consumers who have a long-term goal in mind when they buy stocks and mutual funds and can only accumulate a portfolio by investing bit by bit over an extended period. Customers pay as little as $1.99 per trade to buy or sell securities, and they can open an account with just $20. BuyandHold.com keeps prices down through strict cost control. It executes buy and sell orders just twice a day, and limits its selection of stocks to 5,000 public companies. With ShareBuilder.com and other competitors targeting the same segment, BuyandHold.com must employ savvy marketing to retain its customers and attract new ones in the coming years.

MULTIPLE-CHOICE QUESTIONS ABOUT THE VIDEO

1. Because BuyandHold.com encourages customers to set up an automatic program of investing a small amount on a regular basis, it finds that during market downturns, its customers generally

    a. try to sell as quickly as possible.
    b. continue to buy.
    c. change brokers to lower their costs.
    d. prefer to buy directly from public corporations.
    e. become more like day traders.

2. CEO Peter Breen stresses that helping customers invest a small, set amount every week or month at a low cost offers the benefit of

    a. helping customers achieve short-term profits.
    b. supporting the market during turbulent economic periods.
    c. removing barriers to profiting from Wall Street fluctuations.
    d. enabling customers to reach long-term investment goals.
    e. opening up a new market for mainstream brokerage firms.

3. Larger brokerage firms avoid the segment that BuyandHold.com targets because these firms believe that this segment

    a. lacks the buying power to purchase stocks in larger blocks.
    b. has the authority, but not the willingness to buy stocks.
    c. does not want or need to invest in stocks.
    d. prefers to buy from a smaller brokerage firm.
    e. is unsophisticated and uneducated.

4. While BuyandHold.com's customers pay a lower price for trades, they sacrifice the ability to

    a. indicate specific stocks for purchase or sale.
    b. buy or sell every day.
    c. receive detailed portfolio statements.
    d. learn more about investing.
    e. time their trading based on current market conditions.

ANSWERS TO MULTIPLE-CHOICE QUESTIONS ABOUT THE VIDEO

1. b

2. d

3. a

4. e

CASE 8.2 IKEA TARGETS DO-IT-YOURSELFERS

This case discusses how a retailer uses several segmentation variables to select an appropriate target market. Most students will be familiar with IKEA stores or at least know the IKEA brand.

The first question asks whether IKEA's targeting strategy is concentrated or undifferentiated, and why. The retailer is using a concentrated targeting strategy because it is targeting a single market segment (consumers who want fashionable, affordable, and functional furniture). In contrast, an undifferentiated targeting strategy would mean directing one marketing mix to the entire market rather than a particular segment. IKEA is using concentrated targeting because it allows the company to better understand the needs of a specific customer group and concentrate its marketing efforts on satisfying their needs in a way that is profitable.

The second question asks students to consider which segmentation variables that IKEA is using and why are these appropriate. The company is using geographic variables (such as country and city), psychographic variables (such as interest in stylish furniture), and behavioral variables (such as the benefit of saving money by assembling furniture at home). These are appropriate because they enable IKEA to divide the entire retail market for furniture into distinct segments that can more profitably be targeted.

Question 3 asks about the combination of techniques that IKEA might apply when preparing sales forecasts for North America. Students' answers will vary, but all should recognize the importance of using more than one technique to avoid inaccuracies and biases that may result from using only one technique. A customer forecasting survey will be less cost-effective than time-series analysis methods, regression analysis methods, and market tests. IKEA also can apply executive judgment as a reality check.

CHAPTER 9

Consumer Buying Behavior

TEACHING RESOURCES QUICK REFERENCE GUIDE

Resource	Location
Purpose and Perspective	IRM, p. 153
Guide for Using Color Transparencies	IRM, p. 154
Lecture Outline	IRM, p. 154
Notes for Class Exercises, Debate Issue, and Chapter Quiz	IRM, p. 160
Class Exercise 1	IRM, p. 162
Class Exercise 2	IRM, p. 163
Debate Issue	IRM, p. 164
Chapter Quiz	IRM, p. 165
Answers to Discussion and Review Questions	IRM, p. 166
Comments on the Cases	IRM, p. 169
Case 9.1	IRM, p. 169
Video	Tape 1/DVD 1, Segment 9
Video Information	IRM, p. 169
Multiple-Choice Questions About the Video	IRM, p. 170
Case 9.2	IRM, p. 171
Transparency Acetates	Transparency package
Examination Questions: Essay	TB, p. 241
Examination Questions: Multiple-Choice	TB, p. 241
Examination Questions: True-False	TB, p. 265
Author-Selected Multiple-Choice Test Items	TB, p. 671
HMClassPrep Presentation Resources	CD-ROM
PowerPoint Slides	Instructor's website

Note: Additional resources are updated periodically and may be found on the accompanying student and instructor websites at http://www.prideferrell.com/.

PURPOSE AND PERSPECTIVE

We begin this chapter by defining buying behavior and consumer buying behavior. We examine how the customer's level of involvement affects the type of problem solving employed and discuss the types of consumer problem-solving processes, including routinized response behavior, limited problem solving, extended problem solving, and impulse buying. We then analyze the major stages of the consumer buying decision process: problem recognition, information search, evaluation of alternatives, purchase, and postpurchase evaluation. Next, we discuss in detail the situational, psychological, and social influences on the consumer decision-making process. Situational influences include physical surroundings, social surroundings, time perspective, purchase reason, and the buyer's momentary mood and condition. The primary psychological influences on consumer behavior are perception, motives, learning, attitudes, personality and self-concept, and lifestyles. Forces that other people exert on buying behavior are called social influences. Social influences include the influence of roles, families, reference groups and opinion leaders, social class, and culture and subcultures.

GUIDE FOR USING COLOR TRANSPARENCIES

There are two groups of color transparencies. The transparencies identified by a double number are the same as the figures in the text. The transparencies labeled with a number and a letter are illustrations that do not appear in the text, but they can be used as additional examples of concepts discussed.

Figure 9.1   Consumer Buying Decision Process and Possible Influences on the Process
Figure 9.2   Maslow's Hierarchy of Needs
Figure 9A   Chapter 9 Outline
Figure 9B   Key Definitions: Buying Behavior, Level of Involvement
Figure 9C   Children Decide or Influence the Purchase of Products in Many Product Categories
Figure 9D   Types of Consumer Problem Solving
Figure 9E   Levels of Involvement and Consumer Problem-Solving Types
Figure 9F   Fish or Birds?
Figure 9G   Discussion Issue: How Do Reference Groups Affect Purchase Decisions?
Figure 9H   Subcultural Differences in Movie-Going Behavior
Figure 9I   On What Part of the Consumer Buying Decision Process Does This Olay Ad Focus?
Figure 9J   This Visine Advertisement Is Focused On Problem Recognition
Figure 9K   On Which Stage(s) of the Consumer Buying Decision Process Does this NAPA Ad Focus?

LECTURE OUTLINE

(Transparency Figure 9A: Chapter Outline)

Buying behavior is the decision processes and acts of people involved in buying and using products. *Consumer buying behavior* refers to the buying behavior of ultimate consumers.

(Transparency Figure 9B)

I.   **Level of Involvement and Consumer Problem-Solving Processes**
    A.   *Level of involvement* is an individual's intensity of interest in a product and the importance he or she places on a product.

(Transparency Figure 9B)

        1.   Levels of involvement are classified as low, high, enduring, and situational.
        2.   A consumer's level of involvement is a major determinant of the type of problem-solving process employed.
    B.   *Routinized response behavior* is the type of consumer problem-solving process that requires very little search-and-decision effort; it is used for products that are low priced and bought frequently.

(Transparency Figure 9D)

    C.   *Limited problem solving* is a type of consumer problem-solving process that buyers use when they purchase products occasionally or need information about unfamiliar brands in a familiar product category; it requires a moderate amount of time for information gathering and deliberation.

D.   *Extended problem solving* is the consumer problem-solving process employed when unfamiliar, expensive, or infrequently bought products (such as a car, home, and college education) are purchased; buyers use many criteria to evaluate brands and spend more time searching for information and deciding on the purchase.

(Transparency Figure 9E)

E.   *Impulse buying*, in contrast, is an unplanned buying behavior involving a powerful urge to buy something immediately.

II.   **Consumer Buying Decision Process**

A.   The *consumer buying decision process* is a five-stage purchase decision process that includes problem recognition, information search, evaluation of alternatives, purchase, and postpurchase evaluation.

(Transparency Figure 9.1)

1.   The actual act of purchase is only one stage in the process and is a later stage.
2.   Not all decision processes, once initiated, lead to an ultimate purchase; the individual may terminate the process at any stage.
3.   Not all consumer buying decisions include all five stages.

B.   **Problem Recognition**

1.   This stage occurs when a buyer becomes aware of a difference between a desired state and an actual condition.
2.   The individual may be unaware of the problem or need.
3.   Marketers may use sales personnel, advertising, and packaging to trigger recognition of needs or problems.
4.   Recognition speed can be slow or fast.

(Transparency Figure 9J)

C.   **Information Search**

1.   This stage begins after the consumer becomes aware of the problem or need.
2.   The search for information about products will help resolve the problem or satisfy the need.
3.   There are two aspects to an information search: internal search and external search.
    a)   In the *internal search*, buyers first search their memories for information about products that might solve the problem.
    b)   In the *external search*, buyers seek information from outside sources.
        (1)   An external search occurs if buyers cannot retrieve enough information from their memories for a decision.
        (2)   Buyers seek information from friends, relatives, or public sources such as government reports or publications.
4.   Wearout results when consumers begin to pay less attention to repetitious commercials, for example, that supply external information.

D.   **Evaluation of Alternatives**

1.   When successful, an information search yields a *consideration (evoked) set* of products or a group of brands that the buyer views as possible alternatives.
    a)   In this stage, the consumer establishes a set of *evaluative criteria* against which to compare the characteristics of the products in the evoked set.
    b)   The consumer rates and eventually ranks the brands in the consideration set by using the criteria and their relative importance.
2.   Marketers can influence consumers' evaluation by "framing" the alternatives—that is, by the manner in which they describe the alternatives and attributes.

E. **Purchase**
1. The consumer selects the product or brand to be purchased.
2. Product availability, seller choice, and terms of sale may influence the final product selection.
3. The actual purchase is made unless the process has been terminated earlier.

F. **Postpurchase Evaluation**
1. The buyer begins to evaluate the product after purchase, based on many of the criteria used in the evaluation of alternatives stage.
2. *Cognitive dissonance* is a buyer's doubts shortly after a purchase about whether it was the right decision.

(Transparency Figure 9I)

(Transparency Figure 9K)

(Building Customer Relationships: Observing Customers in Their Native Habitats)

III. **Situational Influences on the Buying Decision Process**
A. *Situational influences* are factors resulting from circumstances, time, and location that affect the consumer buying decision process.
1. Can influence a consumer's actions in any stage of the buying process
2. Can shorten, lengthen, or terminate the buying process
B. Situational factors can be divided into five categories: physical surroundings, social surroundings, time perspective, purchase reason, and the buyer's momentary mood and condition.
1. These include store atmosphere, product scarcity, weather, and momentary moods.
2. Marketers go to considerable trouble and expense to create physical settings conducive to purchasing decisions.

IV. **Psychological Influences on the Buying Decision Process**
Psychological influences are those that operate in part to determine people's general behavior, thus influencing their behavior as consumers.

A. **Perception**

(Transparency Figure 9F)

Perception is the process of selecting, organizing, and interpreting information inputs to produce meaning.

1. An individual selects some pieces of information and ignores others.
   a) *Information inputs* are the sensations received through the sense organs.
   b) *Selective exposure* is the process of selecting inputs to be exposed to our awareness while ignoring others.
      (1) An input is more likely to reach a person's awareness if it relates to an anticipated event.
      (2) A person is likely to let an input reach consciousness if the information helps satisfy current needs.
   c) The selective nature of perception also results in selective distortion and selective retention.
      (1) *Selective distortion* is an individual's changing or twisting of received information when it is inconsistent with personal feelings or beliefs.
      (2) *Selective retention* is remembering information inputs that support personal feelings and beliefs and forget-ting inputs that do not.

2. The second step in the perceptual process is perceptual organization—to organize the information that does reach awareness, integrating the new information with what is already known.

3. Third, an individual's interpretation of information inputs, necessary to reduce mental confusion, is the assignment of meaning to what has been organized; interpretation is usually based on what is expected or familiar.

4. Marketers try to influence consumers' perceptions but some-times fail.

   a) A consumer's perceptual process may operate such that a seller's information never reaches the consumer's awareness.

   b) A buyer may receive a seller's information and perceive it differently from the way the marketer intended.

   c) When buyers perceive information inputs that are inconsistent with prior beliefs, they are likely to forget the information quickly.

B. **Motives**

A *motive* is an internal energizing force that directs a person's behavior toward satisfying needs or achieving goals.

1. A buyer's actions at any time are affected not by just one motive but by a set of motives, some stronger than others.

2. Motives affect the direction and intensity of behavior.

   a) *Maslow's hierarchy of needs* are the five levels of needs humans try to satisfy, from most to least important.

(Transparency Figure 9.2)

   b) Once needs at one level are met, humans try to fulfill needs at the next level.

   c) The levels of needs are: physiological needs, safety needs, social needs, esteem needs, and self-actualization needs.

3. *Patronage motives* are motives that influence where a person purchases products on a regular basis.

C. **Learning**

Learning refers to changes in an individual's thought processes and behavior caused by information and experience.

1. The learning process is strongly influenced by the consequences of an individual's behavior; behaviors with satisfying results tend to be repeated.

2. Inexperienced buyers use different types of information than do experienced shoppers familiar with the product and purchase situation.

3. Consumers learn about products directly by experiencing them or indirectly through information from salespeople, friends, relatives, and advertisements.

D. **Attitudes**

An *attitude* is an individual's enduring evaluation of, feelings about, and behavioral tendencies toward an object or idea.

1. Attitudes are learned through experience and interaction with other people.

2. Attitudes remain generally stable, but they can be changed.

3. An attitude consists of three major components: cognitive, affective, and behavioral.

4. Consumers' attitudes toward a firm and its products strongly influence the success or failure of the organization's marketing strategy.

5. Marketers use several approaches to measure consumer attitudes toward dimensions such as prices, package designs, brand names, advertisements, salespeople, repair services, store locations, features of existing or proposed products, and social responsibility activities.

         a)   Direct questioning of consumers

         b)   Projective techniques

         c)   *Attitude scales* are means of measuring consumers' attitudes by gauging the intensity of individuals' reactions to adjectives, phrases, or sentences about an object.

    6.   Changing people's negative attitudes is a long, expensive, and difficult task and may require extensive promotional efforts.

E.   **Personality and Self-Concept**

    1.   *Personality* is a set of internal traits and distinct behavioral tendencies that result in consistent patterns of behavior.

         a)   The uniqueness of one's personality arises from hereditary background and personal experiences.

         b)   When advertisements focus on certain types of personalities, the advertiser uses personality characteristics that are valued positively.

    2.   *Self-concept* is a perception or view of oneself.

         a)   Buyers purchase products that reflect and enhance their self-concept.

         b)   A person's self-concept may influence whether he or she buys a product in a specific product category and may have an impact on brand selection.

F.   **Lifestyles**

Lifestyle is an individual's pattern of living expressed through activities, interests, and opinions.

    1.   Patterns include the way people spend time, extent of interaction with others, and general outlook on life and living.

    2.   People partially determine their lifestyle, but lifestyles are influenced by other factors.

    3.   Lifestyles influence product needs.

V.   **Social Influences on the Buying Decision Process**

Social influences are the forces that other people exert on one's buying behavior.

A.   **Roles**

    1.   A *role* is a set of actions and activities that an individual in a particular position is supposed to perform based on the expectations of both the individual and surrounding persons.

    2.   Each individual has many roles.

B.   **Family Influences**

    1.   An individual's roles, particularly family roles, to some extent influence that person's behavior as a buyer.

(Transparency Figure 9C)

    2.   *Consumer socialization* is the process through which a person acquires the knowledge and skills to function as a consumer.

C.   **Reference Groups and Opinion Leaders**

(Transparency Figure 9G)

    1.   A *reference group* is any group—large or small—that positively or negatively affects a person's values, attitudes, or behaviors.

    2.   Families, friends, church groups, and professional groups are examples of reference groups.

    3.   There are three major types of reference groups: membership, aspirational, and disassociative.

    4.   A reference group is an individual's point of comparison and a source of information.

5. How much a reference group influences a purchasing decision depends on the individual's susceptibility to reference group influence and strength of involvement with the group.
6. Reference group influence may affect the product decision, the brand decision, or both.
7. A marketer sometimes uses reference group influence in advertisements to promote the message that people in a specific group buy the product and are highly satisfied with it.
8. In most reference groups, one or more members stand out as opinion leaders; an *opinion leader* is a reference group member who provides information about a specific sphere that interests reference group participants.

D. **Social Classes**
A *social class* is an open group of individuals with similar social rank.

1. The criteria used to group people into classes vary from one society to another.
2. In our society we group according to many factors, including occupation, education, income, wealth, race, ethnic group, and possessions; analyses of social class in the United States divide people into three to seven categories.
3. To some degree, individuals within social classes develop common patterns of behavior.
4. Because social class influences so many aspects of a person's life, it also affects
   a) Buying decisions
   b) Spending, saving, and credit practices
   c) Type, quality, and quantity of products
   d) Shopping patterns and stores patronized

E. **Culture and Subcultures**
1. *Culture* is the accumulation of values, knowledge, beliefs, customs, objects, and concepts that a society uses to cope with its environments; culture includes
   a) Tangible items such as food, clothing, furniture, buildings, and tools
   b) Intangible concepts such as education, welfare, and laws
   c) The values and a broad range of behaviors accepted by a specific society
2. The concepts, values, and behavior that make up a culture are learned and passed from one generation to the next.
3. Because cultural influences affect the ways people buy and use products, culture affects the development, promotion, distribution, and pricing of products.
4. International marketers must take into account tremendous global cultural differences.
   a) People in other regions of the world have different attitudes, values, and needs.
   b) International marketers must adapt to different methods of doing business and must develop different types of marketing mixes.
5. *Subcultures* are groups of individuals whose characteristic values and behavior patterns are similar and differ from those of the surrounding culture.
   a) Subcultural boundaries are usually based on geographic designations and demographic factors.

(Transparency Figure 9H)

   b) Marketers recognize that the growth in the number of U.S. subcultures has resulted in considerable variation in consumer buying behavior.

(Building Customer Relationships: One Nation, Many Subcultures)

   (1) **African American Subculture**
      (a) Largest racial or ethnic subculture
      (b) Shop more often, use less coupons, prefer ads specifically targeting African Americans

(c)   Research shows a positive response to ads that reflect heritage

(2)   **Hispanic Subculture**

(a)   Within the next ten years, will become the largest ethnic group

(b)   Strong family values, need for respect affects buying trends

(c)   Concern for product quality and strong brand loyalty

(3)   **Asian American Subculture**

(a)   Fastest growing, most affluent, and perhaps most diverse American subculture

(b)   Individual language, religion, and value system of each group influences purchasing decisions

(c)   Some cross-culture traits include an emphasis on hard work, strong family ties, and high value placed on education

NOTES FOR CLASS EXERCISES, DEBATE ISSUE, AND CHAPTER QUIZ

On the following pages, you will find two class exercises, a debate issue, and a chapter quiz. These are formatted in large-size type so that you can use them as class handouts or for making transparencies. Below are the authors' comments on the class exercises, the debate topic for this chapter, and the answers to the chapter quiz.

Comments on Class Exercise 1

The objective of this class exercise is to help students understand how social influences affect their consumption behaviors.

Question 1. As fraternity or sorority members, students may be influenced to stay out late for social reasons, which may conflict with their roles as students, employees, and church members. The demands of a person's many roles may be inconsistent and confusing. Some married students may describe joint decision-making situations and the influence of children. Other likely responses will relate to clothing, restaurant choice, and food or beverage consumption.

Question 2. You may also want to ask "When ordering at a restaurant, do you find that people often order the same thing?" After one person (opinion leader) has decided to order something, others may order the same thing ("I'll take what he/she ordered"). Reference groups clearly affect the choice of clothing and patronage at retail outlets. Some students may indicate that there are places they will not go because of the presence of negative reference groups.

Question 3. The cars that students drive may reflect either their present social status or their desired social status. Social class may also affect what beer, wine, or other beverages students drink. You may also want to ask "How does social class affect where you shop?"

Question 4. Ask students the following: "Have any of you been in other cultures where you saw people doing things that would never be accepted in America?" If you have international students in class, ask them what they find peculiar about the American culture. Discussion may be geared toward views of time and women.

Question 5. Students may be able to identify certain types of food (catfish in the South), clothing (surf wear in the West), vehicles (pickups in the Midwest and Southwest), or accessories (handguns in the East) that are associated with subcultures.

Question 6. Some possible examples include the following:

- *Promotion*: Show upper-class individuals in luxury car ads.

- *Product*: Design products (cars) that meet joint needs of family.

- *Price*: Offer price discounts to students with limited income.

- *Distribution*: Allocate more pickups to Midwest and Southwest.

Comments on Class Exercise 2

For this exercise, each of the stages of the consumer buying decision process should be thoroughly discussed and made available to the students before they answer these questions. There are many possible answers for each question. For example, in Question 1, the recent college graduate reading *Consumer Reports* to compare automobile ratings could be in any of four stages:

- *Problem Recognition*: The consumer suddenly sees his or her present car as inferior compared to the ratings of other cars in the magazine.

- *Information Search*: The consumer has decided to buy a new car and is seeking all possible information to make an intelligent choice.

- *Evaluation of Alternatives*: The consumer has narrowed choices to a few car brands and is comparing them by using the ratings in the magazine.

- *Postpurchase Evaluation*: The consumer has just purchased a new car and is com-paring its ratings to those of some other cars.

Some possible answers to the remaining questions include the following:

1. Problem recognition

2. Postpurchase evaluation

3. Purchase

4. Evaluation of alternatives

5. Problem recognition

6. Problem recognition/postpurchase evaluation

7. It depends. If using the sample leads the person to question the quality of his or her current brand of laundry detergent, then the person is most likely in the problem recognition stage. If the person is looking for another brand, it could be information search. Finally, if a person is trying to decide on a new brand of detergent, the stage is most likely evaluation of alternatives.

DEBATE ISSUE

Is it appropriate for marketers to specifically target children in their advertisements?

CHAPTER QUIZ

Answers to Chapter Quiz 1. d; 2. b; 3. b; 4. c.

Class Exercise 1

IMAGINE THAT YOU ARE GOING OUT TONIGHT. WHICH OF THE FOLLOWING SOCIAL INFLUENCES WILL DETERMINE WHAT YOU WEAR, WHERE YOU GO, WHAT YOU DO, AND WHAT YOU WILL BUY OR CONSUME?

1. **Your role as a student, family member, employee, church member, or fraternity or sorority member.**

2. **Identification with a positive reference group. Disassociation from a negative reference group.**

3. **Membership within a particular social class. Aspirations to be in a different social class.**

4. **Cultural values that accept or reject certain types of behavior. Gender roles: expectations of how men and women should act.**

5. **Membership in a subculture based on geography, age, or ethnic background.**

6. **Knowing how these factors affect your consumption behavior, how can marketers adjust their marketing mixes to meet your needs?**

Class Exercise 2

IN WHICH STAGE OF THE CONSUMER BUYING DECISION PROCESS ARE EACH OF THE FOLLOWING PEOPLE?

1. A recent college graduate reads *Consumer Reports* to compare automobile ratings.

2. On the first day of class, a student finds out that a programmable calculator is needed for the course, but she doesn't own one.

3. After purchasing an evening gown, a woman decides that it is not quite appropriate for her special occasion.

4. A car buyer gets a loan to purchase a new car.

5. A teenager compares numerous compact disc players and narrows the choice down to two players.

6. While on the way to work, a person's automobile stalls and will not start again.

7. At an open-house party, a guest realizes that the host already owns the gift he plans to give.

8. A person receives a sample package of laundry detergent in the mail and uses it to wash a load of clothes.

Debate Issue

IS IT APPROPRIATE FOR MARKETERS TO SPECIFICALLY TARGET CHILDREN IN THEIR ADVERTISEMENTS?

YES

- Children possess billions of dollars in discretionary income and they spend almost all of it.

- Children buy regularly, are responsive to peer pressure, and are heavily influenced by the hours of television advertising they watch each week.

- Researchers estimate that children directly influence billions of dollars in adult purchases each year.

- An astute marketer recognizes the importance of children and acts accordingly by targeting them in their advertisements.

NO

- Recent research has suggested that advertising can have detrimental effects on children.

- By portraying an altered sense of reality, advertising can make children more prone to need gratification.

- Advertising makes children more susceptible to the effects of peer pressure.

- Although children do influence adult purchases, purchase decisions are made by adults.

- Marketers should target advertising toward parents, not young, impressionable children.

Chapter Quiz

1. Which of the following products would probably require extended problem solving before a purchase?

   a. Products purchased frequently
   b. Products to be purchased in the future
   c. Products that are purchased routinely
   d. Expensive products
   e. Products purchased as a result of social influences

2. When in their information search, consumers focus on communication with friends and relatives, they are utilizing _____ sources.

   a. internal
   b. personal
   c. marketer-dominated
   d. direct
   e. organizational

3. Selective exposure refers to

   a. targeting only certain parts of the total market.
   b. admitting only certain inputs into consciousness.
   c. the circumstances or conditions that exist when a consumer is making a purchase decision.
   d. the process of selecting, organizing, and interpreting information inputs to produce meaning.
   e. remembering inputs that support personal feelings and beliefs and forgetting those that do not.

4. Which of the following is the fastest growing, most affluent subculture in the United States?

   a. African Americans
   b. Hispanics
   c. Asian Americans
   d. Native Americans
   e. Italian Americans

ANSWERS TO DISCUSSION AND REVIEW QUESTIONS

1. **How does a consumer's level of involvement affect his or her choice of problem-solving process?**

   The level of involvement determines the importance and intensity of interest in a product in a particular situation. A buyer's level of involvement determines why he or she is motivated to seek information about certain products and brands but virtually ignores others. The extensiveness of the buying decision process varies greatly with the consumer's level of involvement. Routinized response behavior is likely to be used for low involvement products. High involvement products frequently require limited or extended decision making.

2. **Name the types of consumer problem-solving processes. List some products you have bought using each type. Have you ever bought a product on impulse? If so, describe the circumstances.**

   The types of consumer problem-solving processes include routinized response behavior, limited problem solving, and extended problem solving.

   Routinized response behavior occurs when people buy frequently purchased, low-cost items that need very little search-and-decision effort. Examples of routinely purchased products include milk, bread, packaged food products, and laundry services.

   Limited problem solving occurs when consumers buy products only occasionally and when they need to obtain information about an unfamiliar brand in a familiar product category. This type of decision making requires a moderate amount of time for information gathering and deliberation. Purchase decisions might include a new pest control company, a mechanic to install a muffler, or a new "healthy" cereal.

   Extended problem solving comes into play when a purchase involves unfamiliar, expensive, or infrequently bought products, such as cars, homes, or stereo systems.

   Most students probably will indicate that they have bought a product on impulse. Typical impulse products include candy, a compact disc, or a pair of jeans.

3. **What are the major stages in the consumer buying decision process? Are all these stages used in all consumer purchase decisions? Why or why not?**

   The major stages in the consumer buying decision process are problem recognition, information search, evaluation of alternatives, purchase, and postpurchase evaluation.

   Not all consumer decisions include all five stages. The individual may terminate the process at any stage, and not all decisions lead to a purchase. Sometimes individuals engaged in routine behavior eliminate some stages, while those engaged in extended problem solving usually go through all five stages.

4. **What are the categories of situational factors that influence consumer buying behavior? Explain how each of these factors influences buyers' decisions.**

Situational factors can be classified into categories: physical surroundings, social surroundings, time perspective, purchase reason, and the buyer's momentary mood and condition. Physical surroundings, such as location, store atmosphere, aromas, sounds, and lighting can influence buying behavior by creating a setting that is more or less conducive to making purchases. Social surroundings influence buying behavior when a customer feels pressured to behave in a particular way depending on who is in the location where the decision is being made. The amount of time required to become knowledgeable about a product, to search for it, and to buy it all influence the buying decision process. The time of day, week, or year, such as seasons or holidays, also affect the buying decision process. The purchase reason raises the questions of what exactly the product purchase should accomplish and for whom. The buyer's momentary moods can affect a person's ability and desire to search for information, to receive information, or to seek and evaluate alternatives.

5. **What is selective exposure? Why do people engage in it?**

Selective exposure relates to receiving information and then screening it internally with only partial awareness of all of the cues received. We select some inputs and ignore many others because we cannot be conscious of all inputs at one time. An input is more likely to reach awareness if it relates to an antecedent event or to an unmet need. Thus you are more likely to notice a TV advertisement for McDonald's when you are hungry and wondering where to go for lunch.

6. **How do marketers attempt to shape consumers' learning?**

Marketers attempt to influence consumers' learning by getting them to experience products, such as through the use of free samples. Indirect experiences of products through product information from salespeople and advertisements are other avenues by which marketers attempt to influence purchases through the learning process.

7. **Why are marketers concerned about consumer attitudes?**

Consumer attitudes toward a firm and its products strongly influence the success or failure of the organization's marketing program. Negative attitudes among consumers may result in loss of sales, whereas strong positive attitudes may increase sales. Because attitudes play such an important role in determining consumer behavior, marketers seek to measure consumer attitudes toward prices, packaging, branding, advertising, salespeople, services, images, and features of new products. If a significant number of consumers hold negative attitudes toward a firm or its products, the marketing program should be changed to make attitudes more favorable.

8. **In what ways do lifestyles affect the consumer buying decision process?**

A lifestyle is an individual's pattern of living expressed through activities, interests, and opinions. Lifestyles have a strong impact on many aspects of the consumer buying process from problem recognition to postpurchase evaluation. Lifestyles influence product needs, brand preferences, types of media used, and how and where people shop.

9.   **How do roles affect a person's buying behavior? Provide examples.**

A role consists of a set of actions and activities expected of a person holding a certain position within a group, organization, or institution. All individuals assume several roles depending on the number of positions they occupy. These roles might affect whether, what, where, when, or why a person buys. The roles of other persons also influence purchasing behavior. Marketers want to know not only who does the actual buying but also who influences the purchase decisions. Consider the types of clothes you buy and wear depending on whether you are going to work, going to class, going to church, or going to a gym. You and the people in these places know what types of clothing are appropriate for each place.

10.   **What are family influences, and how do they affect buying behavior?**

Family influences have a very direct impact on the consumer buying decision process. Parents teach children how to cope with a variety of problems, including purchasing decisions. Children often gain consumer socialization, the process through which a person acquires the knowledge and skills needed to function as a consumer, from their parents. Through observation of family buying practices and choice of brand names, children are influenced to use some of these techniques or products when they establish their own families. The extent to which family members participate in the buying process also affects who will be allowed input later in a person's life when consumer buying decisions must be made.

11.   **What are reference groups? How do they influence buying behavior? Name some of your own reference groups.**

A reference group is a group an individual identifies so strongly with that he or she takes on many of the values, attitudes, or behaviors of group members. The group can be large or small, and usually an individual will have several reference groups. The effect of reference groups on purchasing behavior depends on the type of product, the person's susceptibility to the group's influence, and the strength of the person's involvement with the group.

12.   **How does an opinion leader influence the buying decision process of reference group members?**

An opinion leader is viewed as being well informed about a sphere of interest and is willing and able to share information with followers. An opinion leader is viewed as having values and attitudes that are similar to followers and thus can be trusted by the followers.

13.   **In what ways does social class affect a person's purchase decisions?**

Individuals within social classes often exhibit common consumer behavior patterns; they share similar attitudes, values, and possessions. Social class influences a person's attitudes, perceptions, motives, personality, and learning process, all of which affect purchasing decisions. Marketers thus need to be aware of the impact of social class on consumer behavior.

14.   **What is culture? How does it affect a person's buying behavior?**

Culture is everything in our surroundings that is made by human beings, including tangible and intangible items. Culture influences what we wear and eat, where we live, and how we live. It affects the ways we buy and use products and influences the satisfaction we receive from products. Because culture determines the ways products are purchased and used, it affects the entire marketing mix.

15. **Describe the subcultures to which you belong. Identify buying behavior that is unique to one of your subcultures.**

This question lets students probe the unique subculture to which they belong. Students should be encouraged to relate the particular features of their subculture to their purchasing behavior.

COMMENTS ON THE CASES

[o|o] *CASE 9.1 BUILDING CUSTOMER EXPERIENCES AT BUILD-A-BEAR*

This case shows students how the founder of a fast-growing retail chain uses her knowledge of consumer behavior to stimulate in-store purchasing. Students who live near a Build-A-Bear store may be familiar with the premise. You may wish to ask students who have never seen this store to collect background information on the company before discussing the case.

The first question asks which situational influences students expect to be most important for consumers in a Build-A-Bear Workshop. Physical surroundings are critical, because these encourage customers to participate in creating and buying a stuffed animal. Social surroundings are also important, because the attitude and behavior of salespeople and other customers can influence the in-store purchasing decision. Momentary moods may play a key but less important role, because they affect the buyer's reaction to creating and buying the product.

The second question asks about the role that learning plays in shaping the behavior of Build-A-Bear's customers. Once customers have moved through the entire process of creating a stuffed animal in the store, they are more likely to return to make and buy more for themselves or for others if they found the experience satisfying. Knowing this, the CEO mandates three weeks of training for all salespeople so they can become skilled in the production process and in making the experience fun and fulfilling for customers.

The third question asks how Build-A-Bear influences the level of involvement that customers attach to stuffed animals, and asks students to consider whether the level of involvement differs for children and for parents. Build-A-Bear makes stuffed animals into high-involvement products by allowing customers to participate in the memorable experience of creating and personalizing their chosen products. For example, customers can select from different types of fur, stuffing, clothing, and so on, and work with store personnel to actually produce the finished product. Customers are even encouraged to register a name for each stuffed animal, adding to the personality that customers perceive in their products. The level of involvement may differ between children and parents, depending on who is participating in creating the bears and for what occasions.

Video Information

Company:	Build-A-Bear
Location:	Tape 1/DVD 1, Segment 9
Length:	3:19

Video Overview: Maxine Clark drew on her insights into consumer behavior—honed through 25 years of retail management experience and by analyzing her own reactions as a shopper—when she opened the first Build-A-Bear Workshop. Clark believes that consumers want an interactive, memorable experience when they make a purchase. Her Build-A-Bear Workshops are designed to engage customers by inviting them to directly participate in the playful experience of crafting one-of-a-kind stuffed animals. Although the stores employ high-tech touches such as a computerized registry of stuffed animals and their owners, which is used to collect information for the company's database, the emphasis is on making the entire experience fun and unforgettable. Clark says that her customers are not just putting together a teddy bear—they're creating a new friend.

MULTIPLE-CHOICE QUESTIONS ABOUT THE VIDEO

1. The physical surroundings of each Build-A-Bear store are designed to influence the consumer buying process by

    a. boosting the store into the consideration set of shoppers.
    b. reducing cognitive dissonance among parents of younger customers.
    c. allowing customers to have an interactive, memorable experience.
    d. facilitating the internal search for information about similar products.
    e. limiting the shopper's ability to make an impulse purchase.

2. Although teddy bears are typically low-involvement products, Build-A-Bear's products inspire higher involvement because they

    a. are symbols of a new and unique high-end brand.
    b. are closely linked to social influences.
    c. play an important role in consumer socialization among family members.
    d. are created and personalized through memorable buying experiences.
    e. appeal to routinized response behavior.

3. Maxine Clark believes that customers want their shopping experiences to be

    a. quick and convenient.
    b. cost-effective.
    c. differentiated by high-tech touches.
    d. familiar and basic.
    e. interactive and entertaining.

4. To reinforce the notion that each individually-created stuffed animal is special, Build-A-Bear asks all buyers to

    a. earn special discounts by referring other customers to the store.
    b. register their names and the names of their stuffed animals.
    c. buy only one stuffed animal at a time.
    d. hold special events like birthday parties in local stores.
    e. visit other Build-A-Bear stores when they travel.

ANSWERS TO MULTIPLE-CHOICE QUESTIONS ABOUT THE VIDEO

1. c

2. d

3. e

4. b

CASE 9.2 AUTOTRADER.COM FUELS ONLINE BUYING OF USED CARS

The objective of this case is to show students how a dot-com company used its knowledge of consumer buying behavior to build a sizable business selling used cars on the web. Most students are interested in cars and familiar with buying from online retailers or auction sites, so they are likely to find this case engaging.

The first question asks how AutoTrader has helped potential car buyers learn how to buy cars online. The company applied its knowledge of psychological influences on buying to encourage learning through informative television commercials showing step-by-step how to use the AutoTrader web site. It also encouraged positive attitudes and involvement through its online "Slide into Your Ride" promotion and its online newsletter.

The second question asks in which stage of the consumer buying process AutoTrader's television commercials would be most likely to influence potential car buyers to use AutoTrader's web site, and why. Students should realize that car buying generally involves extended problem solving because the product is so costly. They should be able to make a convincing case that the company's commercials are most influential in the information search stage of the buying process (because consumers seeking used cars need to find out what cars are available and what buying options are available). Students may also make a case for the commercials being influential in the purchase stage (because consumers are ready to buy and open to learning where and how to make the purchase).

The third question asks students to consider why it is important for AutoTrader to influence first-time buyers' perceptions of its site through online promotions such as "Slide into Your Ride." AutoTrader wants first-time buyers to remember its website when they are getting ready to buy a used car and to associate the site with convenience and other positive benefits. This promotion was designed to take advantage of selective exposure, reaching first-time buyers during the months when they typically buy cars before going back to college.

CHAPTER 10

Business Markets and Buying Behavior

TEACHING RESOURCES QUICK REFERENCE GUIDE

Resource	Location
Purpose and Perspective	IRM, p. 173
Guide for Using Color Transparencies	IRM, p. 174
Lecture Outline	IRM, p. 175
Notes for Class Exercises, Debate Issue, and Chapter Quiz	IRM, p. 180
Class Exercise 1	IRM, p. 182
Class Exercise 2	IRM, p. 183
Debate Issue	IRM, p. 184
Chapter Quiz	IRM, p. 185
Answers to Discussion and Review Questions	IRM, p. 186
Comments on the Cases	IRM, p. 188
Case 10.1	IRM, p. 188
Video	Tape 1/DVD 1, Segment 10
Video Information	IRM, p. 189
Multiple-Choice Questions About the Video	IRM, p. 189
Case 10.2	IRM, p. 190
Transparency Acetates	Transparency package
Examination Questions: Essay	TB, p. 273
Examination Questions: Multiple-Choice	TB, p. 273
Examination Questions: True-False	TB, p. 294
Author-Selected Multiple-Choice Test Items	TB, p. 671
HMClassPrep Presentation Resources	CD-ROM
PowerPoint Slides	Instructor's website

Note: Additional resources are updated periodically and may be found on the accompanying student and instructor websites at http://www.prideferrell.com/.

PURPOSE AND PERSPECTIVE

In this chapter, we first describe the major types of business markets, including producer, reseller, government, and institutional markets. Next, we look at several dimensions of business buying, such as the characteristics of transactions with business customers, the attributes of business customers and some of their primary concerns in making purchase decisions, business buying methods, and the major types of business purchases. Then we discuss characteristics of demand for business products. We also cover the business (organizational) buying decision process. In this section, we analyze the major participants in business buying decision processes through an examination of the buying center. Then we examine the stages of the business buying decision process and the factors that affect that process. Finally, we discuss industrial classification systems and their usefulness to business marketers in planning marketing strategies.

GUIDE FOR USING COLOR TRANSPARENCIES

There are two groups of color transparencies. The transparencies identified by a double number are the same as the figures in the text. The transparencies labeled with a number and a letter are illustrations that do not appear in the text, but they can be used as additional examples of concepts discussed.

Figure 10.1	Business (Organizational) Buying Decision Process and Factors That May Influence It
Figure 10A	Chapter 10 Outline
Figure 10B	Key Definitions: Business Markets, Business Buying Behavior
Figure 10C	Types of Business Markets
Figure 10D	Business Products Imported and Exported from China
Figure 10E	Types of Business Purchases
Figure 10F	Purchases from Minority-Owned Businesses Are Increasing
Figure 10G	Media Spending by Firms Serving Business Markets
Figure 10H	Is Merrimack College a Part of Institutional Markets or Government Markets? Why?
Figure 10I	At Which Type of Market Is This Advertisement Aimed? Why?

LECTURE OUTLINE

(Transparency Figure 10A: Chapter Outline)

I.   **Business Markets**

(Transparency Figure 10B)

A *business market* consists of individuals or groups that purchase a specific kind of product for resale, direct use in producing other products, or use in general daily operations.

(Transparency Figure 10C)

A.   **Producer Markets**
   1.   *Producer markets* are individuals and organizations that purchase products for the purpose of making a profit by using them to produce other products or by using them in their operations.

(Transparency Figure 10D)

   2.   A wide range of industries make up the producer markets, including agriculture, forestry, fisheries, mining, construction, transportation, communication, and utilities.
B.   **Reseller Markets**
   1.   *Reseller markets* consist of intermediaries who buy finished goods and resell them for profit.
   2.   Resellers do not change the physical characteristics of the product except for occasional minor alterations.
   3.   Wholesalers purchase products for resale to retailers, to other wholesalers, and to producers, governments, and institutions.
   4.   Retailers purchase products for resale to final consumers.
   5.   When making purchase decisions, resellers consider several factors.
      a)   Level of demand to determine quantity and price levels
      b)   Amount of space required for the product
      c)   Suppliers' ability to provide adequate quantities when and where wanted
      d)   Ease of placing orders
      e)   Availability of technical assistance and training programs

f)   Whether the product complements or competes with products the firm currently handles

C.   **Government Markets**

1.   *Government markets* include federal, state, county, and local governments that buy goods and services to support their internal operations and to provide products to their constituencies.

2.   The government spends billions of dollars on a wide range of goods and services.

3.   The types and quantities of products that government markets purchase reflect societal demands on government agencies.

4.   Many firms do not try to sell to the government because of the complex buying procedures necessitated by the government's public accountability.

5.   Government purchases are made through bids or negotiated contracts.

6.   Government markets, although complex, can be very lucrative.

D.   **Institutional Markets**

1.   *Institutional markets* are organizations with charitable, educational, community, or other nonbusiness goals; examples include churches, colleges, hospitals, and civic clubs.

2.   Because institutions have different goals and fewer resources than other markets, marketers may use special marketing activities to serve this segment.

(Transparency Figure 10H)

(Transparency Figure 10I)

II.   **Dimensions of Marketing to Business Customers**

A.   **Characteristics of Transactions with Business Customers**

1.   Transactions between businesses tend to be much larger than consumer transactions.

a)   Suppliers often must sell their products in large quantities to make profits.

b)   Cultivating customers who place orders may be an unprofitable use of resources.

2.   Businesses' sales generally are negotiated less frequently than consumer sales.

a)   Some business purchases involves expensive items, such as computers.

b)   Other products, such as raw materials and component parts, are used continuously in production and may need frequent replenishing.

c)   The contract regarding terms of sale of these items is likely to be a long-term agreement.

3.   Long negotiating periods requiring considerable marketing time and selling effort may be necessary to finalize purchase decisions.

a)   Orders are frequently large and expensive.

b)   Purchased items may be custom built.

c)   Several people or departments within the purchasing organization may be involved in the transaction.

4.   *Reciprocity*, whereby two organizations agree to buy from each other, is used to a limited extent in cases where it is not prohibited by the Federal Trade Commission.

B.   **Attributes of Business Customers**

1.   Business customers differ from consumers in that they are better informed about the products they purchase.

2.   They demand detailed information before buying to be sure products meet the organization's needs.

3.   They seek psychological satisfaction from organizational advancement and financial rewards.

4. Agents who consistently exhibit rational business buying behavior are likely to attain personal goals because they are performing their jobs in ways that help their firms achieve organizational objectives.

C. **Primary Concerns of Business Customers**
1. Price is very important to business customers.
   a) Price influences operating cost and costs of goods sold, which in turn affects the selling price and profit margin, and ultimately the organization's ability to compete.
   b) A buyer of capital equipment views price as the amount of investment necessary to obtain a certain level of return or savings.
2. Level of product quality is also of concern.
   a) A product must meet specifications so that its use will not result in malfunction for the ultimate consumer.
   b) Obtaining a product that meets but does not exceed specifications is important to avoid excess costs.
3. Business buyers value service.
   a) The services that suppliers provide may be the primary element that differentiates one product offering from another.
   b) Often the mix of services is likely to be the major avenue through which a marketer can gain a competitive advantage.
   c) Typical services desired by consumers:
      (1) Market information
      (2) Inventory maintenance
      (3) On-time delivery
      (4) Repair services
   d) Communication channels that allow customers to ask questions, complain, submit orders, and trace shipments are an indispensable service component.

(Ethics and Social Responsibility: Is It Ethnical to Buy Business from Your Customers?)

D. **Methods of Business Buying**
1. Description is commonly used when the products are standardized according to certain characteristics and are normally graded using such standards.
2. Inspection is necessary when items have unique characteristics and vary in condition.
3. Sampling occurs when one item is taken from the lot and assumed to represent the characteristics of the entire lot.
4. Negotiation of contracts may be executed through several means.
   a) Sellers submit bids, and the buyer negotiates terms with those who submit the most attractive bids.
   b) Buyers may be able to provide only a general description of the desired item.
   c) Contracts may specify a base price and provisions for payment of additional costs and fees.

(Tech Know: Online Auctions Click with Businesses)

E. **Types of Business Purchases**

(Transparency Figure 10E)

1. In a *new-task purchase*, the organization makes an initial purchase of an item to be used to perform a new job or solve a new problem.
2. A *straight rebuy purchase* is a routine purchase of the same products under approximately the same terms by a business buyer.

3.   In a *modified rebuy purchase*, a new-task purchase is changed on subsequent orders or when the requirements of a straight-rebuy purchase are modified.

F.   **Demand for Business Products**
Several characteristics distinguish demand for business products from consumer demand. The demand for different types of business products also varies.

(Transparency Figure 10G)

1.   **Derived Demand**
a)   *Derived demand* is the demand for business products derived from the demand for consumer products.
b)   Business customers purchase products to be used directly or indirectly in the production of goods and services to satisfy consumers' needs.
c)   When consumer demand for a product changes, a wave is set in motion that affects demand for all firms involved in the production of that product.

2.   **Inelastic Demand**
a)   *Inelastic demand* is a demand that is not significantly altered by a price increase or decrease.
b)   When a sizable price increase for a component part represents a large proportion of the product's cost, demand may become more elastic; the price increase of the component part causes the price at the consumer level to rise sharply.
c)   The inelasticity characteristic applies to market or industry demand for the business product but not to the demand for an individual supplier.

3.   **Joint Demand**
a)   *Joint demand* involves two or more items used in combination to produce a product.
b)   With joint demand, shortages of one item may jeopardize sales of all the jointly demanded products.

4.   **Fluctuating Demand**
a)   The demand for business products may fluctuate enormously because it is derived from consumer demand.
b)   When a business marketer's customers change their inventory policies, the firm may notice substantial changes in demand.
c)   Significant price increases or decreases can lead to surprising changes in demand in the short run.

III.   **Business Buying Decisions**
Business (organizational) buying behavior refers to the purchase behavior of producers, government units, institutions, and resellers.

(Transparency Figure 10B)

A.   **The Buying Center**
1.   The *buying center* is a group of people within an organization, including users, influencers, buyers, deciders, and gatekeepers, who make business purchase decisions.
a)   Users are organizational participants who actually use the product being acquired.
b)   Influencers often are technical personnel who help develop the specifications and evaluate alternative products for possible use.
c)   Buyers select the suppliers and negotiate the terms of the purchases.
d)   Deciders actually choose the products and vendors.
e)   Gatekeepers control the flow of information to and among people who occupy the other roles in the buying center.

2.   The number and structure of an organization's buying centers are affected by the organization's size, its market position, the volume and types of products purchased, and the firm's managerial philosophy.

B.   **Stages of the Business Buying Decision Process**

(Transparency Figure 10.1)

1.   First stage: One or more individuals in the business recognize that a problem or need exists.

2.   Second stage: The development of product specifications requires that buying center participants assess the problem or need and determine what will be necessary to resolve or satisfy it.

3.   Third stage: This stage involves searching for potential products to solve the problem and locating suppliers of such products.

   a)   Some organizations engage in *value analysis*, an evaluation of each component of a potential purchase: quality, design, materials, and so on.

   b)   Some vendors can be eliminated because they cannot supply needed quantities or because they have poor delivery or service records.

   c)   The products on the list generated in the search stage are evaluated to determine which ones (if any) meet the product specifications; firms evaluate current and potential suppliers as well, using *vendor analysis*.

4.   Fourth stage: Results of deliberations and assessments in the third stage are used during the fourth stage to select the product to be purchased and the supplier from which to buy it. The product is ordered.

   a)   *Multiple sourcing* is the selection and use of several vendors.

   b)   *Sole sourcing* is a situation in which an organization decides to use only one supplier.

5.   Fifth stage: The product's and supplier's performances are evaluated.

C.   **Influences on the Business Buying Decision Process**

1.   Environmental factors are forces such as competitive and economic factors, political forces, legal and regulatory factors, technological changes, and sociocultural issues.

2.   Business factors include the company's objectives, purchasing policies, and resources as well as the size and composition of the buying center.

3.   Interpersonal factors refer to the relationships among the people in the buying center.

4.   Individual factors are the personal characteristics of participants in the buying center, such as age, personality, educational level, and tenure and position in the organization.

IV.   **Using Industrial Classification Systems**

A.   **Identifying Potential Organizational Customers**

1.   Much information about business customers is based on industrial classification systems.

   a)   The *Standard Industrial Classification (SIC) system* is the federal government's system for classifying selected economic characteristics of industrial, commercial, financial, and service organizations.

   b)   The *North American Industry Classification System (NAICS)* is replacing the SIC system. The NAICS is a single industry classification system that all three NAFTA partners (the United States, Canada, and Mexico) will use to generate comparable statistics among all three countries.

      (1)   NAICS is similar to the International Standard Industrial Classification (ISIC) system used in Europe and other parts of the world.

      (2)   NAICS divides industrial activity into 20 sectors and is more comprehensive and more up-to-date.

            (3)   NAICS will also provide more information about the service industry and high-tech products.

        c)   Industrial classification systems are ready-made tools that allow marketers to divide organizations into groups based mainly on the types of goods and services provided.

2.   In conjunction with an industrial classification system, organizational marketers can use *input-output data*, which tell what types of industries purchase the products of a particular industry.

        a)   A major source of input-output data is the *Survey of Current Business*, published by the Office of Business Economics, U.S. Department of Commerce.

        b)   After finding out which industries purchase the major portion of an industry's output, a marketer must determine the industrial classification for those industries.

        c)   Next, the industrial marketer can ascertain the number of firms that are potential buyers.

3.   Locating Organizational Customers

        a)   A firm may identify and locate potential customers by using state or commercial industrial directories, such as *Standard and Poor's Register*.

           (1)   These publications contain information such as name, industrial classification, address, telephone number, and annual sales.

           (2)   Marketers develop lists of potential customers by desired geographic location.

        b)   A firm may also employ the services of a commercial data company, such as Dun & Bradstreet.

           (1)   This type of service is more expedient, but more expensive as well.

           (2)   A commercial data company can provide, for every company on an industrial classification list, its name, location, sales volume, number of employees, types of products handled, names of executive officers, and other pertinent information.

B. **Estimating Purchase Potential**

In addition to deriving a list of potential customers, marketers must determine which ones to pursue, a decision usually based on estimated purchase potential.

(Transparency Figure 10F)

1.   A marketer must first find a relationship between the size of potential customers' purchases and a variable available in industrial classification data, such as number of employees.

2.   Establishing a relationship will probably involve a survey of a random sample of potential customers.

3.   After estimating purchase sizes of potential customer segments, the marketer selects the customers to include in the target market.

4.   There are several limitations to the use of industrial classification data to estimate purchase potential.

        a)   A few industries do not have designations.

        b)   Double counting may occur when products are shipped between two establishments within the same firm.

        c)   Some business data may be understated as a result of Bureau of the Census limitations.

        d)   Lag time between collection of data and availability of information is usually significant.

NOTES FOR CLASS EXERCISES, DEBATE ISSUE, AND CHAPTER QUIZ

On the following pages, you will find two class exercises, a debate issue, and a chapter quiz. These are formatted in large-size type so that you can use them as class handouts or for making transparencies. Below are the authors' comments on the class exercises, the debate topic for this chapter, and the answers to the chapter quiz.

Comments on Class Exercise 1

The objective of this class exercise is to show students that business buying behavior has many similarities to consumer buying behavior.

Question 1. If you ask enough students, you will eventually have all of these criteria listed. Although businesses are more likely to develop formal written specifications about these concerns, final consumers also find these to be important concerns for nearly any high-involvement product category.

Question 2. Examples might include the following:

- Description: mail-order products (clothing, personal computers)

- Inspection: car, furniture, house, or any used item

- Sampling: grocery food items, mail samples, ice cream

- Negotiation: car, house, or any used item

Question 3. The situations roughly match as follows:

- New-task purchase: Extended decision making

- Modified rebuy: Limited decision making

- Straight rebuy: Routine decision making

Question 4. You might want to ask "Who plays what roles in the family when a PlayStation video game machine is purchased?" Children (and perhaps their parents) are the users and influencers. The mother may be the decider and the father the buyer. Older children may be the gatekeepers who control the flow of information to the parents. Grandparents might also be the buyers, while the parents may play the roles of deciders and gatekeepers. The point is that, to be successful, marketers must target the entire buying center (or family). Focusing an entire sales presentation on the user may not be effective if the decider is not persuaded.

Comments on Class Exercise 2

The purpose of this exercise is to allow students to demonstrate their understanding of different purchasing methods. Each product is typically purchased by the following methods:

1.	Grain	**sampling**
2.	Used vehicles	**inspection**
3.	Office space	**inspection, negotiation**
4.	Oranges	**description, sampling**
5.	Bulldozer	**negotiation**
6.	Computer and printer	**inspection**
7.	Office furniture	**inspection**
8.	Pens and pencils	**description**
9.	Eggs	**description**
10.	Assembly line equipment	**inspection, negotiation**

DEBATE ISSUE

Because reciprocity can promote favoritism and sometimes threaten competitive activity, should it be completely banned?

CHAPTER QUIZ

Answers to Chapter Quiz 1. d; 2. c; 3. b; 4. d.

Class Exercise 1

ALTHOUGH BUSINESS BUYING BEHAVIOR MIGHT SEEM QUITE DIFFERENT FROM YOUR BUYING BEHAVIOR, THE TWO ARE MORE SIMILAR THAN YOU MAY THINK. AS YOU ANSWER THE FOLLOWING QUESTIONS, THINK ABOUT HOW SIMILAR OR DISSIMILAR THE BUSINESS BUYING PROCESS IS TO YOUR OWN.

1. When you buy a new shirt, compact disc, stereo, television, or car, which of the following are the most important to you?

   - Quality
   - Product information
   - Product availability
   - On-time delivery
   - Service
   - Repair services
   - Credit
   - Price

2. Give examples of products that you buy (or may buy) based on

   - Description
   - Sampling
   - Inspection
   - Negotiation

3. Match the business purchase situation with the consumer goods buying situation. How or why are they related?

   - New-task purchase
   - Modified rebuy
   - Straight rebuy
   - Limited decision making
   - Routine decision making
   - Extended decision making

4. How is the buying center of a business similar to the following purchasing roles that family members play?

   - Users
   - Buyers
   - Gatekeepers
   - Influencers
   - Deciders

Class Exercise 2

BUSINESS PURCHASES CAN BE MADE BY SEVERAL METHODS, INCLUDING DESCRIPTION, INSPECTION, SAMPLING, AND NEGOTIATION. WHICH METHOD IS MOST OFTEN USED FOR EACH OF THE FOLLOWING PRODUCTS?

1. Grain
2. Used vehicles
3. Office space
4. Oranges
5. Bulldozer
6. Computer and printer
7. Office furniture
8. Pens and pencils
9. Eggs
10. Assembly line equipment

Debate Issue

BECAUSE RECIPROCITY CAN PROMOTE FAVORITISM AND SOMETIMES THREATEN COMPETITIVE ACTIVITY, SHOULD IT BE COMPLETELY BANNED?

YES

- The Federal Trade Commission and the Justice Department monitor reciprocal agreements and stop those that are anti-competitive.

- Reciprocal agreements influence purchasing agents to deal only with certain suppliers.

- Reciprocal agreements can lower the morale of purchasing agents and lead to less than optimal purchases.

NO

- Reciprocal agreements help lower the purchasing costs for both parties.

- Reciprocity occurs most often among small businesses and is thus less likely to threaten competition.

- Reciprocal agreements are a good means of ensuring high-quality service and an adequate supply of needed materials.

- Reciprocity is a means of establishing long-term relationships built on trust and cooperation.

Chapter Quiz

1. Mike, a purchasing agent, recently placed an order with the Kahn Corporation. Mike's company has ordered these same products before under the same terms of sale. What type of purchase does this situation represent?

    a. New-task
    b. Repetitive
    c. Institutional
    d. Straight rebuy
    e. Modified rebuy

2. Best Tires is a manufacturer and marketer of tires for new passenger cars. In recent years, the company's business has declined because of the overall decrease in consumer demand for new cars. In this case, the demand for Best Tires' products is said to be _____ since it depends on the demand for new cars.

    a. inelastic
    b. fluctuating
    c. derived
    d. elastic
    e. nonderived

3. During the search for products and evaluating possible suppliers stage of the business buying decision process, marketers sometimes use _____ analysis to examine the quality, design, materials, and possibly item reduction in order to acquire the product in the most cost effective way.

    a. cost
    b. value
    c. profit
    d. strategic
    e. SWOT

4. Which one of the following countries will not be included in the data presented in the new industrial classification system that is replacing the SIC?

    a. Mexico
    b. Canada
    c. United States
    d. Japan
    e. All but one NAFTA country

ANSWERS TO DISCUSSION AND REVIEW QUESTIONS

1. **Identify, describe, and give examples of the four major types of business markets.**

   The four major types of business markets are producer markets, reseller markets, government markets, and institutional markets.

   The producer market consists of individuals and business organizations that purchase products to make a profit by using them to produce other products or by using them in their operations. Farmers are a producer market because they purchase farm machinery, fertilizer, seed, and livestock to carry out their tasks.

   The reseller market consists of intermediaries, such as wholesalers and retailers, that buy finished goods and resell them to make a profit. Sears is such a reseller.

   Government markets consist of federal, state, county, and local governments that, taken together, spend billions of dollars annually for goods and services to support their internal operations and their constituencies.

   Institutional markets are organizations that seek to achieve goals other than the normal business goals of profit, market share, or return on investment.

2. **Regarding purchasing behavior, why might business customers generally be considered more rational than ultimate consumers?**

   Business customers usually seek and obtain more information about the product before purchasing than do ultimate consumers. They may give special attention to information about the product's functional features, specifications, and technical attributes. Most business customers seek advancement within the organization and greater financial and psychological rewards. By performing the purchasing function in a way that helps their firms achieve organizational objectives, business buyers can further the attainment of their personal goals.

3. **What are the primary concerns of business customers?**

   Many of the primary considerations of business customers when making purchasing decisions fall into the areas of quality level, service, and price. Quality level is maintained by purchasing a product that meets a set of delineated characteristics called specifications. Products that exceed specifications may cost more without providing offsetting benefits.

   Suppliers' service to business customers influences these customers' costs, sales, and profits. Some of the most commonly desired services include market information, maintaining an inventory, on-time delivery, repair services, and replacement parts. Open communication channels are also important.

   Price influences operating costs and costs of goods sold and thus affects the selling prices and profit margins.

4. **List several characteristics that differentiate transactions involving business customers from consumer transactions.**

   Business customer transactions differ from consumer transactions in several ways. Orders tend to be larger, there are longer negotiation periods, reciprocity sometimes plays a role in the process, and business customers tend to be more informed about the products they purchase.

5. **What are the commonly used methods of business buying?**

    Most business customers use one or more of the following methods: description, inspection, sampling, and negotiation. Products that are commonly standardized and normally graded using such standards may be purchased on the basis of a description of their desired characteristics. Certain products, especially those that are large, expensive, and have unique characteristics, will probably have to be inspected by the purchasers before a decision is reached. When buying decisions are based on sampling, the purchaser assumes that the sample product taken from the lot is representative of the entire lot. Negotiated contracts occur when sellers submit bids and the buyer discusses terms with those who submit the most attractive bids.

6. **Why do buyers involved in a straight rebuy purchase require less information than those making a new-task purchase?**

    The straight rebuy purchase is a routine procedure. The specifications and terms have been worked out, and all major problems should have been resolved. Conversely, in a new-task purchase, a business makes an initial purchase of an item that requires the development of product specifications, vendor specifications, and procedures for future purchases.

7. **How does demand for business products differ from consumer demand?**

    Demand for business products differs from consumer demand in that it is

    (a) derived, (b) inelastic, (c) joint, or (d) fluctuating.

8. **What are the major components of a firm's buying center?**

    The major components or roles of a buying center are users, influencers, buyers, deciders, and gatekeepers. One person may perform several of these roles.

9. **Identify the stages of the business buying decision process. How is this decision process used when making straight rebuys?**

    The stages of the business buying decision process are (1) recognizing the problem, (2) establishing product specifications to solve the problem, (3) searching for products and suppliers and evaluating products with respect to specifications, (4) selecting and ordering the most appropriate product, and (5) evaluating product and supplier performance. This decision process is not used for routine, straight rebuy purchases.

10. **How do environmental, business, interpersonal, and individual factors affect business purchases?**

    The level of influence of these factors varies with the buying situation, the type of product being purchased, and whether the purchase is new-task, modified rebuy, or straight rebuy.

11. **What function does an industrial classification system help marketers perform?**

    An industrial classification system is a ready-made tool that allows marketers to divide organizations into groups based mainly on the types of goods and services provided.

12. **List some sources that a business marketer can use to determine the names and addresses of potential customers.**

    One approach to identifying and locating potential customers is to use government directories or commercial organizational directories such as *Standard and Poor's Register* and *Dun & Bradstreet's Market Identifiers* or *Million Dollar Directory*. Lists of potential customers can be developed by desired geographic location.

    Use of the services of a commercial data company, such as Dun & Bradstreet, is more expedient but also more expensive. This service can provide the business marketer with a list of firms and pertinent information about the resources of each firm.

COMMENTS ON THE CASES

▣ *CASE 10.1 VIP DESK BRINGS CONCIERGE SERVICES TO BUSINESS MARKETS*

This case helps students understand the profit potential of satisfying the needs of business customers (and their customers). Because students are unlikely to know much about VIPdesk or concierge services in general, you may want to have them gather background information before discussing the case in class.

The first question asks whether VIPdesk's business customers are members of producer markets, reseller markets, government markets, or institutional markets? Its customers can be categorized as members of producer markets, because they buy goods and services (such as VIPdesk's concierge services) in the process of producing other products or operating their businesses. When a company rewards employees by offering access to VIPdesk's services, it is buying the service as part of its operations—specifically, to motivate higher employee performance. When a bank offers VIPdesk's services to credit card customers, it is buying the service to incorporate into its product (the credit card).

The second question asks about the primary concerns of a credit card company that is considering the use of VIPdesk's services for its cardholders and how VIPdesk is addressing these concerns. Students may identify several primary concerns, including price, quality, and service. VIPdesk is addressing price concerns by charging the businesses a flat annual fee to offer concierge services to their customers. It is addressing quality concerns by hiring experienced concierges to work part-time during peak periods and utilize their knowledge of local resources to satisfy requests from callers in the area. It is addressing service concerns by offering a choice of three levels of service to satisfy the needs of each business's customers.

Question 3 asks how a credit card company might use methods of description, inspection, sampling, and negotiation when making a buying decision about offering VIPdesk's services to customers. The company might ask VIPdesk to describe the characteristics of its three service levels in terms of how the credit card company's customers would reach a concierge and how much personal attention they would receive at each level. This would help the credit card company weigh the benefits its customers receive against the flat fee the company would pay. Also, the company might request the opportunity to inspect VIPdesk's facilities and observe how its concierges work and handle inquiries. With sampling, the company might arrange to have a sample of its managers, employees, or customers receive the VIPdesk's services for a limited period for evaluation purposes. Finally, the company might negotiate the flat-free pricing and level of service that VIPdesk would provide.

Video Information

Company: VIPdesk

Location: Tape 1/DVD 1, Segment 10

Length: 5:24

Video Overview: Mary Naylor, founder of VIPdesk.com, has adapted the hotel concierge concept to the Internet age. When a company wants to provide its employees or customers with easy access to concierge services, it can hire VIPdesk.com for as little as 25 cents per person per year. Contracted by phone or Internet, VIPdesk.com's concierges will arrange for reservations at restaurants, reserve theater tickets, or perform other helpful tasks. Naylor keeps costs low by employing home-based employees to supplement its call-center employees when demand rises.

MULTIPLE-CHOICE QUESTIONS ABOUT THE VIDEO

1. As part of the business market that CEO Mary Naylor is targeting, MasterCard's Alice Droogan thinks that VIPdesk.com's pricing
    a. is appropriate for the company's pricing strategy.
    b. should be more volume-driven to stimulate higher demand.
    c. is reasonable for the service's value as a customer loyalty enhancement.
    d. includes a reasonable markup of the firm's variable and fixed costs.
    e. should be periodically discounted to enable its users to attract new customers.
2. Banks that offer their MasterCard Platinum cardholders access to VIPdesk.com's services are
    a. trying to justify a higher demand-based pricing strategy.
    b. seeking to differentiate their credit cards form competing cards.
    c. applying differential pricing to account for price sensitivity variances.
    d. stimulating comparison discounting to avoid parity positioning.
    e. seeking to pass the breakeven point and achieve profitability.
3. The reason Van Kempen and other companies offer employees free access to VIPdesk.com's concierge service is
    a. they want employees to evaluate the services before customers begin using them.
    b. the services play an important role as price leaders.
    c. to enhance their professional pricing.
    d. to strengthen loyalty among their shareholders.
    e. to reward employees good performance.
4. Mary Taylor helps business customers put the pricing of VIPdesk.com's services into perspective by
    a. emphasizing that the price per person is less than the cost of a key chain.
    b. comparing her services and pricing to the services and prices of competitors.
    c. offering personal testimonials form satisfied users in a range of industries.
    d. showing how volume usage will lead to profitability in a short time.
    e. offering to provide sample services to top management for a limited time.

ANSWERS TO MULTIPLE-CHOICE QUESTIONS ABOUT THE VIDEO

1. a

2. e

3. c

4. a

CASE 10.2 WEBMD DELIVERS ONLINE SERVICES TO HEALTH-CARE PROVIDERS

This case illustrates some of the opportunities and challenges that high-tech companies face in marketing to businesses in the health-care industry. Students are unlikely to know much about the process, problems, and benefits of exchanging medical and financial data in the health-care field. Therefore, you may want to ask the class to conduct background research before you discuss this case.

The first question asks which of the environmental influences that can affect the business buying process are creating opportunities for WebMD. Competitive factors are important: WebMD is becoming stronger by acquiring key competitors, which gives it the resources and capabilities to offer more products. Technological changes are also important: WebMD's sophisticated systems and web sites enable the company to serve both business customers and consumers in a cost-effective manner. In addition, legal and regulatory forces are a key influence, because WebMD can help the medical industry comply with standards for electronic exchange of information. Students may make a convincing case for other environmental influences, as well.

Question 2 asks which of the organizational influences that can affect the business buying process could pose threats for WebMD. One potential threat is that a customer will have the resources to create its own electronic processing systems rather than contracting with WebMD. A second threat related to resources is the unwillingness of health-care providers to commit financial resources to buying WebMD's services unless they can see a long-term benefit such as higher efficiency. Students may be able to identify additional organizational influences that may be threats.

In question 3, students are asked whether a customer that prefers multiple sourcing would welcome WebMD's acquisition of Medifax-EDI if the customer previously contracted for services from both companies. No, the acquisition probably would not be welcomed because it eliminates one of the sources from which this customer likes to buy. The purpose of multiple sourcing is to reduce the possibility of disruptions. Students may also recognize that sole sourcing will make the customer much more dependent on WebMD, even if the acquisition results in the customer paying less for WebMD's services. This is a good opportunity to discuss the advantages and disadvantages of sole sourcing compared with multiple sourcing, from the customer's viewpoint and from WebMD's viewpoint.

CHAPTER 11

Product Concepts

TEACHING RESOURCES QUICK REFERENCE GUIDE

Resource	Location
Purpose and Perspective	IRM, p. 191
Guide for Using Color Transparencies	IRM, p. 192
Lecture Outline	IRM, p. 192
Notes for Class Exercises, Debate Issue, and Chapter Quiz	IRM, p. 197
Class Exercise 1	IRM, p. 199
Class Exercise 2	IRM, p. 200
Debate Issue	IRM, p. 201
Chapter Quiz	IRM, p. 202
Answers to Discussion and Review Questions	IRM, p. 203
Comments on the Cases	IRM, p. 205
Case 11.1	IRM, p. 205
Video	Tape 2/DVD 2, Segment 11
Video Information	IRM, p. 206
Multiple-Choice Questions About the Video	IRM, p. 206
Case 11.2	IRM, p. 207
Transparency Acetates	Transparency package
Examination Questions: Essay	TB, p. 299
Examination Questions: Multiple-Choice	TB, p. 299
Examination Questions: True-False	TB, p. 320
Author-Selected Multiple-Choice Test Items	TB, p. 671
HMClassPrep Presentation Resources	CD-ROM
PowerPoint Slides	Instructor's website

Note: Additional resources are updated periodically and may be found on the accompanying student and instructor websites at http://www.prideferrell.com/.

PURPOSE AND PERSPECTIVE

This chapter covers fundamental concepts relating to (1) definition of a product, (2) consumer and business product classification schemes, (3) product mix and product line concepts, (4) product life cycles, (5) product adoption processes, and (6) the reasons some products fail. It provides definitions and examines the basic relationships necessary for understanding the role of products in the marketing mix. Students often believe that products are related more to production than to marketing. We point out that products can be goods, services, ideas, or all three. Many real-world examples are presented to illustrate product concepts.

GUIDE FOR USING COLOR TRANSPARENCIES

There are two groups of color transparencies. The transparencies identified by a double number are the same as the figures in the text. The transparencies labeled with a number and a letter are illustrations that do not appear in the text, but they can be used as additional examples of concepts discussed.

Part 5 Opener	Product Decisions
Figure 11.1	The Concepts of Product Mix Width and Depth Applied to Selected United States Procter & Gamble Products
Figure 11.2	The Four Stages of the Product Life Cycle
Figure 11.3	Distribution of Product Adopter Categories
Figure 11A	Chapter 11 Outline
Figure 11B	Key Definitions: Good, Service, Idea
Figure 11C	Classification of Products
Figure 11D	Characteristics of Convenience Shoppers Online
Figure 11E	Do All of These Products Have Product Life Cycles?
Figure 11F	Why Wi-Fi?
Figure 11G	Product Adoption Process
Figure 11H	What Type of Product Is Being Provided by Amtrak
Figure 11I	Is Ben & Jerry's Ice Cream a Convenience, Shopping, or Specialty Product? Why?

LECTURE OUTLINE

(Transparency Part 5 Opener)

(Transparency Figure 11A: Chapter Outline)

I. **What Is a Product?**
   A. A product is everything, both tangible and intangible, that a buyer receives in an exchange.
   B. A product can be either tangible or intangible and includes functional, social, and psychological utilities or benefits.
   C. A product can be an idea, a service, a good, or any combination of the three, including supporting services such as installation, guarantees, product information, and promises of repair or maintenance.

(Transparency Figure 11B)

   1. A *good* is a tangible physical entity.
   2. A *service* is an intangible result of the application of human and mechanical efforts to people or objects.
   3. An *idea* is a concept, philosophy, image, or issue.

(Transparency Figure 11H)

   D. When buyers purchase a product, they are really buying the benefits and satisfactions that they think the product will provide.
II. **Classifying Products**
   Products fall into two general categories—*consumer products* and *business products*.

(Transparency Figure 11C)

   A. **Consumer Products**
      Consumer products are products purchased to satisfy personal and family needs; they are categorized according to how buyers generally behave when purchasing a specific item.

1.   **Convenience Products**

(Transparency Figure 11D)

a)   *Convenience products* are relatively inexpensive, frequently purchased items for which buyers exert only minimal purchasing effort.

b)   The buyer spends little time planning the purchase of a convenience item or comparing available brands or sellers.

c)   A convenience product normally is marketed through many retail outlets.

d)   Because sellers experience high inventory turnover, per-unit gross margins can be relatively low.

e)   Producers of convenience products can expect little promotional effort at the retail level.

2.   **Shopping Products**

a)   *Shopping products* are items for which buyers are willing to expend considerable effort in planning and making the purchase.

b)   Buyers allocate considerable time to comparing stores and brands in prices, product features, qualities, services, and perhaps warranties.

c)   Although shopping products are purchased less frequently and are more expensive than convenience products, buyers of shopping products are not extremely loyal to their brands.

d)   Shopping products require fewer retail outlets than convenience products.

e)   Because shopping products are purchased less frequently, causing lower inventory turnover, marketing channel members expect to receive higher gross margins.

f)   Usually, the producer and the marketing channel members expect some cooperation from each other in providing parts and repair services and performing promotional activities.

3.   **Specialty Products**

a)   *Specialty products* have one or more unique characteristics, and buyers are willing to expend considerable effort to obtain them.

b)   Buyers actually plan the purchase of a specialty product; they know exactly what they want and will not accept a substitute.

c)   Specialty items often are distributed through a limited number of retail outlets.

d)   Like shopping products, specialty products are purchased infrequently, causing lower inventory turnover; thus gross margins must be relatively high.

(Transparency Figure 11I)

4.   **Unsought Products**

a)   *Unsought products* are products purchased to solve a sudden problem, products of which customers are unaware, and products that people do not necessarily think about buying.

b)   Examples include emergency medical services and automobile repairs.

B.   **Business Products**

Business products are purchased to use in a firm's operations, to resell, or to use in the manufacture of other products; they are classified according to their characteristics and intended uses in an organization.

1.   **Installations**

a)   *Installations* include facilities and nonportable major equipment.

b)   Facilities are items such as office buildings, factories, and warehouses.

c)   Major equipment usually is used for production purposes.

          d)   This equipment is usually expensive and intended to be used for a considerable period of time.

          e)   Marketers of installations frequently must provide a variety of services, including training, repairs, maintenance assistance, and may even help finance the purchase.

2.   **Accessory Equipment**

          a)   *Accessory equipment* does not become a part of the final physical product but is used in production or office activities.

          b)   Compared with major equipment, accessory items usually are much cheaper, purchased routinely with less negotiation, and treated as expense items rather than as capital items because they are not expected to last as long.

          c)   Sellers do not have to provide the multitude of services expected of installations marketers.

3.   **Raw Materials**

          a)   *Raw materials* are basic materials that become part of a physical product.

          b)   Other than the processing required to transport and physically handle the product, raw materials have not been processed when a firm buys them.

          c)   Raw materials often are bought in large quantities according to grades and specifications.

4.   **Component Parts**

          a)   *Component parts* become a part of the physical product and are either finished items ready for assembly or products that need little processing before assembly.

          b)   Buyers purchase component parts according to their own specifications or industry standards.

          c)   Component parts suppliers must provide consistent quality and on-time deliveries.

5.   **Process Materials**

          a)   *Process materials* are used directly in the production of other products.

          b)   Unlike component parts, process materials are not readily identifiable.

          c)   Process materials are purchased according to industry standards or the purchaser's specifications.

6.   **MRO Supplies**

          a)   *MRO supplies* are maintenance, repair, and operating items that facilitate an organization's production and operations but do not become part of the finished product.

          b)   Supplies are commonly sold through numerous outlets and are purchased routinely.

7.   **Business Services**

          a)   *Business services* are the intangible products that many organizations use in their operations and include financial, legal, marketing research, information technology, and janitorial services.

          b)   Purchasers must decide whether to provide their own services internally or to obtain them from outside the organization.

          c)   This decision depends largely on the costs associated with each alternative and how frequently the services are needed.

III. **Product Line and Product Mix**

    A.   A *product item* is a specific version of a product that can be designated as a distinct offering among an organization's products.

    B.   A *product line* is a group of closely related product items that are considered a unit because of marketing, technical, or end-use considerations.

1. Marketers must understand buyers' goals if they hope to come up with the optimal product line.
2. Specific items in a product line usually reflect the desires of different target markets or different consumer needs.

C. A *product mix* is the composite, or total, group of products that an organization makes available to customers.

(Transparency Figure 11.1)

1. The *width of product mix* is the number of product lines a company offers.
2. The *depth of product mix* is the average number of different products offered in each product line.

IV. **Product Life Cycles and Marketing Strategies**

Product life cycle is the progression of a product through four stages: introduction, growth, maturity, and decline.

A. **Introduction**

(Transparency Figure 11.2)

1. The *introduction stage* of the product life cycle begins at a product's first appearance in the marketplace, when sales start at zero and profits are negative.
    a) Developing and introducing a new product can cost millions of dollars, and the risk of new product failure is quite high.
    b) During the introduction stage, potential buyers must be made aware of the new product's features, uses, and advantages.
2. Most new products start off slowly and seldom generate enough sales to bring immediate profits.
    a) As buyers learn about the new product, marketers should be alert for product weaknesses and make corrections quickly to prevent the product's early demise.
    b) Marketing strategy should be designed to attract the segment that is most interested and has the fewest objections.

B. **Growth**

1. During the *growth stage*, sales rise rapidly and profits reach a peak and start to decline.
2. This stage is critical to a product's survival because competitive reactions to the product's success during this period will affect the product's life expectancy.
3. Profits begin to decline late in the growth stage as more competitors enter the market, driving prices down and creating the need for heavy promotional expenses.
4. As sales increase, management must support the momentum by adjusting the marketing strategy.
    a) The goal is to establish and fortify the product's market position by encouraging brand loyalty.
    b) Gaps in geographic market coverage should be filled during the growth period.
    c) Promotion expenditures may be slightly lower than during the introductory stage but are still quite substantial.
    d) After recovering development costs, a business may be able to lower prices.

(Tech Know: Nokia: Phone Fun and Games)

C. **Maturity**

1. During the *maturity stage*, the sales curve peaks and starts to decline and profits continue to fall.
2. This stage is characterized by intense competition as many brands are now in the market.

a) Competitors emphasize improvements and differences in their versions of the product.
b) Weaker competitors are squeezed out or lose interest.
3. Because many products are in the maturity stage of their life cycles, marketers must know how to deal with these products and be prepared to adjust their marketing strategies.
4. Three general objectives can be pursued during the maturity stage:
a) Generate cash flow.
b) Maintain share of market.
c) Increase share of customer—the percentage of each customer's needs being met by the firm.

D. **Decline**
1. During the *decline stage*, sales fall rapidly.
a) When this happens, the marketer considers pruning items from the product line to eliminate those not earning a profit.
b) The marketer may also cut promotion efforts, eliminate marginal distributors and, finally, plan to phase out the product.
c) An organization can justify maintaining a product as long as it contributes to profits or enhances the overall effectiveness of a product mix.
2. In this stage, marketers must determine whether to eliminate the product or try to reposition it to extend its life.
a) During a product's decline, outlets with strong sales volumes are maintained and unprofitable outlets are weeded out.
b) Spending on promotion efforts is usually considerably reduced.
3. Many firms lack the resources to renew a product's demand and are forced to consider harvesting or divesting the product or the strategic business unit (SBU).
a) The harvesting approach employs a gradual reduction in marketing expenditures and a less resource-intensive marketing mix.
b) The divesting approach involves withdrawing all marketing support from the declining product or SBU; the firm may arrange for another firm to acquire the product.
4. Because most businesses have a product mix consisting of multiple products, a firm's destiny is rarely tied to one product.

(Transparency Figure 11E)

V. **Product Adoption Process**
A. The *product adoption process* includes the stages the buyers go through in accepting a product.

(Transparency Figure 11G)

1. The five stages of the adoption process are awareness, interest, evaluation, trial, and adoption.

(Transparency Figure 11F)

a) First stage: Awareness is when a buyer becomes aware of the product's existence.
b) Second stage: Interest is when the buyer seeks information and is receptive to learning about the product.
c) Third stage: Evaluation is when the buyer considers the product's benefits and decides whether to try it.

        d)   Fourth stage: Trial is when the buyer examines, tests, or tries the product to determine if it meets his or her needs.

        e)   Fifth stage: Adoption is when the buyer purchases the product and can be expected to use it again whenever the need for this general type of product arises.

    2.   Entering the adoption process does not mean the person will eventually adopt the product—rejection can occur at any stage.

(Building Customer Relationships: Kodak Pictures a Digital Future)

  B.   When an organization introduces a new product, people do not begin the adoption process at the same time, nor do they move through it at the same speed.

(Transparency Figure 11.3)

    1.   *Innovators* are the first adopters of new products. They enjoy trying new things and tend to be venturesome.

    2.   *Early adopters* are the careful choosers of new products. They are viewed as the people to check with by people in the remaining adopter categories.

    3.   *Early majority* are those people adopting new products just before the average person. They are deliberate and cautious in trying new products.

    4.   *Late majority* includes skeptics who adopt new products when they feel it is necessary.

    5.   *Laggards* are the last adopters. They distrust new products, and when they finally adopt the innovation, it may have been replaced by a new product.

VI. **Why Some Products Fail and Others Succeed**

  A.   In general, consumer products fail more often than business products.

  B.   Products fail for a variety of reasons.

    1.   One of the most common reasons a product fails is failure to match product offerings to customer needs.

    2.   Ineffective or inconsistent branding has also been blamed for product failures.

    3.   New products sometimes fail because of poor timing, technical or design problems, overestimation of market size, poor promotion, or insufficient distribution.

  C.   When examining the problem of product failure, it is important to distinguish the degree of failure.

    1.   Absolute failure occurs when an organization loses money on a new product because it is unable to recover development, production, and marketing costs; therefore, the product is usually deleted.

    2.   Relative product failure occurs when a product returns a profit, but does not meet a company's profit or market share objectives; repositioning or improving the product might make this product a success.

  D.   For a new product to be successful, it must provide a significant and perceivable benefit to a sizable number of customers.

  E.   Effective planning and management are also critical to launch a new product that will be successful.

NOTES FOR CLASS EXERCISES, DEBATE ISSUE, AND CHAPTER QUIZ

On the following pages, you will find two class exercises, a debate issue, and a chapter quiz. These are formatted in large-size type so that you can use them as class handouts or for making transparencies. Below are the authors' comments on the class exercises, the debate topic for this chapter, and the answers to the chapter quiz.

Comments on Class Exercise 1

This exercise is designed to help students understand how properly classifying consumer products affects marketing efforts.

1. Answers will vary. The idea is to have students determine the degree of brand loyalty they exhibit for each product category so that they can answer the next question.

2. Responses to these questions will vary, but similarities should emerge. The differences should help make the point that the classification is dependent on the target market and individual consumer perceptions. For instance, some might see shampoo as a specialty good for which only one brand will do; life insurance should seem like an obvious unsought good, but some may see suits and dresses as unsought goods.

3. Product classifications relate to marketing mix as follows:

	Convenience	Shopping	Specialty	Unsought
Profit margin	Low	Medium	High	High
Manufacturer or retail promotion	Manufacturer	Both	Both	Both
Distribution intensity (No. of retail outlets)	High	Medium	Low	Low
More self-service or personal selling	Self-service	Personal selling	Personal selling	Personal selling

Comments on Class Exercise 2

The goal of this exercise is for students to apply the product life cycle to existing products. Answers:

1. VCRs — maturity
2. Digital display watches — decline
3. Blue jeans — maturity
4. Laptop computers — maturity
5. DVD players — growth
6. Wine coolers — decline
7. Fax machines — maturity
8. Minivans — growth
9. Compact discs — growth
10. Palm handhelds — growth
11. Skateboards — maturity
12. Mobile homes — maturity
13. Bottled water — maturity
14. Fur coats — decline
15. Peanut butter — maturity

DEBATE ISSUE

In terms of product management, can following the product life cycle (PLC) philosophy be detrimental?

CHAPTER QUIZ

Answers to Chapter Quiz 1. b; 2. d; 3. b; 4. c.

Class Exercise 1

1. List the brand name of the product you usually prefer for each of the following product categories:

    - Car/truck
    - Compact disc player
    - Suit or dress
    - Soft drink

    - Bicycle
    - Life insurance
    - Shampoo
    - Toothpaste

2. Which of these brands are you

    a. likely to buy frequently?
    b. willing to spend considerable effort to obtain?
    c. willing to accept substitutes for?

    Based on this information, group the eight products into the following product classifications: convenience, shopping, specialty, or unsought.

3. How does the classification influence the marketing mix factors?

	Convenience	Shopping	Specialty	Unsought
Profit margin				
Manufacturer or retail promotion				
Distribution intensity (No. of retail outlets)				
More self-service or personal selling				

Class Exercise 2

IN WHAT STAGES OF THE PRODUCT LIFE CYCLE ARE THE FOLLOWING PRODUCTS?

1. VCRs
2. Digital display watches
3. Blue jeans
4. Laptop computers
5. DVD players
6. Wine coolers
7. Fax machines
8. Minivans
9. Compact discs
10. Palm handhelds
11. Skateboards
12. Mobile homes
13. Bottled water
14. Fur coats
15. Peanut butter

Debate Issue

IN TERMS OF PRODUCT MANAGEMENT, CAN FOLLOWING THE PRODUCT LIFE CYCLE (PLC) PHILOSOPHY BE DETRIMENTAL?

YES

- **Difficult to determine specific stage of PLC**

- **"Self-fulfilling prophecy"**

- **Self-fulfilling prophecy can cause the PLC to be shortened and thus curtail profit potential**

- **Self-fulfilling prophecy can have significant effects on product mix**

NO

- **Must be accompanied by other analytical techniques**

- **Can properly plan for new product development or improvement**

- **Better able to determine when a product should be harvested or receive reinvestment**

- **Proper marketing strategies will facilitate optimal resource allocation**

Chapter Quiz

1. **An example of a convenience product is**

   a. stereo equipment.   d. a bicycle.

   b. gasoline.   e. athletic shoes.

   c. a motorcycle.

2. **What measure of the product mix involves the number of product lines a company offers?**

   a. Quality   d. Width

   b. Consistency   e. Size

   c. Depth

3. **In which stage of the product life cycle do profits peak?**

   a. Introduction   d. Termination

   b. Growth   e. Maturity

   c. Decline

4. **Depending on the length of time it takes them to adopt a new product, people can be divided into five major adopter categories: early adopters, early majority, late majority, laggards, and**

   a. late adopters.   d. middle adopters.

   b. nonadopters.   e. middle majority.

   c. innovators.

ANSWERS TO DISCUSSION AND REVIEW QUESTIONS

1. **List the tangible and intangible attributes of a pair of Nike athletic shoes. Compare the benefits of the Nike shoes with those of an intangible product, such as a hairstyling in a salon.**

    This question is intended to get students to recognize that product benefits are more than the visible, tangible attributes. Tangible attributes of a pair of Nike shoes include the quality of the leather and other materials, inside supports, cushioned heels, and long-lasting soles. Intangible attributes include product image, the fact that these shoes are a prized possession for a special group of consumers, and identification with athletic, fitness-oriented individuals.

    The attributes of a pair of shoes are more visible than are the attributes of a hairstyle. One who markets a hairstyling service must deal with intangible characteristics such as image, fashion, and confidence.

2. **A product has been referred to as a "psychological bundle of satisfaction." Is this a good definition of a product? Why or why not?**

    Products do provide psychological benefits as well as satisfaction, but they are more than this simple definition implies. The tangible and intangible attributes include functional, social, and psychological utilities of all parts of the product. Stating that a product is a "psychological bundle of satisfaction" does not make it explicit that some products provide mechanical and functional features that help accomplish a task but do not necessarily provide a great deal of psychological stimulation. For example, a car's fan belt is desired for the functional benefits it provides; these benefits are probably more important than psychological aspects.

3. **Is a personal computer sold at a retail store a consumer product or a business product? Defend your answer.**

    The classification of products into the business or consumer class depends on the buyer's purpose and intent. If a personal computer is purchased for a consumer's home use, it is a consumer product. If it is purchased for a business office, it is an industrial or business product.

4. **How do convenience products and shopping products differ? What are the distinguishing characteristics of each type of product?**

    Convenience products (milk, pay telephones, and gasoline) are purchased at the closest retail facility. Shopping products (clothing and furniture) are purchased after comparisons and alternatives have been evaluated. Distinguishing characteristics include frequency of purchase, time of consumption, searching time, margins, and product adjustment. Convenience products rank lower than shopping products in terms of searching time, margins, adjustment, and time of consumption. Convenience products also are replaced more often than shopping products.

5. **In the category of business products, how do component parts differ from process materials?**

    Component parts become a part of the physical product and are either finished items ready for assembly or products that need little processing before assembly. Although they become part of a larger product, component parts often can be identified and distinguished easily.

    Process materials are used directly in the production of products; unlike component parts, they are not readily identifiable.

6. **How does an organization's product mix relate to its development of a product line? When should an enterprise add depth to its product lines rather than width to its product mix?**

   Product mix is the composite of products that a firm sells. The product line includes a group of products closely related in terms of marketing, technical, or end-use considerations. For example, toothpaste is a product Procter & Gamble sells; Gleem II and Crest are the two brands in the product line. A firm should add depth to the product line when there is greater opportunity to profit by building on current marketing expertise and consumers' acceptance in a particular market. Launching new products to add to the marketing mix may require new marketing channels, promotion, pricing techniques, and production facilities. Many firms have expanded by increasing the width of their product mixes and depth of their product lines.

7. **How do industry profits change as a product moves through the four stages of its life cycle?**

   During the introduction stage, profits are negative. The firm should break even as the growth stage is reached, and profits should increase rapidly and show the highest profit-to-sales ratio during late growth. Profits decline during maturity and usually drop further during the decline stage.

8. **What is the relationship between the concepts of product mix and product life cycle?**

   Most firms are not tied to a single product. They often have a number of products in the product mix, and different products are usually at different stages of the product life cycle. This means that new products must be introduced and the life of existing products prolonged to meet organizational sales goals.

9. **What are the stages in the product adoption process, and how do they affect the commercialization phase?**

   The stages of the product adoption process are the stages buyers must go through before they accept a product. The first stage is awareness, when the buyer becomes aware of the product. The second stage is interest, when the buyer seeks information and is receptive to learning about the product. The third stage is evaluation, when the buyer considers the product's benefits and decides whether to try it. The fourth stage is trial, when the buyer examines, tests, or tries the product to determine if it meets his or her needs. The fifth stage is adoption, when the buyer purchases the product and can be expected to use it again whenever the need for this general type of product arises. This adoption model has several implications when a new product is being launched. First, the company must promote the product to create widespread awareness of its existence and its benefits. At the same time, marketers should emphasize quality control and provide solid guarantees to reinforce buyer opinion during the evaluation stage. Finally, production and physical distribution must be linked to patterns of adoption and repeat purchases.

10. **What are the five major adopter categories that describe the length of time required for a consumer to adopt a new product, and what are the characteristics of each?**

    Innovators are the first to adopt a new product; they enjoy trying new products and tend to be venturesome. Early adopters choose new products carefully and are viewed as "the people to check with" by people in the remaining adopter categories. People in the early majority adopt just prior to the average person; they are deliberate and cautious in trying new products. Late majority people, who are quite skeptical of new products, eventually adopt new products because of economic necessity or social pressure. Laggards, the last to adopt a new product, are oriented toward the past; they are suspicious of new products, and when they finally adopt the innovation, it may already have been replaced by a new product.

11. **In what ways does the marketing strategy for a mature product differ from the marketing strategy for a growth product?**

For a mature product, the sales curve starts to peak and decline, meaning the marketing strategy must be different than for a growth product. For a mature product, advertising and dealer-oriented promotions are typical. Marketers must also take into account that the buyers' knowledge of the product has attained a high level. Marketers sometimes expand into global markets and, often, products are adapted to more precisely meet the needs of global customers. Suggesting new uses for the product is also another approach for a mature product. Offering dealers of the product promotional incentives is another way to market a mature product. Pricing changes may also occur, and advertising tends to focus on what makes a mature product different from the competition. In the growth stage, a typical marketing strategy is to encourage strong brand loyalty. Marketers try to strengthen the product's market share and develop a competitive niche by emphasizing the product's benefits. Aggressive pricing is also used at this phase. Providing product variations may also occur at this stage.

12. **What are the major reasons for new-product failure?**

Some new products fail for a variety of reasons. One of the most common reasons is the company's failure to match product offerings to customer needs. When products do not offer value and do not have the features customers want, they fail in the marketplace. Sometimes new products fail because of poor timing. Ineffective or inconsistent branding has also been blamed for product failures. Other reasons for new-product failure include: technical or design problems, overestimation of market size, poor promotion, and insufficient distribution.

COMMENTS ON THE CASES

CASE 11.1 SONY'S PLAYSTATION PLAYS ON AND ON

This case examines a firm that may be of considerable interest to students because its products are growing in popularity. To introduce this case, you might ask students to indicate with a show of hands how many have bought one of the Sony game consoles (PSOne, PlayStation 2 or PlayStation 3). Ask these students why they chose a Sony console rather than one of the competing products, especially the Xbox and the GameCube. Focus their attention on the factors that influence consumer choices rather than on the technical aspects of the products.

The first question asks how PlayStation 2 can be classified as a product. Based on the categories in the text, students should be able to classify it as a consumer product (not purchased by organizations) and, more specifically, as a shopping product or specialty product. Students who call it a shopping product will say that buyers expend considerable effort to obtain one of these game consoles. Students who call it a specialty product will say that buyers know exactly what they want and are unlikely to accept a substitute. This is a good opportunity to show students that product classification depends on product usage and buyer motivation.

The second question asks students to which product adopter groups is Sony most likely to promote PlayStation 3, and why. Most students will respond with "innovators" and/or "early adopters" because people in the first category are adventuresome in their buying habits (and therefore would have fewer objections to overcome), and people in the second category often have significant influence over consumers in the other categories.

The third question asks students to assess where the PSOne and the PlayStation 2 are in their life cycles, and what this implies for Sony's marketing strategy. Some students may argue that the PSOne is in the decline stage, while others may argue that the PSOne is in late maturity. Students will recognize that reducing the price and renaming the product PSOne (as opposed to its original PlayStation name) are ways to extend the life cycle, encourage buying, and differentiate this much older product from newer versions with updated technology and more sophisticated capabilities. Either way, Sony is unlikely to invest much time or money in marketing the PSOne. The PlayStation 2 is probably in the maturity stage, where it faces strong competition for market share. Sony may have to continue its promotional expenditures, even if more moderately than for the PlayStation 3, to protect share and channel relationships. Discussion of this question will help students appreciate the factors that characterize each life cycle stage and the strategic implications of each stage.

Video Information

Company: Sony

Location: Tape 2/DVD 2, Segment 11

Length: 1:45

Video Overview: This video briefly looks at the excitement surrounding the launch of the PlayStation 2 and some of the games that can be played on it. Although the video concentrates on one product, *Madden 2001*, it can help students recognize the importance of related and/or supporting products during the launch of a new product.

MULTIPLE-CHOICE QUESTIONS ABOUT THE VIDEO

1.   For Sony, the PlayStation 2 game console represents a

   a.   product item.
   b.   product line.
   c.   product mix.
   d.   business product.
   e.   convenience product.

2.   Sony's PlayStation 2 is *best* categorized as a(n)

   a.   installation.
   b.   component part.
   c.   convenience product.
   d.   shopping product.
   e.   unsought product.

3.   According to the video, which of the following is one of the strongest features of games played on the Sony PlayStation 2?

   a.   Color
   b.   Sound
   c.   Realism
   d.   Price
   e.   Distribution

ANSWERS TO MULTIPLE-CHOICE QUESTIONS ABOUT THE VIDEO

1.   a

2.   d

3.   c

CASE 11.2 DELL MIXES IT UP WITH COMPUTERS, ELECTRONICS, AND MORE

In this case, students learn how and why Dell is widening its product mix. The goal is to stimulate discussion of the basic concepts of product decision making and the product adoption process. Students are likely to be interested in this case because they know the Dell name in connection with personal computers.

The first question asks how the Dell DJ music player can be classified as a product. It is most likely a shopping product because consumers are willing to expend considerable effort in planning and completing its purchase. Also, the Dell DJ is not widely available (compared to convenience products) and is purchased less frequently. The Dell DJ is a direct competitor to the Apple iPod; the iPod is far better known and is more likely to be a specialty product for which buyers will accept no substitutes.

Question 2 asks students whether customers are likely to be willing to purchase consumer electronics like home theater systems direct from Dell. Students who say "yes" may argue that Dell has a good reputation, its products are not pioneers, and customers probably need less education and assistance in the buying process. Therefore, customers should feel comfortable buying direct from Dell rather than from a local retailer. Students who say "no" may argue that Dell made its name in personal computers and customers may not have the same positive associations when the brand is extended to home theater systems. Moreover, home theater systems are not as common as personal computers and, as a result, customers still need information and assistance as they make their buying decisions for this expensive product. Customers may also want to see a product demonstration before buying a home theater system, making them reluctant to buy direct. This question is a good opportunity for class discussion of the effect of the product adoption process and a wider product mix on customer buying decisions.

Question 3 asks students to consider how wide Dell's product mix can be without hurting the credibility of the organization. Can the company successfully market Dell motorcycles or Dell frozen pastries? Students should recognize that an excessively wide product mix—covering an array of dissimilar products—can raise questions in customers' minds about what the brand stands for. On the other hand, Dell may be able to add many product lines that are closely related to computers, including additional consumer electronics products. Ask students to suggest product lines that Dell might add without hurting its credibility and contrast those with lines that could hurt its credibility. Is the class in complete agreement? You can use this question to illustrate the challenges that companies face in making decisions about their product lines and product mix.

CHAPTER 12

Developing and Managing Products

TEACHING RESOURCES QUICK REFERENCE GUIDE

Resource	Location
Purpose and Perspective	IRM, p. 209
Guide for Using Color Transparencies	IRM, p. 210
Lecture Outline	IRM, p. 210
Notes for Class Exercises, Debate Issue, and Chapter Quiz	IRM, p. 216
Class Exercise 1	IRM, p. 218
Class Exercise 2	IRM, p. 219
Debate Issue	IRM, p. 220
Chapter Quiz	IRM, p. 221
Answers to Discussion and Review Questions	IRM, p. 222
Comments on the Cases	IRM, p. 225
Case 12.1	IRM, p. 225
Video	Tape 2/DVD 2, Segment 12
Video Information	IRM, p. 226
Multiple-Choice Questions About the Video	IRM, p. 226
Case 12.2	IRM, p. 227
Transparency Acetates	Transparency package
Examination Questions: Essay	TB, p. 327
Examination Questions: Multiple-Choice	TB, p. 327
Examination Questions: True-False	TB, p. 351
Author-Selected Multiple-Choice Test Items	TB, p. 671
HMClassPrep Presentation Resources	CD-ROM
PowerPoint Slides	Instructor's website

Note: Additional resources are updated periodically and may be found on the accompanying student and instructor websites at http://www.prideferrell.com/.

PURPOSE AND PERSPECTIVE

This chapter examines several ways to improve an organization's product mix, including managing existing products through line extensions and product modifications. Next, we discuss how firms develop new products, from idea generation to commercialization. After development of new products, the process of product differentiation through quality, design, and support services is discussed. We discuss the goals and timing of product positioning and repositioning, as well as when a product should be deleted from the product mix. Finally, we discuss the organizational alternatives in managing products, including the product manager, market manager, and venture team approaches.

GUIDE FOR USING COLOR TRANSPARENCIES

There are two groups of color transparencies. The transparencies identified by a double number are the same as the figures in the text. The transparencies labeled with a number and a letter are illustrations that do not appear in the text, but they can be used as additional examples of concepts discussed.

Figure 12.1	Phases of New-Product Development
Figure 12.3	Stages of Expansion into a National Market During Commercialization
Figure 12.4	Hypothetical Perceptual Map for Pain Relievers
Figure 12.5	Product Deletion Process
Figure 12A	Chapter 12 Outline
Figure 12B	Key Definitions: Product Differentiation, Product Quality, Product Positioning
Figure 12C	Three Approaches to Differentiating Products
Figure 12D	Kellogg: An Example of How a Company Benefits from New Product Development
Figure 12E	Organizational Forms for Managing Products
Figure 12F	Are You Ready for a Hybrid?
Figure 12G	Will Product Adoption of Digital Video Recorders (DVRs) Be Fast or Slow?
Figure 12H	Is the McDonald's McGriddle a Line Extension or a New Product?
Figure 12I	What Are the Major Dimensions of the Positioning of the MINI?

LECTURE OUTLINE

(Transparency Figure 12A: Chapter Outline)

I. **Managing Existing Products**

An organization can overcome weaknesses and gaps in its existing product mix through line extension or product modification.

A. **Line Extensions**
1. A *line extension* is the development of a product closely related to one or more products in the existing product line but designed specifically to meet somewhat different needs of customers.
2. Line extensions are more common than new products because they are a less expensive, lower risk alternative for increasing sales.
3. A line extension may focus on a different market segment or on increasing sales within the same market segment by more precisely satisfying the needs of people in that segment.

(Transparency Figure 12H)

B. **Product Modifications**
1. *Product modification* means changing one or more characteristics of a firm's product; it differs from a line extension in that the original product is removed from the line.
2. Product modification is less risky than new-product development.
3. Three conditions must exist for product modification to improve the firm's product mix.
   a) The product must be modifiable.
   b) The customer must be able to perceive that a modification has been made.
   c) The modification should make the product more consistent with customers' desires.

4. There are three major ways to modify products.
   a) **Quality Modifications**
      (1) *Quality modifications* are changes relating to a product's dependability and durability, usually executed by altering the materials or the production process.
      (2) Reducing quality may allow the firm to lower its price and direct the item at a different target market.
      (3) Increasing quality may allow the firm to charge a higher price by creating customer loyalty and lowering customer sensitivity to price.
      (4) Some companies have been able to both increase quality and reduce cost of a product.
   b) **Functional Modifications**
      (1) *Functional modifications* are changes that affect a product's versatility, effectiveness, convenience, or safety; they usually require that the product be redesigned.
      (2) These modifications can make a product useful to more people and thus enlarge its market.
      (3) These changes can place the product in a favorable competitive position by providing benefits that other brands do not offer and help the firm achieve a progressive image.
   c) **Aesthetic Modifications**
      (1) *Aesthetic modifications* change the sensory appeal of a product by altering its taste, texture, sound, smell, or appearance.
      (2) Aesthetics of a product can differentiate it from competing brands to gain market share.
      (3) The major drawback in using aesthetic modifications is that their value is subjective.

II. **Developing New Products**
   A. A firm develops new products as a means of enhancing its product mix and adding depth to a product line.

(Transparency Figure 12D)

(Transparency Figure 12F)

(Transparency Figure 12G)

1. Developing and introducing new products is frequently risky and expensive.
2. Failure to introduce new products is also risky.
3. The term "new product" can have more than one meaning.
   a) A new product can be an innovative product that has never been sold by any organization.
   b) It can also be a product that a given firm has not marketed previously, although similar products may have been available from other companies.
   c) A product can be viewed as new when it is brought to one or more markets from another market.
   B. Before a product is introduced, it goes through the seven phases of the *new-product development process*; a product may be dropped at any stage of this process.

(Transparency Figure 12.1)

1. **Idea Generation**
   a) *Idea generation*, the first step in the development process, occurs when firms seek product ideas to achieve organizational objectives.
   b) Firms trying to maximize product mixes effectively usually develop systematic approaches to new-product development.
   c) New ideas may be generated internally or externally.
2. **Screening**
   a) In phase two, *screening*, the most promising ideas are selected for further review.
   b) Ideas are analyzed to determine whether they match the organization's objectives, resources, and abilities.
   c) The potential market, the needs and wants of buyers, possible environmental changes, and possible cannibalizations of current products are also analyzed and weighed.
   d) Using a checklist of new-product requirements to ensure a systematic approach, more ideas are rejected during screening than in any other stage.
3. **Concept Testing**
   a) Stage three is *concept testing*, in which a sample of potential buyers is presented with a product idea to determine their attitudes and initial buying intentions regarding the product.
   b) A firm can test more than one concept for the same product before it invests considerable resources in research and development.
   c) The results of concept testing can be used to find out which aspects of the product are most important to potential customers.
   d) Concept tests include a brief written or oral description of the concept followed by a series of questions on the product's advantages, disadvantages, and price.
4. **Business Analysis**
   a) During stage four, *business analysis*, the product idea is evaluated to determine its potential contribution to the firm's sales, costs, and profits.
   b) Marketers evaluate how well the product fits with the firm's existing product mix, the strength of market demand for the product, the types of environmental and competitive changes to be expected, and how these changes might affect the product's future sales, costs, and profits.
   c) For many product ideas, this analysis is challenging because forecasting accurately is difficult, especially for completely new products.
5. **Product Development**
   a) In stage five, *product development*, the firm finds out if it is technically feasible to produce the product and if it can be produced at costs low enough to make the final price reasonable.
      (1) The idea or concept is converted into a prototype, or working model, that should reveal the tangible and intangible attributes associated with the product in consumers' minds.
      (2) The functionality of the prototype must be tested, including performance, safety, and convenience.
      (3) The specific level of product quality is determined based on what price the target market views as acceptable and on the quality level of the firm's own and competing products.
   b) This phase can be lengthy and expensive; thus a relatively small number of product ideas are put into development.

6. **Test Marketing**
    a) Stage six, *test marketing*, is the limited introduction of the product in geographic areas chosen to represent the intended market to gauge the extent to which potential customers will actually buy it.
    b) Test marketing is not an extension of the development stage, but a sample launching of the entire marketing mix.
    c) Test marketing provides several important benefits.
        (1) It minimizes the risk of product failure.
        (2) It lets marketers expose a product in a natural marketing environment to obtain a measure of its sales performance.
        (3) It allows marketers to identify any weaknesses in the product itself or in other aspects of the marketing mix.
        (4) Marketers can experiment in different test areas with advertising, price, and packaging variations.
    d) Test marketing is also expensive and involves risks.
        (1) Competitors may try to "jam" the testing program by increasing promotion of their own products.
        (2) Competitors may copy the product in the testing stage and rush to introduce a similar product.
    e) Many companies use simulated test marketing to avoid these risks.
    f) Not all products that are test marketed are actually launched.
7. **Commercialization**

(Transparency Figure 12.3)

    a) Stage seven, *commercialization*, is the phase of planning for full-scale manufacturing and marketing and preparing budgets.
    b) Marketing management analyzes the results of test marketing to find out what changes in the marketing mix are needed before the product is introduced.
    c) The organization refines plans for production, quality control, distribution, and promotion.
    d) Enormous amounts of money spent during this stage on marketing and manufacturing may not be recovered for several years.
    e) Products are usually launched through an introduction process called a "roll-out"—stages that start in a set of geographic areas and gradually expand into adjacent areas.
        (1) Gradual introduction reduces the risk of introducing a new product and provides additional benefits.
        (2) However, a gradual introduction allows competitors to monitor the product's performance.

III. **Product Differentiation through Quality, Design, and Support Services**

(Transparency Figure 12B)

Product differentiation is the process of creating and designing products so that customers perceive them as different from competing products. The three physical aspects of product differentiation that companies must consider are product quality, product design and features, and product support services.

(Transparency Figure 12C)

A.   **Product Quality**

Product *quality* refers to the overall characteristics of a product that allow it to perform as expected in satisfying customer needs. Expectations and perceptions of quality vary by customer.

(Transparency Figure 12B)

1.   *Level of quality* is the amount of quality possessed by a product.
2.   *Consistency of quality* is the degree to which a product is the same level of quality over time. It can also be compared across competing products.

B.   **Product Design and Features**

1.   *Product design* refers to how a product is conceived, planned, and produced; it involves the total sum of all the product's physical characteristics.
   a)   One component of design is *styling*, the physical appearance of a product.
   b)   Most consumers seek out products that look good and function well.
2.   *Product features* are specific design characteristics that allow a product to perform certain tasks. These can differentiate a firm's products from those of its competitors.
3.   For a brand to have a sustainable competitive advantage, marketers must determine the product designs and features that customers desire.

(Ethics and Social Responsibility: Lying to Customers)

C.   **Product Support Services**

1.   *Customer services* include any human or mechanical efforts or activities a company provides that add value to a product.
2.   Customer services can include delivery, installation, financing, customer training, warranties, repairs, and more.
3.   Providing good customer service may be the only way a firm can differentiate its products when all products in a market have essentially the same quality, design, and features.

IV.   **Product Positioning and Repositioning**

A.   *Product positioning* refers to the decisions and activities intended to create and maintain a certain concept of a product in the customers' minds.

(Transparency Figure 12B)

B.   Marketers try to position a product so that it seems to possess the characteristics most desired by the target market.

C.   Product position is the result of customers' perceptions of a product's attributes relative to those of competing brands.

1.   Marketers sometimes analyze product positions by developing "perceptual maps," as shown in Figure 12.4; these are created by questioning a sample of consumers about their perceptions of products, brands, and organizations with respect to two or more dimensions.

(Transparency Figure 12.4)

2.   Using a perceptual map, marketers can compare how consumers perceive their brands compared to ideal points representing customer desires.

D.   Product positioning is part of a natural progression when market segmentation is used.

E.   Positioning can be designed to compete head to head or to avoid it.
1.   Head-to-head positioning may be appropriate if the product's performance characteristics are at least equal to those of competitive brands, if the product is priced lower, or even when the price is higher if the product's performance characteristics are superior.
2.   Positioning to avoid competition may be best when the product's performance characteristics do not differ significantly from competing brands, when the brand has unique characteristics, or when marketers want to keep a new brand from cannibalizing sales of their existing brands.
F.   If a product has been planned properly, its features and brand image will give it the distinct appeal needed. If buyers can easily identify the benefits, they are more likely to purchase the product.
G.   Positioning decisions are not just for new products.
1.   Evaluating the positions of existing products is important because a brand's market share and profitability may be strengthened by product repositioning.
2.   Repositioning can be accomplished by physically changing the product, its price, its distribution, or its promotion.

(Transparency Figure 12I)

V.   **Product Deletion**
Product deletion is the process of eliminating a product from the product mix when it no longer satisfies a sufficient number of customers.

(Transparency Figure 12.5)

A.   A weak product is a drain on potential profitability and the marketer's time and resources.

(Building Customer Relationships: General Motors Takes Slow-Selling Products Off the Road)

B.   It is often difficult to drop a product over the protests of management, salespeople, and loyal customers.
C.   Instead of letting a weak product become a financial burden, a firm should periodically and systematically review and analyze its contribution to the firm's sales for a given time frame.
D.   There are three ways to delete products.
1.   A phase-out lets \the product decline without changing the marketing strategy.
2.   A run-out calls for increased marketing efforts in core markets, deletion of some marketing expenditures, or price reductions to exploit any strengths left in the product.
3.   An immediate drop is the best strategy when losses are too great to prolong its life.

VI.   **Organizing to Develop and Manage Products**
There are several alternatives to the traditional functional form of business organization.

(Transparency Figure 12E)

A.   The Product Manager Approach
1.   A *product manager* is the person within an organization responsible for a product, product line, or several distinct products that make up a group.
2.   A *brand manager* is responsible for a single brand.
3.   Product or brand managers operate cross-functionally to coordinate the activities, information, and strategies involved in marketing an assigned product.
4.   This approach is used by many large, multiple-product companies in the consumer packaged-goods business.

    B.   The Market Manager Approach
        1.   A *market manager* is responsible for managing the marketing activities that serve a particular group of customers.
        2.   This approach is effective when a firm uses different types of activities to market products to diverse customer groups.
    C.   The Venture Team Approach
        1.   The *venture team* is a cross-functional team that creates entirely new products that may be aimed at new markets.
        2.   Venture teams, unlike product managers or market managers, are responsible for all aspects of a product's development.
        3.   Venture teams work outside established organizational divisions and have greater flexibility to apply innovative approaches to new products and markets, which lets the company take advantage of opportunities in highly segmented markets.
        4.   Companies are increasingly using such cross-functional teams for product development to boost product quality.

NOTES FOR CLASS EXERCISES, DEBATE ISSUE, AND CHAPTER QUIZ

On the following pages, you will find two class exercises, a debate issue, and a chapter quiz. These are formatted in large-size type so that you can use them as class handouts or for making transparencies. Below are the authors' comments on the class exercises, the debate topic for this chapter, and the answers to the chapter quiz.

Comments on Class Exercise 1

This exercise asks students to create new product ideas using the first four phases of the new-product development process.

Your class or group is a venture team, designed to create entirely new products. Students work for the _____ company (you or students decide).

1.   *Idea generation.* Ask students to think of something they wish were available that isn't. Reviewing recent advances in areas such as telecommunications or thinking about things they've seen in science fiction or futuristic movies may help stimulate discussion. You can classify ideas in terms of product modifications (quality, function, or aesthetics). Caution the class not to criticize any ideas at this stage.

2.   *Screening.* Product development moves from the general to the specific. This phase gets more detail-oriented and requires that students' creative ideas now show some practicality. (You may want to allow some leeway on technical feasibility because you may not know if it can be done or not.) Some may develop ideas that are workable but are not needed or wanted by consumers. Remind students that more ideas are rejected in this stage than in any other.

3.   *Concept testing*

    a.   Concept testing is most likely to occur through focus groups but can be done in other ways.

    b.   Not all new product ideas have to be concept tested.

4.   *Business analysis*

    a.   Some products may generate initial interest but produce no long-term profits. An example is no-run pantyhose, which can be made but would produce diminishing demand.

b. Another firm may produce a similar product and capitalize on its superior market position. Regulatory and social forces may not allow continued sales of some questionable products.

c. Secondary data for product categories may help estimate sales potential and typical industry costs. An experiment or survey could measure consumer buying intentions.

Comments on Class Exercise 2

The goal of this exercise is to help students understand product positioning—that is, customers' perceptions of a product's attributes—by considering the position of several products. Possible answers:

1. Volvo automobiles — **safe**
2. Keds athletic shoes — **inexpensive, simple comfort**
3. Mont Blanc writing instruments — **more expensive**
4. Diet Coke — **superior taste**
5. Hampton Inn — **for business travel**
6. Dom Perignon champagne — **premium taste**
7. Curtis Mathes television sets — **better quality**
8. Avis Rent-A-Car — **more responsive**
9. Just For Men haircolor — **for men only**
10. Subway sandwiches — **alternative fast food**

DEBATE ISSUE

Is test marketing always necessary when launching a new product?

CHAPTER QUIZ

Answers to Chapter Quiz 1. b; 2. c; 3. a; 4. a.

Class Exercise 1

YOUR CLASS OR GROUP IS A VENTURE TEAM DESIGNED TO CREATE ENTIRELY NEW PRODUCTS. YOU WORK FOR THE _____ COMPANY.

1. *Idea generation.* You can get ideas for new products for the company from personnel, customers, competitors, ad agencies, consultants, and private research firms. One method you can use now is brainstorming ideas. Make a list of possible product ideas.

2. *Screening.* Pick the ones you think are most feasible.

   a. Do you really think that this product can be made and marketed? What kinds of resources (financial and technological) would be required?

   b. Does the product fit with the nature and wants of buyers? Do people really care about what the product offers?

3. *Concept testing*

   a. How could you best present the product concept to consumers to get their reactions?

   b. Is it necessary to conduct concept testing on each product?

4. *Business analysis.* Determine potential for profit.

   a. Is demand strong enough to justify entering the market, and will demand endure?

   b. How might environmental and competitive changes affect future results?

   c. How could research be used to help estimate sales, costs, and profits?

Class Exercise 2

DESCRIBE THE FOLLOWING BRANDS' RELATIVE POSITIONING IN THEIR PRODUCT CATEGORIES:

1. Volvo automobiles

2. Keds athletic shoes

3. Mont Blanc writing instruments

4. Diet Coke

5. Hampton Inn

6. Dom Perignon champagne

7. Curtis Mathes television sets

8. Avis Rent-A-Car

9. Just For Men haircolor

10. Subway sandwiches

Debate Issue

IS TEST MARKETING ALWAYS NECESSARY WHEN LAUNCHING A NEW PRODUCT?

YES

- Reduces risk of product failure
- Provides opportunity to refine various marketing mix components (variations in promotion, price, packaging, and distribution)
- Allows a firm to "preview" the product's performance in the marketplace relative to competitors
- Based on test marketing results, some products are not commercialized.

NO

- Unnecessary if previous stages of introduction process were performed accurately
- Invalid possibly because of competitive interference
- Tips off competitors about firm's new products
- Competitors can monitor test marketing.
- In some cases, the costs of a product failure may be less than the cost of test marketing.

Chapter Quiz

1. _____ is the development of a product that is closely related to one or more products in a firm's existing product line but is designed specifically to meet somewhat different customer needs.
   a. Quality modification
   b. Line extension
   c. Aesthetic modification
   d. Feature modification
   e. Product mix modification

2. What steps in developing new products involves determining whether the product idea is compatible with company objectives, needs, and resources on a general level?
   a. Product development
   b. Evaluation of competitors' efforts
   c. Screening
   d. Idea generation
   e. Business analysis

3. Three major ways in which marketers engage in product differentiation are
   a. product quality, product design and features, and product support services.
   b. product quality, product support services, and packaging.
   c. product support services, product design and features, and product positioning.
   d. product positioning, product quality, and product management.
   e. product positioning, product design and features, and product promotion.

4. When a company is introducing a new brand in a market where it already has one or more brands, which type of product positioning is *most likely* to be used?
   a. Positioning to avoid competition
   b. Head-to-head competition
   c. Parallel positioning
   d. Segmented positioning
   e. Counter-positioning

ANSWERS TO DISCUSSION AND REVIEW QUESTIONS

1. **What is a line extension, and how does it differ from a product modification?**

   A line extension is development of a product closely related to existing products in the line, but the product meets different customer needs. A product modification means changing one or more characteristics of a product. A product differentiation differs from a line extension in that the original product does not remain in the line.

2. **Compare and contrast the three major approaches to modifying a product.**

   Any product modification changes one or more of a product's characteristics. The three major ways to modify a product are to alter its quality, function, or aesthetics. Changes affecting a product's dependability and durability are quality modifications. Functional modifications are those that affect a product's versatility, effectiveness, convenience, or safety. Quality modifications usually can be made by altering materials or the production process. Functional modifications usually require that the product be redesigned. Aesthetic modifications are less tangible than either quality or functional ones because they change the way a product tastes, sounds, smells, or looks rather than how it actually works. Although consumers usually perceive quality and functional changes as improvements, aesthetic modifications are more subjective and therefore more risky.

3. **Identify and briefly explain the seven major phases of the new-product development process.**

   The seven major phases of new-product development are idea generation, screening, concept testing, business analysis, product development, test marketing, and commercialization. Idea generation is the activity in which business and other organizations look for product ideas that will help them accomplish their objectives. New product ideas can come from internal sources such as marketing managers, researchers, sales personnel, engineers, or other organizational personnel. They can also be generated outside the company from customers, competitors, advertising agencies, management consultants, and private research organizations. In the screening phase, products with the greatest potential are selected for further consideration. Product ideas are analyzed to determine whether they fit the organization's objectives and resources and whether or not the organization can produce and market the product.

   Concept testing is a low-cost procedure to determine consumers' initial reaction to a product idea. During concept testing, a small sample of potential buyers is presented with a product idea through a written or oral description to discover their attitudes and initial buying intentions regarding the product. Concept testing is followed by the business analysis phase, in which the product idea is evaluated to determine its potential contribution to the firm's sales, costs, and profits. Marketers evaluate how well the product fits with the existing product mix, the strength of market demand for the product, the types of environmental and competitive changes to be expected, and how these changes might affect the product's future sales, costs, and profits.

   Product development is the phase in which the organization discovers the technical feasibility of producing the product and whether or not it can be produced at costs that will result in a reasonable final price. The company creates a prototype and then performs laboratory tests on performance, safety, convenience, and other functional qualities. If the tests indicate that the product merits test marketing, marketers begin to make decisions regarding branding, packaging, labeling, pricing, and promotion.

Test marketing involves a limited introduction of a product in geographic areas chosen to represent the intended market. The goal is to determine the reactions of probable buyers. The last phase of product development is commercialization, the stage in which plans for full-scale manufacturing and marketing are refined and settled, and budgets for the product are prepared. During this phase the organization has expenditures for plant, equipment, personnel, advertising, personal selling, and other types of promotion.

4. **Do small companies that manufacture just a few products need to be concerned about developing and managing products? Why or why not?**

Any manufacturing firm, regardless of size or number of products, must be concerned about developing and managing products. This may be especially critical to a firm with just a few products, because the firm's profits (and sales) are derived entirely from this product. To maintain its current position, the firm must continuously seek ways to improve its product and thus remain competitive; otherwise, customers will turn to substitute products that provide similar benefits. Managing the product involves more than product modification; it also includes designing appropriate promotion, pricing, and distribution strategies that are based on an appraisal of environmental factors such as economic, technological, social, consumer, and legal/political forces.

5. **Why is product development a cross-functional activity within an organization? That is, why must finance, engineering, manufacturing, and other functional areas be involved?**

Long-range strategic planning strengthens the firm's commitment to product development. Such commitment involves various functional areas in the process of commercializing a product idea. To develop the product successfully, a firm typically needs several years and considerable resources (which is a capital budgeting problem). The legal function is essential in obtaining patents and copyrights, clearing brand names, and so on. Engineering needs to develop the product idea into a product that customers want (based on marketing information) and that the firm is capable of producing (production). The financial commitment for developing product prototypes, acquiring appropriate production equipment, testing the product in the market, and launching the product may be substantial; thus, the financial function is necessary to obtain needed capital and maintain the proper cash flows.

6. **What is the major purpose of concept testing, and how is it accomplished?**

Concept testing allows an organization to determine consumers' initial reactions to a product idea before investing considerable resources in research and development. To determine initial attitudes and buying intentions about a product, marketers present a small sample of potential buyers with the product idea, either in written or oral form. Concept tests consist of a brief description of the concept followed by a series of questions on the product's attractiveness, benefits, advantages over competitors, price, and possible improvements. Product development personnel use the test results to identify those product characteristics that potential customers find most valuable.

7. **What are the benefits and disadvantages of test marketing?**

Benefits:

- Marketers can expose a product in a natural environment to gauge its sales performance.

- Marketers can identify perceived weaknesses in the product or other parts of the marketing mix.

- Marketers can experiment with variations in the advertising, price, and packaging in different test markets.

- Marketers can measure the extent of brand awareness, brand switching, and repeat purchases that result in variations in the marketing mix.

Disadvantages:

- Test marketing can be expensive.

- Test marketing can delay new product introduction.

- Competitors may emerge with their own similar product as a result of the new product in a test market.

- Competitors may skew the results of the marketing measurements by offering sales and promotions or increasing the advertising on their own current product line.

- Test markets may yield erroneous results and cause full-fledged introductions of new products that will not be successful.

8. **Why can the process of commercialization take a considerable amount of time?**

    Organizations usually launch a product in stages, beginning in a limited geographic area and gradually expanding to include other areas. Using this process, known as a roll-out, means taking years to market a product on a national scale. For example, a product may first be marketed in only one city, then in the state in which the city is located, then in adjacent states, and eventually in remaining states. At any time during this process, the company may decide to make changes that slow the operation even more, such as packaging, advertising, or price changes. Gradual product introduction is often necessary because it takes time to establish a system of wholesalers and retailers, to develop a distribution network, and to manufacture the product in required quantities.

9. **What is product differentiation, and how can it be achieved?**

    Product differentiation is the process of creating and designing products so that customers perceive them differently from competing products. The issue of customer perception is critically important in differentiating products. Product differentiation can be achieved through the use of product quality, product design and features, and product support services. These are areas where companies can focus their attention to create real differences between their products and other companies' products. In terms of quality, the level and consistency of quality are important. In terms of product design and features, the styling, or physical appearance of the product, or the product features are important. In terms of product support services, customer service is important.

10. **Explain how the term *quality* has been used to differentiate products in the automobile industry in recent years. What are some makes and models of automobiles that come to mind when you hear the terms *high quality* and *poor quality*?**

    We have heard the phrase "Quality is Job 1" in commercials for Ford automobiles and references to "commitment to quality" on Chrysler commercials. While the term "quality" has varied definitions, we usually associate high quality with Mercedes-Benz, Infiniti, Lexus, Cadillac, or Lincoln and low quality with the ill-fated Yugo.

11. **What is product positioning? Under what conditions would head-to-head product positioning be appropriate? When should head-to-head positioning be avoided?**

   Product positioning refers to the decisions and activities intended to create and maintain a certain concept of the firm's product (relative to competitive brands) in customers' minds. Head-to-head product positioning is appropriate when the product's characteristics are at least equal to those of competitive brands, if the product is lower priced, or if the product is higher priced but its performance is superior to its competitors' offerings. Positioning to avoid competition may be better when the product is not significantly better, when the brand has unique characteristics, or when marketers want to keep a new brand from cannibalizing sales of their existing brands.

12. **What types of problems does a weak product cause in a product mix? Describe the most effective approach for avoiding such problems.**

   Weak products reduce an organization's profitability in several ways. First, they drain resources that could be used to modify stronger products or develop new ones. Second, because fewer marginal products are manufactured, per-unit production costs increase. Third, the negative feelings customers may develop toward a weak product may be transferred to other company products, thereby reducing sales. The most effective approach for avoiding such problems is to employ a periodic systematic review in which each product is evaluated to determine its value to the organization's product mix. The review analyzes not only a product's contribution to current sales, but includes projections of future sales, costs, and profits. It considers the merits of changing the marketing strategy to improve the product's performance and provides an organization with the information it needs to determine when to delete a product. Once a decision is made to delete a product, a firm can use a phase-out approach, a run-out approach, or can drop the product immediately.

13. **What type of organization might use a venture team to develop new products? What are the advantages and disadvantages of such a team?**

   The venture team approach is appropriate for new products, especially those designed for markets with which the company is unfamiliar. A venture team offers several advantages. The responsibility for all product development remains with a group that develops the product from inception to commercialization. Usually, the organizational chart is horizontal rather than vertical; this cuts across all formal organizational lines. Finally, all functional areas are involved. Disadvantages of the venture team are that it disrupts the formal organizational system and does not offer complete continuity. After the product is developed, team members may return to their functional areas, or they may join a new or existing division to manage the product.

COMMENTS ON THE CASES

CASE 12.1 CALI COSMETICS POSITIONS PRODUCTS WITH OLIVE OIL

This case provides an opportunity to study how a relatively small international firm has positioned its products, a line of cosmetics with olive oil as a primary ingredient. In the very competitive cosmetics industry, product differentiation is crucial to establishing a competitive position in such a crowded market.

The first question asks whether Oliva beauty products are line extensions, modified products, or new products for the Cali family. Based on the information supplied in the case, the Oliva line would appear to be line extensions or modifications (depending on the specific product) to products marketed at the Cali family's Beauty Farm spa for many years.

Question 2 asks students to describe the positioning of Oliva beauty products. Based on the information supplied in the case, Cali Cosmetics appears to be positioning its beauty products as different from competitors because of Cali's use of olive oil, which the company promotes as having healthy, regenerative, and moisture-balancing attributes. Additionally, the company's promotion of its association with a well-established spa and the family's history further distinguish the products in the minds of consumers, perhaps giving the products a more prestigious image.

The third question asks students to assess Cali Cosmetics' strategy for differentiating its products from those of competitors. Responses may vary, but the question should help students recognize the importance of product differentiation and positioning, particularly in a market as intensely competitive as the cosmetics industry. Cali's efforts to differentiate its products by associating them with a natural and healthy ingredient, as well as with the family's well-established spa, may help the Oliva line stand out in a crowded and competitive marketplace. Even so, with so many new "natural" cosmetics and products associated with spas or well-known celebrities being introduced, Cali Cosmetics will have to work hard to ensure that its products fulfill customers' expectations of the product based on their position and image in order to succeed.

Video Information

Company: Cali Cosmetics

Location: Tape 2/DVD 2, Segment 12

Length: 2:29

Video Overview: This case examines a small Italian firm that markets a line of cosmetics that contain olive oil. The firm's history and products provide an opportunity to study product positioning in the highly competitive cosmetics industry.

MULTIPLE-CHOICE QUESTIONS ABOUT THE VIDEO

1. Cali Cosmetics' use of olive oil as a primary ingredient in its beauty products represents an attempt to _____ its products as natural and healthful.
    a. improve
    b. modify
    c. differentiate
    d. reposition
    e. intensify
2. Cali Cosmetics markets cosmetics based on recipes used in the family's spa known as the
    a. Baronessa's Castle.
    b. Beauty Castle.
    c. Beauty Farm.
    d. Beauty Spa.
    e. Castle Spa.

3.   According to the video, Cali Cosmetics' Olivia line of beauty products can be sold in all of the following *except*

a.   department stores.
b.   discount stores.
c.   florist shops.
d.   grocery stores.
e.   specialty boutiques .

ANSWERS TO MULTIPLE-CHOICE QUESTIONS ABOUT THE VIDEO

1.   c

2.   c

3.   b

CASE 12.2 USING THE 3RS TO DRIVE PRODUCT INNOVATION AT 3M

The purpose of this case is to show how 3M uses a structured process for new product development. The company has a reputation for creating and commercializing innovative products. Students should be familiar with Post-it notes and Scotch-Brite scouring pads, as well as with 3M's adhesive tapes and other products.

In the first question, students are asked why 3M would apply quality improvement techniques to the design of new products. According to the case, 3M believes that quality improvement more closely connects the company with its market because of the focus on the customer's perspective. The company also believes that quality improvement increases the chances for new product success. Finally, by teaching its customers to use quality improvement methods, 3M is building closer relationships with them and demonstrating a strong commitment to their success.

The second question asks about the effect that the 3M Acceleration program is likely to have on each stage of the new product development process. This program is designed to move the most potentially profitable ideas out of the screening stage more quickly. Ideally, these ideas will speed through successive stages in the process (concept testing, business analysis, product development, test marketing, and commercialization). Students may say that the acceleration would become most pronounced after the business analysis has been completed and management can see the profit potential of each idea more clearly. Ask students to consider whether 3M should accelerate certain stages in the process, such as test marketing, and what might happen if a product is rushed through a stage without sufficient time to study and analyze the results.

Question 3 asks students to evaluate 3M's goals of launching twice the number of new products and triple the number of successful products compared with previous years. Are these goals practical and attainable? How might these goals affect the efforts of 3M's Lead User Teams? Students should recognize that these are ambitious goals designed to challenge employees and instill a sense of urgency and purpose. Striving to meet the goals—even if they are not completely attainable—will counteract internal inertia and complacency; it will also motivate 3M employees to work diligently and creatively. With more products in development, the Lead User Teams will be challenged to more closely monitor emerging trends and thoroughly understand what their customer segments need today and tomorrow.

CHAPTER 13

Branding and Packaging

TEACHING RESOURCES QUICK REFERENCE GUIDE

Resource	Location
Purpose and Perspective	IRM, p. 229
Guide for Using Color Transparencies	IRM, p. 230
Lecture Outline	IRM, p. 230
Notes for Class Exercises, Debate Issue, and Chapter Quiz	IRM, p. 238
Class Exercise 1	IRM, p. 241
Class Exercise 2	IRM, p. 242
Debate Issue	IRM, p. 243
Chapter Quiz	IRM, p. 244
Answers to Discussion and Review Questions	IRM, p. 245
Comments on the Cases	IRM, p. 249
Case 13.1	IRM, p. 249
Video	Tape 2/DVD 2, Segment 13
Video Information	IRM, p. 249
Multiple-Choice Questions About the Video	IRM, p. 250
Case 13.2	IRM, p. 251
Transparency Acetates	Transparency package
Examination Questions: Essay	TB, p. 357
Examination Questions: Multiple-Choice	TB, p. 357
Examination Questions: True-False	TB, p. 381
Author-Selected Multiple-Choice Test Items	TB, p. 671
HMClassPrep Presentation Resources	CD-ROM
PowerPoint Slides	Instructor's website

Note: Additional resources are updated periodically and may found on the accompanying student and instructor websites at http://www.prideferrell.com/.

PURPOSE AND PERSPECTIVE

This chapter defines and discusses branding, packaging, and labeling. It begins with a discussion of the value of branding and then discusses brand loyalty, which includes three levels: brand recognition, brand preference, and brand insistence. Brand equity, types of brands (manufacturer, private distributor, and generic), and brand name selection are discussed. We also deal with methods of protecting brands, covering such issues as trademarks and protecting a brand from becoming generic. This section also examines branding policies—individual branding, family branding, and brand extensions. Brand licensing is also discussed. The strategy of co-branding and its advantages and disadvantages are also discussed.

Next, we examine major packaging issues including the functions of packaging, packaging strategies, and various types of packaging. The chapter ends with a discussion of labeling, including legal labeling requirements.

GUIDE FOR USING COLOR TRANSPARENCIES

There are two groups of color transparencies. The transparencies identified by a double number are the same as the figures and tables in the text. The transparencies labeled with a number and a letter are illustrations that do not appear in the text, but they can be used as additional examples of concepts discussed.

Figure 13.1	Major Elements of Brand Equity
Figure 13.2	Consumers' Perceptions of Store and Manufacturers' Brands for Selected Product Groups
Table 13.1	The World's Most Valuable Brands
Table 13.2	Companies That Spend the Most on Packaging
Figure 13A	Chapter 13 Outline
Figure 13B	Key Definitions: Brand, Brand Equity
Figure 13C	Persons Who Try to Stick with Well-Known Brand Names
Figure 13D	Brand Trade Characters Are Sometimes Used to Aid in Creating Favorable Brand Associations Which Help to Build Brand Equity
Figure 13E	Has the Silk Brand Name Helped This Brand Achieve an 80% Market Share?
Figure 13F	Requirements of an Effective Brand Name
Figure 13G	Putting Your Name Brand on a Stadium: What Are the Benefits and the Costs?
Figure 13H	Why Is Morton Salt Using Its Trade Character on the Package and in This Advertisement?
Figure 13I	Why Is This Organization Concerned About Possible Fraudulent Labeling?

LECTURE OUTLINE

(Transparency Figure 13A: Chapter Outline)

I. **Branding**
    A. **Definitions of Branding Terms**
        1. A *brand* is a name, term, symbol, design, or other feature that identifies one seller's good or service as distinct from those of other sellers.

(Transparency Figure 13B)

        2. A *brand name* is that part of a brand that can be spoken, including letters, words, and numbers; a brand name is often a product's only distinguishing characteristic.
        3. A *brand mark* is an element of a brand that cannot be spoken, often a symbol or design.
        4. A *trademark* is a legal designation indicating that the owner has exclusive use of the brand or part of that brand and that others are prohibited by law from using it.
        5. A *trade name* is the full legal name of an organization rather than the name of a specific product.
    B. **Value of Branding**
        1. To Buyers
            a) Brands help buyers identify specific products that they like and do not like, which facilitates the purchase of those items that satisfy individual needs.
            b) A brand helps a buyer evaluate the quality of products, especially when the person lacks the ability to judge a product's characteristics; that is, a brand may symbolize a certain quality level to a purchaser, and the person in turn lets that perception of quality represent the quality of the item.

(Transparency Figure 13E)

      c)   A brand helps reduce a buyer's perceived risk of purchase.

      d)   A brand can give buyers the psychological reward that comes from owning a brand that symbolizes status.

2.   To Sellers

      a)   Sellers' brands identify each firm's products, which makes repeat purchasing easier for consumers.

      b)   To the extent that buyers become loyal to a specific brand, the firm's market share for that product achieves a certain level of stability, which allows the firm to use its resources more efficiently.

      c)   When a firm develops some degree of customer loyalty to a brand, it can maintain a fairly consistent price for the product instead of having to cut the price repeatedly to attract customers.

C.   **Brand Loyalty**

1.   *Brand loyalty* is a customer's favorable attitude toward a specific brand, which affects the likelihood of consistent purchase of this brand when the need arises for a product in that product category; brand loyalty can be categorized into three levels.

(Transparency Figure 13C)

      a)   *Brand recognition* occurs when a customer is aware that a brand exists and views it as an alternative to purchase if his or her brand is unavailable or if the other available brands are unfamiliar to the customer.

      b)   *Brand preference* is a stronger degree of brand loyalty. A customer definitely prefers one brand over competitive offerings and will purchase the brand if available, but will not go out of his or her way to find it.

      c)   *Brand insistence* is the strongest degree of brand loyalty, in which a customer strongly prefers a specific brand, will accept no substitute, and will go to great lengths to acquire it.

2.   Although brand loyalty is a challenge to build, it makes a significant contribution to a sustainable competitive advantage.

3.   Brand loyalty seems to be on the decline.

      a)   This is due in part to marketers' increased reliance on sales, coupons, and other promotions, and in part to the array of similar products from which customers can choose.

      b)   Several recent studies indicate that brand loyalty is declining for all age groups and especially among consumers 50 and over.

D.   **Brand Equity**

(Transparency Figure 13.1)

1.   *Brand equity* is the marketing and financial value associated with a brand's market strength.

(Transparency Figure 13B)

(Transparency Figure 13G)

2.   The elements of brand equity include proprietary brand assets, such as patents and trademarks, as well as brand name awareness, brand loyalty, perceived brand quality, and brand association.

(Transparency Table 13.1)

      a)   Awareness of a brand name leads to familiarity, and familiar brands are more likely to be viewed as more reliable and of more acceptable quality.

       b)   Customers with brand loyalty are less vulnerable to competitors' actions and provide brand visibility and reassurance to potential new customers.

       c)   Perceived brand quality helps to support a premium price, allowing a marketer to avoid severe price competition because a brand name can actually stand for and be used to judge actual quality.

       d)   Marketers associate a particular lifestyle or certain personality with a specific brand to appeal to consumers who can relate to the image.

(Transparency Figure 13D)

3.   Although brand equity is difficult to measure, one company will pay a premium to purchase a brand from another company because it is less risky than developing its own.

(Transparency Figure 13H)

E.   **Types of Brands**

1.   *Manufacturer brands* are initiated by producers and ensure that producers are identified with their products at the point of purchase.

       a)   A manufacturer brand usually requires that a producer get involved with distribution, promotion, and (to some extent) pricing decisions.

       b)   The producer tries to stimulate demand for the product, which tends to encourage intermediaries to make the product available.

2.   *Private distributor brands* (or private brands, store brands, or dealer brands) are initiated and owned by resellers; manufacturers are not identified on the products.

(Transparency Figure 13.2)

       a)   Retailers and wholesalers use private distributor brands to develop more efficient promotion, generate higher gross margins, and change store images.

       b)   Private distributor brands give retailers or wholesalers freedom to purchase products of a specified quality at the lowest cost without disclosing the identity of the manufacturer.

       c)   Traditionally, private brands have appeared in packaging that directly imitates the packaging of competing manufacturers' brands without significant legal ramifications; but the legal risks are increasing for private brands.

       d)   Some private brands are produced by companies that specialize in making only private distributor brands, while other private brands are made by producers of manufacturer brands.

          (1)   Both find it difficult at times to ignore the opportunities that come from producing private distributor brands.

          (2)   If a producer decides not to produce a private brand for a reseller, a competitor probably will.

          (3)   Also, the production of private distributor brands allows the producer to use excess capacity during periods when its own brands are at nonpeak production.

3.   *Generic brands* indicate only a product category and do not include the company name or other identifying terms.

       a)   Generic brands are usually sold at lower prices than are comparable branded items.

(Building Customer Relationships: The Power of Private Distributor Brands)

       b)   Sales of generic brands account for less than half of a percent of all grocery sales.

F. **Selecting a Brand Name**

(Transparency Figure 13F)

1. Marketers should consider a number of factors when selecting a brand name.
    a) The name should be easy for customers to say, spell, and recall.
    b) If possible, the brand name should suggest the product's uses and special characteristics in a positive way and avoid negative or offensive references.
    c) If a marketer intends to use a brand for a product line, the brand must be designed to be compatible with all products in the line.
    d) A brand should be designed so that it can be used and recognized in all types of media.
    e) Brand names can be created from single or multiple words, initials, numbers, or combinations of these.
    f) To avoid terms that have negative connotations, marketers sometimes use fabricated words that have no meaning.
2. Brand names can be created internally by the organization, by outside consultants, or by hiring a company specializing in brand name development.
3. Even though branding considerations apply to both goods and services, there are some special dimensions of service branding.
    a) The brand name of a service is usually the same as the company name.
    b) Service brands must be flexible enough to encompass a variety of current services as well as new ones that a company might offer in the future.
    c) Service marketers often use a symbol along with a brand name to make the brand distinctive and to convey an image.

G. **Protecting a Brand**

1. Marketers should take steps to protect their exclusive rights to a brand.
    a) Marketers should design a brand name that they can protect easily through registration; this protects trademarks for ten years and allows them to be renewed indefinitely.
    b) The company should be certain that the selected brand is unlikely to be considered as infringement on any brand already registered with the U.S. Patent and Trademark Office.
2. Using some of the following methods, a marketer must guard against letting a brand name become a generic term used to refer to a general product category because generic terms cannot be protected as exclusive brand names.
    a) Firms can spell the name with a capital letter.
    b) They can use the name as an adjective to modify the name of the general product class.
    c) Including the word "brand" just after the name is helpful.
    d) Firms can indicate that the brand is trademarked with the symbol ®.
3. In 1988, the Trademark Law Revision Act was enacted to increase the value of the federal registration system relative to foreign competitors and to protect consumers from counterfeiting, confusion, and deception.
4. In many foreign countries brand registration is not possible. The first firm to use a brand in such a country automatically has the rights to it.
5. Brand counterfeiting is harmful because the usually inferior counterfeit product undermines consumers' confidence in their loyalty to the brand and reduces the brand owners' revenues from marketing their legitimate products.

H.   **Branding Policies**
1.   In establishing branding policies, the firm must decide whether to brand its products at all.
   a)   When an organization's product is homogeneous and similar to competitors' products, it may be difficult to brand.
   b)   Raw materials are hard to brand because of the homogeneity of these products and their physical characteristics.
2.   If a firm chooses to brand its products, it may opt for one or more branding policies.
   a)   *Individual branding* is a policy of naming each product differently.
      (1)   A major advantage of individual branding is that when an organization introduces a poor product, the negative images associated with it do not contaminate the company's other products.
      (2)   Individual branding policies may facilitate the use of market segmentation when a firm wishes to enter many segments of the same market; separate, unrelated names can be used with each brand aimed at a specific segment.
   b)   In *family branding*, all of the firm's products are branded with the same name or at least part of the name; family branding is beneficial because the promotion of one item with the family brand promotes the firm's other products.
   c)   In *brand-extension branding*, a firm uses one of its existing brand names as part of a brand for an improved or new product that is usually in the same product category as the existing brand.
3.   Marketers share a common concern that if a brand is extended too many times or extended too far away from its original product category, the brand can be significantly weakened.
4.   Branding policy is influenced by the number of the firm's products, the characteristics of its target markets, the competing products available, and the firm's resources.

I.   **Co-Branding**
   Co-branding is the use of two or more brands on one product; marketers employ co-branding to capitalize on the brand equity of multiple brands.

1.   The two brands can be owned by the same company.
2.   Co-branding capitalizes on the trust and confidence customers have in the brands involved.
3.   The brands should not lose their identities, and it should be clear to customers which brand is the main brand.
4.   When a co-branded product is unsuccessful, both brands are implicated in the product failure.
5.   To gain customer acceptance, the brands involved must represent a complementary fit in the minds of buyers.
6.   Co-branding can help an organization differentiate its products from those of its competitors.
7.   Co-branding can also take advantage of the distribution capabilities of co-branding partners.

J.   **Brand Licensing**
   Brand licensing is an agreement whereby a company permits another organization to use its brand on other products for a licensing fee.

1.   A growing number of companies are letting approved manufacturers use their trademarks on other products for a licensing fee.
2.   Advantages of licensing include extra revenue, low cost, free publicity, new images, and trademark protection.

3. Disadvantages of licensing include lack of manufacturing control and too many unrelated products bearing the same name.

II. Packaging

Packaging involves the development of a container and a graphic design for a product.

A. Packaging Functions

1. Packaging protects the product or maintains its functional form by reducing damage that could affect its usefulness and increase costs.
2. The size or shape of a package may relate to the product's storage, convenience of use, or replacement rate.
3. Packaging promotes a product by communicating its features, uses, benefits, and image.

B. Major Packaging Considerations

1. Marketers should conduct research to determine exactly how much customers are willing to pay for package designs.
2. Developing tamper-resistant packaging is very important.
3. Marketers should consider how much consistency among their package designs is desirable.
   a) If a firm's products are unrelated or aimed at vastly different target markets, no consistency may be the best policy.
   b) With *family packaging*, a firm designs similar packaging for all its products or includes one major design element in every package; sometimes this approach is used only for lines of products.
4. Marketers must consider the package's promotional role.
   a) The package can be used to attract customers' attention and encourage them to examine the product.
   b) Through verbal and nonverbal symbols, the package can inform potential buyers about the product's content, features, uses, advantages, and hazards.
   c) A firm can create desirable images and associations by using certain colors, designs, shapes, and textures in packages.
   d) A package may perform a promotional function when it is designed to be safer or more convenient to use if such characteristics stimulate demand.
   e) To develop a package that has definite promotional value, a designer must consider size, shape, texture, color, and graphics.
      (1) Beyond the obvious minimal limitation that the package must be large enough to hold the product, a package can be designed to appear taller or shorter.
      (2) The shape of the package can help communicate a particular message.
      (3) Color on packages is often used to attract attention; people associate certain feelings and connotations with specific colors.
5. Marketers must consider whether to develop packages that are environmentally responsible. Marketers must carefully balance society's desires to preserve the environment against consumers' desires for convenience.

(Tech Know: Technology Brings Eye Catching Colors to Packaging)

C. Packaging and Marketing Strategy

(Transparency Table 13.2)

1. Packaging can be a major component of a marketing strategy.
   a) A new cap or closure, a better box or wrapper, or a more convenient container size may give a firm a competitive advantage.

b) The right type of package for a new product can help it gain market recognition very quickly.

c) Marketers should view packaging as a major strategic tool for convenience products.

2. **Altering the Package**

Marketers alter packaging for a number of reasons.

a) A package may be redesigned because new product features need to be highlighted.

b) Packages may be altered to make the product safer or more convenient to use.

c) Marketers may change a package because new packaging materials become available.

d) Marketers may alter a package to reposition an existing product.

3. **Secondary-Use Packaging**

A secondary-use package is one that can be reused for purposes other than its initial use.

a) Secondary-use packages can be viewed by customers as adding value to products.

b) Secondary-use packaging can be used to stimulate unit sales.

4. **Category-Consistent Packaging**

Category-consistent packaging is used to package products in line with the packaging practices associated with a particular product category.

5. **Innovative Packaging**

Innovative packaging such as a unique cap, design, applicator, or other feature will sometimes be used by marketers to make the product completely distinctive.

a) Using innovative packaging can be effective if the innovation makes the product safer or easier to use.

b) Unique packages sometimes make brands stand out next to their competitors.

c) Using innovative packaging usually requires a considerable amount of resources.

6. **Multiple Packaging**

Marketers sometimes package products in twin packs, tri-packs, six-packs, or other forms of multiple packaging.

a) Multiple packaging is likely to increase demand because it increases the amount of the product available at the point of consumption.

b) Multiple packaging is not appropriate for infrequently used products.

c) Multiple packaging can make products easier to handle and store, and facilitate special price offers.

d) Multiple packaging may increase consumer acceptance of a product by encouraging buyers to try it several times.

7. **Handling-Improved Packaging**

Packaging may be changed to make it easier to handle in the distribution channel.

a) Changes made might involve the outer carton, special bundling, shrinkwrapping, or palletizing.

b) Sometimes the shape of a package may be changed to facilitate handling.

c) Outer containers are sometimes changed so that they will more easily proceed through automated warehousing systems.

D. **Criticisms of Packaging**

1. Some packages suffer from functional problems; they do not work well or are inconvenient.

2. Certain types of packages have a questionable impact on the environment.

3.   Much packaging criticism focuses on safety problems such as packages with sharp edges or those using aerosol propellants.

4.   Sometimes packages are perceived as deceptive.

    a)   Shapes, colors, or designs sometimes make a product appear larger than it actually is.

    b)   Inconsistent use of size designations can lead to customer confusion.

    c)   Sometimes the cost of the package is higher than the cost of the product itself.

III. **Labeling**

    A.   *Labeling* involves providing identifying, promotional, legal, or other information on package labels.

    1.   Labels carry varying amounts of information.

    2.   A label can be part of the package itself or a separate feature attached to the package.

    3.   The type of information a label contains may include several things:

    a)   The brand name and mark

    b)   The registered trademark symbol

    c)   Package size and content

    d)   Product features

    e)   Nutritional information

    f)   Type and style of product

    g)   Number of servings

    h)   Care instructions

    i)   Directions for use

    j)   Safety precautions

    k)   The name and address of the manufacturer

    l)   Expiration dates

    m)   Seals of approval

    n)   Other facts

    4.   For many products, the label includes a *universal product code (UPC)*, which is a series of electronically readable lines identifying a product and providing inventory and pricing information.

    5.   Labels can facilitate the identification of a product by displaying the brand name in combination with a unique graphic design.

    6.   By drawing attention to products and their benefits, labels can strengthen an organization's promotional efforts by containing these items:

    a)   The offer of a discount

    b)   Larger package size at the same price

    c)   Information about a new or improved product feature

    7.   Federal laws and regulations specify information that must be included on labels of certain products.

    a)   Garments must be labeled with the name of the manufacturer, country of manufacture, fabric content, and cleaning instructions.

    b)   Nonedible items like shampoo and detergent must include both safety precautions and directions for use.

    8.   The 1966 Fair Packaging and Labeling Act focuses on mandatory labeling requirements, voluntary adoption of packaging standards by firms within industries, and the provision of power to the Federal Trade Commission and the Food and Drug Administration to establish and enforce packaging regulations.

(Transparency Figure 13I)

9.   The Nutrition Labeling Act of 1990 requires the FDA to review food labeling and packaging, focusing on nutrition content, label format, ingredient labeling, food descriptions, and health messages, regulating much of the labeling on more than 250,000 products.
    a)   Any food product for which a nutritional claim is made must have nutrition labeling.
    b)   Information on food labels must include:
        (1)   Number of servings per container
        (2)   Serving size
        (3)   Number of calories per serving
        (4)   Number of calories derived from fat
        (5)   Number of carbohydrates
        (6)   Amounts of specific nutrients, such as vitamins

B.   The use of new technology in the production and processing of food has led to additional food labeling issues. The FDA now requires specific logos for irradiated food products and has issued voluntary guidelines pertaining to biotech ingredients.

C.   Despite legislation to make labels as accurate and informative as possible, questionable labeling practices persist. For example, the FDA amended its regulations to forbid producers of vegetable oil from making "no cholesterol" claims on their labels.

D.   Another area of concern is "green labeling."
    1.   Consumers who are committed to making environmentally responsible purchasing decisions are sometimes fooled by labels.
    2.   Several manufacturers have been accused of "greenwashing" customers, using misleading claims to sell products by playing on customers' concern for the environment.

E.   Of concern to many manufacturers are the Federal Trade Commission's guidelines regarding "Made in U.S.A." labels.
    1.   The FTC requires that all, or virtually all, of a product's components be made in the United States if the label says "Made in U.S.A."
    2.   The FTC considered changing the standard to "substantially all," but rejected the idea.

NOTES FOR CLASS EXERCISES, DEBATE ISSUE, AND CHAPTER QUIZ

On the following pages, you will find two class exercises, a debate issue, and a chapter quiz. These are formatted in large-size type so that you can use them as class handouts or for making transparencies. Below are the authors' comments on the class exercises, the debate topic for this chapter, and the answers to the chapter quiz.

Comments on Class Exercise 1

The purpose of this exercise is to reinforce an understanding of brand components and policies and the functions of packaging.

1.   Students often get these components mixed up, particularly the first two. Coke cans offer a good chance to explain the difference between the brand name Coca-Cola and the script design that makes up the brand mark. The students will usually note the trademark registration ®. The trade name—the official name of the company—is marked on the back of the can. The fact that "Coke" is referred to generically may also bring up the point that firms spend a great deal of resources to retain brand name rights.

2. Replaceable caps (on 16-oz. drinks) help preserve taste; airtight containers and expiration dates help ensure freshness. Package sizes are generally produced in amounts that meet individual consumer needs (e.g., 2-oz. candy bars; 12-oz. drinks, five sticks of gum) for appropriate prices. A production orientation might only produce one size, for instance. Most students are so accustomed to the packages of these items that they rarely recognize the role of communication. Effective packaging rein-forces successful promotional campaigns by reminding consumers of the benefits and image produced by advertisements at the point of purchase.

3. Coca-Cola products are good examples of individual and brand-extension branding, although students may be unaware that besides Coke, many bottlers also produce other soft drinks that do not carry the Coke brand name. Examples are Fresca and Barq's Root Beer. Some candy bars may provide examples of family branding (Nestlé or Hershey's).

4. Usually, students will violate one of these guidelines, which points to why some consulting firms now specialize in developing new company or brand names.

Comments on Class Exercise 2

The purpose of this exercise is to have students consider the importance of the major requirements of an effective brand name.

1. *Easy to say, spell, and recall:*

    Tide detergent

    Biz detergent

    Zee paper towels

    Tone soap

    Jif peanut butter

    Pert shampoo

2. *Communicates major product benefits:*

    No-Yolks pasta

    Clean & Clear (skin care products)

    Dustbuster (hand-held vacuum)

    Quick-Lash mascara

    Reach toothbrush

    Carpet-Fresh (rug and room deodorizer)

3. *Suggests product uses or special features:*

    Glass Works (glass cleaner)

    Mop & Glo (floor cleaner)

    Soft Scrub (cleanser)

4.   *Distinctive enough to set it apart from competitors:*

Orville Redenbacher (popcorn)

Reebok (athletic shoes)

Häagen-Dazs (ice cream)

Molly McButter (butter substitute)

Yoplait (yogurt)

DEBATE ISSUE

Should fast-food restaurants use environmentally responsible packaging even when such packaging is less effective in preserving product quality?

CHAPTER QUIZ

Answers to Chapter Quiz 1. e; 2. d; 3. c; 4. d.

Class Exercise 1

1. Look at the nearest snack food wrapper or soft drink container and identify the

   a. brand name.

   b. brand mark.

   c. trademark.

   d. trade name.

2. Using the wrapper or container, explain how packaging performs three functions: protection, convenience, and communication.

3. Is the manufacturer of the product using individual, family, or brand-extension branding?

4. You work for a firm that is introducing a new chocolate candy bar that contains an extra amount of caffeine. Develop a brand name that

   a. is easy for customers to say, spell, and recall.

   b. positively suggests uses and special characteristics.

   c. indicates major product benefits.

   d. can be protected easily through registration.

Class Exercise 2

IN DEVELOPING A BRAND NAME, IT IS IMPORTANT TO CONSIDER THE REQUIRE-MENTS OF AN EFFECTIVE CHOICE. FOR EACH OF THE FOLLOWING REQUIREMENTS, GIVE SEVERAL EXAMPLES OF BRAND NAMES THAT SATISFY THAT REQUIREMENT.

1. **Easy to say, spell, and recall**

2. **Communicates major product benefits**

3. **Suggests product uses or special features**

4. **Distinctive enough to set the product apart from competing brands**

Debate Issue

SHOULD FAST-FOOD RESTAURANTS USE ENVIRONMENTALLY RESPONSIBLE PACKAGING EVEN WHEN SUCH PACKAGING IS LESS EFFECTIVE IN PRESERVING PRODUCT QUALITY?

YES

- Traditionally, fast-food marketers have used too much packaging, which creates unnecessary amounts of garbage going into landfills.

- Traditionally, the type of materials used were not biodegradable.

- Fast-food marketers must focus on the long-term impact on the environment rather than on product packaging that provides the greatest amount of customer satisfaction when the product is consumed.

NO

- A fast-food marketer should use a package that allows the customer to receive the highest-quality food product at the point of purchase.

- Proper disposal of a package, after the customer no longer needs it, is not the responsibility of the fast-food organization.

- Most fast-food customers prefer to have the highest-quality food product, even if the package is not environmentally responsible.

Chapter Quiz

1. Compared to creating and developing a brand from scratch, a firm sometimes buys a brand from another company at a premium price because outright purchase is
   a. more challenging strategically.
   b. less time consuming.
   c. less risky.
   d. less expensive.
   e. less expensive and less risky.

2. Which of the following laws was enacted by Congress in 1988 to strengthen trademark protection?
   a. Brand Protection Act
   b. Lanham Act
   c. Trademark Infringement Act
   d. Trademark Law Revision Act
   e. U.S. Patent and Trademark Act

3. To use co-branding effectively, which one of the following is probably *least* important?
   a. The brands involved should represent a complementary fit in a customer's mind.
   b. The brands that are teamed together should not lose their individual identities.
   c. The brands involved should be owned by two or more organizations.
   d. To avoid confusion on the part of customers, co-branding should be done in a way so that it is obvious which brand is the main brand or key brand.
   e. The co-branded product should be able to benefit from the distribution system of both brands involved.

4. To promote an overall company image, packages of Pillsbury cake and cookie mixes have similar designs and colors. This approach is known as
   a. family branding.
   b. brand managing.
   c. line consistency.
   d. family packaging.
   e. product grouping.

ANSWERS TO DISCUSSION AND REVIEW QUESTIONS

1. **What is the difference between a brand and a brand name? Compare and contrast the terms *brand mark* and *trademark*.**

   A brand is a name, term, symbol, design, or a combination of these that identifies a seller's products and differentiates them from competitors' products. A brand name is that part of a brand that can be spoken, including letters, words, and numbers.

   A brand mark is the element of a brand that cannot be spoken, such as a symbol or design. A trademark is a legal designation indicating that the owner has exclusive use of a brand or part of a brand and that others are prohibited by law from using it.

2. **How does branding benefit consumers and marketers?**

   Brands aid buyers by helping them identify specific products that they like and do not like, which in turn facilitates the purchase of items that satisfy individual needs. A brand also helps a buyer evaluate the quality of products, especially when the person lacks the ability to judge a product's characteristics. Brands identify a seller's products, which facilitates repeat purchases by consumers. To the extent that buyers become loyal to a specific brand, the firm's market share for that product achieves a certain level of stability. A stable market share places a firm in a position to use its resources more efficiently. When a firm develops some degree of customer loyalty for a brand, it can charge a premium price for the product. Branding helps an organization introduce a new product that carries the name of one or more of its existing products. Branding facilitates promotional efforts because each branded product indirectly promotes all the firm's other products that are similarly branded.

3. **What are the three major degrees of brand loyalty?**

   Brand loyalty is the customer's favorable attitude toward a specific brand. The three levels of brand loyalty are brand recognition, brand preference, and brand insistence. Brand recognition, the mildest form of brand loyalty, exists when a customer is aware that the brand exists and views it as an alternative to purchase. Brand preference, a stronger degree of brand loyalty, exists when a customer definitely prefers one brand over competitive offerings; however, if the brand is not available, the customer will accept a substitute. Brand insistence, the strongest degree of brand loyalty, exists when a customer not only strongly prefers a specific brand, but will not accept a substitute.

4. **What is brand equity? Identify and explain the major elements of brand equity.**

   Brand equity is the marketing and financial value associated with a brand's strength in the market. Four major elements underlie brand equity: brand name awareness, brand loyalty, perceived brand quality, and brand associations. Being aware of a brand leads to brand familiarity, resulting in increased levels of comfortableness with the brand. Customers are more likely to choose familiar brands over unfamiliar ones. Brand loyalty allows an organization to keep its existing customers, and loyal customers reassure potential new ones. Customers associate a certain level of perceived overall quality with a brand. A brand name can even substitute for actual judgment of quality when customers are themselves unable to make quality judgments about products and rely on the brand as an indicator of quality. The final component of brand equity is the set of associations linked to a brand. Positive associations contribute significantly to a brand's equity.

5. **Compare and contrast manufacturer brands, private distributor brands, and generic brands.**

   Manufacturer brands are initiated by producers and ensure that producers are identified with their products at the point of sale. These brands usually require a producer to become involved in distribution, promotion and, to some extent, pricing decisions. Manufacturer brands include Green Giant, Apple Computer, and Levi's jeans.

   Private distributor brands are initiated and owned by resellers or retailers and do not identify the manufacturer or producer. Private brands are used to develop more efficient promotion, generate higher gross margins, and improve store images. These brands include IGA (Independent Grocers' Alliance), Sears' Craftsman, and Wal-Mart's "Sam's Choice" beverages and snacks.

   A generic brand indicates only the category of the product (such as aluminum foil, tissue, or peanut butter) and does not include the company name or manufacturer. Generic brands are usually sold at lower prices than are comparable brand names.

6. **Identify the factors a marketer should consider in selecting a brand name.**

   When selecting a brand, marketers must consider a number of factors. The brand name should be easy to say, spell, and remember. To avoid consumer confusion, brands should be compatible with those of other products in the product line. Choosing a name that suggests the product's uses and special characteristics as well as indicating the product's major benefits is important. Marketers try to select a brand that is distinctive enough to set it apart from competitors but avoids negative or offensive implications. Finally, marketers strive to choose a brand that can be used and recognized in all types of media. Because service brands are usually the same as the company name, service marketers do not always have the flexibility to choose a brand that meets all of the above criteria.

7. **The brand name Xerox is sometimes used generically to refer to photocopying, and Kleenex is used to refer to tissues. How can the manufacturers protect their brand names, and why would they want to?**

   A generic term is used to refer to a general product category. Generic terms cannot be protected as exclusive brand names. To keep a brand name from becoming a generic term, the firm should spell it with a capital letter and use it as an adjective to modify the name of the general product class. An organization can deal with this problem directly by advertising that its brand is a trademark and should not be used generically. The firm can also indicate that the brand is trademarked by placing the symbol ® next to the brand name.

   If these brand names are not protected by their owners, then companies will lose their rights to be the sole users of these names. The terms can then be used generically, as has been the case for "aspirin" and "elevator."

8. **What is co-branding? What major issues should be considered when using co-branding?**

   Co-branding is the use of two or more brands on one product. Marketers employ co-branding to capitalize on the brand equity of multiple brands. The brands used for co-branding can be owned by the same company or by different companies. Some issues to consider when using co-branding are that the brands not lose their identities, and it should be clear to customers which brand is the main brand. It is important for marketers to understand that when a co-branded product is unsuccessful, both brands are implicated in the product failure. To gain customer acceptance, the brands involved must represent a complementary fit in the minds of buyers. Co-branding can help an organization differentiate its products from those of its competitors. By using the product development skills of a co-branding partner, an organization can create a distinctive product. Co-branding can also take advantage of the distribution capabilities of co-branding partners.

9. **What are the major advantages and disadvantages of brand licensing?**

   Brand licensing involves an agreement whereby a company allows approved manufacturers to use its trademark on other products for a licensing fee.

   The advantages of licensing include

   - Extra revenue earned from the licensing fee

   - Low-cost or free publicity

   - New images that potentially give new life to a brand

   - Trademark protection

   Disadvantages of licensing may be

   - Lack of manufacturing control that could hurt the company's reputation; that is, if inferior products bear a company's brand, consumers may extend negative opinions to the firm's own products as well.

   - Consumers may be confused by too many unrelated products carrying the same name.

   - Agreements may fail because of poor timing, inappropriate distribution channels, or mismatching product and name.

10. **Describe the functions a package can perform. Which function is most important? Why?**

    A package can perform several functions, including protection, economy, convenience, and promotion. First, packaging materials are needed to protect the product or to maintain it in functional form. The package should effectively reduce damage that could affect the product's usefulness and increase costs (economy). Second, consumers may be concerned with convenience. Third, packaging can promote a product by communicating its features, uses, benefits, and image.

11. **What are the main factors a marketer should consider when developing a package?**

    When making packaging decisions, marketers must take into account a variety of issues. Cost is a critical consideration when developing a package. Some available processes and designs are very expensive, so before making packaging decisions, marketers engage in research to determine how much customers are willing to pay for packages. Because packaging must comply with the Food and Drug Administration's packaging regulations, marketers make sure that packages are tamper resistant. When new technology is developed or new legislation is passed, marketers modify packages to protect consumers and comply with the law. Another consideration is how much consistency of packaging there should be among the various products an organization markets. If products are aimed at different target markets, marketers may opt for no consistency, but if the desire is to promote an overall company image, a firm may package all its products in a similar way, an approach known as family packaging. A package's promotional role is an important consideration because packages inform potential buyers about the product's content, features, uses, advantages, and hazards along with creating a product image. Marketers try to choose features that enhance a package's promotional value. The size and shape of a package must lend itself to easy handling by wholesalers and retailers, or they may refuse to carry the product. Finally, marketers must consider the issue of environmentally responsible packaging, attempting to balance concern for the environment with consumers' preference for convenience.

12. **In what ways can packaging be used as a strategic tool?**

Because a package has the potential for giving a product a competitive edge, marketers often regard packaging as an important strategic tool. Altering a package can make a product more convenient or safer, promote a new feature, or assist product repositioning. A secondary-use package, one that can be reused for purposes other than its initial use, can stimulate sales. Because certain product categories are characterized by recognizable types of packaging, an organization often uses these traditional shapes and colors when introducing a brand in one of those categories to facilitate easy recognition by potential buyers. Sometimes an innovative package design attracts consumers by distinguishing a brand from its competitors, resulting in increased sales. For certain types of products, multiple packaging is used to increase demand. This strategy is based on the belief that if consumers have more of a product at home, they will use more and want more. In addition, multiple packs can make products easier to handle and simplify special price offers. Handling-improved packaging facilitates distribution and shelving, making a product more attractive to those who handle and sell it.

13. **What are the major criticisms of packaging?**

Several aspects of packaging evoke criticism. The simplest criticism is that some packages just don't work well. Environmental irresponsibility, such as lack of biodegradability, is a growing packaging criticism. Some critics focus on safety issues, such as containers with sharp edges or aerosol containers that contain health hazards. Finally, packaging is sometimes criticized as being deceptive. For example, certain shapes or colors may make a product appear larger than it actually is.

14. **What are the major functions of labeling?**

Marketers use labeling in a variety of ways. By highlighting the brand with an eye-catching graphic design, the label can facilitate product identification. Labels serve a descriptive function, specifying the product's source, contents, major features, use, and care. For certain products, labels can be strictly informative, furnishing specific product grade, nutritional content, and number of servings. Through the use of attention-getting graphics, labels also serve a valuable promotional function.

15. **In what ways do regulations and legislation affect labeling?**

New labeling requirements, either for the food industry in nutritional labeling, or for other products to warn of hazardous use, may require a company to redesign its packaging. This could mean additional costs, which must be considered in establishing the price to the consumer. An entire industry may be impacted by new governmental regulations requiring labeling where it has never occurred before. The new labeling may provide opportunities for different producers and different products to engage in competitive marketing. Also, labeling regulations may change because of new guidelines that are challenged, causing a compromise in labeling. For example, the FTC ordered New Balance to stop making the "Made in U.S.A." claim on its athletic shoe labels because some components (rubber soles) are made in China.

COMMENTS ON THE CASES

CASE 13.1 PLUMPJACK WINERY POURS OUT CORK CONTROVERSY

In this case, students learn how a unique approach to packaging is providing a distinctive marketing angle for a small California winery. Since students may not know the PlumpJack brand, and they may be unaware of the controversy over cork, you may want to request that students conduct some background research before discussing the case.

The first question asks whether PlumpJack's screw-top bottles can be considered category-consistent packaging. No, these bottles are not consistent with closure methods used by most wineries that market high-end wine products. Instead, PlumpJack is using its unusual screw tops to help its wines stand out among competitors.

The second question asks whether U.S. customers are likely to view PlumpJack wines as inexpensive, lower-quality wines, even though the actual quality of PlumpJack wines may be improved through the use of screw-top caps. PlumpJack is using a number of marketing elements to avoid this misperception and reinforce the high-quality image it wants to project. For example, the price of wine sold in a screw-top bottle is slightly higher than the price of same wine sold in a corked bottle. As another example, PlumpJack is using publicity to educate customers about the benefits of screw-top caps. It is also relying on consumer learning to shape attitudes and behaviors by selling wine in a two-pack so consumers can compare the taste of the wine in the screw-top bottle with the taste of the wine in the traditional bottle.

In the third question, students are asked whether they would recommend that PlumpJack sell its screw-top wines singly instead of in a twin-pack with corked wines. Students who support continuing the twin-pack approach may stress the ability to have buyers taste and compare the wine from each bottle. They may also point to the attention that this unusual packaging arrangement is attractive in the wine world. Students who support selling the bottles individually may say that the price of a two-pack could detract from higher sales. They may also say that consumers who are accustomed to buying wine in traditional corked bottles should be able to purchase the wine packaged that way, rather than being forced to also buy the wine in a screw-top bottle.

The fourth question asks students to suggest how PlumpJack could use labeling to promote its innovative packaging. One possibility is to use labeling to include educational information explaining the benefits of screw tops. Another is to add a hang-tag calling attention to the screw top that compares its benefits to those of cork closures. A third possibility is to use a special, brightly-colored sticker or even an entirely different label to make the screw-top wine stand out on store shelves. Students likely will offer a variety of other ideas.

Video Information

Company:	PlumpJack Winery
Location:	Tape 2/DVD 2, Segment 13
Length:	2:20

Video Overview: PlumpJack Winery has taken the unusual step of packaging its luxury wine in a screw-top bottle. This type of bottle is typically associated with lower-quality wines in the United States, but PlumpJack's owners say that cork closures are outdated. Screw-top bottles eliminate the musty, mildewy taste that some wine drinkers notice when they buy a cork-top bottle, and they also avoid dangerous chemicals that may be in the cork. In addition, increasing the number of screw-top bottles will help save the existing supply of cork. Finally, winery officials note that screw-top closings enable customers to conveniently close and store unused wine without the fuss of trying to force a cork back into the bottle.

MULTIPLE-CHOICE QUESTIONS ABOUT THE VIDEO

1. Which of the following reasons does PlumpJack Winery *not* use for justifying the replacement of corks with screw tops?
   a. To avoid the musky, mildewy taste that corks sometimes impart to wine
   b. To reduce the expense of importing cork
   c. To save the world's cork supply
   d. To allow consumers to easily close and store unfinished bottles of wine
   e. To avoid dangerous chemicals that may taint cork

2. According to the video, bad cork may affect up to _____ of all wine.
   a. 40 percent
   b. 30 percent
   c. 20 percent
   d. 10 percent
   e. 7 percent

3. The Internet is influencing wine packaging because
   a. shipping wine to buyers by air can compromise the cork tops.
   b. cork can be shipped more quickly and cheaply from distant sources.
   c. screw tops can be shipped more quickly and cheaply from distant sources.
   d. bottles can be shipped more quickly and cheaply from distant sources.
   e. shipping cork to producers by air can compromise cork quality.

4. PlumpJack says its new screw-top bottles are
   a. a permanent change to the winery's packaging and marketing efforts.
   b. temporary until the world's cork supply is replenished.
   c. an experiment on the advice of scientists and winemakers.
   d. designed to allow resellers to transport wine more easily.
   e. designed to enhance the flavor of wines stored for short time periods.

ANSWERS TO MULTIPLE-CHOICE QUESTIONS ABOUT THE VIDEO

1. b

2. e

3. a

4. c

CASE 13.2 THE HARLEY DAVIDSON BRAND ROARS INTO ITS SECOND CENTURY

The purpose of this case is to show how product quality and brand image can affect a company's long-term success. When Harley-Davidson tried to expand too quickly, quality suffered and sales dropped. Once the company improved quality and focused on encouraging brand insistence, it was able to boost brand equity.

The first question asks what Harley-Davidson's employees might do to measure brand equity as they mingle with customers at motorcycle rallies. Students' answers will vary, although all are likely to realize that determining the extent of brand awareness among motorcycle buyers is the most basic component of brand equity. Students may suggest that company employees ask Harley owners and non-owners alike about their perceptions of the brand's quality and their reasons for these perceptions. Employees can also consider brand perceptions in the context of customers' and non-customers' lifestyle elements (as evidenced by personal appearance, motorcycle customization, interests, and so forth). This question helps students understand the difficulty of precisely gauging the value of a particular brand.

The second question asks students whether Harley-Davidson should continue family branding or move to individual branding for new models of motorcycles. Most students will argue that family branding has been successful and, given its strong brand equity, Harley-Davidson should continue as the family brand. Some students may argue that putting individual brands on new motorcycle models could help the company appeal to younger customers or customers in other segments who currently do not have an affinity for Harley-Davidson. What are the advantages and disadvantages of using individual brands to insulate the company from possible product failures or the consequences of targeting new customers who are unlike current customers? Students are likely to have strong opinions on this question, making for lively classroom discussion.

In question 3, students consider the questions that Harley-Davidson should ask of a company that wants to license its brand for items of clothing. The purpose of this question is to help students think through the potential problems that licensing can cause for a successful brand. For example, Harley-Davidson would want to ask questions related to quality, to ensure that both manufacturing and marketing are handled with care and in a way that is consistent with the brand's image. The company would also want to ask about specific apparel items on which the brand would appear, to ensure that the brand is not used inappropriately. Students are likely to suggest additional questions, as well.

CHAPTER 14

Services Marketing

TEACHING RESOURCES QUICK REFERENCE GUIDE

Resource	Location
Purpose and Perspective	IRM, p. 253
Guide for Using Color Transparencies	IRM, p. 254
Lecture Outline	IRM, p. 254
Notes for Class Exercises, Debate Issue, and Chapter Quiz	IRM, p. 260
Class Exercise 1	IRM, p. 262
Class Exercise 2	IRM, p. 263
Debate Issue	IRM, p. 264
Chapter Quiz	IRM, p. 265
Answers to Discussion and Review Questions	IRM, p. 266
Comments on the Cases	IRM, p. 269
Case 14.1	IRM, p. 269
Video	Tape 2/DVD 2, Segment 14
Video Information	IRM, p. 269
Multiple-Choice Questions About the Video	IRM, p. 270
Case 14.2	IRM, p. 270
Transparency Acetates	Transparency package
Examination Questions: Essay	TB, p. 387
Examination Questions: Multiple-Choice	TB, p. 387
Examination Questions: True-False	TB, p. 410
Author-Selected Multiple-Choice Test Items	TB, p. 671
HMClassPrep Presentation Resources	CD-ROM
PowerPoint Slides	Instructor's website

Note: Additional resources are updated periodically and may found on the accompanying student and instructor websites at http://www.prideferrell.com/.

PURPOSE AND PERSPECTIVE

We begin with a discussion of the nature of services, focusing on the growing importance of service industries in our economy. We address the unique characteristics of services—intangibility, inseparability of production and consumption, perishability, heterogeneity, client-based relationships, and customer contact. We next present issues associated with developing marketing mixes for services. Then we focus on service quality, addressing customer evaluation of service quality and the four factors affecting service quality: customer expectations, quality specifications, employee performance, and management of service expectations. Finally, we define nonprofit marketing and examine the development and control of nonprofit marketing strategies.

GUIDE FOR USING COLOR TRANSPARENCIES

There are two groups of color transparencies. The transparencies identified by a double number are the same as the figures in the text. The transparencies labeled with a number and a letter are illustrations that do not appear in the text, but they can be used as additional examples of concepts discussed.

Figure 14.1	The Tangibility Continuum
Figure 14.2	Service Quality Model
Figure 14A	Chapter 14 Outline
Figure 14B	Unique Service Characteristics
Figure 14C	Categories of Services
Figure 14D	Key Definitions: Search Qualities, Experience Qualities, Credence Qualities
Figure 14E	Customers' Familiarity with Their Own Managed Health Care Plans
Figure 14F	How Would an Online Brokerage Service Provider Use This Information?
Figure 14G	Expanding the Availability of Bank Services: Do you Prefer a Human or an Electronic Teller?
Figure 14H	How Do the Service Characteristics of Intangibility and Inseparability Affect the Marketing Strategy of Universities Like Bentley?
Figure 14I	Which Dimension(s) of Service Quality Does This Advertisement for Liberty Mutual Address?

LECTURE OUTLINE

(Transparency Figure 14A: Chapter Outline)

I.   **The Nature and Importance of Services**
  A.   A *service* is an intangible product involving a deed, a performance, or an effort that cannot be physically possessed.
  B.   Services as products should not be confused with customer service, which involves any service activity that adds value to the product.
  C.   Service industries account for over half of the U.S. gross domestic product (GNP) and about 80 percent of U.S. non-farm jobs.
  D.   Economic growth and lifestyle changes have led to the expansion of the service sector, including consumer and business services.

II.   **Characteristics of Services**

(Transparency Figure 14B)

There are six distinguishing characteristics of services that differentiate them from goods.

  A.   **Intangibility**

(Transparency Figure 14.1)

Intangibility means a service is unperceivable by the senses.

  1.   A service cannot be seen, touched, tasted, or smelled.
  2.   A service cannot be physically possessed by a consumer.
  B.   **Inseparability of Production and Consumption**
Inseparability of production and consumption means that a service is produced and consumed at the same time.

(Transparency Figure 14H)

  1.   Customers want a specific type of service.
  2.   Customers expect the service to be provided in a specific way by a specific individual.

C.   **Perishability**
     Perishability means that storing unused service capacity for future use is impossible.

     1.   Goods marketers can handle supply-demand problems through production scheduling and inventory techniques; service providers cannot.
     2.   Service providers can plan for demand that fluctuates according to day of the week, time of day, or season.

D.   **Heterogeneity**
     Heterogeneity is variation in quality.

(Transparency Figure 14G)

     1.   Quality of manufactured goods is easier to control with standardized procedures.
     2.   Variations can occur with services provided by different organizations, the same organization, different people, or the same person and are therefore very difficult to control.
     3.   Heterogeneity usually increases as the degree of labor-intensiveness increases.
     4.   Services that are people-based are susceptible to fluctuations in quality.

E.   **Client-Based Relationships**
     Client-based relationships result in satisfied customers who use a service repeatedly over time.

     1.   The success of many services depends on creating and maintaining interactions with customers that result in client-based relationships.
     2.   A concentrated effort to provide quality services builds a relationship in which customers become very loyal and are unlikely to switch to a competitor.

F.   **Customer Contact**
     Customer contact comprises the necessary interaction between the provider and the customer needed to deliver the service.

     1.   Customer contact varies depending on the service.
     2.   Satisfied employees lead to satisfied customers.
     3.   Service organizations must train employees to perform customer-oriented behavior and reward them for success.

III. **Developing and Managing Marketing Mixes for Services**
     The characteristics of services require that marketers consider additional issues when it comes to the four major marketing mix variables—product, distribution, promotion, and price.

(Transparency Figure 14C)

(Building Customer Relationships: Segmentation Blurred by Combining Marketing Efforts in Car Rental Services)

A.   **Development of Services**
     1.   A service offered by an organization is generally a package, or bundle, of services consisting of a core service and one or more supplementary services.
          a)   A core service is the basic service experience or commodity that a customer expects to receive.
          b)   A supplementary service is a supportive one related to the core service and used to differentiate the service bundle from that of competitors.
     2.   Heterogeneity results in variability in service quality and makes it difficult to standardize service delivery.
     3.   The heterogeneity advantage to marketers is that it allows them to customize their services to match the specific needs of individual customers.

(Transparency Figure 14F)

4.   The expense of some customized services leaves marketers with a dilemma: how to provide service at an acceptable level of quality in an efficient and economic manner and still satisfy individual customer needs.
   a)   Some marketers provide standardized packages to cope with the problem.
   b)   This leads to highly specified actions and activities the service provider provides.
5.   Intangibility makes it difficult for customers to evaluate a service prior to purchase.
   a)   Intangibility requires service marketers to market promises to customers.
   b)   Customers are forced to place some degree of trust in the service provider to perform the service in a manner that meets or exceeds those promises.
   c)   Marketers also employ tangible cues to help assure customers about the quality of the service, such as well-groomed, professional-appearing contact personnel, and clean, attractive physical facilities.
6.   The fact that customers take part in the production of a service means that other customers can affect the outcome of a service.
7.   Some of the challenges of service design may be overcome by relying on the behavioral studies.

B.   **Distribution of Services**
Marketers deliver services in a variety of ways.

1.   In some instances, customers go to a service provider's facility.
2.   Some services are provided at the customer's home or business.
3.   Some services are delivered primarily at "arm's length," without face-to-face contact.
4.   Marketing channels for services are usually short and direct, meaning that the producer delivers the service directly to the end user, but some services use intermediaries.
5.   Inventory management is very important to service providers, especially balancing supply and demand.
   a)   Inseparability and level of customer contact contribute to the challenges of demand management.
   b)   In some instances, appointments and reservations are used to schedule service delivery.
   c)   To increase the supply of a service, marketers use multiple service sites and increase the number of contact service providers at each site.
   d)   To make delivery more accessible to customers and to increase the supply of a service as well as to reduce labor costs, some service providers have decreased the use of contact personnel and replaced them with equipment. This can create a lack of personalization.

C.   **Promotion of Services**
1.   The intangibility of services results in several promotion-related challenges to service marketers.
   a)   It may not be possible to depict the performance of a service in an advertisement.
   b)   It may not be possible to depict the performance of a service in a store display.
2.   Promotion of services typically includes tangible cues that symbolize the service.
3.   While these symbols have nothing to do with the actual service, they make it much easier for customers to understand the intangible attributes associated with the service.
4.   To add tangibility, ads for services often show pictures of facilities, equipment, and service personnel.
5.   Service providers are more likely to promote price, guarantees, performance documentation, availability, and training and certification of contact personnel than goods marketers.

6.   Use of concrete, specific language makes the services more tangible in the minds of customers.

7.   Promoters are also careful not to promise too much, because customers' expectations may be raised to unattainable levels.

8.   Contact personnel, through their actions, can be directly or indirectly involved in the personal selling of a service.

9.   Since many services cannot be experienced beforehand, or before an extended period of time, offering some services such as insurance on a trial basis cannot be done.

10.   Because of the heterogeneity and intangibility of services, word-of-mouth communication is important in service promotion.

D.   **Pricing of Services**

1.   Prices of services can be established on several different bases.

   a)   The performance of specific tasks

   b)   Hourly, daily, or some other amount of time rates

   c)   Demand-based pricing, so that when demand for the service is high, the price is high.

      (1)   The perishability of services means that when demand is low, the unused capacity cannot be stored and is lost forever.

      (2)   Some services are very time-sensitive in that a significant number of customers desire the service at a particular time. This is the peak demand.

      (3)   Providers of time-sensitive services often use demand-based pricing to manage the problem of balancing supply and demand, charging top prices during peak demand.

   d)   Services offered to customers in bundles leave marketers to decide whether to offer the services at one price, separately priced, or to use a combination of the methods.

2.   Because of the intangibility of services, customers rely heavily at times on price as an indicator of quality.

   a)   If customers perceive the services in a category as being similar in quality, and if the quality of the services is difficult to judge even after purchase, customers may seek the lowest-priced provider.

   b)   If quality varies, customers may rely on the price-quality association.

3.   Under certain conditions, marketers may be limited with respect to setting prices.

   a)   Market conditions may limit prices for certain services.

   b)   State and local government regulations may reduce price flexibility.

IV. **Service Quality**

Service quality is defined as customers' perception of how well a service meets or exceeds their expectations; marketers are thus forced to examine quality from the customer's point of view.

A.   **Customer Evaluation of Service Quality**

1.   Service quality is difficult to evaluate because services do not possess *search qualities*—that is, tangible attributes that can be judged before the purchase (such as color, style, size, feel, or fit).

(Transparency Figure 14D)

2.   Service quality must be judged on

   a)   *experience qualities*, or attributes that can be judged only during purchase or consumption of a service.

   b)   *credence qualities*, or attributes that consumers are unable to evaluate even after purchasing and consuming a service because of lack of knowledge or skill.

(Transparency Figure 14E)

3. Marketers must learn how customers evaluate service quality on tangibles, reliability, responsiveness, assurance, and empathy, all of which have links to employee performance.

B. **Delivering Exceptional Service Quality**

(Transparency Figure 14.2)

1. Providing high-quality service on a consistent basis is very difficult.
2. Organizations can take steps to increase the likelihood of providing high-quality service with an understanding of the following four factors that affect service quality: analysis of customer needs, meeting service quality specifications, employee performance, and management of service expectations.
3. **Analysis of Customer Expectations**
    By analysis of customer expectations, a service can be designed to meet or exceed those expectations.

    a) The difference between a desired level of service and an acceptable level of service is a customer's zone of tolerance.
    b) Customer needs and expectations are determined through marketing research, comment cards, and daily interaction.

4. **Service Quality Specifications**
    Service quality specifications are goals set in terms of employee or machine performance to help ensure good service delivery.

    a) The specifications must be tied to needs expressed by customers.
    b) To provide high-quality service successfully, managers must become role models with a commitment to quality.

5. **Employee Performance**
    Employee performance is critical to customer perceptions of service quality.

    a) Customer-contact employees in most service industries are often the least-trained and lowest-paid members of the organization.
    b) Evaluations and compensation systems help ensure that customer-contact employees perform their jobs well.

6. **Management of Service Expectations**
    Service companies must manage service expectations to ensure that customers have realistic expectations of what the company can provide.

    a) Service expectations are very significant in customer evaluations of service quality.
    b) Expectations can be set through promises in advertising and external communication.
    c) To deliver on promises made, a company needs to have good internal communication among its departments.
    d) Customers tell four times as many people about bad service as they do about good service.

(Transparency Figure 14I)

V. **Nonprofit Marketing**
    Nonprofit marketing includes marketing activities conducted by individuals and organizations to achieve some goal other than ordinary business goals of profit, market share, or return on investment. Nonprofit marketing is divided into two categories: nonprofit-organization marketing and social marketing.

A. **How Is Nonprofit Marketing Different?**
1. Although the chief beneficiary of the business enterprise is the owner, the beneficiaries of the nonprofit enterprise include clients, members, and the public at large.
2. Nonprofit marketing offers greater opportunities for creativity than most for-profit business organizations.
3. Nonprofit marketing may be controversial.
   a) The controversial nature of a nonprofit organization may require the marketing manager to make more value judgments about participation.
   b) Marketing does not attempt to state what an organization's goals should be or to debate the issue of nonprofit versus business goals; marketing attempts only to provide a body of knowledge and concepts to help further the organization's goals.

B. **Nonprofit Marketing Objectives**
1. The basic aim of nonprofit organizations is to obtain a desired response from a target market.
2. Nonprofit marketing objectives should be stated in terms of serving perceived needs and wants of a target public rather than in terms of a product because the product may become obsolete, leaving the organization without an objective or purpose.

C. **Developing Nonprofit Marketing Strategies**
1. **Target Markets**
   The marketer first must pinpoint the target market.

   a) The *target public* is a collective of individuals who have an interest in or concern about an organization, a product, or a social cause.
   b) Once an organization is concerned about exchanging values or obtaining a response from the public, it is viewing the public as a market.
   c) The nonprofit organization target market includes client publics and general publics.
      (1) The *client public* is the direct consumer of the product; most of the attention in developing a marketing strategy is directed toward the client public.
      (2) The *general public* is the indirect consumer of the product.

2. **Developing a Marketing Mix**
   a) The product in a nonprofit organization typically deals with ideas and services more often than with goods.
      (1) Problems in developing a product configuration evolve when an organization fails to define what is being provided.
      (2) The marketing of ideas and concepts is more abstract and much effort is required to present benefits.

   (Ethics and Social Responsibility: Nonprofits Benefit from Brand Savvy)

   b) Distribution, or the availability of nonprofit products, is necessary for exchange to take place.
      (1) If the product is an idea, selecting the right media (the promotional strategy) to communicate the idea will facilitate distribution.
      (2) By nature, services consist of assistance, convenience, and availability. Availability is part of the total service (product).
      (3) The traditional concept of the marketing channel may need to be revised for nonprofit marketing.
   c) Promotion is used widely in nonprofit organizations to communicate with clients and the public.
      (1) Direct mail is the primary means of fundraising for social services.

(2)   Personal selling is used widely, although it may be called by another name, such as recruiting or fund-raising.

(3)   Sales promotion is used widely when nonprofit organizations undertake special events to obtain funds, communicate ideas, or provide services.

d)   The broadest definition of price (valuation) must be used to develop the nonprofit marketing strategy. Price should be viewed as the exchange of something of value for something else of value.

(1)   *Opportunity cost* is the value of the benefit given up by selecting one alternative over another.

(2)   Financial price may or may not be charged for a nonprofit product.

(3)   Pricing strategies of nonprofit organizations often place the public's and clients' welfare before matching costs with revenue.

NOTES FOR CLASS EXERCISES, DEBATE ISSUE, AND CHAPTER QUIZ

On the following pages, you will find two class exercises, a debate issue, and a chapter quiz. These are formatted in large-size type so that you can use them as class handouts or for making transparencies. Below are the authors' comments on the class exercises, the debate topic for this chapter, and the answers to the chapter quiz.

Comments on Class Exercise 1

This exercise focuses on how recognizing the characteristics of services can enhance services marketing strategies.

Question 1. You pay for a ticket that gets you a seat to watch a game, which otherwise is not tangible (possessible). In effect, you buy a memory of the ball game. Thus, to gain customer loyalty, it is important that everything influencing that memory be positive. Setting tickets prices, then, is highly related to how consumers perceive the value of the ballgame experience. More tangible products, such as food and souvenirs, are bought and should contribute positively to the experience. Sports teams make great efforts to increase tangibility by arranging events where fans meet the players (shake hands, obtain autographs). Promotional campaigns with memorable slogans are also efforts to increase tangibility.

Question 2. Busch Stadium management spends extensive time training personnel to deal with unruly fans and to stop problems before they happen. Food selection includes a wide variety of quality food (pizza, Mexican, varieties of ice cream). Bad food makes bad memories, and lack of vending availability or slow food service means missed innings. Narrow rows, dirty or crowded restrooms, and limited food offerings do little to make fans want to go to a game when the team is losing. Some students may argue that having a winning team is most important, but the point should be emphasized that because team performance varies, the rest of the experience should be standardized at a high quality level.

Question 3. Ticket sales cannot be inventoried and sold at a later time. Sales promotions may be used to fill the park to capacity on slow nights or at games against weaker teams.

Question 4. Any part of the service that involves people (players, attendants, vendors, food service providers) will be subject to varying levels of performance. Clearly, this means that attention should be paid to personnel selection, training, and compensation. Good service comes from meeting or exceeding customers' expectations of consistent quality.

Comments on Class Exercise 2

By focusing on consumer outcomes, this exercise is designed to have students think about the types of businesses these companies are actually in and the markets they are truly serving.

There are no right or wrong answers for this exercise; outcomes sought will vary depending on the customer. Possible answers:

1. Banks—investment opportunities, convenience, peace of mind

2. Plumbing repairs—24-hour service, trouble-free plumbing

3. Education—opportunities, social development, learning

4. Hospitals—surgery, emergency care, wellness

5. Police protection—peace of mind, crime reduction, emergency service

6. Legal counseling—legal advice, estate planning, legal representation

7. L.A. Lakers basketball—entertainment, excitement

8. State Farm Auto Insurance—fast claim handling, peace of mind, protection from loss

9. Dry cleaning—clean clothing, convenience, image enhancement

10. Utilities—efficient repairs, uninterrupted service

DEBATE ISSUE

Does Domino's Pizza sell a service rather than a good?

CHAPTER QUIZ

Answers to Chapter Quiz 1. a; 2. a; 3. b; 4. e.

Class Exercise 1

THE ST. LOUIS CARDINALS BASEBALL ORGANIZATION IS OWNED BY ANHEUSER-BUSCH, WHICH ALSO OPERATES BUSCH STADIUM, HOME OF THE CARDINALS. DESPITE BEING LOCATED IN A RELATIVELY SMALL MARKET, THE CARDINALS HAVE SET ATTENDANCE RECORDS. MUCH OF THIS SUCCESS IS THE RESULT OF EFFECTIVE SERVICES MARKETING AT THE BALLPARK, WHICH MAKES ATTEND-ING GAMES AN ENJOYABLE EXPERIENCE FOR FANS, WHETHER THE CARDINALS WIN OR LOSE.

1. What part of your experience at a baseball game is primarily intangible? What are you paying for when you go to a ballgame?

2. Consumers have difficulty separating the producer (the Cardinals and Busch Stadium) from the consumption experience (which includes fan behavior, food vending, seats, or bleachers). Why would this be important for the management at Busch Stadium to understand? In other words, can you go see a winning team play but not enjoy the game, or vice-versa?

3. Busch Stadium holds around 55,000 fans. What difference does it make that services are highly perishable? How would this influence sales promotion activity?

4. What aspects of the baseball game experience are susceptible to heterogeneity? What does this say about the importance of employing high-quality personnel?

Class Exercise 2

FOR EACH OF THE FOLLOWING SERVICES, WHAT IS THE OUTCOME SOUGHT BY THE BUYER?

1. Banks
2. Plumbing repairs
3. Education
4. Hospitals
5. Police protection
6. Legal counseling
7. L.A. Lakers basketball
8. State Farm Auto Insurance
9. Dry cleaning
10. Utilities

Debate Issue

DOES DOMINO'S PIZZA SELL A SERVICE RATHER THAN A GOOD?

YES

- Consumers are buying guaranteed speedy delivery, which is a service.

- Domino's has redefined the pizza industry as a service because it delivers a hot, recently prepared pizza to the customer's doorstep.

NO

- Advertising campaign stresses quality and freshness.

- Consumers are buying a hot, fresh pizza with their choice of toppings— tangible things implying that Domino's is selling a tangible good.

Chapter Quiz

1. The necessary interaction between service provider and customer that allows a service to be delivered is called

   a. customer contact.
   b. service exchange.
   c. marketing.
   d. relationship marketing.
   e. service contact.

2. This type of communication is important in service promotion because of heterogeneity and the intangibility of services.

   a. Word-of-mouth
   b. Newspaper
   c. Television
   d. Radio
   e. Internet

3. Consumers' service expectations are influenced by advertising, word-of-mouth communication, and

   a. recommendations from friends.
   b. past experiences with the service.
   c. news stories about the service.
   d. the tangibles of the service.
   e. credence qualities.

4. Distribution for nonprofit organizations is

   a. unimportant because physical movement does not take place.
   b. not an important decision variable.
   c. coordinated by middlemen.
   d. inefficient rather than efficient.
   e. typically characterized by short channels.

ANSWERS TO DISCUSSION AND REVIEW QUESTIONS

1. **How important are services in the U.S. economy?**

    Services are very important to the U.S. economy, leading some people to call the United States the world's first service economy. Service industries account for over half of the country's gross domestic product and about 80 percent of its non-farm jobs. More than one-half of new businesses are service businesses, and service employment is expected to continue to grow.

2. **Identify and discuss the major service characteristics.**

    Services are intangible, inseparable, heterogeneous, perishable, involve customer contact, and have client-based relationships. Intangibility causes problems such as impossibility to store, inability to protect through patents, inability to display or readily communicate, and pricing difficulty. Inseparability means that the consumer is involved in production, and centralized mass production is difficult. Heterogeneity makes it difficult to standardize or control the quality of the service produced. Perishability means that the service cannot be stockpiled or inventoried.

3. **For each marketing mix element, which service characteristics are most likely to have an impact?**

    For the marketing mix elements of creation, distribution, promotion and pricing, the service characteristics of intangibility, inseparability of production and consumption, perishability, heterogeneity, client-based relationships, and customer contact would relate in these ways. For service development, heterogeneity results in variability in service quality and makes it difficult to standardize service delivery. However, heterogeneity provides one advantage to service marketers, in that they can customize their services to match the specific needs of individual customers. The characteristic of intangibility makes it difficult for customers to evaluate a service prior to purchase. Intangibility requires service marketers like hair stylists to market promises to customers. Marketers employ tangible cues to help assure customers about the quality of the service, such as neat, clean, professional-looking contact personnel. Inseparability of production and consumption and the level of customer contact also influence the development and management of services. The fact that the customers take part in the production of a service means that other customers can affect the outcome of a service. Service marketers attempt to reduce this problem by encouraging customers to cooperate in sharing the responsibility of maintaining an environment that allows all participants to receive the intended benefits of the service.

    Distribution of services is impacted by the service characteristics of inseparability and level of customer contact. In some instances, service marketers use appointments and reservations as approaches for scheduling the delivery of services. To increase the supply of a service, marketers use multiple service sites and increase the number of service providers at each site. Customer contact can also be a problem, especially when a business changes a high-contact service into a low-contact service. That can negatively impact customer service.

    Promotion of services is impacted by the service characteristic of intangibility since this characteristic results in several promotion-related challenges. Since it may not be possible to depict the actual performance of a service in an advertisement or display in a store, explaining the service to customers can be difficult. This results in promotion of price, guarantees, performance documentation, availability, and use of specific, concrete language. Customer contact can also be impacted since service contact people can be directly or indirectly involved in the personal selling of a service. Intangibility makes experiencing a service prior to purchase difficult, making promotion more difficult. Heterogeneity also can make promotion challenging.

Pricing of services is affected by the perishability of services. Since services cannot be stored, pricing often fluctuates to account for lack of or too much demand. The inseparability of services is also a concern, leading to bundled services. Marketers must decide when to bundle and when not to bundle services based on customer desires. The intangible nature of services also leaves customers relying heavily at times on price as an indicator of quality. Many customers view higher-priced products as having higher quality.

4. **What is service quality? Why do customers experience difficulty in judging service quality?**

Service quality can be defined as customers' perceptions of how well a service meets or exceeds their expectations. Customers, not organizations, judge service quality; therefore, service marketers must judge quality from their customers' viewpoint. Service organizations first discover what customers expect and then produce service products that meet or exceed those expectations.

Because services are intangible, customers cannot see, feel, taste, or hear them, and judging their quality is thus extremely difficult. Although goods have tangible attributes that can be judged before purchase, services must be judged only during purchase and consumption.

5. **Identify and discuss the five components of service quality. How do customers evaluate these components?**

*   The *tangibles* component includes the physical evidence of the service. Customers evaluate these through the appearance of the facilities, the appearance of service personnel, and the tools or equipment used to provide the service.

*   The *reliability* component includes the consistency and dependability in performing the service. Customers evaluate this through criteria such as accurate billing or recordkeeping and on-time performance of services.

*   The *responsiveness* component includes the willingness or readiness of employees to provide the service. Evaluation of this component depends on the returning of customer phone calls, providing prompt service, or handling of urgent requests.

*   The *assurance* component includes the knowledge/competence of employees and their ability to convey trust and confidence. This component is evaluated through the perceived knowledge and skills of the employees, the company's name and reputation, and the personal characteristics of the employees.

*   The *empathy* component includes the caring and individual attention provided by employees. Evaluation criteria include the listening skills of the employee, the sincere caring about the customer's interests, and personalized attention.

6. **What is the significance of tangibles in service marketing?**

Tangibles include the facilities, employees, or communications associated with a service. They help to form a part of the product and are often the only aspects of a service that can be viewed prior to purchase. For example, the tangibles associated with a rock concert might be its communications (radio advertisements), facilities (stadium or convention center where the concert will be held), and the employees (ticket sales representatives). Since these elements are experienced prior to the actual service itself (concert), marketers must pay close attention to them and make sure they are consistent with the image of the service product.

7. **How do search, experience, and credence qualities affect the way customers view and evaluate services?**

    Search qualities can be viewed prior to purchase. Experience qualities (satisfaction, courtesy, and so forth) can be assessed only after purchase. Credence qualities cannot be assessed even after purchase and consumption. Because services are mainly intangible, there are few search qualities to evaluate. Because the product cannot be seen or touched prior to purchase, experience qualities are often the key means of assessing satisfaction. To illustrate, an airline's performance is best evaluated after passengers arrive at their final destinations. Credence qualities are usually based on reputation and image. For example, it is hoped that the image of a doctor or lawyer is related to past performance and that the product (performance) has consistency. In the long run, experience qualities are probably the most important in evaluating services.

8. **What steps should a service company take to provide exceptional service quality?**

    To deliver exceptional service quality, an organization should first analyze the needs and expectations of its customers. Methods of determining these needs and expectations can include marketing research, such as surveys and focus groups, comment cards, or asking employees who have close contact with customers. Next, the organization should establish goals or standards to help ensure that these customer needs and expectations are satisfied. After service quality standards are set, organizations should take steps to ensure that customer-contact employees perform their jobs well; this involves training, providing them with information about customers, informing them about service expectations, and basing compensation on customer-oriented measures of performance such as friendliness and customer satisfaction. Finally, service organizations must manage service expectations. Through advertising and internal communication, services set realistic service expectations and make sure they deliver what they promise.

9. **How does nonprofit marketing differ from marketing in for-profit organizations?**

    Nonprofit marketing is conducted by individuals and organizations devoted to some goal other than the ordinary goals of business, which are profit, market share, or return on investment. Business marketing is usually conducted for the benefit of an owner, shareholder, or manager. Examples of nonprofit marketing would be marketing aimed at increasing contributions to a particular charity or at encouraging people to recycle. These nonprofit enterprises benefit clients, members, or the public at large. In addition, nonprofit marketing often allows more opportunity for creativity than most business organizations.

10. **What are the differences among clients, publics, and customers? What is the difference between a target public and a target market?**

    Clients are often considered as those individuals directly involved in an exchange transaction with a nonbusiness organization. Publics involve members of society who may have an interest in the exchange transaction between private parties. The term "customer" is used synonymously with "client." If a nonbusiness organization views the entire society as the group to which it directs its message and with which to exchange, then the general public becomes the same as the target market.

11. **Discuss the development of a marketing strategy for a university. What marketing decisions must be made as the strategy is developed?**

   The development of a marketing strategy for a university would consist of pinpointing a target market (defined in terms of the types of students the university would serve) and developing a marketing mix. The marketing mix would relate to the product (the types of educational programs offered), promotion (including the advertising and personal selling activities of the university), availability or distribution (where the university is located and its various branches), and the price (tuition and other expenses of attending a university).

COMMENTS ON THE CASES

CASE 14.1 THE NEW WAVE OF MARKETING AT NEW ENGLAND AQUARIUM

This case illustrates the diverse marketing challenges that nonprofit organizations face in achieving their goals. Students outside the Boston area may be less familiar with the New England Aquarium. However, they may know about a local aquarium or another nonprofit organization in the area that has similar goals and challenges.

Question 1 asks students who can be considered the Aquarium's client public. In this case, the client public consists of all the members and non-members who visit the Aquarium and take advantage of its offerings.

The second question asks what other marketing efforts, apart from the web and community meetings, would help Maureen Hentz attract new Aquarium volunteers. Students may suggest a number of different techniques. One sample answer: Hentz might send letters or e-mails inviting current and previous employees, volunteers, and interns to refer qualified people for open positions. Remind students that as a nonprofit organization, the Aquarium's resources are very limited, which rules out expensive programs.

The third question asks how the Aquarium might use pricing to manage its attendance. The case states that the weekend is the Aquarium's busiest attendance period. One idea, therefore, is to set a lower admission fee on weekdays (or selected hours during weekdays) to attract visitors who would otherwise come on the weekend. Students should be able to offer additional ideas.

Video Information

Company:	The New England Aquarium
Location:	Tape 2/DVD 2, Segment 14
Length:	11:09

Video Overview: With a mission to "present, promote, and protect" the world of the water, The New England Aquarium is an enduring landmark in the Boston area. It traces its roots back to 1969, when a group of Boston citizens banded together around their mutual commitment to the ocean. The aquarium hosts 1.3 million visitors annually and provides one of the largest volunteer pools in the country-over 1,00 volunteers that log in over 100,000 hours in a given year. Since the aquarium wants to appeal to a extremely diverse customer base-characteristic of the greater Boston area-it aims to build a work force of paid and unpaid staff that reflects the diversity of the surrounding community. Maureen Hentz, director of volunteer programs, is working proactively to recruit from different ages, races, ethnicity, physical abilities, and socioeconomic levels. The aquarium hopes to be known as a leader in diversity, a place where people are free to express their opinions and feel comfortable with their respective differences.

MULTIPLE-CHOICE QUESTIONS ABOUT THE VIDEO

1. The New England Aquarium, which was founded in 1969 by Boston natives, has a mission statement to

    a. have the largest aquarium in the New England area.
    b. present the most exotic sea creatures.
    c. present, promote, and protect the world of the water.
    d. educate customers about sea creatures and sea life.
    e. promote the protection of sea creatures.

2. According to Maureen C. Hentz, the Director of the Volunteer Programs, used to consist of

    a. stay at home mothers who wanted something to do while their kids were at school.
    b. the spouses of all the employees.
    c. the children of all the employees.
    d. church group volunteers.
    e. none, which is why they are working on diversifying the program.

3. Maureen Hentz feels diversity encompasses

    a. race and ethnicity differences.
    b. race, socioeconomic, ethnicity, levels of ability, and age.
    c. mainly varying levels of age and gender differences.
    d. various levels of abilities, race, and ethnicity
    e. race, age ,and gender

4. Currently, the biggest challenge for the New England Aquarium is

    a. trying to diversify the amount of sea life maintained.
    b. keeping the employee turnover rate down.
    c. trying to market to the community.
    d. not become complacent.
    e. trying to gain more interns for the summer.

ANSWERS TO MULTIPLE-CHOICE QUESTIONS ABOUT THE VIDEO

1. d

2. a

3. e

4. a

CASE 14.2 AARP USES NEW NAME TO REACH BROADER TARGET MARKET

This case introduces students to the challenges that AARP faces in attracting new members among the baby-boom generation. Students will probably know the AARP name but may have little knowledge of the organization's scope, purpose, and activities. You may wish to ask students to gather some background data on AARP before discussing this case in class.

Question 1 asks students to identify the dimensions of service quality that are being addressed by AARP's new marketing efforts. According to the case, these include physical evidence of the service (as evidenced by its newly-designed magazines), willingness or readiness to provide the service (as evidenced by its advertising campaign and its mall tours), knowledge and competence (as evidenced by the content of its different magazines), and empathy (as evidenced by the switch to three magazines geared to the needs of specific membership segments).

Question 2 asks how AARP is coping with the challenges of marketing intangible services. One way it copes is by using tangible cues to represent the quality of its intangible services. For example, the new magazines are tangible evidence of AARP's responsiveness to the differing needs of differing segments. The mall tours are also tangible reminders that AARP is a strong national voice for seniors. In addition, the official AARP name no longer contain the word "retired," sending a signal that the organization serves both working and non-working seniors.

Question 3 asks students to suggest other steps that AARP might take to demonstrate reliability, responsiveness, assurance, or empathy. Students will offer a variety of creative ideas. For example, AARP might use promotion to publicize its advocacy efforts on behalf of certain member segments as a way of demonstrating empathy or, in the case of urgent requirements, demonstrating responsiveness. It might also provide employees as expert speakers on local and regional programs for seniors as a way of demonstrating assurance.

CHAPTER 15

Marketing Channels and Supply Chain Management

TEACHING RESOURCES QUICK REFERENCE GUIDE

Resource	Location
Purpose and Perspective	IRM, p. 273
Guide for Using Color Transparencies	IRM, p. 274
Lecture Outline	IRM, p. 274
Notes for Class Exercises, Debate Issue, and Chapter Quiz	IRM, p. 280
Class Exercise 1	IRM, p. 282
Class Exercise 2	IRM, p. 283
Debate Issue	IRM, p. 284
Chapter Quiz	IRM, p. 285
Answers to Discussion and Review Questions	IRM, p. 286
Comments on the Cases	IRM, p. 288
Case 15.1	IRM, p. 288
Video	Tape 2/DVD 2, Segment 15
Video Information	IRM, p. 289
Multiple-Choice Questions About the Video	IRM, p. 290
Case 15.2	IRM, p. 291
Transparency Acetates	Transparency package
Examination Questions: Essay	TB, p. 417
Examination Questions: Multiple-Choice	TB, p. 417
Examination Questions: True-False	TB, p. 438
Author-Selected Multiple-Choice Test Items	TB, p. 671
HMClassPrep Presentation Resources	CD-ROM
PowerPoint Slides	Instructor's website

Note: Additional resources are updated periodically and may be found on the accompanying student and instructor websites at http://www.prideferrell.com/.

PURPOSE AND PERSPECTIVE

This chapter explores marketing channels and supply chain management. We begin by examining the functions of marketing channels, including creating utility and facilitating exchange efficiencies. We also examine the justification for intermediaries. We divide types of marketing channels into those for consumer products and those for business products. Then, we explore the intensity of market coverage. Next, we introduce the fundamentals of supply chain management, including channel leadership, cooperation, and conflict, as well as vertical and horizontal channel integration. The chapter concludes by examining the legal ramifications of selected channel management practices.

GUIDE FOR USING COLOR TRANSPARENCIES

There are two groups of color transparencies. The transparencies identified by a double number are the same as the figures and tables in the text. The transparencies labeled with a number and a letter are illustrations that do not appear in the text, but they can be used as additional examples of concepts discussed.

Part 6 Opener	Distribution Decisions
Figure 15.1	Efficiency in Exchanges Provided by an Intermediary
Figure 15.2	Typical Marketing Channels for Consumer Products
Figure 15.3	Typical Marketing Channels for Business Products
Table 15.2	Key Tasks in Supply Chain Management
Figure 15A	Chapter 15 Outline
Figure 15B	Key Definitions: Marketing Channel, Marketing Intermediary
Figure 15C	Legal Issues in Channel Management
Figure 15D	Is This Product Distributed Though Multiple Marketing Channels?
Figure 15E	Are iPods Distributed Through Intensive, Selective, or Exclusive Distribution?

LECTURE OUTLINE

(Transparency Part 6 Opener)

(Transparency Figure 15A: Chapter Outline)

The *distribution* component of the marketing mix focuses on the decisions and actions involved in making products available to customers when and where they want to purchase them.

I.   **The Nature of Marketing Channels**
   A.   **Marketing Channel Concepts**
      1.   A *marketing channel* (also called a channel of distribution) is a group of individuals and organizations that directs the flow of products from producers to customers. The major role of marketing channels is to make products available at the right time at the right place in the right quantities.

(Transparency Figure 15B)

      2.   Some marketing channels are direct—from producer straight to customer—but most channels have *marketing intermediaries* that link producers to other intermediaries or to ultimate consumers through contractual arrangements or through the purchase and reselling of products.
         a)   Wholesalers buy and resell products to other wholesalers, to retailers, and to industrial customers.
         b)   Retailers purchase products and resell them to ultimate consumers.
      3.   Although distribution decisions need not precede other marketing decisions, they are a powerful influence on the rest of the marketing mix.
         a)   Channel decisions are critical because they determine a product's market presence and buyers' accessibility to the product.
         b)   Channel decisions have additional strategic significance because they entail long-term commitments. It is usually easier to change prices or promotional efforts than to change marketing channels.

B. **Marketing Channels Create Utility**
   Marketing channels create three types of utility: time, place, and possession.

   1. Time utility—created by having products available when the customer wants them
   2. Place utility—created by making products available in locations where customers wish to purchase them
   3. Possession utility—means the customer has access to the product to use or to store for future use
   4. Channel members sometimes create form utility by assembling, preparing, or otherwise refining the product to suit individual customer needs.

C. **Marketing Channels Facilitate Exchange Efficiencies**

   (Transparency Figure 15.1)

   1. Marketing intermediaries can reduce the costs of exchanges by efficiently performing certain services or functions. Intermediaries provide valuable assistance because of their access to, and control over, important resources used in the proper functioning of marketing channels.
   2. Despite these efficiencies, the press, consumers, public officials, and other marketers freely criticize intermediaries, especially wholesalers.
      a) Critics accuse wholesalers of being inefficient and parasitic.
      b) Buyers often wish to make the distribution channel as short as possible, assuming that the fewer the intermediaries, the lower the price will be.
      c) Because suggestions to eliminate them come from both ends of the marketing channel, wholesalers must be careful to perform only those marketing activities that are truly desired.
   3. Critics who suggest that eliminating wholesalers would lower customer prices do not recognize that this would not eliminate the need for services that wholesalers provide. Although wholesalers can be eliminated, the functions they perform cannot.

D. **Marketing Channels Form a Supply Chain**
   An important function of the marketing channel is the joint effort of all channel members to create a supply chain, a total distribution system that serves customers and creates a competitive advantage.

   1. *Supply chain management* refers to long-term partnerships among marketing channel members working together to reduce inefficiencies, costs, and redundancies in the entire marketing channel and to develop innovative approaches, in order to satisfy customers.
      a) Supply chain management involves manufacturing, research, sales, advertising, shipping and, most of all, cooperation and understanding of tradeoffs throughout the whole channel to achieve the optimal level of efficiency and service.
      b) Table 15.2 outlines the key tasks involved in supply chain management.

   (Transparency Table 15.2)

      c) Whereas traditional marketing channels tend to focus on producers, wholesalers, retailers, and customers, the supply chain is a broader concept that includes facilitating agencies, such as shipping companies, communication companies, and other organizations that take part in marketing exchanges.
   2. Supply chain management is helping more firms realize that optimizing the supply chain costs through partnerships will improve all members' profits.
   3. Supply chains start with the customer and require the cooperation of channel members to satisfy customer requirements.

(Tech Know: U.S. Armed Forces Revamp Their Supply-Chain Management Strategies)

    4.   Technology has dramatically improved the capability of supply chain management on a global basis.

    5.   Supply chain management should not be considered just a new buzzword. Reducing inventory and transportation costs, speeding order cycle times, cutting administrative and handling costs, and improving customer service—these improvements provide rewards for "all" channel members.

II. **Types of Marketing Channels**

  A.   **Channels for Consumer Products**

(Transparency Figure 15.2)

    1.   As shown in Figure 14.2, a channel moves goods directly from producer to consumers.

    2.   Channel B, which moves goods from the producer to a retailer and then to customers, is a frequent choice of large retailers, since it allows them to buy in quantity from manufacturers.

    3.   A long-standing channel, especially for consumer products, channel C takes goods from the producer to a wholesaler, then to a retailer, and finally to consumers.

    4.   Channel D—through which goods pass from producer to agents to wholesalers to retailers and then to consumers—is frequently used for products intended for mass distribution, such as processed foods.

    5.   For some consumer goods, a long channel may be the most efficient distribution channel. When several channel members perform specialized functions, costs may be lower than when one channel member tries to perform them all.

  B.   **Channels for Business Products**

(Transparency Figure 15.3)

    1.   Channel E illustrates the direct channel for business products. Business customers like to communicate directly with producers, especially when expensive or technically complex products are involved.

    2.   In the second business products channel, channel F, an *industrial distributor* facilitates exchanges between the producer and customer. An industrial distributor is an independent business that takes title to products and carries inventories.

        a)   Industrial distributors offer sellers several advantages, such as performing the needed selling activities in local markets at relatively low cost to a manufacturer and reducing a producer's financial burden by providing customers with credit services.

        b)   Using industrial distributors has several disadvantages, such as the fact that they may be difficult to control, and they often stock competing brands.

    3.   The third channel for business products, channel G, employs a manufacturer's agent, an independent businessperson who sells complementary products of several producers in assigned territories and is compensated through commissions.

        a)   Using manufacturers' agents can benefit a business marketer because these agents possess considerable technical and market information and have an established set of customers.

        b)   The use of manufacturers' agents is not problem-free; even though straight commissions may be cheaper, the seller may have little control over manufacturers' agents.

    4.   Channel H includes both a manufacturer's agent and an industrial distributor.

C. **Multiple Marketing Channels and Channel Alliances**
    To reach diverse target markets, manufacturers may use several marketing channels simultaneously, with each channel involving a different set of intermediaries.

(Transparency Figure 15D)

1. *Dual distribution* is the use of two or more marketing channels for distributing the same products to the same target market.
2. A *strategic channel alliance* exists when the products of one business organization are distributed through the marketing channels of another.

III. **Intensity of Market Coverage**
     In addition to deciding which marketing channels to use to distribute a product, marketers must determine the intensity of coverage a product should get—that is, the number and kinds of outlets in which it will be sold.

A. **Intensive Distribution**
    1. In *intensive distribution*, all available outlets for distributing a product are used.
    2. Intensive distribution is appropriate for convenience products.

B. **Selective Distribution**
    1. In *selective distribution*, only some available outlets in an area are chosen to distribute a product.
    2. Selective distribution is appropriate for shopping products.
    3. Selective distribution is desirable when a special effort—such as customer service from a channel member—is important.

C. **Exclusive Distribution**
    1. In *exclusive distribution*, only one outlet is used in a relatively large geographic area.
    2. Exclusive distribution is suitable for products purchased rather infrequently, consumed over a long period of time, or requiring service or information to fit them to buyers' needs.
    3. Exclusive distribution is often used as an incentive to sellers when only a limited market is available for products.

(Transparency Figure 15E)

IV. **Supply Chain Management**
A. **Channel Leadership, Cooperation, and Conflict**
    Each channel member performs a different role in the system and agrees (implicitly or explicitly) to accept certain rights, responsibilities, rewards, and sanctions for nonconformity.

    1. **Channel Leadership**
        a) Although many marketing channels are determined by consensus, some are organized and controlled by a dominant member, or *channel captain* (also called a channel leader). The channel captain may be a producer, wholesaler, or retailer.
        b) To attain desired objectives, the captain must possess *channel power*, the ability to influence another channel member's goal achievement.
    2. **Channel Cooperation**
        a) Channel cooperation is vital if each member is to gain something from other members.
        b) There are several ways to improve channel cooperation.
            (1) If a marketing channel is viewed as a unified supply chain competing with other systems, individual members will be less likely to take actions that create disadvantages for other members.

       (2)   Channel members should agree to direct efforts toward common objectives so channel roles can be structured for maximum marketing effectiveness, which in turn can help members achieve individual objectives.

(Building Customer Relationships: Partnering with Channel Members)

       (3)   A critical component in cooperation is a precise definition of each channel member's tasks.

3.   **Channel Conflict**

    a)   Channel conflicts may arise from self-interest, misunderstandings about role expectations, communication difficulties, and intermediaries' overemphasis on competing products or diversification into product lines traditionally handled by other intermediaries.

    b)   Although there is no single method for resolving conflict, partnerships can be reestablished if two conditions are met.

       (1)   The role of each channel member must be specified.

       (2)   Channel members must institute certain measures of channel coordination, which requires leadership and benevolent exercise of control.

    c)   To prevent channel conflict from arising, producers, or other channel members, may provide competing resellers with different brands, allocate markets among resellers, define policies for direct sales to avoid potential conflict over large accounts, negotiate territorial issues between regional distributors, and provide recognition to certain resellers for their importance in distributing to others.

B.   **Channel Integration**

1.   Channel functions may be transferred between intermediaries and to producers and even customers.

2.   Various channel stages may be combined under the management of a channel captain either horizontally or vertically.

    a)   **Vertical Channel Integration**

       (1)   *Vertical channel integration* combines two or more stages of the channel under one management. This may occur when one member of a marketing channel purchases the operations of another member or simply performs the functions of another member, eliminating the need for that intermediary.

       (2)   Whereas members of conventional channel systems work independently, participants in vertical channel integration coordinate efforts to reach a desired target market.

       (3)   Integration has been successfully institutionalized in marketing channels called *vertical marketing systems (VMSs)*, in which a single channel member coordinates or manages channel activities to achieve efficient, low-cost distribution aimed at satisfying target market customers. Most vertical marketing systems take one of three forms:

          (a)   A "corporate VMS" combines all stages of the marketing channel, from producers to consumers, under a single owner.

          (b)   In an "administered VMS," channel members are independent, but a high level of interorganizational management is achieved by information coordination.

          (c)   Under a "contractual VMS," the most popular type of vertical marketing system, channel members are linked by legal agreements spelling out each member's rights and obligations.

b) **Horizontal Channel Integration**
(1) Combining organizations at the same level of operation under one management constitutes *horizontal channel integration*. An organization may integrate horizontally by merging with other organizations at the same level in a marketing channel.
(2) Although horizontal integration permits efficiencies and economies of scale in purchasing, marketing research, advertising, and specialized personnel, it is not always the most effective method of improving distribution.

V. **Legal Issues in Channel Management**
A. **Dual Distribution**

(Transparency Figure 15C)

1. Some companies may use dual distribution by utilizing two or more marketing channels to distribute the same products to the same target market.
2. Courts do not consider this practice illegal when it promotes competition, but they view as a threat to competition a manufacturer that uses company-owned outlets to dominate or drive out of business independent retailers or distributors that handle its products.

B. **Restricted Sales Territories**
1. To tighten control over distribution of its products, a manufacturer may try to prohibit intermediaries from selling its products outside designated sales territories.
2. Although courts have deemed restrictive sales territories a restraint of trade among intermediaries handling the same brands, they have also held that exclusive territories can actually promote competition among dealers handling different brands.

C. **Tying Agreements**
1. When a supplier (usually a manufacturer or franchiser) furnishes a product to a channel member with the stipulation that the channel member must purchase other products as well, a *tying agreement* exists. A related practice is "full-line forcing," in which a supplier requires that channel members purchase the supplier's entire line to obtain any of the supplier's products.
2. The courts accept tying agreements when the supplier alone can provide products of a certain quality, when the intermediary is free to carry competing products as well, and when a company has just entered the market. Most other tying agreements are considered illegal.

D. **Exclusive Dealing**
1. When a manufacturer forbids an intermediary to carry products of competing manufacturers, the arrangement is called *exclusive dealing*.
2. The legality of an exclusive dealing contract is generally determined by applying three tests.
a) If the exclusive dealing blocks competitors from as much as 10 percent of the market, if the sales revenue involved is sizable, and if the manufacturer is much larger (and thus more intimidating) than the dealer, the arrangement is considered anticompetitive.
b) If dealers and customers in a given market have access to similar products or if the exclusive dealing contract strengthens an otherwise weak competitor, the arrangement is allowed.

E. **Refusal to Deal**
1. For more than 75 years, the courts have held that producers have the right to choose channel members with which they will do business (and the right to reject others).
2. Within existing distribution channels, however, suppliers may not legally refuse to deal with wholesalers or dealers just because these wholesalers or dealers resist policies that are anticompetitive or in restraint of trade.

NOTES FOR CLASS EXERCISES, DEBATE ISSUE, AND CHAPTER QUIZ

On the following pages, you will find two class exercises, a debate issue, and a chapter quiz. These are formatted in large-size type so that you can use them as class handouts or for making transparencies. Below are the authors' comments on the class exercises, the debate topic for this chapter, and the answers to the chapter quiz.

Comments on Class Exercise 1

The objective of this class exercise is to aid student understanding of the dimensions of channel selection and their possible relationships with channel conflict.

Question 1. These manufacturers have the resources to control their own channels and apparently have altered objectives to include increased coverage in new segments. Many manufacturers suggest that since outlet stores are located outside metro areas, they are not competing directly with retailers. The buyer behavior of outlet store shoppers is different from that of upscale department store shoppers: for outlet store shoppers, price is the deciding factor and customer service is unimportant. Because most items in an outlet store are past season, retailers are usually unwilling to carry them (product attributes are different). The economy and social forces (environmental forces) may encourage people to shop for value rather than for status.

Question 2. If market coverage is seen as a continuum, then these manufacturers have moved from a selective or exclusive intensity to a more intensive coverage. As coverage intensifies, customer service is decreased (particularly at outlet stores). Additionally, consumers' perceptions of brand quality typically decrease as coverage intensity increases.

Question 3. Retailers expect manufacturers to supply relatively exclusive rights to distribute their branded goods. In the case of outlet stores, manufacturers have deviated from their role as producer to the role of retailer. (This might be a good time to define wholesaling and retailing.) Additionally, it appears that some manufacturers are selling some new items through outlet stores. It is also likely that manufacturers did not effectively or honestly communicate their distribution intentions to retailers.

Question 4. If retailers try to use coercive power, they will most likely hurt themselves by eliminating some of their best-selling brands. The conflict might be resolved by specifying the roles of each channel member (i.e., who sells what season's merchandise).

Comments on Class Exercise 2

The purpose of this exercise is to improve students' understanding of the intensities of market coverage. Answers:

1.	Potato chips	**intensive**
2.	Gucci handbags	**exclusive**
3.	Large-screen televisions	**selective**
4.	Rolex watches	**exclusive**
5.	Clinique cosmetics	**selective**
6.	Carbonated beverages	**intensive**
7.	Range Rover vehicles	**exclusive**
8.	Stereo systems	**selective**
9.	Levi jeans	**selective**
10.	IBM personal computers	**selective**
11.	Gasoline	**intensive**
12.	Cannondale bicycles	**selective**
13.	Jaguar automobiles	**exclusive**
14.	Nintendo video games	**selective**
15.	Reebok shoes	**selective**

DEBATE ISSUE

Does cutting out the intermediary cut costs?

CHAPTER QUIZ

Answers to Chapter Quiz 1. e; 2. d; 3. d; 4. e.

Class Exercise 1

MANY MANUFACTURERS SELL PRODUCTS IN OUTLET STORES AT 25 TO 70 PERCENT OFF RETAIL PRICES. RETAILERS DO NOT LIKE THE ADDED COMPETITION FROM THEIR OWN SUPPLIERS DESPITE MANUFAC-TURERS' CLAIMS THAT THEY ARE ONLY SELLING LAST SEASON'S MERCHANDISE.

1. How could business objectives, buyer behavior, product attributes, or environmental forces affect a manufacturer's decision to distribute through outlet stores?

2. By selling in outlet stores, how have these manufacturers changed their intensity of market coverage? How is customer service different at an outlet store?

3. Which of the following may be responsible for the conflict between manufacturers and retailers?
   - Lack of clear communication
   - Deviation from role expectations
   - Diversification into product lines traditionally handled by other intermediaries

4. Should retailers develop store brands, refuse to stock certain items, or focus their buying power on one supplier or group of suppliers? How should the conflict be resolved?

Class Exercise 2

IDENTIFY THE INTENSITY OF MARKET COVERAGE FOR EACH OF THE FOLLOWING PRODUCTS:

1. Potato chips
2. Gucci handbags
3. Large-screen televisions
4. Rolex watches
5. Clinique cosmetics
6. Carbonated beverages
7. Range Rover vehicles
8. Stereo systems
9. Levi jeans
10. IBM personal computers
11. Gasoline
12. Cannondale bicycles
13. Jaguar automobiles
14. Nintendo video games
15. Reebok shoes

<u>Debate Issue</u>

DOES CUTTING OUT THE INTERMEDIARY CUT COSTS?

<u>YES</u>

- Intermediaries make a significant profit on the products they carry.

- Some wholesalers are inefficient and tend to be parasitic.

- Eliminating intermediaries can cut these costs and decrease the time it takes for products to reach consumers.

- Companies that are truly concerned about customer service will eliminate intermediaries and take responsibility for performing their tasks.

<u>NO</u>

- Intermediaries make significantly less profit than retailers.

- Wholesalers survive by providing certain functions more efficiently than other channel members.

- Producers would have to provide additional functions, often at greater expense and time than using wholesalers.

- To survive, wholesalers must be more efficient and more customer-focused than alternative marketing institutions.

Chapter Quiz

1. In a simple economy of five producers and five consumers, there would be _____ transactions possible without an intermediary and _____ transactions possible with one intermediary.

   a. ten; twenty-five
   b. thirty; ten
   c. twenty-five; fifteen
   d. sixteen; eight
   e. twenty-five; ten

2. Nationally distributed consumer convenience products are *most likely* distributed through which of the following channels?

   a. Producer, consumers
   b. Producer, agents, wholesalers, retailers, consumers
   c. Producer, wholesalers, consumers
   d. Producer, wholesalers, retailers, consumers
   e. Producer, industrial distributor, wholesalers, retailers, consumers

3. Honey Farms is a maker of fine chocolates. The company's latest product, Fudge-Dipped Strawberries, is the premier product in its Fudge-Dipped line. The product is very expensive and targeted to upscale consumers. Which form of distribution would Honey Farms be likely to use for its new product?

   a. Intensive
   b. Selective
   c. Targeted
   d. Exclusive
   e. Premier

4. Goodyear allows companies like Sears and Discount Tire to distribute and discount its tires. This action significantly increases the possibility of channel _____ with independent Goodyear dealers.

   a. understanding
   b. power
   c. leadership
   d. communication
   e. conflict

ANSWERS TO DISCUSSION AND REVIEW QUESTIONS

1. **Describe the major functions of marketing channels. Why are these functions better accomplished through combined efforts of channel members?**

   The major functions of marketing channels include creating utility and facilitating exchange efficiencies. Marketing channels create time utility by making products available when customers want them, place utility by having them where customers can purchase them, and possession utility by providing customers the opportunity to use or store products. Because intermediaries are specialists at the services they provide, they can make exchanges more efficient. By dividing responsibilities, each channel member becomes expert at what each does, making the marketing channel more efficient and therefore providing more reliable service to ultimate consumers.

2. **Can one channel member perform all the channel functions? Explain your answer.**

   One channel member cannot always perform all channel functions most efficiently. The member may lack the capacity or facilities needed to perform each function, so it may be more efficient for other channel members to perform some or even all of the channel functions.

3. **"Shorter channels are usually a more direct means of distribution and therefore are more efficient." Comment on this statement.**

   Shorter marketing channels are not always the most efficient method of distribution. If this statement were true, there would be no need for wholesalers, and all products would flow directly from producers to consumers. Durable household goods and convenience goods such as candy and gum are by their nature usually sold in convenient locations. Without longer channels, it would cost the producers more to get their products directly to the many outlets that sell the products.

4. **List several reasons why consumers often blame intermediaries for distribution inefficiencies?**

   To consumers, intermediaries are not always visible in the distribution system and therefore are not worth what they cost. Throughout history, form utility has been perceived as having more value for consumers than time and place utility. However, many consumers do not realize that if the intermediaries are eliminated, either the producer or the consumer must perform the intermediaries' functions, leading to higher prices if the producer must perform those functions. Many people believe that intermediaries are parasitic and therefore contribute to inefficiency. In other words, consumers do not understand the role and function of intermediaries.

5. **Compare and contrast the four major types of marketing channels for consumer products. Through which type of channel is each of the following products most likely to be distributed: a) new automobiles, b) saltine crackers, c) cut-your-own Christmas trees, d) new textbooks, e) sofas, and f) soft drinks?**

   The first type of consumer product channel is from producer directly to consumer. Although this type of channel is the simplest, it is not always the cheapest or most efficient. The second type of channel is producer to retailer to consumer and is efficient when large retailers can buy in large quantities from producers. The third channel, producer to wholesaler to retailer to consumer, is one of the most traditional types and is practical for producers of goods that sell to hundreds of thousands of consumers. The last type of consumer products distribution channel is from producer to agent to wholesaler to retailer to consumer. This method is most often used by producers of mass-marketed products.

   The specified products are most likely to be distributed as follows:

a)   New automobiles—producer to retailer to consumer

b)   Saltine crackers—producer to food broker to wholesaler to retailer to consumer

(In some cases, the producer may sell to a wholesaler, without using a broker. Also, when a very large retailer like Wal-Mart is involved, producer to retailer to consumer channel is employed.)

c)   Cut-your-own Christmas trees—producer to consumer

d)   New textbooks—producer to retailer to consumer

e)   Sofas—producer to wholesaler to retailer to consumer, or possibly producer to retailer to consumer

f)   Soft drinks—producer to retailer to consumer

(Usually, soft drinks are bottled locally.)

6.   **Outline the four most common channels for business products. Describe the products or situations that lead marketers to choose each channel.**

The first type of channel for business products is direct from producer to organizational customer. Expensive and technically complex products such as computers and aircraft are often sold through direct channels. A second business distribution channel is from producer to industrial distributor to industrial buyer. This channel is used when a product has broad market appeal, is easily stocked and serviced, is sold in small quantities, and is needed rapidly. The third business channel is from producer to manufacturers' agent to organizational buyer. This channel is effective for highly seasonal products. The last common channel for business products is from producer to agent to industrial distributor to organizational buyer. This type of channel is practical when the organizational marketer wants to cover a large geographic area but does not maintain a sales force, or when a marketer wants to enter a new geographical region without expanding its existing sales force.

7.   **Describe an industrial distributor. What types of products are marketed through an industrial distributor?**

An industrial distributor is an independent business that takes title to products and carries inventories. The industrial distributor usually carries standardized organizational products, such as maintenance supplies and tools. The functions of an industrial distributor vary with the number of links in the channel.

8.   **Under what conditions is a producer most likely to use more than one marketing channel?**

A producer uses more than one marketing channel to reach diverse target markets, such as when the same product is directed to both consumers and organizational buyers. In other cases, companies may sell similar products under different brand names through multiple channels, a practice called *dual distribution*.

9.   **Explain the differences among intensive, selective, and exclusive methods of distribution.**

In intensive distribution, the product is distributed through many outlets for the convenience of customers; examples of products likely to be distributed intensively include candy, gum, and soft drinks. Selective distribution employs only some available outlets in an area and is used for typewriters, stereos, and other products that buyers want to compare in terms of price, design, and style. Exclusive distribution employs only one outlet in a relatively large geographic area. It is typically used for specialty products that are purchased infrequently or require a high degree of adjustment to buyers' needs, such as Rolex watches and Jaguar automobiles.

10. **"Channel cooperation requires that members support the overall channel goals to achieve individual goals." Comment on this statement.**

Cooperation is required of all channel members to provide an integrated system that will deliver the products customers desire. Failure of one link in the channel could cause customer dissatisfaction and therefore channel failure.

11. **Name and describe firms that use (a) vertical integration and (b) horizontal integration in their marketing channels.**

Firms that use vertical integration in their marketing channels include Kentucky Fried Chicken, Exxon, and Safeway. All these firms combine two or more stages of their distribution channels under one management. For example, Kentucky Fried Chicken delivers food products and supplies to its own franchise operators.

Firms that use horizontal integration include Wal-Mart, IGA, and Sears. These firms combine institutions at the same level in the channel. For instance, Wal-Mart integrates horizontally by adding more retail outlets, and IGA integrates horizontally by taking over or adding more wholesale outlets.

12. **Explain the major characteristics of each of the three types of vertical marketing systems (VMSs): corporate, administered, and contractual.**

A vertical marketing system (VMS) is coordinated or managed by a single channel member to achieve efficient, low-cost distribution aimed at satisfying target market customers. A corporate VMS combines all channel stages from producers to consumers under a single ownership. An administered VMS is a centrally coordinated system with a channel leader to establish strategy. In a contractual VMS, channel members are linked by legal agreements that spell out each member's rights and obligations.

13. **Under what conditions are tying agreements, exclusive dealing, and dual distribution judged illegal?**

Tying agreements exist when a supplier furnishes a product to a channel member with the stipulation that the channel member purchase other products as well. Most tying agreements are illegal unless the supplier alone can provide a particular quality of products, the intermediary is free to carry competing products, or the company has just entered the market. Exclusive dealing occurs when a manufacturer forbids an intermediary to carry products of competing manufacturers. It is considered illegal if it blocks competitors from as much as 10 percent of the market, the sales revenue involved is sizable, and the manufacturer is much larger than the dealer. Dual distribution occurs when a producer distributes the same product through two or more different channel structures. It is not usually considered illegal unless it inhibits competition. For example, a manufacturer might use a company-owned outlet to drive independent firms out of business.

COMMENTS ON THE CASES

CASE 15.1 SMARTER CHANNEL MANAGEMENT AT SMARTERKIDS

This case illustrates the evolution of a company that began as a dot-com retailer and, through a merger, became the key consumer channel for a larger company. As a result, the current SmarterKids web site differs from the web site as shown in this video. Because students are unlikely to know much about

SmarterKids, you may want to ask them to check the web site and do other background research before discussing this case in class.

Question 1 asks students to describe Excelligence's approach to channel integration. According to the case, Excelligence is vertically integrated because it manufactures many of the toys that it markets through SmarterKids. With two stages of the marketing channel under one corporate management, Excelligence can better coordinate activities, control costs, and ensure a sufficient supply of products.

In question 2, students are asked whether SmarterKids should use the direct selling "party plan" channel in addition to online retailing. Students who support the party plan may say that like-minded parents would appreciate a convenient way of seeing toys and hearing other parents' comments before buying from SmarterKids. They may also say that this is an opportunity for the children to play with the toys and for parents to make buying decisions based on how their children react. Students who do not support using this channel may say that it could put more emphasis on party-givers than on building connections with the SmarterKids brand. In addition, they may note that using the party plan prevents SmarterKids from collecting and analyzing the kind of detailed customer-by-customer data it needs to guide purchasing and marketing activities.

Question 3 asks about the conditions under which a toy manufacturer would be just as interested in marketing its products through SmarterKids as it would through Toys "R" Us. SmarterKids caters to a more sophisticated (and potentially more loyal) customer base of parents who want to buy quality educational toys. Therefore, once SmarterKids has tested and recommended a manufacturer's products, those products will probably enjoy steady sales. Also, a manufacturer selling through SmarterKids doesn't have to worry about aisle and shelf placement, as it does with Toys "R" Us. Instead, it can rely on SmarterKids to highlight its toys according to age-appropriateness, product category, and relation to the child's development. Finally, Toys "R" Us may demand a lower price because of its potentially higher volume, whereas selling to SmarterKids could bring in higher profit margins. Students may offer other ideas, as well.

Video Information

Company:	SmarterKids
Location:	Tape 2/DVD 2, Segment 15
Length:	4:29

Video Overview: SmarterKids.com is out to solve a universal problem for parents: finding toys that teach children and keep them entertained as well. This Boston-based company helps connect children with toys that are best suited for their needs. Parents fill out a confidential form about their children's interest and abilities, and the site creates a customized storefront for that child. SmarterKids.com adds value by saving parents time; it creates a better shopping experience than aimlessly browsing the web for nameless products. SmarterKids reviews some 4,000 toys, books, and software programs for quality assurance. The site also provides homework help, a directory of tutors, and phone, email, and support.

MULTIPLE-CHOICE QUESTIONS ABOUT THE VIDEO

1. According to the video, SmarterKids' primary value proposition over traditional brick-and-mortar toy stores is

    a.   a wider selection.
    b.   greater convenience.
    c.   significantly lower cost.
    d.   the ability to cater to specialty educational markets.
    e.   superior brand recognition.

2. What type of company is SmarterKids.com?

    a.   toy wholesaler.
    b.   Internet retailer.
    c.   toy manufacturer.
    d.   land-based retailer.
    e.   private school offering enrichment opportunities.

3. All of the following are added values that Smarterkids.com offers to its customers except

    a.   It creates customer profiles.
    b.   It conducts toy, game, and book testing.
    c.   It offers free delivery.
    d.   It creates personalized recommendations.
    e.   It offers fun and exciting educational products.

4. What does the CEO of Smarterkids.com say is the company's key to success?

    a.   better product.
    b.   better prices.
    c.   trust.
    d.   an exclusive arrangement with Toys-R-Us.
    e.   endorsement by the National Education Association (NEA).

5. What service does Smarterkids.com offer its customers that makes it unique?

    a.   free gift wrapping for all purchases.
    b.   a match of products and services that will help a child grow.
    c.   a frequent buyer discount program.
    d.   coupons for children's products and services in the local area.
    e.   referrals by pediatricians and children's dentists.

ANSWERS TO MULTIPLE-CHOICE QUESTIONS ABOUT THE VIDEO

1.   b

2.   b

3.   c

4.   c

5.   b

CASE 15.2 GRAINGER WIRES THE CHANNEL FOR BUSINESS PRODUCTS

In this case, students see how an industrial distributor established a comprehensive online catalog site. Because students may not be familiar with Grainger or its operations, you may wish to have them collect background information prior to discussing the case.

Question 1 asks why a competing industrial distributor would even consider investing in a portal designed by Grainger. One reason is to avoid the expense and headache of setting up a separate, proprietary website. A second reason is to band together with other distributors as a way of lowering costs and thereby improving margins. On the other hand, competitors didn't invest because they may have worried about Grainger's ability to control or dominate the portal, among other concerns.

Question 2 asks whether Grainger is in a position to be a channel captain. Because of its size, Grainger is in a good position to serve as a channel captain for business products. Its huge buying capacity, supplier contacts, and customer relationships provide it with significant channel power.

Question 3 asks students to explain why a hospital would buy from Grainger instead of buying directly from producers. First, the hospital may not buy in sufficient quantities or place orders frequently enough to deal directly with producers. Second, the hospital may require special services (such as delivery of different orders to different buildings or departments) that producers are unprepared or unwilling to provide. Third, the hospital may prefer to deal with one of Grainger's local distribution branches rather than trying to arrange orders and obtain service from a producer located some distance away.

CHAPTER 16

Wholesaling and Physical Distribution

TEACHING RESOURCES QUICK REFERENCE GUIDE

Resource	Location
Purpose and Perspective	IRM, p. 293
Guide for Using Color Transparencies	IRM, p. 294
Lecture Outline	IRM, p. 294
Notes for Class Exercises, Debate Issue, and Chapter Quiz	IRM, p. 301
Class Exercise 1	IRM, p. 303
Class Exercise 2	IRM, p. 304
Debate Issue	IRM, p. 305
Chapter Quiz	IRM, p. 306
Answers to Discussion and Review Questions	IRM, p. 307
Comments on the Cases	IRM, p. 310
Case 16.1	IRM, p. 310
Video	Tape 2/DVD 2, Segment 16
Video Information	IRM, p. 310
Multiple-Choice Questions About the Video	IRM, p. 311
Case 16.2	IRM, p. 312
Transparency Acetates	Transparency package
Examination Questions: Essay	TB, p. 445
Examination Questions: Multiple-Choice	TB, p. 445
Examination Questions: True-False	TB, p. 473
Author-Selected Multiple-Choice Test Items	TB, p. 671
HMClassPrep Presentation Resources	CD-ROM
PowerPoint Slides	Instructor's website

Note: Additional resources are updated periodically and may be found on the accompanying student and instructor websites at http://www.prideferrell.com/.

PURPOSE AND PERSPECTIVE

This chapter explores many of the organizations and activities that are involved in making products available to customers when and where they want them. We begin with a discussion of the nature of wholesaling. We examine the services wholesalers offer producers and retailers and classify wholesalers based on the activities they perform in the marketing channel. Next, we consider how physical distribution activities are integrated into marketing channels and contribute to overall marketing strategies. We discuss physical distribution activities in detail, beginning with the three aspects of order processing: order entry, order handling, and order delivery. We note the importance of efficient inventory management and materials handling. We consider the essential processing functions a warehouse performs and differentiate among private warehouses, public warehouses, and distribution centers. Then we discuss the five major modes of transportation, analyze transportation selection criteria, and explain how two or more modes of transportation may be combined for greater efficiency. Finally, we examine the strategic relationship of physical distribution to other elements in the marketing mix.

GUIDE FOR USING COLOR TRANSPARENCIES

There are two groups of color transparencies. The transparencies identified by a double number are the same as the figures and tables in the text. The transparencies labeled with a number and a letter are illustrations that do not appear in the text, but they can be used as additional examples of concepts discussed.

Table 16.1	Major Wholesaling Functions
Figure 16.1	Types of Merchant Wholesalers
Table 16.2	Services That Limited-Service Wholesalers Provide
Figure 16.2	Types of Agents and Brokers
Table 16.3	Services That Agents and Brokers Provide
Figure 16.3	Proportional Cost of Each Physical Distribution Function as a Percentage of Total Distribution Costs
Figure 16.4	Proportion of Intercity Freight Carried by Various Transportation Modes
Table 16.4	Typical Transportation Modes for Various Products
Table 16.5	Relative Ratings of Transportation Modes by Selection Criteria
Figure 16A	Chapter 16 Outline
Figure 16B	Key Definitions: Wholesaling, Physical Distribution
Figure 16C	How Can FedEx and Similar Organizations Help Its Business Customers to Use Physical Distribution-Related Services Strategically?
Figure 16D	Why Would a Multimodal Shipping Capability Be Important to a Company That Does Business in Several Countries?

LECTURE OUTLINE

(Transparency Figure 16A: Chapter Outline)

I.   **The Nature of Wholesaling**
    A.   **Wholesaling Concepts**
        1.   *Wholesaling* refers to all transactions in which products are bought for resale, for making other products, or for general business operations.

(Transparency Figure 16B)

        2.   A *wholesaler* is an individual or organization that facilitates and expedites exchanges that are primarily wholesale transactions.
        3.   Distribution of all goods requires wholesaling activities, whether a wholesaling firm is involved or not.

(Transparency Table 16.1)

    B.   **Services Provided by Wholesalers**
        1.   Wholesalers provide essential services to both producers and retailers.
            a)   Services Provided to Producers
                (1)   By initiating sales contacts with a producer and by selling diverse products to retailers, wholesalers serve as an extension of the producer's sales force.
                (2)   Wholesalers often pay for transporting goods; they reduce a producer's warehousing expenses and inventory investment by holding goods in inventory; they extend credit and assume losses from buyers who turn out to be poor credit risks; and when they buy a producer's entire output and pay promptly or in cash, they are a source of working capital.
                (3)   Wholesalers serve as conduits for information within the marketing channel.

(4)   Many producers would prefer more direct interaction with retailers, but wholesalers are more likely to have closer contact with retailers because of their strategic position in the marketing channel.

b)   Services Provided to Retailers
(1)   Wholesalers support retailers by assisting with marketing strategy, especially the distribution component.
(2)   They help retailers select inventory.
(3)   They are often specialists on market conditions and experts at negotiating final purchases.
(4)   They can reduce a retailer's burden of looking for and coordinating supply sources.
(5)   If the wholesaler purchases for several different buyers, expenses can be shared by all customers.

2.   By buying in large quantities and delivering to customers in smaller lots, wholesalers are able to perform physical distribution activities efficiently.

3.   The distinction between services performed by wholesalers and those performed by other businesses has blurred in recent years.

C.   **Types of Wholesalers**
1.   **Merchant Wholesalers**

(Transparency Figure 16.1)

Merchant wholesalers are independently owned businesses that take title to goods, assume risks associated with ownership, and generally buy and resell products to other wholesalers, business customers, or retailers.

a)   *Full-service wholesalers* perform the widest possible range of wholesaling functions.
(1)   Customers rely on full-service wholesalers for product availability, suitable assortments, breaking large quantities into smaller ones, financial assistance, and technical advice and service.
(2)   Types of Full-Service Wholesalers
(a)   *General-merchandise wholesalers* carry a wide product mix but offer limited depth within product lines.
(b)   *Limited-line wholesalers* carry only a few product lines but offer an extensive assortment of products within those lines.
(c)   *Specialty-line wholesalers* offer the narrowest range of products, usually a single product line or a few items within a product line.
(d)   *Rack jobbers* are full-service, specialty-line wholesalers that own and maintain display racks in supermarkets, drugstores, and discount and variety stores.

b)   *Limited-service wholesalers* provide fewer marketing services than full-service wholesalers and specialize in just a few functions.
(1)   Limited-service wholesalers take title to merchandise but often do not deliver merchandise, grant credit, provide marketing information, store inventory, or plan ahead for customers' future needs.
(2)   Types of Limited-Service Wholesalers

(Transparency Table 16.2)

(a)   *Cash-and-carry wholesalers* are intermediaries whose customers— usually small businesses—pay cash and furnish transportation.

        (b) *Truck wholesalers*, sometimes called truck jobbers, transport a limited line of products directly to customers for on-the-spot inspection and selection.

        (c) *Drop shippers*, also known as desk jobbers, take title to goods and negotiate sales but never take actual possession of products.

        (d) *Mail-order wholesalers* use catalogs instead of sales forces to sell products to retail and business customers.

2. **Agents and Brokers**

    a) Agents and brokers negotiate purchases and expedite sales but do not take title to products.

(Transparency Figure 16.2)

        (1) *Agents* represent either buyers or sellers on a permanent basis.

        (2) *Brokers* are intermediaries that buyers or sellers employ temporarily.

    b) Although agents and brokers perform even fewer functions than limited-service wholesalers, they are usually specialists in particular products or types of customers and can provide valuable sales expertise.

    c) Types of Agents

(Transparency Table 16.3)

        (1) *Manufacturers' agents* are independent intermediaries that represent two or more sellers and usually offer customers complete product lines.

        (2) *Selling agents* market either all of a specified product line or a manufacturer's entire output.

        (3) *Commission merchants* receive goods on consignment from local sellers and negotiate sales in large, central markets.

    d) A broker's primary purpose is to bring buyers and sellers together. Thus, brokers perform fewer functions than other intermediaries.

3. **Manufacturers' Sales Branches and Offices**

    a) *Sales branches* are manufacturer-owned intermediaries that sell products and provide support to the manufacturer's sales force.

    b) *Sales offices* are manufacturer-owned operations that provide services normally associated with agents.

    c) Manufacturers may set up these branches or offices to reach their customers more effectively by performing wholesaling functions themselves.

II. **The Nature of Physical Distribution**

  A. Physical Distribution Concepts

    1. *Physical distribution*, also known as logistics, refers to the activities used to move products from producers to consumers and other end users.

(Transparency Figure 16B)

    a) These activities include order processing, inventory management, materials handling, warehousing, and transportation.

    b) Planning an efficient physical distribution system is crucial to developing an effective marketing strategy because it can decrease costs and increase customer satisfaction.

    2. Physical distribution deals with the physical movement and storage of products and supplies both within and among marketing channel members. Physical distribution systems must meet the needs of both the supply chain and customers.

3.   Within the marketing channel, physical distribution activities are often performed by a wholesaler, but they may be performed by the producer or retailer or outsourced. *Outsourcing* is the contracting of physical distribution tasks to third parties who do not have managerial authority within the marketing channel.

B.   **Physical Distribution Objectives**

    1.   **Meeting Standards of Customer Service**

        a)   In physical distribution, availability, timeliness, and quality are important dimensions of customer service.

            (1)   Availability—the percentage of orders that can be filled directly from a company's existing inventory

            (2)   Timeliness—how quickly the product is shipped to the customer

            (3)   Accuracy—whether the product the customer ordered is the product that is shipped to the customer

        b)   Customers seeking a high level of customer service may also want sizable inventories, efficient order processing, availability of emergency shipments, progress reports, post-sale services, prompt replacement of defective items, and warranties.

        c)   Companies must also examine the service levels competitors offer and match or exceed those standards when the costs of providing the services can be justified by the sales generated.

    2.   **Reducing Total Distribution Costs**

        a)   Although physical distribution managers try to minimize the costs associated with order processing, inventory management, materials handling, warehousing, and transportation, decreasing the costs in one area often raises them in another.

(Transparency Figure 16.3)

        b)   A total-cost approach to physical distribution enables managers to view physical distribution as a system rather than a collection of unrelated activities.

            (1)   The total-cost approach involves analyzing the costs of all distribution alternatives, even those considered too impractical or expensive.

            (2)   A distribution system's lowest total cost is never the result of using a combination of the cheapest functions. Instead, it is the lowest overall cost compatible with the company's stated service objectives.

        c)   Physical distribution managers must be sensitive to the issue of cost tradeoffs.

    3.   **Reducing Cycle Time**

        An important goal of physical distribution involves reducing *cycle time*, the time it takes to complete a process; doing so can reduce costs and/or increase customer service.

C.   **Functions of Physical Distribution**

    1.   **Order Processing**

        a)   *Order processing* is the receipt and transmission of sales order information. Efficient order processing facilitates product flow.

        b)   Order processing entails three main tasks: order entry, order handling, and order delivery.

            (1)   Order entry begins when customers or salespeople place purchase orders via telephone, mail, e-mail, or website.

            (2)   Once an order is entered, it is transmitted to a warehouse, where product availability is verified, and to the credit department where prices, terms, and the customer's credit rating are checked. If approved, the order is assembled.

(3) When the order has been assembled and packed for shipment, the warehouse schedules delivery with an appropriate carrier.

   c) Whether to use a manual or an electronic order-processing system depends on which method provides the greatest speed and accuracy within cost limits.

      (1) Manual processing suffices for small-volume orders and is more flexible in certain situations.

      (2) Most companies use *electronic data interchange (EDI)*, which uses computer technology to integrate order processing with production, inventory, accounting, and transportation.

2. **Inventory Management**

Inventory management involves developing and maintaining adequate assortments of products to meet customers' needs.

(Tech Know: TAL Manages JCPenney Shirt Inventory)

   a) Because a firm's investment in inventory usually represents a significant portion of its total assets, inventory decisions have a major impact on physical distribution costs and the level of customer service provided.

      (1) When too few products are carried in inventory, the result is "stockouts," or shortages of products, which in turn result in brand switching, lower sales, and loss of customers.

      (2) When too many products are carried, costs increase, as do risks of product obsolescence, pilferage, and damage.

   b) To determine when to order, a marketer calculates the "reorder point," the inventory level that signals the need to place a new order. To calculate the reorder point, the marketer must know the order lead time, the usage rate, and the amount of safety stock required.

      (1) Order lead time—average time lapse between placing the order and receiving it

      (2) Usage rate—rate at which a product's inventory is used or sold during a specific time period

      (3) Safety stock—amount of extra inventory that a firm keeps to guard against stockouts resulting from above-average usage rates and/or longer than expected lead times

      (4) Reorder point = (order lead time x usage rate)

      (5) + safety stock

   c) Efficient inventory management with accurate reorder points are crucial for firms that use a *just-in-time (JIT)* approach, in which supplies arrive just as they are needed for use in production or for resale.

3. **Materials Handling**

Materials handling, the physical handling of products, is an important factor in warehouse operations, as well as in transportation from points of production to points of consumption.

   a) Efficient procedures and techniques for materials handling minimize inventory management costs, reduce the number of times a good is handled, improve customer service, and increase customer satisfaction.

   b) Product characteristics often determine handling.

   c) Unit loading and containerization are two common methods used in materials handling.

      (1) Unit loading—one or more boxes are placed on a pallet or skid; these units can then be efficiently loaded by mechanical means.

(2) Containerization—the consolidation of many items into a single large container, which is then sealed at its point of origin and opened at its destination.

4. **Warehousing**

a) *Warehousing*, the design and operation of facilities for storing and moving goods, is another important physical distribution function.

b) The basic distribution functions that warehouses perform include receiving, identifying, sorting, and dispatching goods to storage; holding goods in storage until needed; recalling and assembling stored goods for shipment; and dispatching shipments.

c) By using the right type of warehouse, a company may reduce transportation and inventory costs or improve service to customers; the wrong warehouse may drain company resources.

d) Types of Warehouses

(1) *Private warehouses* are operated by companies for the purpose of shipping and storing their own products.

(a) A firm usually leases or purchases a private warehouse when its warehousing needs in a given geographic market are substantial and stable enough to warrant a long-term commitment to a fixed facility.

(b) Private warehouses are also appropriate for firms that require special handling and storage and that want control of warehouse design and operation.

(c) When sales volumes are fairly stable, ownership and control of a private warehouse may provide benefits, such as property appreciation; however private warehouses have fixed costs and limited flexibility.

(2) *Public warehouses* lease storage space and related physical distribution facilities as an outsource service to other companies.

(a) Public warehouses sometimes provide such distribution services as receiving, unloading, inspecting, and reshipping products; filling orders; providing financing; displaying products; and coordinating shipments.

(b) They are especially useful to firms with seasonal production or low-volume storage needs, have inventories that must be maintained in many locations, are testing or entering new markets, or own private warehouses but occasionally require additional storage space.

(c) Many public warehouses furnish security for products being used as collateral for loans, a service provided at either the warehouse or at a "field public warehouse," the site of the owner's inventory location.

(d) Public warehouses also provide "bonded storage," a warehousing arrangement in which imported or taxable products are not released until the products' owners pay U.S. customs duties, taxes, or other fees.

e) *Distribution centers* are large, centralized warehouses that receive goods from factories and suppliers, regroup them into orders, and ship them to customers quickly, the focus being on the movement of goods rather than storage.

(1) They are designed and located for rapid flow of products.

(2) Benefits include improved customer service and product availability, minimized delivery time, lower transportation costs, and lower inventory costs.

5.   **Transportation**

(Transparency Figure 16C)

a)   *Transportation*, the movement of products from where they are made to where they are used, is the most expensive physical distribution function.

b)   **Transportation Modes**

There are five basic transportation modes, each offering distinct advantages.

(Transparency Figure 16.4)

(1)   Railroads carry heavy, bulky freight that must be shipped long distances overland.

(2)   Trucks provide the most flexible schedules and routes of all major transportation modes because they can go almost anywhere.

(Transparency Table 16.4)

(3)   Waterways are the cheapest method of shipping heavy, low-value, nonperishable goods.

(4)   Air transportation is the fastest yet most expensive form of shipping.

(5)   Pipelines, the most automated transportation mode, usually belong to the shipper and carry the shipper's products.

c)   **Choosing Transportation Modes**

Distribution managers select a transportation mode based on the combination of cost, speed, dependability, load flexibility, accessibility, and frequency that is most appropriate for their product and generates the desired level of customer service.

(Transparency Table 16.5)

(1)   Speed is measured by the total time a carrier has possession of goods, including the time required for pickup and delivery, handling, and movement between points of origin and destination.

(2)   Dependability of a transportation mode is determined by the consistency of service provided.

(3)   Load flexibility is the degree to which a transportation mode can provide appropriate equipment and conditions for moving specific kinds of goods and can be adapted for moving other products.

(4)   Accessibility refers to a carrier's ability to move goods over a specific route or network.

(5)   Frequency refers to how often a company can send shipments by a specific transportation mode.

d)   **Coordinating Transportation**

(1)   To take advantage of the benefits offered by various transportation modes and to compensate for deficiencies, marketers often combine and coordinate two or more modes. This approach, sometimes called *intermodal transportation*, has become easier in recent years because of new developments within the transportation industry.

(Transparency Figure 16D)

(2)   Specialized outsource agencies provide other forms of transportation coordination.

(a) *Freight forwarders* combine shipments from several organizations into efficient lot sizes.

(b) *Megacarriers* are freight transportation companies that offer several shipment methods, including rail, truck, and air service.

D. **Strategic Issues in Physical Distribution**

1. Physical distribution functions—order processing, inventory management, materials handling, warehousing, and transportation—account for about half of all marketing costs.

2. The strategic importance of physical distribution is evident in all elements of the marketing mix.

a) Product design and packaging must allow for efficient stacking, storage, transport, and tracking.

b) Competitive pricing may depend on a firm's ability to provide reliable delivery or emergency shipments of replacement parts.

c) Promotional campaigns must be coordinated with distribution functions so that advertised products are available to buyers and order-processing departments can handle additional sales orders efficiently.

d) Channel members must consider warehousing and transportation costs, which may influence a firm's policy on stockouts or its choice to centralize (or decentralize) inventory.

(Global Marketing: How OshKosh B'Gosh Brings Bib Overalls from Abroad)

3. Improving physical distribution starts by closing the gap with customers. The entire supply chain must understand and meet customers' requirements.

4. No single distribution system is ideal for all situations, and any system must be evaluated continually and adapted as necessary.

NOTES FOR CLASS EXERCISES, DEBATE ISSUE, AND CHAPTER QUIZ

On the following pages, you will find two class exercises, a debate issue, and a chapter quiz. These are formatted in large-size type so that you can use them as class handouts or for making transparencies. Below are the authors' comments on the class exercises, the debate topic for this chapter, and the answers to the chapter quiz.

Comments on Class Exercise 1

The objective of this exercise is to improve students' recognition of various types of wholesalers. Answers:

1. Broker

2. Drop shipper

3. Selling agent

4. Mail-order wholesaler

5. Cash-and-carry wholesaler

6. Truck wholesaler

7. Commission merchant

8. Manufacturers' agent

Comments on Class Exercise 2

The objective of this class exercise is to help students understand the role of physical distribution activities in achieving superior customer service.

Question 1. It is important to prioritize customer demands to know which services customers are more willing to pay for. Additionally, tradeoffs must be considered between those things that some customers want but whose costs might outweigh the benefits. In Part A, the most expensive services are likely to be emergency shipping, maintaining inventories, and after-sale service. However, these costs must be weighed against the consumer goodwill they will provide. In Part B, ask students, "What would happen if Domino's didn't have the 30-minute guarantee?" If no service objectives are set, it affects both employees (who don't try as hard) and customers (who receive inconsistent service). In Part C, press students to determine if their prices take into account the costs of handling particularly small or large orders or emergency orders. Likewise, are the costs of potential lost sales from lower performance levels considered?

Question 2. A related question to ask would be "What types of problems do you have when ordering at a fast-food restaurant?" Students can especially identify with this question. Problems can be overcome by properly handling complaints, offering customers progress reports, checking inventory/credit before completing an order, offering substitutes, and electronic order processing.

Question 3. Stockouts usually mean lost sales. Reorder points and using a marketing information system can reduce problems, as can heavily stocking items that are sold most often.

DEBATE ISSUE

With respect to inventory management, is it better to have an "overstock" than a "stockout"?

CHAPTER QUIZ

Answers to Chapter Quiz 1. c; 2. c; 3. e; 4. d.

Class Exercise 1

Type of Wholesaler	Takes Possession of Products	Delivers Merchandise to Customers	Provides Credit	Takes Title to Products	Common Products Carried
1. _____	No	No	No	No	Used in industrial equipment
2. _____	No	No	Yes	Yes	Building materials
3. _____	Sometimes	Yes	Yes	No	Textiles
4. _____	Yes	No	Sometimes	Yes	Office supplies
5. _____	Yes	No	No	Yes	Groceries and office supplies
6. _____	Yes	Yes	No	Yes	Perishables
7. _____	Yes	Yes	Sometimes	No	Agricultural commodities
8. _____	Sometimes	Sometimes	No	No	Apparel and accessories

Class Exercise 2

YOU ARE OPERATING A NEW OFFICE SUPPLY DELIVERY SERVICE IN TOWN AND MUST SET THE PHYSICAL DISTRIBUTION POLICIES FOR THE FIRM. YOUR MAIN OBJECTIVE IS TO DECREASE COSTS WHILE INCREASING SERVICE. YOU MUST DETERMINE WHAT LEVEL OF CUSTOMER SERVICE IS ACCEPTABLE YET REALISTIC. WHILE DOING SO, YOU MUST KEEP IN MIND THE NEEDS OF YOUR PRIMARY TARGET MARKET.

1. In terms of customer service, which of the following are likely to be most important to your target market?

   - Availability
   - Quality
   - Progress reports
   - After-sale service
   - Replacement of defective items
   - Timeliness
   - Sizable inventories
   - Warranties and guarantees
   - Emergency shipments
   - Efficient order processing

   a. Which of these are going to be most costly to provide?

   b. Develop service standards that are specific, measurable, and appropriate for delivery (i.e., How long will delivery take?)

   c. How much will you charge for delivery and other services?

2. In terms of order processing, why do some firms have problems with order entry, order handling, and order delivery? How are you going to prevent and overcome such problems?

3. If your inventory is kept too low, stockouts will occur. What will consumers do when faced with a stockout situation? How might reorder points, electronic equipment, and JIT help avoid stockouts?

Debate Issue

WITH RESPECT TO INVENTORY MANAGEMENT, IS IT BETTER TO HAVE AN "OVERSTOCK" THAN A "STOCKOUT"?

YES

- An overstock allows a firm to serve its customers, which helps to build and maintain strong customer relationships.

- When you tell a customer that you don't have the product, you are indirectly sending the customer to one of your competitors.

- An overstock helps to maximize sales revenues.

NO

- If your inventory is perishable, an overstock can be expensive. An extra 1,000 pounds of bananas, if unsold, can be expensive.

- An overstock requires a firm to have a larger inventory. Holding a larger inventory increases a firm's costs.

- Holding a larger inventory reduces a firm's stock turn rate. A firm generates revenue by turning its inventory, not by holding its inventory.

Chapter Quiz

1. As a wholesaler, Martino, Inc., would be *least likely* to sell its produce items to a

   a. food specialty store.
   b. grocery store.
   c. grocery shopper.
   d. employee cafeteria.
   e. hospital.

2. A manufacturer-owned operation that provides services usually associated with agents is a

   a. facilitating agency.
   b. wholesaler.
   c. sales office.
   d. sales branch.
   e. public warehouse.

3. The contracting of physical distribution tasks to third parties who do not have managerial authority within the marketing channel is known as

   a. illegal.
   b. logistics
   c. warehousing.
   d. wholesaling.
   e. outsourcing.

4. Morgan Steel Company leases a warehouse in Jacksonville, Alabama, to serve Deep South markets that were large enough and stable enough to make a long-term commitment to fixed facilities. This is a

   a. flexible warehouse.
   b. dispatching center.
   c. distribution center.
   d. private warehouse.
   e. public warehouse.

ANSWERS TO DISCUSSION AND REVIEW QUESTIONS

1. **What is wholesaling?**

    Wholesaling refers to all transactions in which products are bought for resale, for making other products, or for general business operations.

2. **What services do wholesalers provide to producers and retailers?**

    For producers, wholesalers serve as an extension of the producer's sales force. Wholesalers also provide services such as financial assistance, storage, and transportation, and they are excellent sources of information and working capital.

    Wholesalers help retailers select inventory and negotiate final purchases. Wholesalers also provide transportation, storage, information, materials handling, and warehousing. Because they provide the fastest delivery at the lowest cost, they create time and place utilities.

3. **What is the difference between a full-service merchant wholesaler and a limited-service merchant wholesaler?**

    A merchant wholesaler is an independently owned business that takes title to goods, assumes risks associated with ownership, and generally buys and resells products to other wholesalers, organizational customers, or retailers. Full-service merchant wholesalers perform the widest possible range of wholesaling functions, whereas limited-service merchant wholesalers provide fewer functions and specialize in just a few functions.

4. **Drop shippers take title to products but do not accept physical possession of them, whereas commission merchants take physical possession of products but do not accept title. Defend the logic of classifying drop shippers as wholesale merchants and commission merchants as agents.**

    Drop shippers are classified as wholesale merchants because they take title and assume risk of product ownership, although they do not take physical possession. Commission merchants take physical possession but do not assume the risk associated with product ownership; they return unsold merchandise to the owner. Product ownership therefore differentiates agents from merchants and determines the classifications of drop shipper and commission merchant.

5. **Why are manufacturers' sales offices and branches classified as wholesalers? Which independent wholesalers are replaced by manufacturers' sales branches? Which independent wholesalers are replaced by manufacturers' sales offices?**

    Manufacturers' sales offices and branches are classified as wholesalers by the U.S. Census of Business because their main function is to perform wholesaling activities. Manufacturers' sales branches serve the same functions as merchant wholesalers, and manufacturers' sales offices serve essentially the same function as agents.

6. **Discuss the cost and service tradeoffs involved in developing a physical distribution system.**

    The main objective of physical distribution is to decrease costs while increasing service. Companies often give customer service high priority, and service may be as important in attracting customers as the cost of the company's product. On one hand, the large inventories and rapid transportation essential for high levels of customer service drive up costs. On the other hand, reduced inventories and slower, cheaper methods of transportation result in customer dissatisfaction and lost sales. Therefore, the overall objective of a service policy should be to improve customer service to the point where an increase in sales from the service will just offset any increase in distribution costs associated with the service.

7. **What factors must physical distribution managers consider when developing a customer service mix?**

There are several factors a physical distribution manager should consider when developing a customer service mix. Because service needs vary from customer to customer, the manager must first analyze and adapt to customer preferences. The manager should also examine the service levels competitors offer. Then the manager may try to identify and correct the causes of customer complaints and billing and shipping errors.

8. **What are the main tasks involved in order processing?**

There are three main order-processing tasks. Order entry begins when customers or salespeople place purchase orders by mail, e-mail, telephone, or website. Order handling involves verifying product availability, approving the credit purchase, and filling the order. Order delivery involves scheduling pickup with an appropriate carrier.

9. **Discuss the advantages of using an electronic order-processing system. Which types of organizations are most likely to utilize electronic order processing?**

Order processing can be performed manually or electronically. Because they let a company integrate order processing, production, inventory control, accounting, and transportation planning into a total information system, electronic data interchange systems have distinct advantages over manual processing. Such a system can function as an information system that links marketing channel members and outsourcing firms together. It reduces paperwork for all members of the supply chain and allows them to share information on invoices, orders, payments, inquiries, and scheduling.

10. **Explain the tradeoffs inventory managers face when reordering products or supplies. How is the reorder point computed?**

When reordering merchandise, inventory managers face tradeoffs based on the amount of safety stock being carried. Large safety stocks ensure product availability, improvements of customer service, and lower order-processing costs because orders are placed less frequently. Small safety stocks result in higher order-processing costs through frequently reordering but lower the overall cost of carrying inventory. The reorder point is computed by multiplying the lead time by the usage rate and adding the safety stock.

11. **How does a product's package affect materials handling procedures and techniques?**

Packaging's protection functions have a strong impact on physical distribution. Decisions about packaging materials and methods affect the efficiency of physical handling. Materials handling techniques and procedures should maximize a warehouse's usable capacity, reduce the number of times a product is handled, and improve customer service. The design of the package should be coordinated to help meet these objectives. For example, a package's size and shape should allow the goods to be stacked and moved efficiently, and its material and design should ensure the package's ability to withstand rigorous handling.

12. **What is containerization? Discuss its major benefits.**

Containerization is the practice of consolidating many items into a single large container that is sealed at the point of origin and opened at the destination. Containerization broadens the capacities of the transportation system by enabling shippers to transport a wider range of cargoes with speed, reliability, and stable costs. It is energy efficient, decreases the need for expensive security measures, and reduces losses and damage.

13. **Explain the major differences between private and public warehouses. What is a field public warehouse?**

A private warehouse is operated by a company for the purpose of distributing its own products. Private warehouses provide benefits such as property appreciation and tax shelters but also incur fixed costs such as insurance, taxes, maintenance, and debt expenses. They provide little flexibility when a company wishes to move inventories to more strategic locations.

Public warehouses rent storage space and physical distribution facilities to other firms. Public warehouse costs are variable rather than fixed (and therefore are usually lower).

A field public warehouse is established by a public warehouse at the customer's inventory location. The warehouser then becomes the custodian of the products and issues a receipt that can be used as collateral for a loan.

14. **The focus of distribution centers is on the movement of goods. Describe how distribution centers are designed for the rapid flow of products.**

Distribution centers are designed to move goods to customers quickly and efficiently. They are one-story buildings (to eliminate the need for elevators) and have easy access to transportation networks such as major highways. The distribution center is highly automated and computerized to facilitate product flows. It serves customers in regional markets to emphasize quick product grouping and shipping.

15. **Compare and contrast the five major transportation modes in terms of cost, speed, dependability, load flexibility, accessibility, and frequency.**

Railroads can carry heavy, bulky freight that must be shipped long distances overland. Generally, their cost is moderate, speed is average, dependability is average, load flexibility is high, accessibility is high, and frequency is low.

Trucks provide the most flexible schedules and routes because they can go almost anywhere. Costs of distribution are higher because of the small shipments carried. They are fast and dependable and have very high accessibility and high frequency.

Waterways are the cheapest method for shipping heavy, low-value, nonperishable goods. This mode of transportation is slow, however, and cannot serve inland markets without supplementary transport. Their dependability is average, load flexibility is very high, but frequency is low.

Airways are the fastest and most expensive method of shipping. Like waterways, however, air transportation must be supplemented with another transportation method. The capacity of air transport depends on the individual aircraft. Dependability is high, load flexibility is very low, but frequency is very high.

Pipelines are the most automated transportation modes. They are characterized by limited accessibility but are dependable and ensure low product damage and theft. Pipelines move products slowly but continuously. Allowances should be made for shrinkage, usually caused by evaporation. Additionally, costs and flexibility are low, but frequency is very high.

16. **Discuss ways marketers can combine or coordinate two or more modes of transportation. What is the advantage of doing so?**

Containerization allows marketers to consolidate many items into a single, large container that can then be transported efficiently by any of the transportation modes available to distribution managers. Freight forwarders combine shipments for several organizations into efficient lots and buy transportation space from various types of carriers. Megacarriers are freight transportation companies that provide several methods of shipment and often offer warehousing, consulting, and leasing services.

The advantage of coordinating two or more modes of transportation is that it allows physical distribution managers to take advantage of the benefits various carriers offer while compensating for their deficiencies. For example, trucking offers more flexibility but costs more than railways. Combining the two carriers is cheaper than using only trucking and provides more accessibility than railways alone.

COMMENTS ON THE CASES

CASE 16.1 QUICK INTERNATIONAL COURIER DELIVERS TIME-SENSITIVE SHIPMENTS

The objective of this case is to show how a company can build a profitable business by providing logistical services to other firms. Students may know very little about this aspect of physical distribution. Therefore, you may want to ask the class to research the company and the industry before discussing this case.

Question 1 asks whether a company that pays extra for urgent air shipments through Quick International Courier can actually reduce its total distribution costs. If the company is able to lower its inventory levels, reduce safety stock, and reduce the amount of warehouse space needed by using Quick International, it will reduce its overall distribution costs.

In the second question, students are asked to identify the details about materials handling that Quick might have to consider before picking up specialized cargo such as a shipment of bone marrow or a carton of computer chips. Quick would have to consider the characteristics of the products it is being asked to transport, such as packaging, volatility, size and shape, and ability to use containerization or unit loading to expedite handling. It would also have to take security into consideration for dangerous and volatile products being shipped. Students may offer other suggestions as well.

The final question asks whether Quick should expand into air delivery for businesses that serve consumer markets. Students who say yes may note that consumers who buy very expensive goods may be more interested in the speed of delivery than the cost of delivery. However, most students will recognize that consumer products generally do not have the kind of price points or margins to absorb or pass through a cost as significant as Quick's fee for air delivery.

Video Information

Company:	Quick International Courier
Location:	Tape 2/DVD 2, Segment 16
Length:	4:13

Video Overview: Quick International Courier specializes in speeding the most urgent, time-sensitive deliveries to national and international destinations by air. The company picks up shipments from its customers and arranges to place them on commercial flights, then meets the planes and delivers the shipments to recipients—all in the same day. Many high-tech firms use Quick as a way of keeping inventory costs low while providing their customers with a higher level of service. With Quick's special software, businesses can even track the status of their shipments at any hour of the day or night, seven days a week.

MULTIPLE-CHOICE QUESTIONS ABOUT THE VIDEO

1. Quick's business customers like the ability to electronically monitor the progress of their shipments because
   a. they want to lengthen the lead time needed for their reorder point.
   b. most are juggling deliveries within limited warehouse and production space.
   c. this information is vital to the functioning of their entire supply chain.
   d. they prefer to outsource their physical distribution activities to specialists.
   e. most deliveries must connect with other transportation modes to be forwarded to their final destination.

2. Quick places shipments on commercial carriers instead of flying its own aircraft because
   a. this allows more flexibility in scheduling deliveries.
   b. it prefers shipping through megacarriers that reach distant locations.
   c. some customers request the use of specific carriers.
   d. international shipments must travel by commercial carrier for legal reasons.
   e. commercial jets have more cargo space available for priority shipments.

3. Quick customizes its services for nearly every shipment, knowing that
   a. customers want special treatment for their deliveries regardless of content.
   b. computer components must be handled differently from cartons of documents.
   c. premium pricing requires a premium level of service.
   d. the usage rate varies according to the time-sensitivity of each shipment.
   e. a high level of accountability will help build relationships with customers and carriers.

4. One of the main reasons for Quick's rapid growth is
   a. the low cost of outsourcing transportation services.
   b. its ability to provide customers with on-site supervision of physical distribution services.
   c. its intermodal transportation capabilities.
   d. the increase in shipments supported by electronic data interchange.
   e. the increase in global trade.

ANSWERS TO MULTIPLE-CHOICE QUESTIONS ABOUT THE VIDEO

1. c

2. a

3. b

4. e

CASE 16.2 WAL-MART COMPETES USING EFFICIENT, LOW-COST PHYSICAL DISTRIBUTION

This case helps students understand how Wal-Mart effectively and efficiently manages its global supply chain and physical distribution efforts. Students should be very familiar with Wal-Mart and its retailing activities, although they may know little about the retailer's behind-the-scenes logistics.

In the first question, students are asked to explain why physical distribution is so important in Wal-Mart's marketing strategy. Wal-Mart's marketing strategy is to provide low prices on a broad selection of products. With thousands of stores stocking tens of thousands of items, the retailer must manage its inventory efficiently and avoid stockouts if it is to satisfy customers at a profit. Otherwise, customers are likely to start shopping at Kmart and other competing retailers.

The second question asks why Wal-Mart would prefer to deal directly with suppliers rather than buying from wholesalers. First, Wal-Mart is likely to negotiate a better price by dealing directly with manufacturers. In contrast, wholesalers need to mark their products up to achieve an acceptable profit—so Wal-Mart would probably pay more if it bought from wholesalers. Second, Wal-Mart buys in huge quantities that producers are better equipped to handle. Finally, Wal-Mart may believe that it can more efficiently perform some of the functions normally handled by wholesalers.

The third question asks how Retail Link helps Wal-Mart do a better job of managing order processing and inventory management. This network helps the retailer and its suppliers jointly agree on a schedule for future orders and deliveries, based on Wal-Mart's analysis of sales data. In this way, Wal-Mart eliminates the expense and bother of placing smaller or emergency orders while enabling each distribution center to have the inventory levels it needs for forecasted sales.

CHAPTER 17

Retailing and Direct Marketing

TEACHING RESOURCES QUICK REFERENCE GUIDE

Resource	Location
Purpose and Perspective	IRM, p. 313
Guide for Using Color Transparencies	IRM, p. 314
Lecture Outline	IRM, p. 314
Notes for Class Exercises, Debate Issue, and Chapter Quiz	IRM, p. 320
Class Exercise 1	IRM, p. 322
Class Exercise 2	IRM, p. 323
Debate Issue	IRM, p. 324
Chapter Quiz	IRM, p. 325
Answers to Discussion and Review Questions	IRM, p. 326
Comments on the Cases	IRM, p. 329
Case 17.1	IRM, p. 329
Video	Tape 2/DVD 2, Segment 17
Video Information	IRM, p. 329
Multiple-Choice Questions About the Video	IRM, p. 330
Case 17.2	IRM, p. 331
Transparency Acetates	Transparency package
Examination Questions: Essay	TB, p. 479
Examination Questions: Multiple-Choice	TB, p. 479
Examination Questions: True-False	TB, p. 504
Author-Selected Multiple-Choice Test Items	TB, p. 672
HMClassPrep Presentation Resources	CD-ROM
PowerPoint Slides	Instructor's website

Note: Additional resources are updated periodically and may be found on the accompanying student and instructor websites at http://www.prideferrell.com/.

PURPOSE AND PERSPECTIVE

This chapter is devoted exclusively to retailing because retailers are very important intermediaries. Here we focus on retailing fundamentals and the broad strategic decisions that retail institutions must make. First, we overview the nature of retailing. Then we classify the major types of retailers. We also examine several types of direct marketing and analyze the concept of franchising. We cover several strategic issues in retailing, including location, positioning, and store image. We close with a discussion of scrambled merchandising and the wheel of retailing hypothesis.

GUIDE FOR USING COLOR TRANSPARENCIES

There are two groups of color transparencies. The transparencies identified by a double number are the same as the figures and tables in the text. The transparencies labeled with a number and a letter are illustrations that do not appear in the text, but they can be used as additional examples of concepts discussed.

Table 17.2	Top 20 Franchises and Their Startup Costs
Figure 17.1	The Wheel of Retailing
Figure 17A	Chapter 17 Outline
Figure 17B	Key Definitions: Retailing, Franchising
Figure 17C	General Merchandise Retailers
Figure 17D	Traditional Specialty Retailer
Figure 17E	Examples of Category Killers
Figure 17F	Are Retailers Protecting Customers' Personal Information?
Figure 17G	Customers' Reactions to Telemarketing Calls
Figure 17H	Percentage of Online Shoppers Who Have Experienced Problems Sometimes or Frequently
Figure 17I	How to Succeed in Retailing as a Small Business
Figure 17J	Satisfaction Scores for Online Retailers
Figure 17K	What Role Does Yahoo! Shopping Play in Online Retailing?
Figure 17L	If You Had the Financial Resources to Purchase a Franchise, Which Company Would You Select? Why?

LECTURE OUTLINE

(Transparency Figure 17A: Chapter Outline)

I.   **The Nature of Retailing**
   A.   *Retailing* includes all transactions in which the buyer intends to consume the product through personal, family, or household use. A *retailer* is an organization that purchases products for the purpose of reselling them to ultimate consumers.

(Transparency Figure 17B)

   B.   Retailing is important to the national economy.
   C.   Retailers add value, provide services, and assist in making product selections.
      1.   Retailer image can enhance the value of the product.
      2.   Retailers facilitate comparison shopping.
      3.   When retailers offer services, such as technical advice, delivery, credit, and repair services, product value is enhanced.
      4.   Retail sales personnel can demonstrate to customers how a product can address their needs or solve a problem.
   D.   Retailers are the critical link between producers and ultimate consumers because they provide the environment in which exchanges with ultimate consumers occur.
   E.   Traditional retailing is being challenged by direct marketing channels that provide home shopping through catalogs, television, and the Internet.

(Transparency Figure 17F)

   F.   New store formats and advances in information technology are making the retail environment highly dynamic and competitive.

G. The key to success in retailing is to have a strong customer focus and a retail strategy that provides the level of service, product quality, and innovation that consumers desire.

H. Retailers are also finding global opportunities.

II. **Major Types of Retail Stores**

A. **General-Merchandise Retailers**

(Transparency Figure 17C)

General merchandise retailers offer a variety of product lines, stocked in considerable depth.

1. **Department Stores**

Department stores are large retail organizations characterized by wide product mixes and employing at least 25 people.

   a) To facilitate marketing efforts and internal management, related product lines are organized into separate departments.

   b) Department stores are distinctively service oriented.

   c) Typical department stores obtain a large proportion of their sales from apparel, accessories, and cosmetics.

2. **Discount Stores**

Discount stores are self-service, general merchandise outlets that regularly offer brand name and private brand products at low prices.

   a) They accept lower margins in exchange for higher sales volume.

   b) They carry a wide, carefully selected assortment of products, including appliances, housewares, clothes, and toys.

   c) Discount retailing developed on a large scale in the early 1950s.

3. **Supermarkets**

Supermarkets are large, self-service stores that carry a complete line of food products as well as some nonfood products.

   a) They are arranged in departments for maximum efficiency in stocking and handling but have central checkout facilities.

   b) Consumers make more than three-quarters of all grocery purchases in supermarkets.

4. **Superstores**

Superstores—which originated in Europe—are giant retail outlets that carry not only food and nonfood products ordinarily found in supermarkets, but also routinely purchased consumer products.

   a) Superstores sell about four times as many items as supermarkets.

   b) They combine features of both discount stores and supermarkets.

   c) To cut handling and inventory costs, they use sophisticated operating techniques and often have tall shelving that displays entire assortments of products.

5. **Hypermarkets**

Hypermarkets combine supermarket and discount store shopping in one location. They are larger than superstores and carry more products, with 40-50 percent of their space allocated to grocery products and the remaining space to general merchandise.

6. **Warehouse Clubs**

Warehouse clubs are large-scale, members-only selling operations combining cash-and-carry wholesaling and discount retailing.

   a) They offer a broad product mix stacked on pallets or pipe racks.

        b)   To keep prices down, they provide very few services.

    7.   **Warehouse and Catalog Showrooms**

        a)   *Warehouse showrooms* are retail facilities with five basic characteristics: large, low-cost buildings; warehouse materials handling technology; vertical merchandise displays; large, on-premises inventories; and minimum services.

        b)   *Catalog showrooms* are a form of warehouse showroom where consumers shop from catalogs and where products are stored out of buyers' reach.

B.   **Specialty Retailers**

Specialty retailers carry a narrow product mix with deep product lines; they do not sell specialty items unless they complement the overall product mix.

    1.   **Traditional Specialty Retailers**

        (Transparency Figure 17D)

       Traditional specialty retailers are stores that carry a narrow product mix with deep product lines. Sometimes, they may be referred to as "limited-line retailers."

        a)   "Single-line retailers" carry unusual depth in one main product category.

        b)   Although chain specialty stores are increasing in number, most are independently owned.

        c)   Because they are small, specialty stores may have high costs in proportion to sales, and satisfying customers may require carrying some products with low turnover rates.

        d)   Specialty retailers succeed by knowing their customers and providing what they want.

    2.   **Off-Price Retailers**

       Off-price retailers are stores that buy manufacturers' seconds, overruns, returns, and off-season production runs at below-wholesale prices for resale to consumers at deep discounts.

        a)   They offer limited lines of national brand and designer merchandise, usually clothing, shoes, or housewares.

        b)   They charge 20 to 50 percent less than department stores for comparable merchandise, but offer few customer services.

        c)   To ensure a regular flow of merchandise into their stores, off-price retailers establish long-term relationships with suppliers that can provide large quantities of goods at reduced prices.

    3.   **Category Killers**

        (Transparency Figure 17E)

       Category killers are very large specialty stores that concentrate on a major category product and compete on the basis of low prices and enormous product availability.

III. **Direct Marketing**

Direct marketing is the use of the telephone and nonpersonal media to communicate product and organizational information to customers who then can purchase products by mail, telephone, or the Internet.

A.   **Catalog Marketing**

Catalog marketing occurs when an organization provides a catalog from which customers make selections and place orders.

B. **Direct-Response Marketing**

Direct-response marketing occurs when a retailer advertises a product and makes it available through mail or telephone orders.

C. **Telemarketing**

(Transparency Figure 17G)

Telemarketing is the performance of marketing-related activities by telephone.

D. **Television Home Shopping**

Television home shopping presents products to television viewers who can purchase products through toll-free numbers by using credit cards.

E. **Online Retailing**

Online retailing makes products available through computer connections.

(Transparency Figure 17H)

(Transparency Figure 17J)

(Transparency Figure 17K)

(Tech Know: Dell Builds PCs and Profits Through Direct Marketing)

IV. **Other Types of Nonstore Retailing**
   A. **Nonstore Retailing**

   Nonstore retailing is the selling of goods and services outside the confines of the retail facility. This form of retailing accounts for an increasing percentage of retail sales.

   B. **Direct Selling**

   Direct selling is the marketing of products to ultimate consumers through face-to-face sales presentations at home or in the workplace.

   1. The "party plan" is sometimes used in direct selling and can occur in homes or in the workplace.
   2. Benefits of Direct Selling
      a) It gives marketers an opportunity to demonstrate the product in the environment where it would most likely be used.
      b) Customers get personal attention.
      c) Products are presented at convenient times and locations for customers.
   3. Limitations of Direct Selling
      a) Direct selling is the most expensive form of retailing.
      b) Some customers believe that practices of direct sellers are unscrupulous and fraudulent.
      c) Some communities strictly control or prohibit direct selling.
   C. **Automatic Vending**

   Automatic vending is the use of machines to dispense products selected by customers.

   1. It is one of the most impersonal forms of retailing.
   2. Machines need only a small amount of space and no sales personnel, but require frequent servicing and repair.

V. **Franchising**

Franchising is an arrangement whereby a supplier (franchiser) grants a dealer (franchisee) the right to sell products in exchange for some type of consideration, such as a percentage of sales. franchising is rapidly increasing.

(Transparency Figure 17B)

(Transparency Table 17.2)

A. **Major Types of Retail Franchises**
   1. A manufacturer may franchise stores to sell a certain brand-name item (e.g., automobiles).
   2. A producer may license distributors to sell a given product to retailers (e.g., soft drinks).
   3. A franchiser may simply provide a carefully developed and controlled marketing strategy (e.g., fast-food restaurant).

B. **Advantages and Disadvantages of Franchising**
   1. Franchising enables a franchisee to start a business with limited capital and to benefit from the business experience of others.
   2. Franchised outlets are generally more successful than independently owned outlets.
   3. The franchiser gains fast and selective product distribution through franchise arrangements without incurring the high cost of construction and operating its own outlets.

(Global Marketing: Fueling Customers in Thailand with Gas, Coffee, and Convenience)

   4. The franchiser can dictate many aspects of the business, and the franchisee must pay to use the franchiser's name, products, and assistance.

(Transparency Figure 17L)

VI. **Strategic Issues in Retailing**

Consumer purchases are often the result of social influences and psychological factors. A retailer's objective must be to make products available, create a stimulating shopping environment, and develop marketing strategies that will increase store patronage.

A. **Location of Retail Stores**
   1. Location is the least flexible and one of the most important issues because it dictates the limited geographic trading area from which a store draws its customers.
   2. Ease of movement to and from the site is important.
   3. Important characteristics of a site include types of surrounding stores, size and shape of building, and terms of rent, lease, or ownership.
   4. Retailers can choose from among several types of locations.
      a) **Free-Standing Structures**
         (1) Allow retailers to position themselves physically away from or close to their competitors
         (2) Are used frequently by automobile dealers and fast-food restaurants
      b) **Traditional Business Districts**
         Traditional business districts consist of structures usually attached to one another and located in a central part of a town or city. Although some of these districts are old and decaying, a number of communities are preserving and revitalizing them.

    c) **Traditional Shopping Centers**
      (1) *Neighborhood shopping centers* usually consist of several small convenience and specialty stores.
        (a) They serve customers who live less than a 10-minute drive away (2- to 3-mile radius).
        (b) They usually hold product mixes to essential products with limited lines.
      (2) *Community shopping centers* include one or two department stores and some specialty and convenience stores.
        (a) They serve a larger geographic area and draw customers who want specialty products not found in neighborhood shopping centers.
        (b) They include a wide range of product mixes and deep product lines.
      (3) *Regional shopping centers* usually have the largest department stores, widest product mixes, and deepest product lines of all centers.
        (a) They have 150,000 or more consumers in their target markets, including consumers traveling from a distance to find products and prices not available in their hometown.
        (b) Shopping center tenants are more likely to be national chains.
    d) **Nontraditional Shopping Centers**
      (1) Factory outlet malls feature discount and factory outlet stores owned by manufacturers of major brand-name products. They attract customers by offering lower prices for quality products and major brand names.
      (2) Miniwarehouse malls sell space to retailers, wholesalers, or light manufacturers, which then operate retail facilities out of warehouse bays.
      (3) A third type is emerging, one that does not include a traditional anchor department store.
      (4) Some shopping center developers are combining off-price stores with category killers in "power center" formats.

B. **Retail Positioning**
  1. *Retail positioning* involves identifying an unserved or underserved market segment and serving it through a strategy that distinguishes the retailer from others in the minds of those consumers.

(Transparency Figure 17I)

  2. Retailers position themselves in several ways:
    a) As sellers of high-quality, premium-priced products.
    b) As marketers of reasonable-quality products at everyday low prices.

C. **Store Image**
  1. A store image is a functional and psychological picture in the consumer's mind that is acceptable to the store's target market.
  2. *Atmospherics*, the physical elements in a store's design that appeal to consumers' emotions and encourage consumers to buy, helps to create an image and position a retailer.
    a) Exterior elements include the appearance of the storefront, display windows, store entrances, and degree of traffic congestion.
    b) Interior elements include aesthetic considerations such as lighting, wall and floor coverings, dressing facilities, store fixtures, and sensory elements, such as color and sound.
  3. Retailers must determine the atmosphere the target market wants and adjust atmospheric variables accordingly.

4. Store image also depends heavily on the store's reputation for integrity, service, location, product assortment, pricing, promotional activities, and community development.
5. Other influencing factors are target market characteristics such as social class, lifestyle, income, and purchase behavior.

D. **Scrambled Merchandising**
1. *Scrambled merchandising* involves adding unrelated products and product lines to an existing mix.
2. Retailers that adopt this strategy hope to convert stores into one-stop shopping centers, generate customer traffic, realize higher profit margins, and/or increase impulse purchases.
3. It can blur a store's image in consumers' minds.
4. It intensifies competition among traditionally distinct types of stores.

E. **The Wheel of Retailing**
1. The *wheel of retailing* hypothesis holds that new businesses enter the market with low prices, margins, and status and become more elaborate and expensive as they attempt to broaden their customer bases. Finally, they emerge at the high end of the scale, competing with newer discount retailers following the same process.

(Transparency Figure 17.1)

2. The wheel of retailing itself, along with other changes in the marketing environment and buying behavior, requires that retailers adjust in order to survive and compete.

NOTES FOR CLASS EXERCISES, DEBATE ISSUE, AND CHAPTER QUIZ

On the following pages, you will find two class exercises, a debate issue, and a chapter quiz. These are formatted in large-size type so that you can use them as class handouts or for making transparencies. Below are the authors' comments on the class exercises, the debate topic for this chapter, and the answers to the chapter quiz.

Comments on Class Exercise 1

The objective of this class exercise is to help students understand strategic issues in retailing by developing an original retail store concept.

Question 1. Students will typically develop specialty store ideas, since they recognize the difficulty of going head to head with larger chain stores. You may also want your students to think in terms of atypical approaches like vending ("Venda-Bait" sells buckets of fishing bait for $1.50 in the Ozarks; videocassette vending machines in large metro areas) or scrambled merchandising (7-Eleven stores with a Hardee's restaurant or Kmart stores with a Little Caesar's restaurant inside; McDonald's located in nontraditional outlets like campuses or zoos).

Question 2. As students respond to this question, press them to define each location in terms of types of stores and market reached. Offering local examples of each may also help students better understand the concepts. A common oversight by students is a decision to locate in a regional shopping center without considering the likely high lease costs. You might also want to talk about why local stores are vacant; most towns have a retail location that changes owners about once a year. Possible reasons could be poor parking and difficult entry, deteriorating or limited facilities, image of surrounding stores, and the like.

Question 3. Although it is difficult for students to think of an entire product assortment, they should go beyond naming only one type of product to be sold. You can carry this discussion further by asking about retail positioning, atmospherics, and store image.

Comments on Class Exercise 2

The goal of this exercise is to help students understand the importance of having store names that help customers easily identify the type of store. Some of these are effective, others are not. Answers:

1.	The Shape of Things	**hairstyling salon**
2.	The Chicken Oil Company	**restaurant**
3.	Wings 'n' Things	**restaurant**
4.	The Paper Bear	**gift/novelty item shop**
5.	Prioriteas	**upscale foods/beverages**
6.	Specially For You	**florist/gift shop**
7.	The Waist Basket	**fitness center**
8.	Bless Your Heart	**health food restaurant**
9.	Clean And Lean	**laundromat/fitness center**
10.	Bombay Bicycle Club	**restaurant**
11.	The Lollipop	**children's clothing store**
12.	Feather Your Nest	**linens store**
13.	Rolling Thunder	**skating rink**
14.	Creations	**silk-screened T-shirts**
15.	Me Too Wee Two	**adult women and children's clothing**

DEBATE ISSUE

Is franchising the best way to own a business?

CHAPTER QUIZ

Answers to Chapter Quiz 1. b; 2. d; 3. e; 4. a.

Class Exercise 1

ASSUME THAT YOU HAVE BEEN GIVEN AMPLE FUNDS TO INVEST IN A NEW RETAIL VENTURE. BE AS CREATIVE AS POSSIBLE.

1. Determine the type of retail store you want to open. Be specific about the characteristics of the store type. Include product assortment, target market(s), service level, and price level.

2. Where will you locate?

    a. Be sure to consider
        *   Ease of movement in, around, and out of the location
        *   Size and shape of the building
        *   Likely terms of rent or lease
        *   Surrounding stores

    b. Choose whether to locate in a free-standing store or in a
        *   Traditional business district
        *   Neighborhood shopping center
        *   Community shopping center
        *   Regional shopping center
        *   Nontraditional shopping center

3. Describe your product assortment in terms of depth, width, and quality.

    a. Which products will be the most important to consumers?

    b. Will consumers want other complementary products when they shop?

Class Exercise 2

FOLLOWING IS A LIST OF RETAIL BUSINESSES. WHAT TYPES OF PRODUCTS ARE SOLD BY EACH ONE?

1. The Shape of Things
2. The Chicken Oil Company
3. Wings 'n' Things
4. The Paper Bear
5. Prioriteas
6. Specially For You
7. The Waist Basket
8. Bless Your Heart
9. Clean And Lean
10. Bombay Bicycle Club
11. The Lollipop
12. Feather Your Nest
13. Rolling Thunder
14. Creations
15. Me Too Wee Two

<u>Debate Issue</u>

IS FRANCHISING THE BEST WAY TO OWN A BUSINESS?

<u>YES</u>	<u>NO</u>
• Franchisees can start a business with limited capital.	• Franchising does not give entre-preneurs the independence they desire—they are still working for someone else.
• Franchisees can take advantage of the business ex-perience of others.	• In some cases, franchisees are not allowed to make crucial decisions.
• A franchisee usually receives operations and management training.	• The more success-ful the franchisee, the greater the royalties and fees paid to the franchiser.
• Franchised names are usually widely recognized.	• Franchisees are never justly com-pensated for their hard work and success.
• Franchised outlets are generally more successful than independently owned businesses.	

Chapter Quiz

1. Which one of the following is a large-scale, members-only, retailer that combines cash-and-carry whole- saling with discount retailing?
   a. Warehouse showroom
   b. Warehouse club
   c. Catalog showroom
   d. Category killer
   e. Hypermarket

2. Matt's girlfriend tells him she wants a cashmere sweater for Christmas. Matt decides to go to a store that provides the best possible selection of sweaters. His *best* choice would be to shop at a _____ store.
   a. department
   b. catalog
   c. discount
   d. traditional specialty
   e. convenience

3. The primary advantage of automatic vending as a form of retailing is that
   a. it offers a low-cost, personal method of selling products.
   b. it provides continuous service to consumers.
   c. since vending machines must be serviced frequently, the products they sell are always fresh.
   d. vending machines require very few repairs.
   e. it eliminates the need for sales personnel.

4. Jane Down is planning to open an upscale dress boutique. She is evaluating ease of movement to and from sites, vehicular traffic, types of stores in the area, and transportation networks. Which strategic retailing issue is she concerned with at this time?
   a. Location
   b. Product depth
   c. Product mix
   d. Scrambled merchandising
   e. Retail positioning

ANSWERS TO DISCUSSION AND REVIEW QUESTIONS

1. **What value is added to the product by retailers? What value is added by retailers for producers and for ultimate consumers?**

   Retailers add value to products in several ways. Image enhances the value of the product. Through its location, a retailer facilitates comparison shopping. A product's value is increased when the retailer offers services such as delivery, credit, and repair. Retail sales personnel can also demonstrate how products help solve customers' problems. Retailers link producers and ultimate consumers by providing the environment in which exchanges with ultimate consumers take place. Producers have a place to sell their products. Ultimate consumers benefit from the resulting availability of a broad array of products.

2. **Differentiate between the two general categories of retail stores based on breadth of product offering.**

   The two categories of retailing stores based on breadth of product offering are general merchandise retailers and specialty retailers. General merchandise retailers offer a broad variety of product lines. In contrast, specialty retailers emphasize narrow product lines.

3. **What are the major differences between discount stores and department stores?**

   Discount stores are self-service, general merchandise outlets that regularly offer brand-name merchandise at low prices. Department stores are large retail organizations characterized by wide product mixes. These two types of retail outlets differ in several respects. First, discount stores are mass merchandisers; that is, they generally offer fewer customer services than department stores and emphasize low prices, high turnover, and large sales volume. Rather than having structured departments, the discount store uses a central check-out procedure. These stores are often in less convenient locations than department stores.

   Department stores are distinctly service-oriented, offering services such as credit, delivery, personal assistance, returns, and a pleasant atmosphere. They are structured by departments, and different atmospheres can be created in each department. They are located more conveniently than discount stores, usually in a major shopping area.

4. **How does a superstore differ from a supermarket?**

   Supermarkets are large, self-service stores that carry a complete line of food products plus some nonfood products. Superstores are giant retail outlets that combine features of supermarkets and discount houses. They carry all food and nonfood products usually found in supermarkets as well as most consumer products purchased on a routine basis, such as housewares, appliances, and clothing. Superstores also offer services ranging from snack bars and check cashing to dry cleaning and automotive repair.

5. **In what ways are traditional specialty stores and off-price retailers similar? How do they differ?**

   Traditional specialty retailers and off-price retailers are similar in that both are specialty retailers. They often carry similar lines of merchandise and generally offer narrower product mixes than department stores and mass merchandisers.

   Traditional specialty retailers and off-price retailers differ in several respects. Traditional specialty retailers offer more depth in their product lines than off-price retailers because the latter often buy "leftover" merchandise from manufacturers. Traditional specialty retailers offer more services than off-price retailers and usually have an exclusive store image. In addition, off-price stores charge 20 to 50 percent less than traditional retailers for comparable merchandise.

6. **Describe direct marketing and the other two major types of nonstore retailing. List some products you have purchased through nonstore retailing in the last six months. Why did you choose this method for making your purchases instead of going to a retail outlet?**

Direct marketing is the use of telephone, mail, and Internet to communicate product and organizational information to customers. The other two major types of nonstore retailing are direct selling and automatic vending. Direct selling is the marketing of products to ultimate consumers through face-to-face sales presentations at home or in the workplace. Automatic vending is the use of machines to dispense products.

The last parts of this question will elicit individual responses. Students will probably state convenience and availability as their reasons for their choices.

7. **How is door-to-door selling a form of retailing? Some consumers believe direct-response orders bypass the retailer. Is this true?**

Door-to-door selling is a form of retailing because it involves an exchange with ultimate consumers. Direct response orders do not bypass the retailer. A mail-order house makes final exchanges with ultimate consumers and thus can be considered a retailer.

8. **Evaluate the following statement: "Telemarketing, television home shopping, and online retailing will eventually eliminate the need for traditional forms of retailing."**

Student opinions will vary considerably on this question, but there are some issues that ought to surface in their answers. There is little question that telemarketing, television home shopping, and online retailing will change the way consumers acquire products by providing more alternatives. However, these alternatives will probably not altogether replace retail stores and other forms of nonstore shopping. Catalog shopping, for example, has been around for over 100 years, and retail stores have not disappeared. In addition, many consumers want personal service, especially when purchasing products with complex or new technology, or very expensive products. Traditional forms of retailing can provide these services, whereas telemarketing, television home shopping, and online retailing cannot.

9. **If you were opening a retail business, would you prefer to open an independent store or to own a store under a franchise arrangement? Explain your preference.**

There are advantages to both owning an independent store and owning a store under a franchise arrangement. Under a franchise arrangement, a supplier grants a dealer the right to sell products in exchange for some type of consideration. For example, the franchiser can offer equipment, buildings, management know-how, marketing assistance, and an established reputation in exchange for a percentage of sales. With an independent business, however, the owner has complete control over the elements of the retailing mix and is not bound by the franchiser's rules.

10. **What major issues should be considered when determining a retail site location?**

Because of its inflexible nature, the location of a retail outlet is one of the most important strategic issues a retailer must address. Location dictates the limited geographic trading area from which a store can draw its customers. Retailers must evaluate potential locations on the basis of several factors:

a. Ease of movement, including factors such as pedestrian and vehicular traffic, parking, and transportation

b. Site characteristics, such as the types of stores in the area, the lease terms, and the size, shape, and visibility of the lot or building

c. Compatibility with nearby retailers—that is, the degree to which stores complement one another, thereby generating traffic

11. **Describe the three major types of traditional shopping centers. Give an example of each type in your area.**

    a. Neighborhood shopping centers consist of small grocery stores, gas stations, and fast-food restaurants. They serve consumers who live less than a ten-minute drive from the center. A typical neighborhood shopping center might have a Safeway supermarket, an Eckerd drugstore, and a McDonald's fast-food restaurant.

    b. Community shopping centers include one or two department stores and some specialty stores as well as convenience stores. They serve a larger geographic area than neighborhood centers. A community shopping center might be a small mall with a locally owned department store, a Baker's shoe store, a Hallmark card store, and a small drugstore that sells convenience goods.

    c. Regional shopping centers usually have the largest department stores with the widest product mixes and deepest product lines. They target more than 150,000 people and often host special events.

12. **Discuss the major factors that help determine a retail store's image.**

    A retail store's image is a functional and psychological picture in the consumer's mind. A store must project an image that is acceptable to its target market. Seven factors contribute to a retail store's image:

    a. Atmospherics, or physical elements in a store's design that appeal to consumers' emotions and encourage them to buy

    b. Reputation for integrity

    c. Location, including accessibility and surrounding retailers

    d. Merchandise assortment offered

    e. Pricing

    f. Promotional activities

    g. Involvement in community activities

13. **How does atmosphere add value to products sold in a store? How important is atmospherics for convenience stores?**

    The term *atmospherics* describes the physical elements in a store's design that appeal to consumers' emotions and encourage consumers to buy. Atmospherics adds value to products sold in a store in that it enhances the products or the products' benefits by offering the psychological rewards of shopping in pleasant surroundings.

    Although atmospherics is less important in convenience stores than in shopping and specialty stores, convenience retailers should still consider it. For example, a

    7-Eleven would want its atmospherics to convey the image of quick and easy service.

14. **Is it possible for a single retail store to have an overall image that appeals to sophisticated shoppers, extravagant buyers, and bargain hunters? Why or why not?**

    A retail store may have great difficulty presenting an overall image that appeals to sophisticated and extravagant buyers and bargain hunters because these shoppers have different motives. However, a department store may successfully do so because it can tailor atmospherics, pricing, and other store image factors to specific departments, some targeted to extravagant shoppers and others aimed at bargain hunters.

15. **In what ways does the use of scrambled merchandising affect a store's image?**

Scrambled merchandising is the addition of unrelated products and product lines to an existing product mix. Scrambled merchandise can adversely affect a store's image unless it is done carefully. If stores add unrelated products to their product mixes, their established images can become blurred in consumers' minds. On the other hand, a store's objective may include becoming a one-stop shopping outlet, which scrambled merchandising can help accomplish.

COMMENTS ON THE CASES

CASE 17.1 REI SCALES NEW HEIGHTS IN RETAILING

This case looks at the marketing decisions made by a successful retailer that operates as a consumer cooperative, sharing some of the profits with its members. Students who are not familiar with REI stores and its nonstore retailing should conduct background research before analyzing this case.

In question 1, students are asked why REI would locate many of its stores in free-standing structures rather than in shopping centers. One key reason is that any location REI chooses must be able to accommodate its unique store atmospherics. Store space in traditional shopping centers cannot always be configured in the way that REI chooses (such as with climbing walls and demonstration areas). Therefore, REI prefers free-standing structures that can be constructed to its specifications. Students may suggest other reasons, as well.

The second question asks about the likely effect of REI's consumer cooperative structure on the retailer's ability to build customer relationships. Customers who become members are more likely to be loyal because they feel they have an ongoing stake in the company, because they can feel part of the REI community (which includes other customers and REI personnel), and because members receive special prices on certain products. Ask students to discuss how they feel about organizations they join compared with how they feel about organizations from which they buy as non-members. This is an opportunity to explore both the retailer's perspective and the customer's perspective on relationship-building.

The third question asks students to describe REI's retail positioning and explain why it is appropriate for the target market. Students' answers will vary somewhat, but most should recognize that REI serves the segment of customers who have or want an active lifestyle and can afford to buy quality equipment and apparel for outdoor activities. This positioning is supported by the unique store atmospherics and educational programs focusing on specific products or sports, which appeal to the target market.

Video Information

Company: REI

Location: Tape 2/DVD 2, Segment 17

Length: 12:45

Video Overview: Recreational Equipment, Inc (REI), an outdoors sporting goods store, was founded in 1938 in Denver by mountain climbers Lloyd and Mary Anderson. They created the company to supply themselves with high-quality ice axes and other climbing gear. As of 2003, REI had more than 2 million active members and 66 retail stores in the U.S. REI members are able to enjoy special benefits and offers. The management team stresses hiring employees who love the outdoors, are enthusiastic, and who truly like people. The quality of the staff is especially important, since REI believes people are attracted to the store based on the values REI maintains. Training includes an orientation, on the floor training, and training with a buddy or mentor. The customer is the focus of training at REI. Education of REI customers stressed over pressure selling. A five-step procedure was developed to enhance the customers' shopping experience. Each and every employee is reviewed on a continuous basis, starting with a six-month review. Furthermore, REI stays in tune with the outdoors through donating significant pretax profits to environment protection organizations.

MULTIPLE-CHOICE QUESTIONS ABOUT THE VIDEO

1.   Steve Kittel, Director of Training believes that customers come to the store because to them REI

    a.   is the cheapest place to find everything they need.
    b.   has more product offering than any other outdoor company.
    c.   REI is more than just a store, it's a lifestyle.
    d.   has the best customer service around.
    e.   personnel know their products better than their competitors do.

2.   The main methods REI uses to train its employees include

    a.   orientation and floor training.
    b.   orientation, vendor clinics, and lots of buddy shifts.
    c.   orientation, on the floor training, and buddy shifts.
    d.   orientation and buddy shifts.
    e.   orientation and vendor clinic.

3.   When it comes to evaluating employees, REI uses which one of the following methods?

    a.   six month review, then yearly reviews
    b.   one review a year
    c.   every 9 months
    d.   evaluate as needed
    e.   evaluate once every two months

4.   REI management feels it is very important to give back to the environment, since that is what keeps them in business. REI chooses to do this through

    a.   conducting clean-up parties to help parks maintain their natural beauty.
    b.   sponsoring highways surrounding national parks to make sure they stay clean and inviting.
    c.   using only recyclable paper for bags and receipts.
    d.   donating large amounts of pre-tax profits.
    e.   giving discounts to those who attempt to maintain the environment

ANSWERS TO MULTIPLE-CHOICE QUESTIONS ABOUT THE VIDEO

1.   c

2.   b

3.   a

4.   e

CASE 17.2 COSTCO OFFERS LOW PRICES AND MERCHANDISE SURPRISES

The goal of this case is to help students understand how a retailer can attract and retain customers despite strong competition from Wal-Mart and low-amenity store designs. Many students will be familiar with Costco; those who have never been in a Costco store may collect background information before discussing the case.

Question 1 asks students how Costco's atmospherics support its retail positioning. Because Costco is known for low prices, it avoids fancy fixtures and interior design in favor of a bare-bones warehouse look. According to the case, the ever-changing assortment of low-priced products is the store's main focus, drawing customers looking for bargains.

Question 2 asks students to analyze the retail strategy represented by the Costco Home chain. This is a discount specialty retailer because it stocks only low-price home furnishings. Ask students to consider what customers might expect from a retail chain bearing the Costco name and how Costco Home stores are likely to address those expectations. This question provides an opportunity to discuss the issues that arise when a retailer operates stores using different retail strategies (as Costco and Wal-Mart are doing).

Question 3 ask how Costco's retail positioning is likely to be affected by its target profit margin of 14 percent. The case indicates that Costco buys merchandise that sells quickly, to avoid the expense of carrying inventory for long periods. Therefore, customers will not find exactly the same product assortment each time they shop at Costco, supporting the positioning of ever-changing, low-priced merchandise. In addition, Costco's managers are always looking for popular products they can sell at low prices, another way of supporting the retail positioning. Challenge students to respond to a situation in which a Costco buyer gets such a good deal on a product that it would achieve a profit margin of 20 percent if sold at the regular markup. Should the product be priced lower based on the lower cost? Or should Costco accept the higher profit margin on this item? This issue should generate lively classroom discussion.

CHAPTER 18

Integrated Marketing Communications

TEACHING RESOURCES QUICK REFERENCE GUIDE

Resource	Location
Purpose and Perspective	IRM, p. 333
Guide for Using Color Transparencies	IRM, p. 334
Lecture Outline	IRM, p. 334
Notes for Class Exercises, Debate Issue, and Chapter Quiz	IRM, p. 341
Class Exercise 1	IRM, p. 343
Class Exercise 2	IRM, p. 344
Debate Issue	IRM, p. 345
Chapter Quiz	IRM, p. 346
Answers to Discussion and Review Questions	IRM, p. 347
Comments on the Cases	IRM, p. 350
Case 18.1	IRM, p. 350
Video	Tape 2/DVD 2, Segment 18
Video Information	IRM, p. 350
Multiple-Choice Questions About the Video	IRM, p. 350
Case 18.2	IRM, p. 351
Transparency Acetates	Transparency package
Examination Questions: Essay	TB, p. 509
Examination Questions: Multiple-Choice	TB, p. 509
Examination Questions: True-False	TB, p. 534
Author-Selected Multiple-Choice Test Items	TB, p. 672
HMClassPrep Presentation Resources	CD-ROM
PowerPoint Slides	Instructor's website

Note: Additional resources are updated periodically and may be found on the accompanying student and instructor websites at http://www.prideferrell.com/.

PURPOSE AND PERSPECTIVE

This chapter is the first of three dealing with promotion decisions and activities. Its primary objective is to give students an overview of promotion. First, we show how integrated marketing communications provides the maximum informational and persuasive impact on customers. Then, we present a theoretical foundation on which to build an understanding of promotion. Consequently, the first part of this chapter focuses on the nature of integrated marketing communications, the role of promotion in organizations, the communication process, and the objectives of promotion. Next, we introduce the concept of the promotion mix and briefly describe the major elements that constitute it. (Promotion mix elements are discussed in greater detail in Chapters 19 and 20.) Then we analyze a number of factors that affect marketers' decisions when selecting specific ingredients to include in a promotion mix for a product. Finally, we examine some criticisms and defenses of promotion.

GUIDE FOR USING COLOR TRANSPARENCIES

There are two groups of color transparencies. The transparencies identified by a double number are the same as the figures and tables in the text. The transparencies labeled with a number and a letter are illustrations that do not appear in the text, but they can be used as additional examples of concepts discussed.

LECTURE OUTLINE

(Transparency Part 7 Opener)

(Transparency Figure 18A: Chapter Outline)

I. **The Nature of Integrated Marketing Communications**
     A.   *Integrated marketing communications* is the coordination of promotion and other marketing efforts to ensure the maximum informational and persuasive impact on customers.

(Transparency Figure 18B)

         1.   Coordinating multiple marketing tools to produce this synergistic effect requires a marketer to employ a broad perspective.
         2.   A major goal of integrated marketing communications is to send a consistent message to customers.
         3.   Integrated marketing communications provides an organization with a way to coordinate and manage its promotional efforts to ensure that customers receive consistent messages.
         4.   It fosters long-term relationships and efficient use of promotional resources.
     B.   Integrated marketing communications has been increasingly accepted for several reasons.
         1.   Mass media advertising is used less today than in the past because of high cost and unpredictable audiences.
         2.   More precisely targeted promotional tools such as cable TV, direct mail, the Internet, etc., are available.
         3.   Database marketing also allows marketers to be more precise in targeting individual customers.
         4.   Today, a number of promotion-related companies provide one-stop shopping to clients seeking advertising, sales promotion, and public relations, thus reducing coordinating efforts.
         5.   Rising costs have also meant that upper management demands systematic evaluations of communication efforts and reasonable return on investments.

C.   The specific communication vehicles employed and the precision with which they are used are changing as both information technology and customer interests become increasingly dynamic.

II.   **The Role of Promotion**

Promotion is communication that builds and maintains favorable relationships by informing and persuading one or more audiences to view an organization more positively and to accept its products.

A.   The overall role of promotion is to stimulate product demand.

B.   Marketers also indirectly facilitate favorable relationships by focusing information about company activities and products on interest groups, current and potential investors, regulatory agencies, and society in general.

1.   Promotion of responsible use of potentially harmful products

2.   Promotion by companies that help selected groups

3.   Cause-related marketing links purchase of products to philanthropic efforts for one or more causes to help boost sales and generate goodwill.

(Building Customer Relationships: Rivals Team up to Advertise Cereal)

4.   Marketers also sponsor special events, often leading to news coverage

C.   For maximum benefit from promotional efforts, marketers strive for proper planning, implementation, and control of communications.

III.   **Promotion and the Communication Process**

Communication is a sharing of meaning. Implicit in this definition is the notion of transmission of information because sharing necessitates transmission.

A.   As shown in Figure 18.2, communication begins with a *source*—a person, group, or organization that has a meaning it attempts to share with an audience.

(Transparency Figure 18.2)

B.   A *receiver* is an individual, group, or organization that decodes a coded message; an audience is two or more receivers.

C.   To transmit meaning, a source must convert the meaning into a series of signs or symbols representing ideas or concepts; this is called the *coding process* or encoding.

1.   To share meaning, the source should use signs or symbols familiar to the receiver or audience. In marketing, this requires knowing the target market and ensuring that messages—e.g., advertisements—use language understood by the target market.

2.   When coding a meaning, a source needs to use signs or symbols that the receiver or audience uses for referring to the concepts the source intends to convey.

D.   To share an encoded message with a receiver or audience, a source selects and uses a *medium of transmission*, the means of carrying the coded message.

1.   When a source chooses an inappropriate medium of transmission, a coded message may reach the wrong receivers.

2.   If an inappropriate medium is chosen, a coded message may reach the intended receivers in an incomplete form because the intensity of the transmission is weak.

E.   In the *decoding process*, signs or symbols are converted by the receiver into concepts and ideas.

1.   The meaning that a receiver decodes is seldom exactly the same as the meaning the source intended.

2.   When the result of decoding differs from what was coded, noise exists. *Noise*, anything that reduces a communication's clarity and accuracy, has many sources and may affect any or all parts of the communication.

a)   Noise sometimes arises within the medium of transmission itself.

b)   Noise will occur if the source uses signs or symbols that are unfamiliar to the receiver or have a different meaning than the one intended.

c)   A receiver may be unaware of a coded message because his or her perceptual processes block it out.

F.   The receiver's response to a message is *feedback* to the source.

1.   During feedback, the receiver or audience is the source of the message that is directed toward the original source, which then becomes a receiver. Thus, communication can be viewed as a circular process.

2.   During face-to-face communication, such as in a personal selling situation, both verbal and nonverbal feedback can be immediate, enabling communicators to adjust their messages quickly to improve the effectiveness of their communication.

3.   When mass communication like advertising is used, feedback is often slow and difficult to recognize.

G.   Each communication channel is limited on the volume of information it can handle effectively. This limit, called *channel capacity*, is determined by the least efficient component of the communication process.

IV.   **Objectives of Promotion**

Although there are several objectives of promotion, these differ widely from one organization to another and within organizations over time.

A.   **Create Awareness**

1.   A considerable amount of promotion focuses on creating awareness of new products or line extensions.

2.   For existing products, promotional efforts aim to increase awareness of brands, product features, image-related issues, and/or operational characteristics.

B.   **Stimulate Demand**

1.   *Primary demand* is demand for a product category rather than for a specific brand of product.

a)   Primary demand is stimulated through *pioneer promotion*, which informs potential customers about the product: what it is, what it does, how it can be used, and where it can be purchased.

b)   Sometimes an industry trade association uses promotional efforts to stimulate primary demand.

2.   *Selective demand* is demand for a specific brand.

a)   Marketers employ promotional efforts that point out the strengths and benefits of a specific brand.

b)   Advertising campaigns, price discounts, free samples, coupons, consumer contests, and sweepstakes are promotional activities that stimulate selective demand.

C.   **Encourage Product Trial**

1.   Promotion activities are necessary to move customers through the product-adoption process.

2.   Free samples, coupons, test drives or limited free-use offers, contests, and games make product trial convenient and low risk for potential customers.

D.   **Identify Prospects**

1.   Certain types of promotional efforts are directed at identifying customers who are interested in the firm's product and are most likely to buy it.

2.   Advertisements may provide direct response information forms or toll-free response lines.

       3.   Customers who fill out information blanks or call organizations usually have higher interest in products.

  E. **Retain Loyal Customers**

       1.   The costs of retaining customers are usually lower than those for acquiring new ones.

       2.   Common promotional activities directed at retaining loyal customers are frequent-user programs and special offers for existing customers only.

       3.   Reinforcement advertising assures current users that they have made the right choice.

  F. **Facilitate Reseller Support**

       1.   Strong relationships with resellers are important to a firm's ability to maintain a sustainable competitive advantage.

       2.   Use of various promotional methods helps organizations achieve this goal.

  G. **Combat Competitive Promotional Efforts**

       1.   Promotional activities may prevent a sales or market share loss.

       2.   A combative promotional objective is most common in extremely competitive consumer products markets.

  H. **Reduce Sales Fluctuations**

       1.   Demand for many products varies because of climate, holidays, or seasons.

       2.   Promotional activities are designed to stimulate sales during sales slumps or low-demand periods.

V. The Promotion Mix

When an organization combines specific methods to promote a particular product, that combination constitutes the promotion mix for that product. The four possible elements of a *promotion mix* are advertising, personal selling, public relations, and sales promotion. For some products, firms use all four ingredients; for other products, only two or three.

(Transparency Figure 18.3)

  A. **Advertising**

       1.   Advertising is a paid nonpersonal communication about an organization and its products transmitted to a target audience through mass media such as television, radio, the Internet, newspapers, magazines, direct mail, outdoor displays, and signs on mass transit vehicles.

(Transparency Figure 18C)

(Transparency Figure 18D)

       2.   Individuals and organizations use advertising to promote goods, services, ideas, issues, and people.

(Transparency Figure 18H)

       3.   Because advertising is highly flexible, it can reach a large target audience or focus on a small, precisely defined segment.

       4.   Advertising offers several benefits.

          a)   It is extremely cost-efficient when it reaches a vast number of people at a low cost per person.

(Transparency Figure 18E)

          b)   It lets the source repeat the message several times.

          c)   The visibility an organization gains from advertising can enhance its image.

5. Advertising also has several disadvantages.
   a) Even though the cost per person reached may be low, the absolute dollar outlay can be extremely high, thus limiting and sometimes preventing the use of advertising in a promotion mix.
   b) It rarely provides rapid feedback.
   c) It is difficult to measure the effects of advertising on sales.
   d) Advertising ordinarily has less persuasive impact on customers than personal selling.

B. **Personal Selling**
1. Personal selling is a paid personal communication that seeks to inform customers and persuade them to purchase products in an exchange situation.
2. Like advertising, personal selling has both advantages and limitations.
   a) The cost of reaching one person through personal selling is considerably more than through advertising, but personal selling efforts often have greater impact on customers.
   b) Personal selling provides immediate feedback.
3. The salesperson can take advantage of several types of communication in addition to verbal language.
   a) *Kinesic communication*, or body language, includes movement of one's head, eyes, arms, hands, legs, or torso.
   b) *Proxemic communication* occurs when either party varies the physical distance that separates the two parties.
   c) *Tactile communication* is communicating through touching.
4. Management of salespeople is very important in making personal selling effective.

C. **Public Relations**
1. Public relations is a broad set of communication efforts used to create and maintain favorable relationships between an organization and its stakeholders.
2. Public relations uses a variety of tools—annual reports, brochures, event sponsorship, etc.
3. Publicity, another public relations tool, is nonpersonal communication in news story form about an organization, its products, or both, that is transmitted through a mass medium at no charge.
4. Unpleasant situations and negative events may generate unfavorable public relations for an organization; effective marketers have policies and procedures in place to help manage public relations problems.
5. Public relations should not be viewed as a set of tools to be used only during crises, but as an ongoing program.

D. **Sales Promotion**
1. Sales promotion is an activity or material that acts as a direct inducement offering added value or incentive for the product to resellers, salespeople, or customers; examples include free samples, games, rebates, sweepstakes, contests, premiums, and coupons.
2. Marketers spend more on sales promotion than on advertising.
3. Unlike advertising and personal selling, marketers' use of sales promotion tends to be irregular, particularly when used to promote seasonal products.
4. Marketers frequently rely on sales promotion to improve the effectiveness of other promotion-mix ingredients.

E. An effective promotion mix requires the right combination of advertising, personal selling, public relations, and sales promotion.

VI. **Selecting Promotion Mix Elements**
    A.   Marketers vary the compositions of promotion mixes for many reasons.
        1.   A promotion mix can include all four elements, but frequently a marketer selects fewer than four.

(Transparency Figure 18F)

        2.   When making decisions about promotion mixes, marketers should recognize that advertising, personal selling, sales promotion, and public relations messages are limited in the extent to which they can inform and persuade customers and move them closer to making purchases.
        3.   Depending on the type of customers and the products involved, buyers to some extent rely on word-of-mouth communication from personal sources.
            a) *Buzz marketing* is an attempt to create a trend or acceptance of a product through word-of-mouth communications.
            b) Marketers should not underestimate the importance of both word-to-mouth communication and personal influence, nor should they have unrealistic expectations about the performance of commercial messages.
        4.   Consumers are also turning to Internet sources for information and opinions about goods and services as well as about the companies that market them. "Viral marketing" is a strategy designed to get Internet users to pass on ads and promotions to others.
    B.   **Promotional Resources, Objectives, and Policies**
        1.   The size of an organization's promotional budget affects the number and relative intensity of promotional methods included in the promotion mix.
            a) If a company's promotional budget is extremely limited, the firm is likely to rely on personal selling because it is easier to measure a salesperson's contribution to sales than to measure the effect of advertising.
            b) A business must have a sizable promotional budget to use regional or national advertising and sales promotion activities.
        2.   An organization's promotional objectives and policies also influence the types of promotion used.
            a) If a company's objective is to create mass awareness of a new convenience good, its promotion mix is likely to lean heavily toward advertising, sales promotion, and possibly public relations.
            b) If a company hopes to educate consumers about the features of a durable good, its promotion mix may combine a moderate amount of advertising, possibly some sales promotion, and a great deal of personal selling because this is an excellent way to inform customers about such products
            c) If a firm's objective is to produce immediate sales of nondurable services, the promotion mix will probably stress advertising and sales promotion.
    C.   **Characteristics of the Target Market**
    The size, geographic distribution, and demographic characteristics of an organization's target market help dictate the ingredients to be included in a product's promotion mix.

        1.   If the size of the market is limited, the promotion mix will probably emphasize personal selling because it can be effective for reaching a small number of people. When markets for a product consist of millions of customers, organizations rely on advertising and sales promotion.
        2.   If a company's customers are concentrated in a small geographic area, personal selling is more feasible than if the customers are dispersed across a vast area. Advertising may be more practical when the company's customers are numerous and not concentrated.

3. Demographic characteristics such as age, income, or education level may dictate the types of promotional techniques that a marketer selects.

D. **Characteristics of the Product**

1. Generally, promotion mixes for business products concentrate on personal selling, whereas consumer goods promotion relies on advertising. However, this generalization should be treated cautiously; producers of business products do use some advertising to promote goods.

(Transparency Figure 18G)

2. Marketers of seasonal products may have to emphasize advertising, and possibly sales promotion, because off-season sales may be insufficient to support an extensive year-round sales force.

3. A product's price influences the composition of the promotion mix.

    a) High-price products call for more personal selling because consumers associate greater risk with the purchase of such products and usually want the advice of a salesperson.

    b) For low-price convenience items, marketers use advertising rather than personal selling.

4. The stage of the product life cycle affects marketers' decisions regarding the promotion mix.

    a) In the introduction stage, a considerable amount of advertising may be necessary for both business and consumer products to make potential users aware of the new product.

    b) The growth and maturity stages necessitate heavy emphasis on advertising for consumer services, whereas business products often require a concentration of personal selling and some sales promotion.

    c) In the decline stage, marketers usually decrease their promotional activities, especially advertising.

5. The intensity of market coverage at which a product is distributed may influence the composition of its promotion mix.

    a) When a product is marketed through intensive distribution, the firm depends heavily on advertising and sales promotion.

    b) Promotion mixes of products distributed through selective distribution vary considerably.

    c) Products distributed exclusively are promoted primarily through personal selling.

6. A product's use can also affect the combination of promotional methods employed.

E. **Costs and Availability of Promotional Methods**

The costs of promotional methods and the availability of promotional techniques are major factors to analyze when developing a promotion mix.

1. National advertising and sales promotion efforts require large expenditures; however, if they reach extremely large numbers of people, the cost per individual may be quite small.

2. Although there are numerous media vehicles within the United States, a firm may find that no available advertising medium effectively reaches a certain market.

F. **Push and Pull Channel Policies**

One element marketers should consider is whether to use a push policy or a pull policy.

(Transparency Figure 18.4)

1. With a *push policy*, the producer promotes the product to the next institution down the marketing channel.

2. With a *pull policy*, the firm promotes directly to consumers with the intention of developing a strong consumer demand for the products.
3. These policies are not mutually exclusive.

VII. **Criticisms and Defenses of Promotion**
A number of specific criticisms have been lodged against promotional activities.

A. **Is Promotion Deceptive?**
1. Although some promotion is deceptive or misleading, not all promotion should be condemned.
2. The increased number of laws, the efforts of government regulatory agencies, and self-regulation have caused a decrease in deceptive promotion.

(Marketing Citizenship: Truth in Advertising)

B. **Does Promotion Increase Prices?**
1. Promotion is often blamed for higher prices, but if promotion is working to stimulate demand, producing and marketing larger quantities can actually help reduce prices.
2. Promotion can also help keep prices lower by facilitating price competition.

C. **Does Promotion Create Needs?**
1. Critics of promotion claim that promotion manipulates consumers by persuading them to buy products they do not need, but without promotion, many needs would still exist.
2. Marketing does not create needs, but capitalizes on them.

D. **Does Promotion Encourage Materialism?**
Promotions are sometimes criticized for encouraging materialism. Marketers assert that values are instilled at home and promotion does not change people into materialistic consumers.

E. **Does Promotion Help Customers Without Costing Too Much?**
Critics question whether promotion helps consumers enough to be worth the costs. Consumers do benefit, for promotions inform them about a product's uses, features, advantages, prices, or purchase locations.

F. **Should Potentially Harmful Products Be Promoted?**
Organizations are often criticized for promoting products associated with unhealthy activities. Those who defend such promotion argue that as long as it is legal to sell a product, promoting it should also be allowed.

NOTES FOR CLASS EXERCISES, DEBATE ISSUE, AND CHAPTER QUIZ

On the following pages, you will find two class exercises, a debate issue, and a chapter quiz. These are formatted in large-size type so that you can use them as class handouts or for making transparencies. Below are the authors' comments on the class exercises, the debate topic for this chapter, and the answers to the chapter quiz.

Comments on Class Exercise 1

This exercise focuses on how components of the communication process influence the effectiveness of the promotion mix. Pose the exercise questions after the following activity:

Bring a necktie to class for this exercise. Select a student volunteer who knows how to tie a necktie properly. Select another volunteer who knows nothing about tying a necktie. Ask the volunteers to stand back to back in front of the class. Give the tie to the second student, and ask the first student to explain how to tie the tie. Occasionally, you'll have students who can communicate the procedure, but generally the second student is left wearing something less than a perfectly tied tie.

Question 1. This is personal selling in that immediate feedback was available and the source was trying to inform and persuade the receiver through personal communication.

Question 2. As with many problems marketers have with producing meaningful ads and personal sales presentations, the source was very familiar with the uses of the product while the receiver was not. The source must consider the characteristics of the receiver.

Question 3. Invariably, the students will laugh and make other distracting noises. The source may be using signs unfamiliar to the receiver (e.g., "Take one end and wrap it around the other end," without specifying which end or how to wrap it), or the receiver's perceptual processes may block it out (being in front of peers may change willingness or ability to decode information).

Question 4. Personal selling provides *immediate* verbal and nonverbal *feedback*. This circular process allows the salesperson to adapt the presentation so that it is meaningful to the receiver. Conversely, feedback from advertising is often slow and difficult to recognize (even though the audience does often talk back to the television set). Advertisers may not recognize feedback until sales or attitudes change, which may take months during and after the campaign. The advantages of personal selling, then, are the feedback and greater individual impact, despite its high per-person cost. The absolute cost of advertising and poor feedback may preclude some from using it, but its cost efficiency, visibility, and image enhancement make it ideal for some products with mass appeal.

Question 5. Often the first student will be trying to explain something while the second student is still trying to process the last command (and while the audience is offering their advice).

Question 6. Demonstration with body language and touching would have helped.

Comments on Class Exercise 2

This exercise should help students see that promotional efforts cannot always be easily and clearly classified into advertising, public relations, sales promotion, or personal selling. In the real business world, each category often overlaps with the others. The promotional efforts described in the exercise can be classified as follows:

1. Advertising and sales promotion

2. Personal selling

3. Publicity-based public relations

4. Advertising and sales promotion

5. Personal selling and sales promotion

DEBATE ISSUE

Should cigarette and beer companies be allowed to sponsor sporting events?

CHAPTER QUIZ

Answers to Chapter Quiz 1. a; 2. e; 3. e; 4. b.

Class Exercise 1

1. What promotion mix element was this communication process most like?

2. What problems did the source have with the coding process?

3. How did noise affect the decoding process?

4. How is feedback different in a personal selling situation versus using mass communications? What are the pros and cons associated with each form?

5. How does channel capacity affect the ability to properly share meaning? Did the source (and other sources of noise) exceed the receiver's ability to effectively decode all information?

6. How might it have helped if the source had been able to use kinesic and tactile communication? How might the receiver respond with proxemic communication?

Class Exercise 2

THE PROMOTION MIX INCLUDES ADVERTISING, PUBLIC RELATIONS, SALES PROMOTION, AND PERSONAL SELLING. HOW WOULD YOU CLASSIFY EACH OF THE FOLLOWING PROMOTION EFFORTS?

1. McDonald's uses television to tell consumers about free french fries with the purchase of a Big Mac.

2. A Toyota salesperson tells customers about the quality of Michelin tires.

3. CNN has a story about Energizer's latest ad campaign. The story features a commercial with the Energizer bunny.

4. Quaker Oats places an ad in *Good Housekeeping* magazine with a coupon attached.

5. A pharmaceutical salesperson leaves free samples with a physician.

<u>Debate Issue</u>

SHOULD CIGARETTE AND BEER COMPANIES BE ALLOWED TO SPONSOR SPORTING EVENTS?

<u>YES</u>

- Cigarettes: banned from broadcast media, so sporting event sponsorship is an important promotional avenue

- Beer: one of the best ways to reach target market

- Quality of sporting events could suffer without the sponsorship of cigarette and beer companies.

- Freedom of speech is a basic right in America; because the selling of cigarettes and beer is legal, these companies have a right to promote their products.

<u>NO</u>

- Cigarette smoking is dangerous.

- Promotes and legitimizes consumption

- Children cannot escape exposure to promotion at sporting events short of not being present.

- Associating beer and tobacco products with sporting events lowers the image of those events.

Chapter Quiz

1. As Betty Jeffries prepares the script for a radio commercial for her boutique, she is engaging in the _____ stage of the communication process.
   - a. encoding
   - b. sourcing
   - c. decoding
   - d. sending
   - e. receiving

2. The basic promotional objective underlying a magazine advertisement with a direct response information form that requests the reader to complete and mail the form to receive additional information is to
   - a. retain loyal customers.
   - b. facilitate reseller support.
   - c. reduce sales fluctuations.
   - d. stimulate primary demand.
   - e. identify prospects.

3. Communication through the use of brochures, annual reports, event sponsorships, and news stories is referred to as
   - a. advertising.
   - b. personal selling.
   - c. sales promotion.
   - d. publicity.
   - e. public relations.

4. Promotion can help to keep prices lower because
   - a. demand for the product does not increase.
   - b. promotion usually intensifies price competition.
   - c. promotion of prices leads to nonprice competition.
   - d. promotion tends to reduce consumers' price sensitivity.
   - e. promotion tends to stabilize a product's price elasticity of demand.

ANSWERS TO DISCUSSION AND REVIEW QUESTIONS

1. **What does *integrated marketing communications* mean?**

    Integrated marketing communications is the coordination of promotion and other marketing efforts to ensure the maximum informational and persuasive impact on customers. Coordinating multiple marketing tools so they have this kind of synergistic effect requires a marketer to employ a broad perspective. A major goal of integrated marketing communications is to send a consistent message to customers. Because various units both inside and outside of a company have traditionally planned and implemented promotional efforts, the messages customers received have not always been consistent. Integrated marketing communications provides an organization with a way to coordinate and manage its promotional efforts to ensure that customers do receive consistent messages. This approach fosters not only long-term customer relationships, but also the efficient use of promotional resources.

2. **What is the major task of promotion? Do firms ever use promotion to accomplish this task and fail? If so, give several examples.**

    Promotion's major task is to communicate with individuals, groups, or organizations directly or indirectly to facilitate exchanges by influencing one or more of them to accept the organization's products. It is possible to use promotion to accomplish this objective and fail. Inconsistent communications or the use of nonessential information directed toward the organization's audience could lead to failure. Students should be able to provide examples of these occurrences, such as promotion directed toward them for expensive or luxury items in which they have no interest or cannot afford. Items such as champagne, luxury cars, or gourmet restaurants could represent this type of failure in communication.

3. **Define *communication* and describe the communication process. Is it possible to communicate without using all the elements in the communication process? If so, which elements can be omitted?**

    Communication is a sharing of meaning. The communication process involves several steps. First, the source places the meaning into a code, a process sometimes called coding. The source must use signs that are familiar to the receiver or audience and refer to the same concepts or ideas. The coded message is sent through a medium of transmission to the receiver or audience. After the receiver or audience receives the message, the message is decoded and the receiver usually supplies feedback to the source. When the decoded message differs from what was encoded, a condition called noise exists.

    Communication is not possible without using all the elements in the communication process.

4. **Identify several causes of noise. How can a source reduce noise?**

    Noise may arise from faulty printing processes, interference or static in television or radio transmissions, laryngitis, or the use of unfamiliar signs that have multiple meanings.

    A source can reduce noise by employing familiar signs that the audience or receiver uses to refer to concepts or ideas. Signs with multiple meanings are detrimental to the communication process because they result in noise. The choice of the proper medium of transmission is important to avoid noise that arises from reaching the wrong audience or from weak transmissions.

5. **Describe the possible objectives of promotion and discuss the circumstances under which each objective might be used.**

   Promotional objectives vary widely from one organization to another and within organizations over time. A considerable amount of promotion is directed at *creating awareness* of new products, new brands, or brand extensions. Creating awareness is important for existing products when marketers want to increase brand awareness, product feature awareness, awareness of image-related issues, or awareness of operational characteristics. When an organization is the first to introduce an innovative product, it uses pioneer promotion to *stimulate primary demand*. Primary demand is demand for a product category rather than for a specific product. To build selective demand, demand for a specific product, marketers employ promotional efforts based on the strengths and benefits of a specific brand. When customers stall during the evaluation stage of the product adoption process, marketers use certain kinds of promotions to *encourage product trial*. The objective of some promotional activities is to *identify prospective customers* who are interested in the firm's products and are most likely to buy. Because the costs of retaining customers are usually much lower than those of acquiring new ones, one objective of promotion is to *retain loyal customers*. Using some promotional methods helps organizations *maintain strong relationships with resellers*, which is critical to maintaining a competitive advantage. Sometimes marketers use promotions to offset or *combat the effects of a competitor's promotional program*. These types of programs are most commonly used by firms in extremely competitive consumer products markets. Finally, promotional techniques are used to *increase sales during slow periods*, thereby reducing sales fluctuations.

6. **Identify and briefly describe the four promotional methods an organization can use in its promotion mix.**

   Advertising is a paid form of nonpersonal communication about an organization and/or its products that is transmitted to a target audience through a mass medium. *Personal selling* is informing customers and persuading them to purchase products through personal communication in an exchange situation. *Sales promotion* is an activity and/or material that acts as a direct inducement, offering resellers, salespeople, or consumers added value or incentive for the product. *Public relations* is a broad set of communication efforts used to create and maintain favorable relationships between an organization and its publics. Public relations tools can include reports, brochures, and event sponsorship. Publicity, which is part of public relations, is nonpersonal communication in news story form about an organization, its products, or both that is transmitted through a mass medium at no charge.

7. **What forms of interpersonal communication besides language can be used in personal selling?**

   Communication may be accomplished through the use of kinesic, proxemic, or tactile communication. Kinesic communication is body language. Proxemic communication involves varying the physical space between the parties involved in communication. Tactile communication involves touching, such as handshaking.

8. **How do target market characteristics determine which promotional methods to include in a promotion mix? Assume a company is planning to promote a cereal to both adults and children. Along what major dimensions would these two promotional efforts have to differ from each other?**

Market characteristics that influence the composition of the promotion mix include the size, geographic distribution, and demographic characteristics of the market. If a company was promoting a cereal to both adults and children, it would use different advertising and sales promotion efforts for each market. Advertising appeals to children might include cartoon characterizations of the cereal, and the sales promotion might include a small toy. In the adult market, such methods would not be suitable; nutritional information, recipes, or a contest might be appropriate.

9. **How can a product's characteristics affect the composition of its promotion mix?**

Both the type of product being promoted and the characteristics of that product affect the composition of the promotion mix. Whether the product is a business or consumer good will affect the composition of the promotion mix. Whether a consumer good is a durable or nondurable good is another factor. Product characteristics such as seasonality, price, stage of the product's life cycle, intensity of distribution of the product, and uses of the product are also determinants of the promotion mix.

10. **Evaluate the following statement: "Appropriate advertising media are always available if a company can afford them."**

Availability of media is an important consideration in the formulation of a promotion mix. Even given the large number of media vehicles available, it may be difficult to reach a target market. A small, highly specialized market is difficult to reach with any degree of certainty through mass media. In addition, some geographic areas may not be accessible through the use of media.

11. **Explain the difference between a pull policy and a push policy. Under what conditions should each policy be used?**

A pull policy aims promotional efforts directly at consumers with the intention of developing a strong demand for the product. A push policy aims promotional efforts only at the next institution down the marketing channel. A pull policy is sometimes used to introduce convenience goods. A push policy often is used to promote items such as business goods and consumer durables.

12. **Which criticisms of promotion do you believe to be the most valid? Why?**

This is an open-ended question, and students' opinions will vary. In any discussion of this question, it is important that you facilitate a balanced view of promotion, giving equal weight to criticisms as well as defenses.

13. **Should organizations be allowed to promote offensive, violent, sexual, or unhealthy products that can be legally sold and purchased? Support your answer.**

This is an effective question for raising the issue of what is legal and what is ethical with regard to promotional activity. Some of the possible concerns students should consider: a) Does restriction of advertising to appropriate audiences constitute censorship? b) How does the age of the target market relate to how ethical or unethical promotions are? There is a difference between promoting products to children and promoting products to informed adults.

COMMENTS ON THE CASES

CASE 18.1 JORDAN'S FURNITURE

This case offers a real-world example of a highly customer-oriented furniture retailer that uses advertising, personal selling, and public relations in ways that set it apart from competing firms.

The first question asks students to describe the marketing mix of Jordan's Furniture. By now, students should easily recognize that Jordan's Furniture retails furniture at competitive (but now low) prices, distributed through its own stores, and promoted through subtle personal selling, as well as advertising and public relations.

Question 2 asks how the promotional efforts at Jordan's Furniture rise above the "noise" of regular furniture store promotions? Students' responses may vary, but possible answers relate to the fact that Jordan's sales staff are attentive but not pushy; it uses "quirky" ads; and it uses public relations efforts to appeal to its target customers' values and desire for a unique shopping experience.

The third question asks how Jordan's promotional strategy illustrates integrated marketing communications. Students' responses will vary but should demonstrate an understanding of integrated marketing communications, which coordinates promotion and other marketing efforts to ensure maximum informational and persuasive impact on customers. Responses should be specific.

Video Information

Company: Jordan's Furniture

Location: Tape 2/DVD 2, Segment 18

Length: 15:30

Video Overview: This video profiles family-owned Jordan's Furniture, which operates five stores in the state of Massachusetts. Jordan's has been able to achieve outstanding results in sales by using a unique approach focusing on non-aggressive salespeople, after-sales follow-up, and a unique retail experience. The company also spends less on advertising than most other furniture retailers, preferring to use lower-budget "quirky" television ads and support local causes to gain good publicity.

MULTIPLE-CHOICE QUESTIONS ABOUT THE VIDEO

1.   Jordan's Furniture has exceeded industry standards in all of the following categories except

   a.   inventory turnover.
   b.   advertising expenditures.
   c.   employee turnover.
   d.   marketing expenditures.
   e.   sales per square foot.

2.   Which of the following attractions can be found in Jordan's Natick store?

   a.   Rollercoaster
   b.   IMAX theater
   c.   Ice skating rink
   d.   Carousel
   e.   Ferris wheel

3. · Which of the following organizations have recognized Jordan's Furniture with awards?
   a.   Better Business Bureau
   b.   National Home Furnishing Association
   c.   Ernst & Young
   d.   GERS Retail System
   e. · All of the above

ANSWERS TO MULTIPLE-CHOICE QUESTIONS ABOUT THE VIDEO

1.   c

2.   b

3.   e

CASE 18.2 CARB WARS: NEW DIETS TURN THE FOOD INDUSTRY UPSIDE DOWN

This case focuses on promotion within the food industry rather than at a specific firm. To introduce the case you might ask students how many have seen advertisements or sales promotions that promote the low-carbohydrate content of particular food products.

Question 1 asks what promotion mix elements appear to be most effective in promoting the low-carb Atkins diet. Based on the facts presented in the case, advertising and public relations appear to be the promotion mix element with the greatest effect on consumer acceptance of low-carb diets. Some students may also report seeing sales promotion efforts, such as point-of-sale displays and samples, on their own grocery-shopping trips. Personal selling is generally too expensive to use for consumer products such as grocery items.

The second question asks about the key promotion objectives to overcome in dealing with a high-carbohydrate image and declining sales for pasta makers such as Barilla. Responses may vary but should demonstrate a basic understanding of how the marketing objectives described in the text may come into play in a promotion campaign. For Barilla, promotional objectives may relate to increasing awareness of the brand, encouraging product trial, retaining customers already loyal to the brand, facilitating reseller support, and combating competitive promotional efforts, especially by competing products promoting a lower-carb content.

The final question asks students how the coordination of promotion with other marketing efforts can help industries under pressure due to the Atkins phenomenon. Responses may vary but should demonstrate an understanding of the concept of integrated marketing communications and how the elements of the promotion mix can be used to achieve various promotional and organizational objectives. Common responses may relate to coordinating advertising, sales promotion, and public relations efforts or modifying products or introducing new products to compete with low-carb offerings.

CHAPTER 19

Advertising and Public Relations

TEACHING RESOURCES QUICK REFERENCE GUIDE

Resource	Location
Purpose and Perspective	IRM, p. 353
Guide for Using Color Transparencies	IRM, p. 354
Lecture Outline	IRM, p. 354
Notes for Class Exercises, Debate Issue, and Chapter Quiz	IRM, p. 361
Class Exercise 1	IRM, p. 363
Class Exercise 2	IRM, p. 364
Debate Issue	IRM, p. 365
Chapter Quiz	IRM, p. 366
Answers to Discussion and Review Questions	IRM, p. 367
Comments on the Cases	IRM, p. 369
Case 19.1	IRM, p. 369
Video	Tape 2/DVD 2, Segment 19
Video Information	IRM, p. 370
Multiple-Choice Questions About the Video	IRM, p. 370
Case 19.2	IRM, p. 371
Transparency Acetates	Transparency package
Examination Questions: Essay	TB, p. 543
Examination Questions: Multiple-Choice	TB, p. 543
Examination Questions: True-False	TB, p. 571
Author-Selected Multiple-Choice Test Items	TB, p. 672
HMClassPrep Presentation Resources	CD-ROM
PowerPoint Slides	Instructor's website

Note: Additional resources are updated periodically and may be found on the accompanying student and instructor websites at http://www.prideferrell.com/.

PURPOSE AND PERSPECTIVE

This chapter presents a detailed discussion of two promotion mix ingredients—advertising and public relations. First, we focus on the nature and types of advertising. Next, we analyze the major steps in developing an advertising campaign. Then, we discuss who is responsible for developing advertising campaigns. In the second part of the chapter, we focus on the nature of public relations. We first examine a variety of public relations tools. We then focus on the specific public relations tools associated with publicity. Finally, we explore the requirements for using public relations effectively and dealing with unfavorable publicity.

GUIDE FOR USING COLOR TRANSPARENCIES

There are two groups of color transparencies. The transparencies identified by a double number are the same as the figures in the text. The transparencies labeled with a number and a letter are illustrations that do not appear in the text, but they can be used as additional examples of concepts discussed.

Figure 19.1   General Steps in Developing and Implementing an Advertising Campaign
Figure 19.2   Geographic Divisions for *Time* Regional Issues
Figure 19A   Chapter 19 Outline
Figure 19B   Major Types of Advertising Defined
Figure 19C   Key Definitions: Advertising Campaign, Publicity
Figure 19D   Top 10 Product Categories for Ad Spending in the U.S.
Figure 19E   Advertising in the Automotive Industry
Figure 19F   Components of a Print Advertisement
Figure 19G   Illustration Techniques for Advertisements
Figure 19H   Major Types of Publicity-Based Public Relations Methods
Figure 19I   Altoids Understands the Importance of Advertising in Building Its Brand Equity

LECTURE OUTLINE

(Transparency Figure 19A: Chapter Outline)

I.   **The Nature and Types of Advertising**
  A.   *Advertising* is a paid form of nonpersonal communication transmitted through mass media, such as television, radio, the Internet, newspapers, magazines, direct mail, mass transit vehicles, and outdoor displays. Advertising is used to promote goods, services, ideas, images, issues, people, and anything else advertisers want to publicize or foster.

(Transparency Figure 19B)

  B.   Institutional Advertising
    1.   *Institutional advertising* promotes organizational images, ideas, political issues, or socially approved behavior.
    2.   *Advocacy advertising*, a type of institutional advertising, promotes a company's position on a public issue.
  C.   Product Advertising
    1.   *Product advertising* promotes the uses, features, and benefits of products.
    2.   The two types of product advertising are pioneer advertising and competitive advertising.
      a)   *Pioneer advertising* focuses on stimulating demand for a product category (rather than a specific brand) by informing potential customers about the product's features, uses, and benefits, and is employed when the product is in its introductory stage.
      b)   *Competitive advertising* attempts to stimulate demand for a specific brand by indicating a brand's features, uses, and advantages, sometimes through indirect or direct comparisons with competing brands.
        (1)   *Comparative advertising* compares two or more brands on the basis of one or more product characteristics.
        (2)   *Reminder advertising* tells customers that an established brand is still around and reminds consumers about the brand's uses, characteristics, and benefits.

(3)   *Reinforcement advertising* assures current users they have made the right brand choice and tells them how to get the most satisfaction from it.

II.   **Developing an Advertising Campaign**

Several steps are required to develop an *advertising campaign*, which is the creation and execution of a series of advertisements to communicate with a particular target audience. The number of steps and the exact order in which they are carried out can vary according to the organization's resources, the nature of its products, and the types of audiences to be reached.

(Transparency Figure 19C)

(Transparency Figure 19.1)

A.   **Identifying and Analyzing the Target Audience**

1.   The *target audience* is the group of people toward whom advertisements are aimed. A target audience may include everyone in the firm's target market, but at times, marketers may wish to direct a campaign at only a portion of the target market.

2.   Advertisers research and analyze target audiences to establish an information base for a campaign. Information commonly needed includes location and geographic distribution of the target group; the distribution of age, income, race, sex, and education; and consumer attitudes regarding the purchase and use of both the advertiser's products and competing products.

3.   Generally, the more advertisers know about the target audience, the better able they are to develop an effective advertising campaign.

B.   **Defining the Advertising Objectives**

1.   Advertisers should consider what the firm hopes to accomplish with the campaign. To develop a campaign with direction and purpose, they must define their advertising objectives.

2.   Because advertising objectives guide campaign development, advertisers should define them carefully to ensure that the campaign will accomplish what they desire.

(Transparency Figure 19I)

3.   Advertising objectives should be stated in clear, precise, and measurable terms.

a)   Precision and measurability allow advertisers to evaluate advertising success at the campaign's end in terms of whether or not the objectives have been met.

(1)   To provide precision and measurability, advertising objectives should contain benchmarks and indicate how far an advertiser wishes to move from the benchmark.

(2)   An advertising objective should specify a time frame so that advertisers know exactly how long they have to accomplish the objective.

b)   Advertising objectives usually are stated in terms of either sales or communication.

(1)   When an advertiser defines objectives in terms of sales, the objectives focus on increasing absolute dollar sales, increasing sales by a certain percentage, or increasing the firm's market share.

(2)   When objectives are stated in terms of communication, they are designed to increase brand or product aware-ness, make consumers' attitudes more favorable, or increase consumers' knowledge of a product's features.

C.   **Creating the Advertising Platform**

1.   An *advertising platform* consists of issues or selling points an advertiser wishes to include in the advertising campaign.

2.   A marketer's advertising platform should consist of issues that are important to consumers.

a) One of the best ways to determine what those issues are is to survey consumers about what they consider most important in the selection and use of the product involved.

b) Research is the most effective method for determining the issues of an advertising platform, but it is expensive. As a result, the most common way to develop a platform is to base it on the opinions of personnel within the firm and individuals in the advertising agency if an agency is used.

3. Because the advertising platform is a base on which to build the message, marketers should analyze this stage carefully in developing an advertising campaign. If the advertisements communicate information that consumers do not consider important when they select and use the product, the campaign can fail.

D. **Determining the Advertising Appropriation**

1. The *advertising appropriation* is the total amount of money a marketer allocates for advertising for a specific time period.

2. Many factors affect the amount of the advertising appropriation, including size of geographic market, distribution of buyers within the market, type of product advertised, and the firm's sales volume relative to competitors'.

(Transparency Figure 19D)

3. Various techniques are used to determine the advertising appropriation.

a) In the *objective-and-task approach*, marketers initially determine the objectives that a campaign is to achieve and then attempt to list the tasks required to accomplish them. Once the tasks have been determined, their costs are added to ascertain the appropriation needed to accomplish the objectives.

b) In the *percent-of-sales approach*, marketers multiply a firm's past sales, plus a factor for planned sales growth or decline, by a standard percentage based on what the firm traditionally spends on advertising and what the industry averages.

c) In the *competition-matching approach*, marketers try to match their major competitors' appropriations in terms of absolute dollars or to allocate the same percentage of sales for advertising that competitors allocate.

d) In the *arbitrary approach*, a high-level executive in the firm states how much can be spent on advertising for a certain time period.

(Transparency Figure 19E)

E. **Developing the Media Plan**

1. To derive the maximum results from media expenditures, a marketer must develop an effective media plan. A *media plan* sets forth the exact media vehicles to be used and the dates and times the advertisements will appear.

2. The media planner's primary goal is to reach the largest number of persons in the advertising target per dollar spent on media.

a) Reach—the percentage of consumers in the target audience actually exposed to a particular advertisement in a stated period of time

b) Frequency—the number of times these targeted consumers are exposed to the advertisements

3. When selecting media, the planner must first decide which kinds of media to use: radio, television, the Internet, newspapers, magazines, direct mail, outdoor displays, mass transit vehicles, or some combination of these.

4. Media planners must consider many factors when formulating the media plan.

a) They should analyze the location and demographic characteristics of people in the target audience because people's taste in media differ according to demographic groups and locations.

      b)   They should consider the sizes and types of audiences specific media reach.

(Building Customer Relationships: Remodeling Advertising Messages)

5.   The message content sometimes affects the types of media used.
    a)   Print media can be used more effectively than broadcast media to present many issues or numerous details.
    b)   When colors, patterns, and textures are important, media that can yield high-quality reproduction, such as magazines or television, should be used.

6.   The cost of media is an important but troublesome consideration. Media planners should try to obtain the best coverage possible for each dollar spent. A *cost comparison indicator* lets an advertiser compare the costs of several vehicles within a specific medium relative to the number of persons reached by each vehicle.

7.   There are three general types of media schedules.
    a)   Continuous—advertising runs at a constant level with little variation.
    b)   Flighting—advertisements run for set periods of time, alternating with periods in which no ads run.
    c)   Pulsing—a combination of continuous and flighting.

F.   **Creating the Advertising Message**

1.   The basic content and form of an advertising message are a function of several factors.
    a)   A product's features, uses, and benefits affect the content of the message.
    b)   Characteristics of people in the target audience, including gender, age, education, race, income, occupation, lifestyle, and other attributes, influence both the content and the form.
    c)   An advertising campaign's objectives and platform also affect the content and form of its messages.
        (1)   If a firm's advertising objectives involve large sales increases, the message may have to be stated in hard-hitting, high-impact language and symbols; when campaign objectives aim at increasing brand aware-ness, the message may use repetition of the brand name and words and illustrations associated with it.
        (2)   The platform is the foundation on which campaign messages are built.
    d)   Choice of media obviously influences the content and form of the message.
        (1)   Effective outdoor displays and short broadcast spot announcements require concise, simple messages.
        (2)   Magazine and newspaper advertisements can include numerous details and long explanations.
        (3)   Some magazine publishers print *regional issues*, in which advertisements and editorials are different in different geographic regions. A precise message content can be tailored to a particular geographic section of the advertising target.

(Transparency Figure 19.2)

2.   Messages for most advertisements depend on the use of copy and artwork.

(Transparency Figure 19F)

    a)   **Copy**
        Copy is the verbal portion of the advertisement and may include headlines, subheadlines, body copy, and signature. Not all advertising copy contains all of these copy elements.

(1)   The headline is critical because it is often the only part of the copy that people read. It should attract readers' attention and create enough interest to make them want to read the body copy.

(2)   The subheadline links the headline to body copy and sometimes helps explain the headline.

(3)   Body copy consists of an introductory statement or paragraph, several explanatory paragraphs, and a closing paragraph.

(4)   The signature contains the firm's trademark, logo, name, and address, identifying the sponsor. It should be attractive, legible, distinctive, and easy to identify in a variety of sizes.

(5)   Radio copy should be informal and conversational and consist of short, familiar terms, to attract listeners' attention and result in greater impact.

(6)   Television copy should neither overpower nor be overpowered by the visual material.

(7)   A *storyboard* is a mockup combining copy and visual material to show the sequence of major scenes in the commercial.

b)   **Artwork**

Artwork consists of an advertisement's illustration and layout.

(1)   *Illustrations* are often photographs, but they can also be presented as drawings, graphs, charts, and tables. They are used to attract attention, encourage the audience to read or listen to the copy, communicate an idea quickly, or communicate an idea that is difficult to put into words.

(Transparency Figure 19G)

(2)   The *layout* is the physical arrangement of the illustration, headline, subheadline, body copy, and signature.

G.   **Executing the Campaign**

1.   The execution of an advertising campaign requires an extensive amount of planning and coordination.

2.   Implementation requires detailed schedules to ensure that various phases of the work are completed on time. Advertising management personnel must evaluate the quality of work and take corrective action when necessary.

H.   **Evaluating Advertising Effectiveness**

1.   There are a variety of ways to test the effectiveness of advertising.

a)   Measuring achievement of advertising objectives

b)   Assessing the effectiveness of copy, illustrations, or layout

c)   Evaluating certain media

2.   Advertising can be evaluated before, during, and after the campaign.

a)   Evaluations performed before the campaign begins are called *pretests*. To pretest advertisements, marketers sometimes use a *consumer jury*, which consists of a number of persons who are actual or potential buyers of the advertised product.

(1)   During such a test, jurors are asked to judge one or several dimensions of two or more advertisements.

(2)   Such tests are based on the belief that consumers are more likely than advertising experts to know what will influence them.

b)   To measure advertising effectiveness during a campaign, marketers usually rely on inquiries.

(1)   In the initial stages of a campaign, an advertiser may use several advertisements simultaneously, each containing a coupon, form, or toll-free number through which potential customers can request information.

(2) The advertiser records the number of inquiries returned and determines which advertisement generated the most response.

    c) Evaluation of advertising effectiveness after the campaign is called a *posttest*. Advertising objectives often determine what kind of posttest is appropriate.

        (1) If the objectives focus on communication, then the posttest should measure changes in dimensions such as product awareness, brand awareness, or customer attitudes.

        (2) For campaign objectives stated in terms of sales, the posttest should measure changes in dimensions such as sales or market share.

        (3) Posttest methods based on memory include recognition and recall tests.

            (a) In a *recognition test*, individual respondents are shown the actual advertisement and asked whether they recognize it.

            (b) Recall can be measured through either unaided or aided recall methods. An *unaided recall test* is a posttest that asks subjects to identify recently seen ads but does not provide any clues. An *aided recall test* is a posttest that asks subjects to identify recently seen ads and provides clues to jog their memories.

            (c) The major justification for using recognition and recall methods is that individuals are more likely to buy the product if they can remember an advertisement than if they cannot remember it.

III. **Who Develops the Advertising Campaign?**

    A. In very small firms, one or two individuals are responsible for performing advertising activities. Usually, these individuals depend heavily on personnel at local newspapers and broadcast stations for artwork, copywriting, and advice about scheduling media.

    B. In certain large businesses, and especially large retail organizations, advertising departments create and implement advertising campaigns. Depending on the size of the advertising program, an advertising department may consist of a few multiskilled persons or a sizable number of specialists such as copywriters, artists, media buyers, and technical production coordinators.

    C. When an organization uses an advertising agency, the development of the advertising campaign is usually a joint effort of the agency and the firm.

        1. The degree to which each participates in the campaign's total development depends on the working relationship between the firm and the agency. The firm ordinarily relies on the agency for copywriting, artwork, technical production, and formulation of the media plan.

        2. An advertising agency can assist a business in several ways.

            a) An agency, especially a large one, can supply the services of highly skilled specialists—not only copywriters, artists, and production coordinators but also media experts, researchers, and legal advisers.

            b) Agency personnel often have broad experience in advertising and are usually more objective than the firm's employees about the organization's products.

            c) The services of an advertising agency can be obtained at a low or moderate cost because the agency usually receives its compensation through a 15 percent commission paid by the media from which it makes purchases.

IV. **Public Relations**

    A. *Public relations* is a broad set of communication efforts used to create and maintain favorable relationships between an organization and its stakeholders, both internal and external.

        1. Public relations can be used to promote people, places, ideas, activities, and even countries.

        2. Public relations focuses on enhancing the image of the total organization.

3.   Because the public's attitudes toward a firm are likely to affect the sales of its products, it is very important for firms to maintain positive public perceptions.

(Building Customer Relationships: PR Battles)

B.   **Public Relations Tools**
Companies use a variety of public relations tools to convey messages and create images.

1.   Public relations material such as brochures, newsletters, company magazines, and annual reports reach and influence the various stakeholders.
2.   Corporate identity material such as logos, business cards, stationery, and signs are created to make a firm immediately recognizable.
3.   Speeches can affect the organization's image.
4.   Event sponsorship, in which a company pays for part or all of a special event, is an effective means of increasing brand recognition with relatively minimal investment.
5.   *Publicity*, which is a part of public relations, is communication in news story form about an organization, its products, or both, transmitted through a mass medium at no charge.

(Transparency Figure 19C)

a)   The most common publicity-based tool is the *news release*, or press release, which is usually a single page of typewritten copy containing fewer than 300 words and describing a company event or product.

(Transparency Figure 19H)

b)   A *feature article* is a manuscript of up to 3,000 words prepared for a specific publication.
c)   A *captioned photograph* is a photograph with a brief description explaining the picture's content.
d)   A *press conference* is a meeting called to announce major news events.
e)   Publicity-based public relations tools offer several advantages, including credibility, news value, significant word-of-mouth communications, and a perception of being endorsed by the media, as well as a relatively low cost.
f)   Publicity-based public relations tools also have some limitations.
(1)   Marketers cannot control whether the media choose to publish them at all.
(2)   Marketers can control neither the content nor the timing of the communication.

C.   **Evaluating Public Relations Effectiveness**
1.   Because of the potential benefits of good public relations, it is essential that organizations evaluate the effectiveness of their public relations campaigns.
2.   Research can be conducted to determine how well a firm is communicating its messages to target audiences.
a)   "Environmental monitoring" identifies changes in public opinion affecting an organization.
b)   A "public relations audit" is used to assess an organization's image among the public or to evaluate the effect of a specific public relations program.
c)   A "communications audit" may include a content analysis of messages, a readability study, or a readership survey.
d)   A "social audit" measures the extent to which stakeholders view an organization as responsible.
3.   One approach to measuring the effectiveness of publicity-based public relations is to count the number of exposures in the media.

4. Although counting the number of media exposures does not reveal how many people have actually read or heard the company's message or what they though about the message afterward, measuring changes in product awareness, knowledge, and attitudes resulting from the publicity campaign can provide this information.

D. **Dealing with Unfavorable Public Relations**

1. A single negative event that produces unfavorable public relations can wipe out a company's favorable image and destroy positive consumer attitudes that took years to build through expensive advertising campaigns and other types of promotional efforts.

2. To protect its image, an organization needs to prevent unfavorable public relations or at least lessen its effect should it occur.

3. Because negative events can happen to even the most cautious firms, organizations should have predetermined plans in place to handle them when they do occur so as to reduce the adverse impact.

4. By being forthright with the press and public and taking prompt action, firms may be able to convince the public of their honest attempts to deal with the situation, and news personnel may be more willing to help explain complex issues to the public.

NOTES FOR CLASS EXERCISES, DEBATE ISSUE, AND CHAPTER QUIZ

On the following pages, you will find two class exercises, a debate issue, and a chapter quiz. These are formatted in large-size type so that you can use them as class handouts or for making transparencies. Below are the authors' comments on the class exercises, the debate topic for this chapter, and the answers to the chapter quiz.

Comments on Class Exercise 1

The objective of this exercise is to recognize the purpose and uses of advertising and to evaluate the effectiveness of various advertisements.

You can present this exercise in various ways. One way is to bring in copies of magazines or newspapers. A second way is to show the class videotapes of commercials that you supply. Either approach makes for an interesting class discussion. Instructor flexibility is required because your students' answers depend on what medium you select.

Question 1. Review the advertisements and complete the following:

Identify ads that represent:

1. _____Institutional advertising (promotes organizational images, ideas, or political issues)

2. _____Product advertising (promotes the uses, features, images, and benefits of a selected product)

3. _____Pioneer advertising (informs about a product's uses to stimulate primary demand without referring to specific brand)

4. _____Competitive advertising (to stimulate selective demand, points out brand's uses, features, and advantages that benefit consumers)

5. _____Comparative advertising (two or more specified brands are compared on the basis of one or more attributes)

6. _____Reminder advertising (lets consumers know that brand is still around and has certain uses, characteristics, and benefits)

7. _____Reinforcement advertising (assures current users they have made the right brand choice and tells them how to get the most satisfaction from it)

Question 2. Evaluate the effectiveness of each advertisement.

1. Local print or television ads are often cluttered with jumbled attempts at several messages. These advertisers seem to think, "I'm paying for this space, and I'm going to get as much in as I can!"

2. Students are quick to point out that some ads (particularly TV) have little relevance for them. Remind them that they might not be in the target audience.

Comments on Class Exercise 2

The purpose of this exercise is to assess the effectiveness of advertising slogans regarding what they communicate and how memorable they are. After discussing the answers, ask students to consider the factors that help to make a slogan more easily recalled. Answers:

1. "We love to see you smile" — **McDonald's**
2. "Like a rock" — **Chevrolet**
3. "Just push play" — **Dodge Ram**
4. "Always a Low Price. Always" — **Wal-Mart**
5. "It's the Cheesiest" — **Kraft Macaroni & Cheese**
6. "We'll leave the light on" — **Motel 6**
7. "Maybe She's Born with It" — **Maybelline**
8. "Eat Fresh" — **Subway**
9. "You're in Good Hands" — **Allstate**
10. "Think Different" — **Apple Computers**
11. "For all your 2000 body parts" — **Lever 2000**
12. "Drivers Wanted" — **Volkswagen**
13. "Eat More Chicken" — **Chick-fil-A**
14. "Think outside the bun" — **Taco Bell**
15. "M'm M'm Good" — **Campbell's**

DEBATE ISSUE

Is using celebrities in an ad campaign a good way to stimulate brand appeal?

CHAPTER QUIZ

Answers to Chapter Quiz 1. c; 2. a; 3. a; 4. a.

CLASS EXERCISE 1

REVIEW THE ADVERTISEMENTS AND COMPLETE THE FOLLOWING:

1. Identify ads that represent:

   a. Institutional advertising

   b. Product advertising

   c. Pioneer advertising

   d. Competitive advertising

   e. Comparative advertising

   f. Reminder advertising

   g. Reinforcement advertising

2. Evaluate the effectiveness of each advertisement:

   a. Does it have a clear objective?

   b. Are the issues or selling points important to the target audiences?

Class Exercise 2

IDENTIFY THE COMPANY OR BRAND THAT IS ASSOCIATED WITH EACH SLOGAN.

1. "We love to see you smile"
2. "Like a rock"
3. "Just push play"
4. "Always a Low Price. Always"
5. "It's the Cheesiest"
6. "We'll leave the light on"
7. "Maybe She's Born with It"
8. "Eat Fresh"
9. "You're in Good Hands"
10. "Think Different"
11. "For all your 2000 body parts"
12. "Drivers Wanted"
13. "Eat More Chicken"
14. "Think outside the bun"
15. "M'm M'm Good"

<u>Debate Issue</u>

IS USING CELEBRITIES IN AN AD CAMPAIGN A GOOD WAY TO STIMULATE BRAND APPEAL?

<u>YES</u>	<u>NO</u>
• Reinforces and legitimizes use of the product	• Good at stimulating awareness but not brand appeal
• Especially effective when celebrity is spokesperson over a long time period	• Celebrities are paid so consumers don't trust what they say
• Breeds familiarity and trust between celebrity and customers	• Trust further dampened when celebrity endorses two different products
• Effective with children	• Can backfire if truth of celebrity's lack of use of the product is made public
	• Celebrity can develop a negative image that can rub off on the brand or organization

Chapter Quiz

1. Soft drink companies advertise that their products beat the competition in national "taste tests," and they refer to the rival brands by name. This type of advertising is *best* described as
   a. pioneer.
   b. competitive.
   c. comparative.
   d. defensive.
   e. selective.

2. Advertising campaign objectives that are aimed at making customers' attitudes more favorable are stated in _____ terms.
   a. communication
   b. sales
   c. demand
   d. market
   e. survey

3. Some of the posttest methods for measuring advertising effectiveness are based on how well consumers remember advertising and include recognition and recall tests. What is the basic difference between these two approaches?
   a. The actual ads are shown in the former but not in the latter.
   b. The former method relies on memory alone, and the latter shows the actual ads.
   c. One uses a consumer jury; the other uses random individuals.
   d. The respondents are given class clues in the latter but not in the former.
   e. One is used primarily by the government, and the other is used by private businesses.

4. Which one of the following is *not* an advantage of using publicity-based public relations tools?
   a. Control by media personnel of the content and timing of messages
   b. Credibility
   c. Strong news value
   d. Follow-up word-of-mouth communications
   e. A favorable perception of being endorsed by the media

ANSWERS TO DISCUSSION AND REVIEW QUESTIONS

1. **What is the difference between institutional and product advertising?**

    Institutional advertising promotes organizational images, ideas, and political issues. Product advertising promotes goods and services.

2. **What is the difference between competitive advertising and comparative advertising?**

    Competitive advertising attempts to stimulate selective demand, which is demand for a specific brand. Comparative advertising is a type of competitive advertising that directly compares two or more brands on the basis of one or product attributes.

3. **What are the major steps in creating an advertising campaign?**

    The major steps in the creation of an advertising campaign are the following:

    a.   Identify and analyze an advertising target.

    b.   Define the advertising objectives.

    c.   Create the advertising platform.

    d.   Determine the advertising appropriation.

    e.   Develop the media plan.

    f.   Create the message.

    g.   Evaluate the effectiveness of the advertising.

4. **What is a target audience? How does a marketer analyze the target audience after identifying it?**

    The target audience is the group of people toward whom the advertisements are aimed. After identifying the target audience, the marketer generally analyzes it with regard to location and geographic distribution of persons; distribution of age, income, race, sex, and education; and consumers' attitudes regarding purchase and use of both the advertiser's products and competitors' products. The exact kind of information needed depends on the type of product being advertised, the characteristics of the target, and the type and amount of competition.

5. **Why is it necessary to define advertising objectives?**

    Advertising objectives must be defined to give the development of the campaign direction and purpose.

6. **What is an advertising platform, and how is it used?**

    An advertising platform consists of the basic issues or selling points that an advertiser wishes to include in the advertising campaign. The advertising platform is used as the base from which to develop the message.

7. **What factors affect the size of an advertising budget? What techniques are used to determine an advertising budget?**

    The size of the geographic market and the distribution of the buyers within it influence the amount of an advertising budget. Also, the type of product—industrial, consumer durable, or consumer convenience item—affects the proportion of revenue appropriated for advertising.

Techniques used for determining the advertising budget include the objective-and-task approach, the percent-of-sales approach, the competition-matching approach, and the arbitrary approach. The objective-and-task approach involves determining the objectives of the advertising campaign and ascertaining the tasks necessary to accomplish them. After the tasks are determined, their costs are added to compute the amount of the total appropriation. In the percent-of-sales approach, the marketer simply multiplies the firm's past sales, forecasted sales, or a combination of the two by a standard percentage based on what the firm traditionally has spent on advertising or based on industry averages. In the competition-matching approach, the advertiser tries to match major competitors' appropriations in terms of absolute dollars or percent of sales. In the arbitrary approach, a high-level executive in the firm states how much can be spent on advertising for a certain period.

8. **Describe the steps in developing a media plan.**

First, the planner decides which general kinds of media to use and selects specific subclasses within each medium. Then the planner selects the specific media vehicles to be used. Finally, the planner creates a time schedule showing the dates and/or times the advertisements will run.

9. **What is the function of copy in an advertising message?**

Copy is used to attract readers' attention and create interest. It also identifies a specific desire or problem of consumers, suggests the advertised product as the best way to solve that problem, states the advantages and benefits of the product, indicates why the advertised product is the best for the buyer's particular situation, substantiates the claims and advantages of the product, and asks the buyer to take action.

10. **Discuss several ways to posttest the effectiveness of advertising.**

Posttest evaluation of advertising may be performed in several ways, and the specific dimensions to be tested are determined by the advertising objectives. If the objectives are set in communication terms, posttests may include consumer surveys and experiments. If the objectives are stated in terms of sales, effectiveness can be determined by ascertaining changes in sales or in market share that are attributable to the advertising campaign. However, because of the expense associated with consumer surveys and experiments and the problems in determining the direct effects of advertising on sales, many advertisers use recognition and recall tests to evaluate advertising. In recognition tests, each respondent is shown the actual advertisement and asked if he or she recognizes it. In recall tests, the respondent is not shown the actual advertisement but instead is asked about what advertisements he or she has seen recently.

11. **What role does an advertising agency play in developing an advertising campaign?**

If a firm uses an advertising agency, the development of the advertising campaign is usually a joint effort, with the agency performing such functions as copywriting, artwork, technical production, and formulation of the media plan. The use of an agency provides a firm with highly skilled specialists who are generally more objective than the firm's employees and have more experience in advertising. In addition, the cost to the firm is generally low or moderate.

12. **What is public relations? Who can an organization reach through public relations?**

Public relations is a broad set of communication efforts used to create and maintain favorable relationships between an organization and its stakeholders. Through public relations, organizations can reach internal and external stakeholders including customers, suppliers, employees, stockholders, the media, educators, potential investors, government officials, and society in general.

13. **How do organizations use public relations tools? Give several examples that you have observed recently.**

Organizations can use public relations tools for a single purpose or for several purposes. Public relations tools are used by organizations to make people aware of their products, brands, or activities, but they are also used to create a specific company image. Public relations tools are also used to maintain an organization's positive visibility and to overcome negative images. On the second part of the question, students' answers will vary.

14. **Explain the problems and limitations associated with publicity-based public relations.**

Limitations of publicity-based public relations arise from requirements of media personnel that the messages be newsworthy, timely, and accurate. Many communications that a firm wishes to present through publicity-based public relations do not qualify as newsworthy. Organizations have little control over the content or timing of publicity releases and no control over the locations in which the releases are presented. Therefore, messages sometimes appear in locations or at times that may not reach an organization's target audiences.

15. **In what ways is the effectiveness of public relations evaluated?**

Organizations evaluate the effectiveness of public relations in a variety of ways. Environmental monitoring, public relations audits, communications audits, and social audits are all research methods used to determine how effectively a firm is communicating its messages or images to its stakeholders. Another approach to measuring the effectiveness of publicity-based public relations is to count the number of exposures in the media. Because counting the number of exposures doesn't reveal how many people actually receive the message, organizations also measure changes in product awareness, knowledge, and attitudes resulting from specific public relations campaigns.

16. **What are some sources of negative public relations? How should an organization deal with unfavorable public relations?**

Although public relations is a planned activity, uncontrolled events can result in negative public relations. Some sources of negative public relations can include news stories about unsafe products, accidents involving an organization, such as a plane crash, or controversial actions taken by employees. One way to handle negative public relations is to avoid events (such as accidents) that generate negative publicity. An organization needs a definite set of policies and procedures to deal with coverage of negative events and to lessen their effects. In most situations, the best approach is to facilitate coverage rather than try to hide the event or reduce coverage. If the organization expedites coverage, less misinformation and fewer rumors are likely to result.

COMMENTS ON THE CASES

CASE 19.1 VAIL RESORTS USES PUBLIC RELATIONS TO PUT OUT A FIRE

The purpose of this case is to demonstrate how a real-world company used public-relations tools to address a negative publicity situation.

Question 1 asks what tools Vail Resorts used to respond to the crisis. The company used direct mail to communicate with customers who had already made reservations, as well as travel agents and local hotels, to reassure them that the resort would reopen and be safe to enjoy. The company also chose to be honest and open with the media, employees, and customers, which helped preserve trust in the firm.

Question 2 asks students to evaluate Vail Resorts' response to the crisis. Responses will vary, but should demonstrate an understanding of crisis planning and its importance. Most students will be quick to agree with the company's own assessment that it could have followed its own crisis management plan more closely, particularly in regard to individual responsibility for specific actions. Part of the firm's problem in the first two days of the crisis was confusion surrounding who was responsible for what. Some students might also suggest additional public relations efforts targeted toward communicating the firm's efforts to be environmentally responsible to counter the dramatic criticism leveled by ELF.

Question 3 asks creating a crisis management and disaster recovery plan can help a company protect its reputation, customer relationships, and profits. According to the case, crisis planning can help arm a firm with tools and procedures to manage a crisis and mitigate unfavorable publicity. Creating these plans can help educate employees as to their responsibilities in a crisis so that they can respond more quickly without having to await instructions from others, which could further slow down the firm's response in a disaster. Openness and honesty can help convince the public of the firm's honest efforts to resolve the situation, which may encourage the media to be more willing to help explain complex issues.

Video Information

Subject:	Vail Resorts
Location:	Tape 2/DVD 2, Segment 19
Length:	18:00

Video Overview: This video examines the use of public relations to manage a crisis situation at Vail Resorts, Inc. In October 1998, Vail Mountain resort was the target of an ecoterrorist attack which destroyed several resort structures and chair-lift operator buildings. Despite initial media misinformation and rumors that the resort would be closed for the season, Vail Resorts recovered and had a successful season, due in large part to a well-planned public relations campaign. The company's crisis management and disaster recovery plans are also examined.

MULTIPLE-CHOICE QUESTIONS ABOUT THE VIDEO

1. The radical environmental organization _____ claimed responsibility for the Vail Mountain fires.

    a. People for the Ethical Treatment of Animals
    b. Greenpeace
    c. Rocky Mountain Animal Federation
    d. Earth Liberation Front
    e. Citizens to Protect the Earth

2. For Vail Resorts to respond appropriately to this situation, the most important thing is probably a(n)

    a. effective crisis management plan.
    b. ethical compliance program.
    c. security system.
    d. natural disaster response team.
    e. marketing strategy.

3.   In order to reinforce that Vail Resorts was a viable business after the attack, the company used _____ to contact consumers.

    a.   e-mail
    b.   newspaper ads
    c.   Internet website
    d.   telephone calls
    e.   direct mail

ANSWERS TO MULTIPLE-CHOICE QUESTIONS ABOUT THE VIDEO

1.   d

2.   a

3.   e

CASE 19.2 MICROSOFT: CRAFTING IMAGE THROUGH PUBLIC RELATIONS

This case shows students how Microsoft is using public relations to shape and protect the image of its company and its products. To introduce this case, you might ask how many students use Microsoft products on their own computers and whether any students have chosen to use instead a rival operating system, web-browser, or other software such as Linux or Netscape.

The first question asks about the major public relations tools being used by Microsoft. As indicated in the case, the company is using news releases, newsletters, brochures, speeches, and publicity (through press conferences and giveaways, for example).

Question 2 asks which stakeholders Microsoft wants to reach with its public relations efforts. Microsoft is aiming to reach consumer and business computer users, government officials, the media, stockholders, educators, potential investors, resellers, employees, suppliers, and society in general.

Question 3 asks how Microsoft should evaluate the results of its public relations programs. One way Microsoft can evaluate the results is by counting the number of exposures in the media. A second way is to conduct research to measure awareness and attitudes before and after public relations campaigns are conducted.

The final question asks how Microsoft should have used public relations to communicate its views during and after the anti-trust trial. Students' answers will vary. Ask them to explain their answers in terms of Microsoft's overall public relations objectives and the PR tools it uses. This is a good opportunity to discuss publicity about recent developments in the case and examine how Microsoft is using public relations to manage its image these days.

CHAPTER 20

Personal Selling and Sales Promotion

TEACHING RESOURCES QUICK REFERENCE GUIDE

Resource	Location
Purpose and Perspective	IRM, p. 373
Guide for Using Color Transparencies	IRM, p. 374
Lecture Outline	IRM, p. 374
Notes for Class Exercises, Debate Issue, and Chapter Quiz	IRM, p. 383
Class Exercise 1	IRM, p. 385
Class Exercise 2	IRM, p. 386
Debate Issue	IRM, p. 387
Chapter Quiz	IRM, p. 388
Answers to Discussion and Review Questions	IRM, p. 389
Comments on the Cases	IRM, p. 394
Case 20.1	IRM, p. 394
Video	Tape 2/DVD 2, Segment 20
Video Information	IRM, p. 394
Multiple-Choice Questions About the Video	IRM, p. 395
Case 20.2	IRM, p. 395
Transparency Acetates	Transparency package
Examination Questions: Essay	TB, p. 577
Examination Questions: Multiple-Choice	TB, p. 577
Examination Questions: True-False	TB, p. 602
Author-Selected Multiple-Choice Test Items	TB, p. 672
HMClassPrep Presentation Resources	CD-ROM
PowerPoint Slides	Instructor's website

Note: Additional resources are updated periodically and may be found on the accompanying student and instructor websites at http://www.prideferrell.com/.

PURPOSE AND PERSPECTIVE

This chapter covers in detail two promotion mix elements—personal selling and sales promotion. To help students build a better understanding of the purposes and roles of salespeople, we initially discuss the basic elements of the personal selling process and the types of salespeople used in organizations. We also devote considerable detail to a discussion of sales management decisions and activities including topics such as establishing sales force objectives; determining the size of the sales force; and recruiting, selecting, training, compensating, motivating, routing, scheduling, and controlling salespeople. Next we discuss how sales promotion activities are blended with other elements in a promotion mix. We also cover the objectives for which organizations use sales promotion. Finally, we classify and present major characteristics of a number of sales promotion methods.

GUIDE FOR USING COLOR TRANSPARENCIES

There are two groups of color transparencies. The transparencies identified by a double number are the same as the figures in the text. The transparencies labeled with a number and a letter are illustrations that do not appear in the text, but they can be used as additional examples of concepts discussed.

Figure 20.1	General Steps in the Personal Selling Process
Figure 20A	Chapter 20 Outline
Figure 20B	Key Definitions: Prospecting, Consumer Sales Promotion Methods
Figure 20C	Major Sales Management Decision Areas
Figure 20D	Major Types of Sales Force Compensation Methods
Figure 20E	Average Salaries for Sales and Marketing Positions
Figure 20F	*Sales & Marketing Management* Provides a Yearly Survey of Buying Power and Other Useful Information to Help Sales Managers
Figure 20G	An Examples of a Sales Incentive Program
Figure 20H	Sales Promotions Like This Provide Incentives to Customers

LECTURE OUTLINE

(Transparency Figure 20A: Chapter Outline)

I.   **The Nature of Personal Selling**
Personal selling is paid personal communication that attempts to inform customers and persuade them to purchase products in an exchange situation.

   A.   There are two primary advantages of personal selling.
      1.   Personal selling provides marketers the greatest freedom to adjust a message to satisfy customers' information needs.
      2.   Personal selling is precise of all promotional methods; it enables marketers to focus on the most promising sales prospects.
   B.   A major disadvantage of personal selling is its cost. Generally, it is the most expensive element in the promotion mix.
   C.   Many people earn their living through personal selling activities.
   D.   Personal selling goals vary from one firm to another.
      1.   Typical goals usually involve identifying prospects, persuading them to buy, and keeping customers satisfied.
         a)   Because most potential buyers seek certain types of information before they make a purchase decision, salespeople must ascertain prospects' informational needs and then provide relevant information.
         b)   To achieve this purpose, sales personnel must be well trained in their products and the selling process in general.
      2.   Salespeople must be aware of their competitors.
         a)   They must monitor the development of new products and keep abreast of competitors' sales efforts in their sales territories, how often and when the competition calls on their accounts, and what the competition is saying about their product in relation to its own.
         b)   Salespeople must emphasize the benefits their products provide, especially when competitors' products do not offer those specific benefits.
      3.   For long-run survival, most marketers depend on repeat sales and thus need to keep their customers satisfied.
         a)   Much of this burden falls on salespeople because they are usually closer to customers than anyone else and often provide buyers with information and service after the sale.

b)   Such contact allows a salesperson an opportunity to generate additional sales and offers them a vantage point to evaluate the strengths and weaknesses of the company's product and other marketing mix ingredients.

II.   **Elements of the Personal Selling Process**
No two salespeople use exactly the same selling methods, but many move through a general selling process consisting of seven steps.

(Transparency Figure 20.1)

A.   **Prospecting**
1.   Developing a list of potential customers is called *prospecting*, and it is the first element in the selling process.

(Transparency Figure 20B)

2.   A salesperson seeks the names of prospects from several sources, including company sales records, trade shows, commercial databases, newspaper announcements, public records, telephone directories, trade association directories, among others.
a)   Sales personnel also use responses to advertisements that encourage interested persons to send in information request forms.
b)   Many salespeople use referrals—recommendations from current customers—to find prospects.
3.   After developing the prospect list, a salesperson evaluates prospects to determine if they are able, willing, and authorized to buy the product.

B.   **Preapproach**
1.   Before contacting acceptable prospects, a salesperson finds and analyzes information about each prospects' specific product needs, current use of brands, feelings about available brands, and personal characteristics.
2.   The more information about a prospect that a salesperson has, the more equipped he or she is to develop a presentation that will precisely communicate with the prospect.

C.   **Approach**
The *approach*—the manner in which a salesperson contacts a potential customer—is a critical step in the sales process because the prospect's first impression of the salesperson may be a lasting one with long-term consequences.

1.   During the initial visit, the salesperson strives to develop a relationship rather than just push a product.
a)   The approach must be designed to deliver value to targeted customers.
b)   If the sales approach is inappropriate, the salesperson's efforts are likely to have poor results.
2.   Types of Approaches
a)   In the referral approach, the salesperson explains to a prospect that an acquaintance, an associate, or a relative suggested the call.
b)   In the cold canvass technique, the salesperson calls on potential customers without their prior consent.
c)   In the repeat contact approach, the salesperson mentions a prior meeting.
d)   The type of approach used depends on the salesperson's preferences, the product being sold, the firm's resources, and the prospect's characteristics.

(Ethics and Social Responsibility: Responsible Selling Improves Customer Relationships)

D. **Making the Presentation**
1. During the sales presentation, the salesperson must attract and hold the prospect's attention, stimulate interest, and spark a desire for the product.
2. During the presentation, the salesperson must not only talk but also listen to gain information about the prospect's specific informational needs.

E. **Overcoming Objections**
1. One of the best ways to overcome a prospect's objections is to anticipate and counter them before the prospect has an opportunity to raise them. This approach can be risky because the salesperson may mention some objections that the prospect would not have raised.
2. If possible, the salesperson should handle objections when they arise. An effective salesperson usually seeks out a prospect's objections to answer them because these may keep the prospect from buying.

F. **Closing the Sale**
1. *Closing* is the stage in the selling process when the salesperson asks the prospect to buy the product(s).
2. During the presentation, the salesperson may use a "trial close" by asking questions that assume the prospect will buy the product.
    a) The reactions to such questions usually indicate how close the prospect is to buying.
    b) The trial close allows prospects to indicate indirectly that they will buy the product without having to say the difficult words, "I'll take it."
3. Closing often serves as an important stimulus to uncover hidden objections.

G. **Following Up**
1. If attempts to close the sale are successful, the salesperson must follow up the sale.
2. In the follow-up stage, the salesperson should determine if the order was delivered on time and was installed properly; should learn whether the customer has problems or questions about the product; and should determine the customer's future product needs.

III. **Types of Salespeople**
A. **Order Getters**
1. An *order getter* increases sales by selling to new customers and increasing sales to present customers, which is sometimes called "creative selling."
2. Order-getting activities are sometimes divided into two categories.
    a) **Current-Customer Sales.**
    These sales personnel concentrate on current customers, calling on people and organizations that have purchased products from the firm before.
    b) **New-Business Sales.**
    These sales personnel are responsible for locating prospects and converting them into buyers.

B. **Order Takers**
1. An *order taker* primarily seeks repeat sales.
    a) Order takers generate the bulk of many firms' total sales.
    b) Most order takers handle orders for standardized products that are purchased routinely and do not require extensive sales efforts; however, the role of order takers is changing.

2. Order takers can be classified into two groups.
   a) **Inside Order Takers**
      These salespeople are located in sales offices and receive orders by mail, telephone, and the Internet. That does not mean, however, that inside order takers never communicate with customers face to face.

   b) **Field Order Takers**
      These salespeople travel to customers and often develop interdependent relationships with customers; they may also be referred to as outside order takers.

C. **Support Personnel**
   Support personnel facilitate selling but usually are not involved solely with making sales.

   1. They engage primarily in marketing industrial products, locating prospects, educating customers, building goodwill, and providing service after the sale.
   2. There are three common types of support personnel.
      a) **Missionary Salespeople**
         Missionary salespeople, usually employed by manufacturers, assist the producer's customers in selling to their own customers.

      b) **Trade Salespeople**
         Trade salespeople direct much of their efforts toward helping customers, especially retail stores, promote the products. Food producers and processors commonly employ trade salespeople.

      c) **Technical Salespeople**
         Technical salespeople direct their efforts toward the organization's current customers by providing technical assistance regarding applications of the product, system designs, and installation procedures. Technical sales personnel frequently are employed to sell technical industrial products.

IV. **Managing the Sales Force**

(Transparency Figure 20C)

(Transparency Figure 20F)

Effective sales force management is an important determinant of a firm's success because the sales force is directly responsible for generating an organization's primary inputs—sales revenue.

A. **Establishing Sales Force Objectives**
   1. Sales objectives tell salespeople what they are expected to accomplish during a specified period. They give the sales force direction and purpose.
   2. Sales objectives should be stated in precise, measurable terms and be specific about the time period and geographic areas involved.
   3. Sales objectives usually are established for both the total sales force and each individual salesperson.
      a) Objectives for the entire force are usually stated in terms of sales volume, market share, or profit.
      b) Sales objectives, or quotas, for individual salespeople are commonly stated in terms of dollars or unit sales volume.

B. **Determining Sales Force Size**
   1. The size of the sales force affects the firm's ability to generate sales and profits, the compensation methods used, salespeople's morale, and overall sales force management.

2. Several analytical methods are used to determine the size of the sales force.
   a) One method involves determining how many sales calls per year are necessary for the organization to serve customers effectively and then dividing this total by the average number of dales calls a salesperson makes annually.
   b) A second method is based on marginal analysis, in which additional salespeople are added to the sales force until the cost of an additional salesperson equals the additional sales generated by that person.

C. **Recruiting and Selecting Salespeople**
1. *Recruiting* is a process by which the sales manager develops a list of qualified applicants for sales positions.
2. A set of required qualifications should be established by the sales manager before recruiting to ensure that the recruiting process results in a pool of qualified salespeople.
3. A sales manager must develop determine what set of characteristics best fits his or her company's particular sales tasks.
   a) The sales manager should prepare a job description that enumerates the specific tasks to be performed by salespeople.
   b) The sales manager should analyze the characteristics of the firm's successful as well as ineffective salespeople.
4. A sales manager usually recruits applicants from several sources: departments within the firm, other firms, employment agencies, educational institutions, respondents to advertisements, and individuals recommended by current employees.
5. The process for hiring a sales force varies from one company to another, but companies that are concerned about reducing sales force turnover are likely to have strict recruiting and selection procedures.
6. Recruitment should be a continuous activity aimed at reaching the best applicants, and it should be a systematic process that effectively matches applicants' characteristics and needs with the requirements of specific selling tasks.

D. **Training Sales Personnel**
1. Many organizations have formal training programs; others depend on informal, on-the-job training.

(Building Customer Relationships: Whirlpool Puts Salespeople in the "Real Whirled")

2. A sales training program can concentrate on the company, its products, its selling methods, or all three.
3. Training programs can be aimed at newly hired salespeople, experienced salespeople, or both.
4. Sales training may be performed in the field, at educational institutions, in company facilities, and/or online.
   a) In some firms, recently hired salespeople receive the bulk of their training before being assigned to a specific sales position.
   b) Other business organizations put new recruits into the field immediately and provide formal training only after the new salesperson has gained some experience.
   c) Training programs can be as short as several days or as long as three years or more.
   d) Sales management must determine the frequency, sequencing, and duration of these activities.
5. Sales managers often engage in sales training, whether daily on the job or periodically during sales meetings; training may also be provided by outside companies specializing in training.

E. **Compensating Salespeople**
1. A compensation plan should attract, motivate, and retain the most effective individuals.
    a) It should be designed to give sales management the desired level of control and to provide sales personnel with acceptable levels of freedom, income, and incentive.
    b) It should be flexible, equitable, easy to administer, and easy to understand.
    c) It should facilitate and encourage proper treatment of customers.
2. To create compensation programs, the developers must determine the level of compensation required and the most desirable method of calculating it.
    a) In analyzing the required compensation level, a firm's sales management tries to ascertain a salesperson's value to the company on the basis of the tasks and responsibilities associated with the sales position.
    b) A salesperson's value to the firm is affected by several factors:
        (1) Salaries of other types of personnel in the firm
        (2) Competitors' compensation plans
        (3) Cost of sales force turnover
        (4) Size of nonsalary selling expenses
3. To deliver the required compensation, a firm may have one or more of three basic compensation methods.

(Transparency Figure 20D)

(Transparency Figure 20E)

    a) In a *straight salary compensation plan*, salespeople are paid a specified amount per time period, and this sum remains the same until they receive a pay increase or decrease.
    b) In a *straight commission compensation plan*, salespeople's compensation is determined solely by the amount of their sales for a given period. A commission may be based on a single percentage of sales or on a sliding scale that involves several sales levels and percentage rates.
    c) In a *combination compensation plan*, salespeople are paid a fixed salary and a commission based on sales volume.

F. **Motivating Salespeople**
1. A sales manager should develop a systematic approach for motivating salespeople to obtain high productivity.
2. Effective sales force motivation is achieved through an organized set of activities performed continuously by the company's sales management.
3. Sales personnel, like other people, join organizations to satisfy personal needs and achieve personal goals.
    a) Sales managers must identify those needs and goals and strive to create an organizational climate that allows each salesperson to fulfill them.
    b) Sales contests and other incentive programs can be effective motivators.

(Transparency Figure 20G)

4. Properly designed incentive programs pay for themselves many times over, and sales managers are relying on incentives more than ever.

G. **Managing Sales Territories**
The effectiveness of a sales force that must travel to its customers depends on sales management's decisions regarding sales territories.

1. **Creating Sales Territories**
    a) Sales managers usually try to create territories that have similar sales potential or to develop territories that require about the same amount of work.

        (1)   Territories with equal sales potential usually will be unequal in geographic size. This causes salespeople with larger territories to have to work harder and longer to generate a specific sales volume.

        (2)   Territories that require equal amounts of work will cause salespeople who are compensated totally or partially by commissions to have unequal income potential.

        (3)   Many sales managers try to balance territorial workloads and earning potential by using differential commission rates.

    b)   A territory's size and shape should also help the sales force provide the best possible customer coverage and should minimize selling costs.

  2.   **Routing and Scheduling Salespeople**

Those in charge of routing and scheduling must consider the sequence in which customers are called on, specific roads or transportation schedules to be used, number of calls to be made in a given period, and time of day the calls will occur.

    a)   In some firms, salespeople plan their own routes and schedules, but in other firms, the sales manager handles the task.

    b)   The major goals should be to minimize salespeople's nonselling time and travel expenses and to maximize their selling time.

H.   **Controlling and Evaluating Sales Force Performance**

  1.   To control and evaluate sales force activities properly, sales management needs information, which can be obtained from salespersons' call reports, customer feedback, and invoices.

  2.   The dimensions used to measure a salesperson's performance are determined largely by the sales objectives that the sales manager sets. Indicators of performance used by sales managers include average number of calls per day, average sales per customer, actual sales relative to sales potential, number of new-customer orders, average cost per call, and average gross profit per customer.

  3.   To evaluate a salesperson, a sales manager may compare one or more of these dimensions with a predetermined performance standard.

  4.   After evaluating salespeople, sales managers take corrective action as needed to improve sales force performance.

V.   **The Nature of Sales Promotion**

A.   *Sales promotion* is an activity and/or material that acts as a direct inducement, offering added value or incentive for the product to resellers, salespeople, or consumers.

  1.   It includes all promotional activities other than personal selling, advertising, and public relations.

  2.   Marketers often use sales promotion to facilitate personal selling, advertising, or both; they also use advertising and personal selling to support sales promotions.

  3.   Sales promotion can increase sales by providing extra purchasing incentives.

  4.   When deciding which sales promotion methods to use, marketers must consider several factors, particularly product characteristics and target market characteristics.

  5.   The use of sales promotion has increased dramatically, primarily at the expense of advertising.

    a)   Heightened concerns about value have made customers more responsive to promotional offers, especially price discounts and point-of-purchase displays.

    b)   Due to their size and increasing access to customer information, retailers have gained considerable power in the supply chain and are demanding greater promotional efforts from manufacturers to boost profits.

    c)   Declines in brand loyalty mean that sales promotions aimed at persuading customers to switch brands are more effective.

d)   The stronger emphasis placed on improving short-term results calls for greater use of sales promotion methods that yield quick, but perhaps short-lived, sales increases.

B.   **Consumer Sales Promotion Methods**

Consumer sales promotion methods encourage or stimulate consumers to patronize a specific retail store or try a particular product.

(Transparency Figure 20B)

(Transparency Figure 20H)

1.   **Coupons and Cents-Off Offers**

a)   *Coupons* reduce a product's price and aim to prompt consumers to try new or established products, increase sales volume quickly, attract repeat purchasers, or introduce new package sizes or features.

(1)   Coupons are the most widely used consumer sales promotion technique.

(2)   For best results, coupons should be easy to recognize and state the offer clearly.

(3)   The nature of the product is the prime consideration in setting up a coupon promotion.

(4)   Coupons offer several advantages.

(a)   Print advertisements with coupons are often more effective at generating brand awareness than print ads without coupons.

(b)   Coupons reward present product users, win back former users, and encourage purchases in larger quantities.

(c)   Because they are returned, coupons also let a manufacturer determine whether it reached the intended target market.

(d)   Electronic coupons have even greater advantages, including lower cost per redemption, greater targeting ability, improved data-gathering capabilities, and greater experimentation capabilities.

(5)   Coupons also have drawbacks.

b)   With a *cents-off offer,* buyers pay a certain amount less than the regular price shown on the label or package.

(1)   This method is used to provide a strong incentive to try the product, stimulate product sales, yield short-lived sales increases, and promote products in off-seasons.

(2)   If used on an ongoing basis, cents-off offers can reduce the price for customers who would buy at the regular price and may cheapen the products image.

2.   **Refunds and Rebates**

a)   With *money refunds,* consumers submit proof of purchase and are mailed a specific amount of money. These usually require multiple purchases to qualify for a refund.

b)   With *rebates,* the consumer is sent a specified amount of money for making a single product purchase.

c)   The main drawback is that many people perceive the redemption process as too complicated and that products associated with them are new, untested, or have not sold well, which may result in the offers actually degrading the products' image and desirability.

3.   **Frequent-User Incentives**

a)   Many firms develop incentive programs to reward customers who engage in repeat purchases.

        b)   Frequent-user incentives foster customer loyalty to a specific company or group of cooperating companies that provide extra incentives for patronage.

    4.   **Point-of-Purchase Materials and Demonstrations.**

        a)   *Point-of-purchase (P-O-P) materials* include such items as outside signs, window displays, counter pieces, display racks, and self-service cartons. These items are used to attract attention, inform customers, and encourage retailers to carry particular products.

        b)   *Demonstrations* are a sales promotion method manufacturers use on a temporary basis to encourage trial use and purchase of the product or to show how the product actually works.

    5.   **Free Samples and Premiums**

        a)   *Free samples* are given out to stimulate trial of a product, increase sales volume in the early stages of the product's life cycle, or obtain desirable distribution.

           (1)   Sampling is the most expensive sales promotion method.

           (2)   Distribution of free samples through websites is growing.

        b)   *Premiums* are items offered free or at a minimum cost as a bonus for purchasing a product.

    6.   **Consumer Games, Contests, and Sweepstakes**

        a)   In *consumer contests and games,* individuals compete for prizes based on their analytical or creative skills.

        b)   The entrants in a *consumer sweepstakes* submit their names for inclusion in a drawing for prizes. Sweepstakes are used to stimulate lagging sales.

C.   Trade Sales Promotion Methods

Trade sales promotion methods attempt to persuade wholesalers and retailers to carry a producer's product and market them more aggressively.

    1.   **Trade Allowances**

        a)   A *buying allowance* is a temporary price reduction offered to resellers for purchasing specified quantities of a product.

           (1)   Such offers are used to provide an incentive to handle a new product, achieve a temporary price reduction, or stimulate the purchase of an item in larger than normal quantities.

           (2)   Drawbacks of buying allowances are that resellers may buy "forward," or buy large amounts the keep them supplied for many months, and competitors may match or beat the offers, lowering everyone's profits.

        b)   A *buy-back allowance* is a sum of money that a producer gives to a reseller for each unit the reseller buys after an initial promotional deal is over. This method is a secondary incentive in which the total amount of money resellers can receive is proportional to their purchases during the initial promotional effort.

        c)   A *scan-back allowance* is a manufacturer's reward to retailers based on the number of pieces moved through their scanners during a specific time period.

        d)   A *merchandise allowance* is a manufacturer's agreement to pay resellers certain amounts of money for providing special promotional efforts such as advertising or displays.

    2.   **Cooperative Advertising and Dealer Listings**

        a)   *Cooperative advertising* is an arrangement in which a manufacturer agrees to pay a certain amount of a retailer's media costs for advertising the manufacturer's products. The amount usually allowed is based on the quantities purchased.

        b)   *Dealer listings* are advertisements promoting a product and identifying the names of participating retailers that sell the product.

3. **Free Merchandise and Gifts**
   a) Free merchandise sometimes is offered to resellers that purchase a stated quantity of products. Free merchandise sometimes is used as payment for allowances provided through other sales promotion methods.
   b) A *dealer loader* is a gift given to a retailer that purchases a specified quantity of merchandise.

4. **Premium (Push) Money**
   Premium, or *push*, *money* is additional compensation to salespeople offered by the manufacturer as an incentive to push a line of goods.

5. **Sales Contests**
   A *sales contest* is used to motivate distributors, retailers, and sales personnel through the recognition of outstanding achievements.

NOTES FOR CLASS EXERCISES, DEBATE ISSUE, AND CHAPTER QUIZ

On the following pages, you will find two class exercises, a debate issue, and a chapter quiz. These are formatted in large-size type so that you can use them as class handouts or for making transparencies. Below are the authors' comments on the class exercises, the debate topic for this chapter, and the answers to the chapter quiz.

Comments on Class Exercise 1

The objective for this class exercise is for students to understand and apply the steps used in personal selling.

Prospecting—developing a list of customers. After developing a list, evaluate each prospect on the basis of his/her ability, willingness, and authority to buy the product. Only such prospects (dates, teachers, parents) with potential are pursued further. Although prospecting helps salespeople be more efficient, they should be careful not to prejudge customers before getting adequate information (e.g., a poorly dressed customer may have the ability and desire to buy).

Preapproach—find and analyze information about each prospect's specific product needs, current use of brands, feelings about available brands, and personal characteristics.

Approach—the manner in which a salesperson contacts a potential customer. The first contact is generally to assess buyers' needs and objectives. The prospect's first impression is usually a lasting one with long-run consequences. You might ask, "Why are these two stages so important?" One reason is that a customer-based salesperson will take the time to find out what the customer needs (satisfying those needs occurs in the presentation application of the marketing concept). The second is the importance of the first impression. In most interviews, the company representative makes his/her mind up about the individual in the first few minutes (some say 30 seconds). Whether it is making a sale or getting a date or a job, how one first appears has a significant impact.

Making the presentation—the salesperson must attract and hold the prospect's attention to stimulate interest and stir up a desire for the product (AIDA). Product demonstrations, listening to comments, and observing responses are important.

Overcoming objections—seeking out a prospect's objections in order to address them. One of the best (though risky) ways is to anticipate and counter objections before the prospect has an opportunity to raise them. Otherwise, deal with objections when they occur or at the end of the presentation.

Closing—asking the prospect to buy the product. Methods include "trial close" by asking questions that assume that the prospect will buy the product. A salesperson should try to close at several points during the presentation because the prospect may be ready to buy. Although these steps generally follow this order, they are often intertwined. After students have discussed how they use these steps (with examples), you might ask, "Why is closing so important?" If given a chance to sell, most people can present and overcome objections but are hesitant to close because they are afraid of rejection. If they did a good job of preparing and listening, they should assume that the customer is ready to buy or that objections are only excuses to be overcome.

Follow-up—contacting the customer to learn what problems or questions have arisen. Follow-up may also be used to determine future needs. With the growing importance of relationship marketing, the follow-up is becoming as important as the other steps, if not more so. You might ask, "Why do some of you (or your parents) continue to buy cars from the same dealership?"

Comments on Class Exercise 2

This exercise is relatively straightforward. Almost every student will have had some contact with one or several of these salespeople. However, students usually do not think about the types of selling these people do. Have your students classify each salesperson and then justify their answers. The most likely answers:

1. Missionary salesperson

2. Order getter, new-business sales

3. Inside order taker

4. Order getter, new-business sales

5. Order getter, new-business sales

6. Order getter, new-business sales

7. Trade salesperson

8. Order getter/field order taker

9. Order getter, new-business sales

10. Field order taker

DEBATE ISSUE

Do coupons make consumers more "brand loyal"?

CHAPTER QUIZ

Answers to Chapter Quiz 1.c; 2. e; 3. e; 4. c.

Class Exercise 1

EXPLAIN HOW YOU CAN USE THE SEVEN STEPS OF PERSONAL SELLING IN EVERYDAY ACTIVITIES SUCH AS DATING, ASKING PARENTS FOR MONEY, NEGOTIATING A HIGHER GRADE ON A TERM PROJECT, GETTING A JOB, OR ASKING FOR A PAY RAISE.

PROSPECTING: The salesperson must develop a list of customers.

PREAPPROACH: The salesperson must find and analyze information about each prospect's specific product needs, current use of brands, feelings about available brands, and personal characteristics.

APPROACH: The salesperson adopts a certain manner in contacting a potential customer. The first contact is generally to assess the buyer's needs and objectives. The prospect's first impression is usually a lasting one.

MAKING THE PRESENTATION: The salesperson must attract and hold the prospect's attention to stimulate interest. Product demonstrations, listening to comments, and observing responses are important.

OVERCOMING OBJECTIONS: One of the best ways is to anticipate and counter objections before the prospect has an opportunity to raise them. Otherwise, deal with objections when they occur.

CLOSING: The salesperson asks the prospect to buy the product. Attempt a "trial close" by asking questions that assume the prospect will buy the product. A salesperson should try to close at several points during the presentation.

FOLLOW-UP: The salesperson contacts the customer to learn what problems or questions have arisen. This may also be used to determine future needs.

Class Exercise 2

SALESPEOPLE ARE TYPICALLY CLASSIFIED AS ORDER GETTERS, ORDER TAKERS, AND SUPPORT PERSONNEL. HOW WOULD YOU CLASSIFY THE FOLLOWING SALESPEOPLE?

1. Pharmaceutical salesperson selling to doctors

2. Car salesperson

3. Retail store salesperson

4. Telemarketer soliciting donations for a charity

5. Real estate agent

6. Heavy equipment salesperson

7. Agent for a snack food distributor who only stocks shelves

8. Door-to-door cosmetics sales-person

9. Insurance salesperson

10. Agent for a snack food distributor who fills a retailer's orders

Debate Issue

DO COUPONS MAKE CONSUMERS MORE "BRAND LOYAL"?

YES

- Coupons are a good way to reward present users of a product.
- Present users will use a particular brand more often.
- Coupons encourage consumers to purchase in larger quantities.
- The larger the price reduction, the greater the number of consumers taking advantage of the promotion.

NO

- Many manufacturers offer coupons; consumers will switch brands by buying those products for which they can find coupons.
- Consumers have been trained not to buy without incentives.
- Truly brand-loyal consumers will buy a particular brand with or without a price incentive.
- Temporary price reductions increase sales today at the expense of future sales.

Chapter Quiz

1. The step or stage of the personal selling process in which the salesperson attempts to make a favorable impression, gather information about the customer's needs and objectives, and build a rapport with the prospective customer is called

   a. prospecting.
   b. preapproach.
   c. approach.
   d. making the presentation.
   e. overcoming objections.

2. Marsha Hemlock, a trained engineer, is a salesperson for a chemical manufacturer. She provides current customers with advice about a product's characteristics and applications. She is a(n)

   a. missionary salesperson.
   b. trade salesperson.
   c. field order taker.
   d. inside order taker.
   e. technical salesperson.

3. Which of the sales force compensation methods is easy to administer, yields more predictable selling expenses, and provides sales managers with a large degree of control over salespeople?

   a. Straight commission
   b. Salary plus bonus
   c. Salary and commission
   d. Straight commission and combination
   e. Straight salary

4. A temporary price reduction to resellers for purchasing specified quantities of a product is

   a. premium money.
   b. a merchandise allowance.
   c. a buying allowance.
   d. a buy-back allowance.
   e. a money refund.

ANSWERS TO DISCUSSION AND REVIEW QUESTIONS

1. **What is personal selling? How does personal selling differ from other types of promotional activities?**

   Personal selling is a process of informing customers and persuading them to purchase products through personal communication in an exchange situation. It differs from other types of promotional activities in that it is the most precise method. It allows a marketer to adjust the message to satisfy a customer's information needs and to zero in on the most promising prospects instead of directing promotional efforts at a group of people.

2. **What are the primary purposes of personal selling?**

   The primary purposes of personal selling can be grouped into three general categories: a) to find individuals and/or organizations that are prospective buyers; b) to transform prospects into buyers; and c) to maintain customer satisfaction.

3. **Identify the elements of the personal selling process. Must a salesperson include all these elements when selling a product to a customer? Why or why not?**

   The personal selling process consists of several elements or steps. The first step is prospecting and evaluating. This involves developing a list of potential customers. After developing a list of acceptable prospects, but before contacting a prospect, comes the preapproach step, in which the salesperson finds and analyzes information regarding the prospect's specific product needs, current brands being used, feelings about available brands, and personal characteristics. In the third step, the approach, the salesperson contacts the prospect. During the fourth step, making the presentation, the salesperson must attract and hold the prospect's attention, stimulate interest, and develop desire for the product. The fifth step is overcoming the prospect's objections. The sixth step is closing, in which the salesperson asks the prospect to buy the product or products. The seventh and final element in the selling process is the follow-up. In this stage, the salesperson contacts the buyer to see whether the order was delivered on time and was installed properly if installation was required, to see if the buyer has any problems or questions regarding the product, and to determine the buyer's future product needs. For personal selling to be effective, all seven elements should be included in the selling process.

4. **How does a salesperson find and evaluate prospects? Do you consider any of these methods to be ethically questionable? Explain.**

   A salesperson seeks the names of prospects from several sources, including company sales records, consumers' information requests from advertisements, other customers, newspaper announcements (marriages, births, deaths), public records, telephone directories, and trade association directories. After developing the prospect list, the salesperson evaluates each prospect to determine whether the prospect is able, willing, and authorized to buy the product. After this evaluation, some prospects may be deleted while others are deemed acceptable and are ranked according to their desirability or potential. The question about ethics will elicit varied responses. Some students may perceive the use of sources such as public records, directories, and announcements as unethical. Others may feel that this practice is ethical but that the sources of information are less satisfactory than are sales records and consumers' information requests.

5. **Are order getters more aggressive or creative than order takers? Why or why not?**

   Order getters generally are considered more creative and aggressive than order takers because they are responsible for eliciting sales. These sales may be either new sales or sales to current customers. In either case, the salesperson is responsible for recognizing the potential buyer's needs and then providing the prospect with the necessary information. Order takers, on the other hand, engage in more repetitive tasks that involve perpetuating a long-lasting, satisfying relationship with customers.

6. **Identify several characteristics of effective sales objectives.**

   Sales objectives should be stated in precise, measurable terms and be specific regarding the time period and the geographic areas involved. They are usually established for the total sales force and for each salesperson. These objectives inform salespeople about their accomplishments during a specified time period, provide the sales force with direction and purpose, and provide performance standards for the evaluation and control of sales personnel.

7. **How should a sales manager establish criteria for selecting sales personnel? What do you think are the general characteristics of a good salesperson?**

   A sales manager must develop a set of characteristics that makes people especially well suited for the sales tasks in the particular company. To facilitate this function, the sales manager should 1) prepare a job description that enumerates the specific tasks to be performed by the salesperson and 2) analyze the characteristics of the firm's successful salespeople as well as the ineffective ones. Based on these two areas, the sales manager should be able to develop a set of specific requirements.

   Although for years marketers have attempted to create a comprehensive set of traits that characterize effective salespeople in general, any list of traits should reflect the needs of the company and the characteristics of its products and target market currently.

8. **What major issues or questions should management consider when developing a training program for the sales force?**

   The major issues or questions to consider when developing a sales force training program are the following:

   a. Who should be trained? Training programs can be directed toward the total sales force or toward a segment of it.

   b. When and where should the training occur? Sales training may be performed in the field, at educational institutions, in company facilities, or in several of these locations.

   c. What should be taught? The content of sales training programs can deal with general company background, plans, policies, and procedures; product information regarding features, uses, advantages, problem areas, parts, service, warranties, packaging, sales terms, promotion, and distribution; and selling methods.

   d. How should the information be taught? The specific methods and materials used in a particular sales training program depend on the type and number of trainees, program content, complexity, length of the training program, size of the training budget, location, number of teachers, and the teachers' preferences.

9. **Explain the major advantages and disadvantages of the three basic methods of compensating salespeople. In general, which method would you prefer? Why?**

The straight salary method of compensation provides salespeople with maximum security, gives the sales manager a large degree of control over salespeople, is easy to administer, and yields predictable selling expenses. Its disadvantages include the lack of incentive, the necessity of close supervision of salespeople's activities, and the level of selling expenses during periods of sales decline. Advantages of the straight commission method of salesperson compensation include providing the maximum amount of incentive, the ability to encourage salespeople to sell certain items by increasing the commission rate on these items, and relating selling expenses directly to sales resources. Disadvantages of this method are the lack of control over the sales force, the possibility of inadequate service to smaller accounts, and the decreased predictability of selling expenses. The combination method of compensation provides a certain level of financial security to salespeople, provides some degree of incentive, and yields selling expenses that fluctuate with sales revenue. Unpredictable selling expenses and difficulties in administration are disadvantages of this method. The students' preferences for compensation methods will reflect individual attitudes toward each method and personal level of risk-taking. Because each method has advantages and disadvantages, arguments can be made for any of them.

10. **What major factors should be taken into account when designing the size and shape of a sales territory?**

In designing the size and shape of sales territories, the sales manager considers several major factors. First, the territories must be constructed so that sales potentials can be measured. Second, the shape of territories should facilitate salespeople's activities to provide the best possible coverage of the firm's customers. Third, the territories should be designed to minimize selling costs. Fourth, the density and distribution of customers influence the sales manager's decisions regarding territory size and shape. Fifth, topographical features may affect decisions about the size and shape of territories.

11. **How does a sales manager, who cannot be with each salesperson in the field on a daily basis, control the performance of sales personnel?**

Because a sales manager ordinarily does not travel with each salesperson, information is needed to control the performance of the sales force. This information can be supplied through salespeople's call reports, customer feedback, and invoices. Call reports and work schedules submitted by sales personnel provide the sales manager with detailed information about current interactions with clients and indicate salespeople's plans during a specific future period.

12. **What is sales promotion? Why is it used?**

Sales promotion is an activity and/or material that acts as a direct inducement, offering added value or incentive for the product to resellers, salespeople, or consumers. Sales promotion activities and materials are used to:

a. Identify and attract new customers

b. Introduce a new product

c. Increase the total number of users for an established brand

d. Encourage greater usage among users

e. Educate consumers regarding product improvements

f. Bring more customers into retail stores

g. Stabilize a fluctuating sales pattern

h. Increase reseller inventories

i. Combat or offset competitors' marketing efforts

j. Obtain more and better shelf space and displays

13. **For each of the following, identify and describe three techniques, and give several examples: (a) consumer sales promotion methods and (b) trade sales promotion methods.**

Students' choices for techniques and examples may vary, but they will include any of the following:

a. Consumer sales promotion methods

(1) Coupons are used to build volume for a brand or product when price is an important purchasing determinant. They may be for a specific brand or for a kind of product, and they may be distributed through retailers, as advertisements, or as throwaways. Clippings from newspapers or flyers distributed at shopping malls are examples of retail coupons.

(2) Cents-off offers entice the buyer to receive a certain amount off the regular price as shown on the label or package. These provide a strong incentive to try a product and are used to promote sales of lagging products. Such offers may appear on many convenience items, including toothpaste, detergent, and coffee.

(3) Money refunds and rebates offer a specified amount of money to be sent to the consumer by mail after proof of purchase is established. These are used to promote trial of a product and to require multiple purchases to obtain proof of purchase. Such items as shampoos and razors have offered money refunds and rebates. Rebates are increasingly offered on automobiles.

(4) Frequent-user incentives reward customers who engage in repeat purchases. Examples of frequent-user incentives include frequent-flyer tickets and free food received after a number of food purchases are made at a specific restaurant.

(5) Point-of-purchase displays include outside signs, window displays, counter pieces, display racks, and self-service cartons. These are used to encourage retailers to carry a firm's product.

(6) Demonstrations are supplied by the manufacturer and are good for attracting attention. They frequently show how a product works and sometimes involve the preparation and distribution of the product. An example is the demonstration of a product in an appliance store.

(7) Free samples may be distributed by mail, by door-to-door delivery, in stores, or on packages. This type of promotion is used to stimulate trial of a new or improved product, increase volume quickly in early life cycle stages, and aid in obtaining retail distribution of the product. Recent examples of free samples include soaps and toothpastes.

(8) Premiums are items offered free or at minimal cost as a bonus for purchasing a particular product. They can be placed on or in the package or can be distributed in stores or through the mail. They are used to attract competitors' customers, introduce different sizes of current products, add variety to promotional efforts, and stimulate loyalty. Small toys offered in cereal boxes are examples of premiums.

(9) Consumer contests involve competition for prizes and usually are based on analytical or creative skills. An example of this technique would be to give $100 for writing a jingle for a new shampoo.

(10) Consumer sweepstakes require entrants to submit their names for inclusion in a drawing. Sweepstakes are often sponsored by cigarette manufacturers.

b. Trade sales promotion methods

(1) Buying allowances are temporary price reductions to resellers for the purchase of specified quantities. They are used as an incentive to handle new products, achieve temporary price reductions, or stimulate the purchase of an item in quantities larger than usual.

(2) A buy-back allowance is a secondary sales promotion method given to resellers after an initial promotional deal is over to stimulate repurchase. Such allowances are used to encourage cooperation in the initial transaction and in restocking.

(3) A scan-back allowance is a manufacturer's reward to a retailer based on the pieces that move through the scanner during a given time period. They directly link trade spending to product movement.

(4) Using merchandise allowances, the manufacturer agrees to compensate resellers with certain amounts of money for providing special reseller promotional efforts such as advertisements or displays. This technique is used for high-volume, high-profit, easily handled products.

(5) Cooperative advertising involves an agreement by a manufacturer to pay a certain amount of the retailer's media costs; the amount is based on the quantity of products purchased by the retailer.

(6) A dealer listing is dual-purpose advertising that announces a product or consumer promotion and contains names of participating retailers that carry the product.

(7) Free merchandise may be offered to a reseller that purchases a stated quantity of the same or different products.

(8) Dealer loaders are premiums granted to a retailer for the purchase of specified quantities of merchandise.

(9) Premium, or push, money is used as an incentive to push a line of goods by providing additional compensation to salespeople.

(10) Sales contests use recognition of sales achievement to motivate resellers, retailers, and sales forces.

14. **What types of sales promotion methods have you observed recently? Comment on their effectiveness.**

This is an open-ended question that will enable students to recall some sales promotion methods they have observed. Methods used to promote retail establishments, new products, or established products will probably be more familiar than those used to promote to resellers.

COMMENTS ON THE CASES

[▣◧◧] *CASE 20.1 SELLING BICYCLES AND MORE AT WHEELWORKS*

The purpose of this case is to examine the role of personal selling at Wheelworks, a three-store retailer in suburban Boston. As consumers, students are very familiar with retail sales but may not be aware of the challenges that stores face in managing personal selling as part of the marketing mix. You can encourage discussion by asking whether students would prefer to buy from recognized experts who are intent on educating their retail customers rather than from professional salespeople who have no hands-on experience with the products they're selling.

Question 1 asks students to identify which of the three types of sales force compensation methods Wheelworks is using and whether Wheelworks should change to another method. According to the case, Wheelworks uses a straight salary compensation plan supplemented by seasonal bonuses. Given the retailer's concern about having employees match products to each customer's needs, it should not change to another compensation method.

Question 2 asks how Wheelworks motivates its sales personnel. Financial compensation is one method. In addition, managers create enjoyable working conditions and a climate in which salespeople can satisfy personal needs such as learning more about bicycles and bicycling. They also occasionally appeal to their salespeople's competitive instincts and interest in excelling.

Question 3 asks students to classify Kurt Begemann in terms of the type of salesperson he represents. Begemann is an order getter because his role is to increase sales by selling bicycles and accessories to new and existing customers. To do this, he uses creative selling, which entails recognizing potential buyers' needs and providing the information they need to make an informed purchasing decision.

Finally, students are asked to evaluate Kurt Begemann's statement that "it's better to be seen as a teacher than to be seen as a salesperson." This represents Begemann's interest in helping customers become more knowledgeable about different products and about the sport of bicycling so they can make informed buying decisions. He seems to believe that customers who view him as a salesperson might mistrust him or think he is ready to push products that may not fit their needs.

Video Information

Company:	Wheelworks
Location:	Tape 2/DVD 2, Segment 20
Length:	9:53

Video Overview: Wheelworks operates three bicycle stores, rings up $10.5 million in annual sales, and employs 45 full-time employees. Now that cycling is enjoying higher popularity, Wheelworks must meet higher demand for mountain bikes and many other types of specialized bicycles. The company prefers to pay salespeople a salary plus fringe benefits and seasonal bonuses rather than pay commissions. Management believes that this allows its employees to take the time they need to assess customer needs and suggest appropriate products, rather than trying to earn higher commissions by selling more expensive bicycles.

MULTIPLE-CHOICE QUESTIONS ABOUT THE VIDEO

1. Wheelworks co-founder Clint Paige sums up his role in managing the sales force as a combination of
   a. friend and mentor.
   b. trust tempered by hands-on management.
   c. hard sell and educational support.
   d. teaching and disciplining.
   e. coaching and cheerleading.
2. When Wheelworks determines the size of its sales force, it takes into consideration
   a. variations in sales.
   b. demand for various products in its line.
   c. availability of new products.
   d. the number of calls needed to close a sale.
   e. the size and volume of competing stores.
3. Managers at Wheelworks don't use sales contests and commissions because
   a. they want to motivate higher individual performance.
   b. profit margins are too slim to support such compensation methods.
   c. they want to give salespeople the freedom to do what's right for each customer.
   d. salespeople feel preyed upon when pressured to work for these incentives.
   e. they rely on enthusiastic leadership to motivate salespeople to sell.
4. Because most of the salespeople ride their bicycles to work at Wheelworks, one fringe benefit they particularly appreciate is
   a. flexible scheduling that allows them to continue training for races and other competitive events.
   b. a good health insurance plan.
   c. the opportunity to attend multiple training clinics every month.
   d. reimbursement for outside sales expenses.
   e. bonuses for recruiting new salespeople.

ANSWERS TO MULTIPLE-CHOICE QUESTIONS ABOUT THE VIDEO

1. e

2. a

3. c

4. b

CASE 20.2 IBM REORGANIZES TO IMPROVE SELLING SOLUTIONS

In this case, students can see how important sales management is in a large, well-known organization that today markets primarily to organizational markets.

In the first question, students are asked why it is important for a company like IBM to focus on selling solutions rather than just products. According to the case, this approach permits the company and its sales staff to be proactive in helping customers solve problems with IBM products. For some customers, this may result in custom solutions. With this approach, IBM's salespeople become team members with customers' representatives to find the best product to address specific tasks.

Question 2 asks how changes in the IBM sales force assisted in focusing on customer needs. Reorganizing the company and revising policies helped free up sales staff from paperwork and meetings in order to spend more time working with customers. The new structure also helped sales reps gain more individual and team coaching to help them be more productive and boost their performance.

Question 3 asks students to explain why they think that IBM's restructured sales force was only required to have a single weekly sales meeting to get some coaching help. Responses may vary, but most students will suggest that this arrangement frees up salespeople from mundane tasks in order to have more time to interact with customers to better understand their needs and hopefully sell more products to them. The new arrangement also suggests that the new CEO, who came from sales himself, has confidence in the skills, talent, and abilities of IBM's salespeople and that he believes that weekly coaching is sufficient to monitor and control their activities as long as they are meeting their performance objectives.

CHAPTER 21

Pricing Concepts

TEACHING RESOURCES QUICK REFERENCE GUIDE

Resource	Location
Purpose and Perspective	IRM, p. 397
Guide for Using Color Transparencies	IRM, p. 398
Lecture Outline	IRM, p. 398
Notes for Class Exercises, Debate Issue, and Chapter Quiz	IRM, p. 404
Class Exercise 1	IRM, p. 406
Class Exercise 2	IRM, p. 407
Debate Issue	IRM, p. 408
Chapter Quiz	IRM, p. 409
Answers to Discussion and Review Questions	IRM, p. 410
Comments on the Cases	IRM, p. 412
Case 21.1	IRM, p. 412
Video	Tape 2/DVD 2, Segment 21
Video Information	IRM, p. 413
Multiple-Choice Questions About the Video	IRM, p. 413
Case 21.2	IRM, p. 414
Transparency Acetates	Transparency package
Examination Questions: Essay	TB, p. 609
Examination Questions: Multiple-Choice	TB, p. 609
Examination Questions: True-False	TB, p. 633
Author-Selected Multiple-Choice Test Items	TB, p. 672
HMClassPrep Presentation Resources	CD-ROM
PowerPoint Slides	Instructor's website

Note: Additional resources are updated periodically and may be found on the accompanying student and instructor websites at http://www.prideferrell.com/.

PURPOSE AND PERSPECTIVE

This chapter introduces basic pricing concepts and issues. First, we explore the nature and importance of pricing. Next, we discuss price and nonprice competition. Then, we discuss demand curves, demand fluctuations, and assessment of price elasticity of demand. Next, we explore marginal analysis and breakeven analysis. We also identify and examine various factors that affect marketers' pricing decisions. We group these major factors into eight categories: organizational and marketing objectives, pricing objectives, costs, other marketing mix variables, channel members' expectations, customers' interpretation and response, competition, and legal and regulatory issues. Finally, we examine several issues associated with the pricing of products sold in business markets focusing on price discounting, geographic pricing, and transfer pricing.

GUIDE FOR USING COLOR TRANSPARENCIES

There are two groups of color transparencies. The transparencies identified by a double number are the same as the figures and tables in the text. The transparencies labeled with a number and a letter are illustrations that do not appear in the text, but they can be used as additional examples of concepts discussed.

Part 8 Opener	Pricing Decisions
Figure 21.1	Demand Curve Illustrating the Price-Quantity Relationship and Increase in Demand
Figure 21.2	Demand Curve Illustrating the Relationship Between Price and Quantity for Prestige Products
Figure 21.3	Elasticity of Demand
Figure 21.4	Typical Marginal Cost and Average Total Cost Relationship
Figure 21.5	Typical Marginal Revenue and Average Revenue Relationship
Figure 21.6	Combining the Marginal Cost and Marginal Revenue Concepts for Optimal Profit
Figure 21.7	Determining the Breakeven Point
Figure 21.8	Factors That Affect Pricing Decisions
Table 21.3	Discounts Used for Business Markets
Figure 21A	Chapter 21 Outline
Figure 21B	The Importance of Price-Related Factors on Consumer Brand Choice for Grocery, Health, and Beauty Products
Figure 21C	Class Exercise: Price vs. Nonprice Competition
Figure 21D	Key Definitions: Price Elasticity of Demand, Breakeven Point
Figure 21E	Orbitz Allows People to Save Up to 75% on Hotels
Figure 21F	Ariba Assists Business Customers in Getting the Best Prices from Suppliers

LECTURE OUTLINE

(Transparency Part 8 Opener)

(Transparency Figure 21A: Chapter Outline)

I. **The Nature of Price**
   A. *Price* is the value exchanged for products in a marketing exchange.
      1. Although the price is very evident in most exchange situations, price does not always take the form of money paid. *Barter*, which is the trading of products, is the oldest form of exchange.
      2. Buyers' interest in price relates to their expectations about the usefulness or a product or the satisfaction they may derive from it.
      3. Buyers must decide whether the utility gained in an exchange is worth the buying power sacrificed.
   B. **Terms Used to Describe Price**
      Different terms can be used to describe price for different forms of exchange, e.g., tuition, fines, fees, rent, commissions, tips, dues, deposits, tips, interest, taxes.

   C. **The Importance of Price to Marketers**
      1. Price plays an important role in marketing because it is often the only marketing mix variable that can be changed quickly to respond to changes in demand or to competitors' actions.

(Transparency Figure 21B)

2.   Because price times quantity sold equals revenue, price is important in determining profits.

3.   Because price has a psychological impact on customers, marketers can use it symbolically. A high price can emphasize the quality of a product; a low price can emphasize a bargain.

II.   **Price and Nonprice Competition**

A product offering can compete on a price or nonprice basis.

A.   **Price Competition**

With *price competition*, a marketer emphasizes price as an issue and matches or beats the prices of competitors.

(Building Customer Relationships: Inside the PC Price War)

(Transparency Figure 21E)

1.   A major advantage of price competition is its inherent flexibility. Prices can be adjusted to compensate for an increase in the firm's operating costs, to offset changes in demand, or to counteract a competitor's pricing strategy.

2.   A disadvantage of price competition is that competitors usually benefit from the flexibility to adjust prices by responding quickly and aggressively to price changes.

B.   **Nonprice Competition**

Nonprice competition occurs when a seller decides not to focus on price and instead emphasizes distinctive product features, service, quality, promotion, packaging, or other factors to distinguish its product from competing brands.

(Transparency Figure 21C)

1.   A major advantage of nonprice competition is that a firm can build customer loyalty toward its brand.

2.   If customers prefer a brand because of nonprice factors, it is more difficult for competitors to lure these customers to their brands.

3.   For nonprice competition to work, a company must be able to distinguish its brand through unique product features, higher product quality, promotion, packaging, or excellent customer service; further, buyers must view these product features as important, and the features must be difficult for competitors to imitate.

4.   Even when competing on a nonprice basis, marketers must remain aware of competitors' prices and be prepared to price its brand near or slightly above that of competing brands.

III.   **Analysis of Demand**

Determining the demand for a product is the responsibility of marketing managers, who are aided in this task by marketing researchers and forecasters. Marketing research and forecasting techniques yield estimates of sales potential, or the quantity of a product that could be sold during a specific period.

A.   **The Demand Curve**

1.   For most products, the quantity demanded goes up as the price goes down and goes down as the price goes up. Thus, there is an inverse relationship between price and demand.

2.   The classic *demand curve* is a graph of the quantity of products expected to be sold at various prices, if other factors remain constant.

(Transparency Figure 21.1)

a) The demand curve illustrates that as price falls, the quantity demanded usually rises.

b) Demand depends on other factors in the marketing mix, including product quality, promotion, and distribution.

3. There are many types of demand, and not all conform to the classic demand curve. Prestige products, for example, seem to sell better at high prices than at low ones.

(Transparency Figure 21.2)

B. **Demand Fluctuations**

1. Changes in buyers' needs, variations in the effectiveness of other marketing mix variables, the presence of substitutes, and dynamic environmental factors can influence demand.

2. In some cases, demand fluctuations are predictable, but they are unpredictable in others, creating problems for some companies unless they can learn to anticipate fluctuations and develop new products and prices to respond accordingly.

(Building Customer Relationships: The Ups and Downs of Beef Prices)

C. **Assessing Price Elasticity of Demand**

After identifying the target market's evaluation of price and examining demand to learn whether price is related inversely or directly to quantity, the next step in pricing is to assess price elasticity of demand.

1. *Price elasticity of demand* provides a measure of the sensitivity of demand to changes in prices. (A formal definition is the percentage change in quantity demanded relative to a given percentage change in price.)

(Transparency Figure 21D)

2. If marketers can determine the price elasticity of demand, setting a price is much easier.

(Transparency Figure 21.3)

a) If demand is elastic, a change in price causes an opposite change in total revenue; an increase in price will decrease total revenue, and a decrease in price will increase total revenue.

b) An inelastic demand results in a parallel change in total revenue, and a decrease in price will decrease total revenue.

IV. **Demand, Cost, and Profit Relationships**

A. **Marginal Analysis**

Marginal analysis examines what happens to a firm's costs and revenues when production (or sales volume) is changed by one unit.

1. To determine the costs of production, it is necessary to distinguish among several types of cost.

a) *Fixed costs* do not vary with changes in the number of units produced or sold. *Average fixed cost* is the fixed cost per unit produced, and is calculated by dividing fixed costs by the number of units produced.

b) *Variable costs* do vary directly with changes in the number of units produced or sold. They are usually constant per unit. *Average variable cost* is the variable cost per unit produced.

c) *Total cost* is the sum of average fixed costs and average variable costs times the quantity produced. The *average total cost* is the sum of the average fixed cost and the average variable cost.

d)   *Marginal cost (MC)* is the extra cost a firm incurs when it produces one more unit of a product.

(Transparency Figure 21.4)

e)   Average fixed cost declines as output increases. Average total cost decreases as long as marginal cost is less than the average total cost, and it increases when marginal cost rises above average total cost.

2.   *Marginal revenue (MR)* is the change in total revenue that occurs when an additional unit of a product is sold. The point of maximum profit is the point at which marginal costs are equal to marginal revenues.

(Transparency Figure 21.5)

(Transparency Figure 21.6)

3.   This discussion of marginal analysis may give the false impression that pricing can be highly precise. If revenue (demand) and cost (supply) remained constant, prices could be set for maximum profits. In practice, however, cost and revenue change frequently.

4.   Marginal analysis is to be used only as a model; the marketer can benefit by understanding the relationship between marginal cost and marginal revenue.

B.   **Breakeven Analysis**

1.   The *breakeven point* is the point at which costs of producing the product equal revenue from selling the product.

(Transparency Figure 21D)

2.   To use breakeven analysis effectively, a marketer should determine the breakeven point for each of several alternative prices. This comparative analysis will identify the highly undesirable price alternatives that should be avoided.

(Transparency Figure 21.7)

3.   Breakeven analysis is simple and straightforward, but it assumes that the quantity demanded is basically fixed (inelastic) and that the major task in setting prices is to recover costs.

V.   **Factors Affecting Pricing Decisions**

Pricing decisions can be complex because of the number of factors to be considered.

(Transparency Figure 21.8)

A.   **Organizational and Marketing Objectives**

1.   Marketers should set prices consistent with the organization's goals and mission.

2.   Pricing decisions should also be compatible with the organization's marketing objectives.

B.   **Types of Pricing Objectives**

The types of pricing objectives (discussed in Chapter 22) a marketer uses will have considerable bearing on the determination of prices.

C.   **Costs**

Costs must be an issue when establishing price.

1.   A firm may sell products below cost to match competition, to generate cash flow, or even to increase market share.

2.   In the long run, an organization cannot endure by selling its products below cost.

3.   To maintain market share and revenue, many firms have concentrated on reducing costs.

D. **Other Marketing Mix Variables**
Because of the interrelation of the marketing mix variables, pricing decisions can influence decisions and activities associated with product, distribution, and promotion variables.

1. For many products, buyers associate better product quality with a high price and lower product quality with a low price.
2. Premium-priced products often are marketed through selective or exclusive distribution, whereas lower-priced products in the same product category may be sold through intensive distribution.
3. Bargain prices often are included in advertisements; premium prices are less likely to appear in advertising messages and are more likely to require personal selling efforts.

E. **Channel Member Expectations**
When making pricing decisions, a producer must consider what distribution channel members (e.g., wholesalers and retailers) expect.

1. Channel members often expect producers to give discounts for large orders and prompt payment.
2. At times, resellers expect producers to provide several support services such as sales training, service training, and cooperative advertising, etc.
3. These discounts and support activities have associated costs, and the producer must consider these costs when determining prices.

F. **Customers' Interpretation and Response**
1. Customers' interpretation of and response to a price are to some degree determined by their assessment of what they receive compared with what they give up to make the purchase.
   a) An *internal reference price* with regard to a particular item is a price in the buyer's mind and has been developed through experience with the product.
   b) An *external reference price* is used when an individual does not have much experience with a given item. Comparison prices are provided by others such as retailers or manufacturers.
2. Buyers' perceptions can be characterized according to their degree of value consciousness, price consciousness, and prestige sensitivity.
   a) *Value-conscious* customers are concerned about both price and quality aspects of a product.
   b) *Price-conscious* customers strive to pay low prices.
   c) *Prestige-sensitive* customers focus on purchasing products that signify prominence and status.

G. **Competition**
A marketer must remain aware of the prices competitors charge in order to adjust its price in relation to competitors' prices.

1. When adjusting prices, a marketer must assess how competitors will respond.
2. When an organization is a monopoly and unregulated, the firm can set prices at whatever the market will bear. If the monopoly is regulated, price flexibility is reduced and the regulatory body lets the organization set prices that generate a reasonable but not excessive rate of return.
3. In an oligopolistic market, when one firm cuts price to gain a competitive edge, other firms are likely to cut prices, too, which means that very little is gained through price cuts.
4. In a perfectly competitive market, there is no flexibility in setting prices. The price of the firm's product is determined by the going market price.

H. **Legal and Regulatory Issues**
    Government action, at times, strongly influences marketers' pricing decisions.

    1. The federal government may invoke price controls to curb inflation.
    2. Many regulations and laws affect pricing decisions and activities.
        a) The Sherman Antitrust Act prohibits conspiracies to control prices. Marketers not only must refrain from fixing prices but also must develop independent pricing policies and set prices in ways that do not even suggest collusion.
        b) Both the Federal Trade Commission Act and the Wheeler-Lea Act prohibit deceptive pricing. Marketers must guard against deceiving customers.
    3. If price differentials tend to lessen or injure competition, they are ruled discriminatory and prohibited. The Robinson-Patman and Clayton Acts limit the use of *price discrimination*, the practice of providing price differentials that injure competition by giving one or more buyers a competitive advantage.

VI. **Pricing for Business Markets**
    Business markets consist of individuals and organizations that purchase products for the purpose of resale, using them in their own operations, or for producing other products. Establishing prices for this category of buyers is sometimes different from setting prices for consumers.

(Transparency Table 21.3)

(Transparency Figure 21F)

A. **Price Discounting**
    Producers commonly provide intermediaries with discounts, or reductions, from list prices.

    1. **Trade Discounts**
        Trade, or *functional, discounts* are reductions off the list price that a producer gives an intermediary for performing certain functions, such as selling, transporting, storing, final processing, and providing credit services.

    2. **Quantity Discounts**
        Quantity discounts are deductions from list price for purchasing in large quantities.

        a) *Cumulative discounts* are quantity discounts that are aggregated over a stated period.
        b) *Noncumulative discounts* are one-time reductions in prices based on the number of units purchased, the dollar value of the order, or the product mix purchased.
    3. **Cash Discounts**
        A *cash discount* is a price reduction given to a buyer for paying promptly or in cash.

    4. **Seasonal Discounts**
        A *seasonal discount* is a price reduction to buyers buying goods or services out of season.

    5. **Allowances**
        An *allowance*, such as a trade-in allowance or a promotional allowance, is a price reduction made to increase sales.

B. **Geographic Pricing**
    Geographic pricing involves reductions for transportation costs or other costs associated with the physical distance between the buyer and the seller.

    1. Prices may be quoted F.O.B. factory or F.O.B. destination, depending on who pays for the shipping costs.

a) An *F.O.B. factory* price is the price of the merchandise at the factory, before the shipment; thus the buyer pays shipping costs.

b) An *F.O.B. destination* price indicates that the producer is absorbing the shipping costs.

2. *Uniform geographic pricing* involves charging all customers the same price, regardless of location; this strategy may be used to avoid problems involved with charging each customer a different price.

3. In *zone pricing*, regional prices are set to take advantage of a uniform pricing system; prices are adjusted for major geographic zones as transportation costs increase.

4. *Base-point pricing* is a geographic pricing policy that includes the price at the factory plus freight charges from the base point nearest the buyer. The legality of this approach has been questioned, so the method has been abandoned.

5. With *freight absorption pricing*, a seller absorbs all or part of the actual freight costs for a particular customer or geographic area.

C. **Transfer Pricing**

Transfer pricing occurs when one unit in a company sells a product to another unit.

1. The price is determined by one of four methods: actual full cost, standard full cost, cost plus investment, or market-based cost.
   a) Actual full cost—calculated by dividing all fixed and variable expenses for a period into the number of units produced
   b) Standard full cost— calculated on what it would cost to produce the goods at full plant capacity
   c) Cost plus investment—calculated as full cost, plus the cost of portion of the selling unit's assets used for internal needs
   d) Market-based cost—calculated at the market price less a small discount to reflect the lack of sales effort and other expenses

2. The choice of method depends on the company's management strategy and the nature of the units' interaction.

3. An organization must ensure that transfer pricing is fair to all units that must purchase its goods or services.

NOTES FOR CLASS EXERCISES, DEBATE ISSUE, AND CHAPTER QUIZ

On the following pages, you will find two class exercises, a debate issue, and a chapter quiz. These are formatted in large-size type so that you can use them as class handouts or for making transparencies. Below are the authors' comments on the class exercises, the debate topic for this chapter, and the answers to the chapter quiz.

Comments on Class Exercise 1

This exercise examines price and nonprice competition, pricing objectives, and factors affecting price decisions.

Question 1. Through price cuts, IBM is trying to keep within striking distance of competitors' prices. There are some reports that IBM may introduce its own low-end PCs, perhaps under a different name. At any rate, students should recognize that in the past IBM has not competed on a price basis, focusing instead on distinctive product features, service (for retailers and customers), product quality, and heavy promotion. This generally leads to increased customer loyalty. Unfortunately for IBM, its products have been successfully imitated by competing manufacturers. This has forced IBM to compete on price since PCs have become fairly standardized products. IBM is not as flexible with its price changes as their competitors, and the resulting price war has created difficulties for IBM.

Question 2. Lower-priced products typically require more intense distribution. Ads may need to shift to emphasize price and value. Given the lower margins and more intense distribution, expect less personal selling and more self-service at the retail level.

Question 3. Though not purely oligopolistic, this industry is characterized by matching price cuts.

Comments on Class Exercise 2

Demand-Related Pricing Calculations

A.   Price Elasticity of Demand

Some students may be confused about elasticity of demand. Conceptually, if you raise your prices TR increases, then demand is inelastic. If you raise prices and TR declines, then demand is elastic.

Calculations:

Old price:	$8	Old quantity: 1,000/month
Total revenue:	$8,000	
New price:	$10	New quantity: 900/month
Total revenue:	$9,000	

Price elasticity of demand: $\dfrac{-10\% \text{ (change in qty)}}{+25\% \text{ (change in price)}} = -.4$

Demand is relatively inelastic (if e < 1.0) for this. If you change the new quantity to 700, then e = 1.2.

B.   Breakeven Analysis

Assume that you are selling pizzas for $8. Your fixed costs (rent, salaries, utilities) are $4,800/month. The food cost and other variable costs are 50 percent of the selling price. What is your breakeven point?

Breakeven Point = $4,800/8 – 4 = 1200 units or $9,600.

DEBATE ISSUE

Is price competition more effective than nonprice competition?

CHAPTER QUIZ

Answers to Chapter Quiz 1. d; 2. b; 3. a; 4. e.

Class Exercise 1

PRICES OF PERSONAL COMPUTERS CONTINUE TO DROP BECAUSE OF (A) INCREASED COMPETITION AMONG PC MAKERS, WHICH OPERATE ON NARROW MARGINS; (B) INCREASED CONSUMER KNOWLEDGE AND SOPHISTICATION, WHICH ENCOURAGES MORE CONSUMERS TO USE MAIL-ORDER DISCOUNT PC MARKETERS; AND (C) DECREASED DIFFERENCES IN QUALITY AND PERFORMANCE AMONG COMPETITORS. ALTHOUGH IBM PRICES ARE STILL ABOVE SOME OF THE COMPETITORS, ALL PC MANUFACTURERS HAVE BEEN CUTTING PRICES TO MAINTAIN MARKET SHARE.

1. Do you think IBM should compete through price or nonprice competition? What are the advantages and disadvantages of each approach?

2. If IBM were to continue competing on price, how might other marketing mix variables be affected?

3. If IBM drops its prices in the near future, what can you expect other PC makers to do? What kind of competitive situation is the PC industry (oligopoly, monopolistic, pure competition)? What does this imply for price setting?

Class Exercise 2

DEMAND-RELATED PRICING CALCULATIONS

A. Price Elasticity of Demand

Calculate the price elasticity of demand for a restaurant's pizza under the following conditions:

Old price: $8   Old quantity: 1,000/month
Total Revenue: $8,000

New price: $10   New quantity: 900/month
Total revenue: $9,000

If the new quantity sold per month were 700 (instead of 900), what would be the price elasticity of demand?

B. Breakeven Analysis

Assume you are selling pizzas at $8. Your fixed costs (rent, salaries, utilities) are $4800/month. The food costs and other variable costs are 50 percent of the selling price. What is your break-even point?

Debate Issue

IS PRICE COMPETITION MORE EFFECTIVE THAN NONPRICE COMPETITION?

YES	NO
• Many customers today are very price conscious.	• Price competition breeds price-sensitive customers with little brand loyalty.
• With so many homogeneous products on the market, price is a major means of distinguishing a product from competitive brands.	• Product features and quality are more distinguishing in setting a product apart from its competitors.
• When price competition is used, firms attempt to keep their costs low.	• Nonprice variables should be desirable to buyers as well as difficult to imitate.

Chapter Quiz

1. Price is a key element in the marketing mix because it relates directly to
   a. the size of the sales force.
   b. the speed of an exchange.
   c. quality controls.
   d. the generation of total revenue.
   e. brand image.

2. If the product price is $100, average variable cost $40 per unit, and the total fixed costs are $120,000, what is the breakeven point?
   a. 500 units
   b. 2,000 units
   c. 1,200 units
   d. 300 units
   e. 3,000 units

3. Generally, customers are *most likely* to rely on the price-quality association when
   a. they cannot judge the quality of the product for themselves.
   b. the product is a well-known brand.
   c. customers can judge the product's quality for themselves.
   d. the product is purchased through the use of the Internet.
   e. products are being purchased from well-established retailers that are familiar to customers.

4. Suppose that the watchband department of Timex sells completed watchbands to the finished watch department. The finished watch department is charged the price it would have to pay an outside watchband manufacturer less a discount to reflect low sales and transportation costs. This method of pricing is called _____ pricing.
   a. zone
   b. actual full cost
   c. standard full cost
   d. cost plus investment
   e. market-based cost

ANSWERS TO DISCUSSION AND REVIEW QUESTIONS

1. **Why are pricing decisions important to an organization?**

   Pricing decisions are important to a firm because they relate directly to the generation of total revenue. This ties price into the other elements of business, such as accounting and finance. A change or error in price will send repercussions throughout the company.

   Pricing is also important because it is indirectly related to quantities sold. As the most flexible aspect of the marketing mix, price plays another important role by affecting production and inventory levels. Price even more indirectly influences total costs through its effect on quantities sold.

2. **Compare and contrast price and nonprice competition. Describe the conditions under which each form works best.**

   Both price and nonprice competition are competitive means by which firms attempt to gain market share and profit. They can be used separately or in unison, depending on the situation.

   With price competition, a marketer emphasizes price as an issue and attempts to match or beat the prices of competitors that also are emphasizing low price. A seller that competes on the basis of price has a great deal of flexibility in adjusting to meet competitive pressures. A disadvantage is that the competition can do the same thing.

   Nonprice competition occurs when a seller elects to emphasize distinctive product features, service, quality, promotion, packaging, or other factors to distinguish its product from competing brands. One advantage to this competitive strategy is that a firm can build customer loyalty to its brand. A disadvantage is that it is fairly rigid and inflexible once applied.

3. **Why do most demand curves demonstrate an inverse relationship between price and quantity?**

   Most demand curves have an inverse relationship between price and quantity because the quantity demanded for most products goes up as the price goes down. This means that the demand for most products is elastic—a change in price causes an opposite change in total revenue.

4. **List the characteristics of products that have inelastic demand, and give several examples of such products.**

   Products typically have inelastic demand when people have strong needs and when there are very few substitutes for these products. Examples include many energy products and medicines.

5. **Explain why optimum profits should occur when marginal cost equals marginal revenue.**

   By producing and selling so that marginal costs equal marginal revenue, a firm should obtain optimum profits because, at this point, the production of one additional unit would result in greater costs than the revenue received from an additional unit. This approach to pricing blends the increasing costs and the inefficiencies of production with the price elasticity of the demand schedule.

   This economic concept gives the false impression that pricing can be highly precise. If revenue and cost remain constant, prices can be set for maximum profits. In practice, revenue and cost are constantly changing. In addition, this approach offers little help in pricing new products.

6. **Chambers Company has just gathered estimates for conducting a breakeven analysis for a new product. Variable costs are $7 a unit. The additional plant will cost $48,000. The new product will be charged $18,000 a year for its share of general overhead. Advertising expenditures will be $80,000, and $55,000 will be spent on distribution. If the product sells for $12, what is the breakeven point in units? What is the breakeven point in dollar sales volume?**

The breakeven point equals 40,200 units, or $482,400 in sales.

7. **In what ways do other marketing mix variables affect pricing decisions?**

The product marketing mix variable has an important influence on pricing decisions because price is the value placed on what is exchanged. If the product is perceived as being of very high quality, a high price will correspond with this image.

The place where a product is sold is also vital. It is important to keep the image of the outlet and the product within a similar range.

Promotion is also an important variable to coordinate with price. Price has a psychological impact on customers, as do different advertising media and approaches. It is important to try to coordinate this factor with price.

8. **What types of expectations may channel members have about producers' prices? How might these expectations affect pricing decisions?**

A channel member expects to earn a profit. The amount of time required to handle the product is also a major consideration. Many resellers expect producers to provide several support activities, such as sales training, service training, repair advisory service, cooperative advertising, sales promotions, and perhaps a program for returning unsold merchandise. These activities affect pricing decisions because failure to price the product so that the producer can provide some of these activities may cause resellers to view the product less favorably.

9. **How do legal and regulatory forces influence pricing decisions?**

The state and federal governments can affect pricing decisions through price controls, freezing prices at certain levels, determining price increase rates, and so on. The Sherman, Clayton, and Robinson-Patman Acts have a strong impact on pricing decisions by setting guidelines for pricing activities and making certain activities illegal. Also, the Federal Trade Commission and the Wheeler-Lea Act prohibit deceptive pricing. Marketers must guard against deceiving customers.

10. **Compare and contrast a trade discount and a quantity discount.**

A trade discount is a reduction off the list price that a producer gives an intermediary for performing certain functions: selling, transporting, storing, and so forth. It is usually given as a percentage or series of percentages off the list price. A quantity discount is a reduction for buying in quantity.

The two discounts are similar insofar as they are incentives to an intermediary from a producer. They help reward the intermediary for actions the producer feels are important. They are different because quantity discounts relate only to the size of the order placed, whereas trade discounts deal with compensation based on functions performed.

11. **What is the reason for using the term *F.O.B.*?**

This term relates to geographic pricing and stands for "free on board." It is used to indicate whether the price includes shipping charges. *F.O.B. factory* means that the price of the goods does not include shipping charges; *F.O.B. destination* means the producer pays for shipping.

12. **What are the major methods used for transfer pricing?**

Transfer price—incurred when one unit in an organization sells to another—is determined by one of four methods: actual full cost, standard full cost, cost plus investment, and market-based cost. Actual full cost is calculated by dividing all fixed and variable expenses for a period into the number of units produced. Standard full cost is calculated on what it would cost to produce the goods at full plant capacity. Cost plus investment is calculated as full cost, plus the cost of a portion of a selling unit's assets used for internal needs. Market-based cost is calculated at the market price less a small discount to reflect the lack of sales effort and other expenses.

COMMENTS ON THE CASES

CASE 21.1 JETBLUE'S FLIGHT PLAN FOR PROFITABILITY

The primary objectives of this case are to illustrate 1) that low prices are not necessarily associated with lower-quality offerings, and 2) how a start-up airline is profiting with a low-cost, low-price strategy despite fierce price competition within the industry. JetBlue is based at a seemingly less-desirable airport, flies new rather than old jets, and offers leather seats and other amenities—yet its fares undercut the competition and its jets take off with more passengers, as well. Students who are not familiar with JetBlue may want to research the airline prior to analyzing this case.

Question 1 asks why JetBlue is successful even though price competition has caused many competitors to fail. One reason is that JetBlue's total costs are generally lower than those of the competition, in part because its jets are more fuel-efficient and less costly to maintain. Another reason is the JFK Airport location which allows better on-time performance and therefore keeps travelers satisfied. A third reason is that passengers enjoy the comfort of more legroom, leather seats, and free satellite television.

Question 2 asks students to discuss how JetBlue uses pricing to deal with demand fluctuations. Knowing that demand for a particular flight is high, the airline can charge higher prices. On the other hand, when demand for a particular flight is low, JetBlue sets lower prices to encourage travelers to choose that flight. Thus, JetBlue uses pricing to more effectively manage both high and low demand and better balance its passenger loads.

In Question 3, students are asked to assess the elasticity of demand for business air travel and for vacation air travel. A businessperson's demand for air travel is likely to be relatively inelastic, meaning that a big change in price will probably not have a major effect on demand. This is because business travel is not always discretionary, so price changes have less of an effect than on leisure travel, where demand is likely to be more elastic.

In Question 4, students are asked to discuss other factors that are important to JetBlue's management when making pricing decisions. This is a good opportunity to discuss the role of legal and regulatory issues (such as deregulation), other marketing mix variables, customers' interpretation and response, and competition. In particular, competition is a key factor because major airlines have the choice of undercutting JetBlue's prices and adding more flights to JetBlue's destinations. Both these actions would siphon JetBlue's passengers and hurt its revenues and profits, possibly sending the airline into the kind of downward spiral that has hurt start-ups in the past. Ask students how JetBlue's management might prepare for such contingencies.

Video Information

Company:	JetBlue
Location:	Tape 2/DVD 2, Segment 21
Length:	6:10

Video Overview: JetBlue was founded by David Neeleman, who spent five years crafting a detailed plan for a new low-cost, low-price airline. Neeleman raised a great deal of money to ensure that his start-up would have the financial stability to withstand recession periods and unexpected challenges such as the fall-off in air travel following terrorist attacks. He keeps JetBlue's costs low by buying new, highly fuel-efficient Airbus 320 jets, which are covered by the manufacturer's warranty and therefore do not require costly repairs and servicing. At the same time, he configured the jets to carry less than the maximum passenger load and installed more expensive leather seats and personal video screens to make flying more comfortable for passengers. Finally, JetBlue's highest ticket prices are usually below the lowest prices of competitors, which only adds to the airline's attractiveness.

MULTIPLE-CHOICE QUESTIONS ABOUT THE VIDEO

1. Buying new Airbus jets is more expensive than buying used jets, says David Neeleman, but he chose this approach because the new planes
   a. come equipped with leather seats at no extra cost.
   b. stimulate traffic because of their stylish image.
   c. cost less to operate because they burn less fuel.
   d. can be delivered on a regular schedule geared to JetBlue's expansion plans.
   e. are better suited to long-distance flights to international destinations.

2. When JetBlue sees higher demand for certain flights, it
   a. lowers prices to accommodate more passengers.
   b. raises prices to equalize the load compared with its other flights.
   c. cuts costs to improve profitability.
   d. applies strict requirements such as a three-week advance ticket purchase.
   e. adds flight attendants to ensure the same high level of customer service.

3. Another efficiency that helps JetBlue keep costs down is
   a. buying fuel at volume prices to store in case of supply problems.
   b. hiring newly-trained crews rather than experienced pilots and navigators.
   c. getting its jets back into the air soon after they land.
   d. matching competitors' fares.
   e. maintaining a minimum cash cushion to allow for emergencies.

4. Neeleman says JetBlue has the "best coach product in the industry" because
   a. its ticket prices undercut the ticket prices of competitors.
   b. the airline is demand-driven.
   c. its new Airbus jets make a more polished appearance than older planes.
   d. its planes come fully equipped and carry a five-year warranty.
   e. it has comfortable leather seats, more legroom, and friendly service.

ANSWERS TO MULTIPLE-CHOICE QUESTIONS ABOUT THE VIDEO

1. c

2. b

3. c

4. e

CASE 21.2 PRICELINE.COM LETS ONLINE CUSTOMERS SET PRICES

The purpose of this case is to provide students with the opportunity to assess pricing that is initiated by customers rather than by sellers. To open the discussion, ask students to describe other circumstances or situations in which customers are allowed to initiate the price that they wish to pay for a product.

The first question asks students to consider the effect that name-your-price sites seem to be having on demand for travel services and to explain the implications for price elasticity of demand. In general, name-your-price sites appear to be reducing prices and therefore increasing demand for travel services, especially air travel. Remind students that airline-initiated price wars are also intended to stimulate demand, usually with great success. That is also the idea behind Hotwire, the airline-backed name-your-price site mentioned in the case. Priceline's growth and the sales volume of other name-your-price sites indicates that demand is fairly elastic for travel services.

Question 2 asks if the pricing facilitated by Priceline.com results in price or non-price competition. The pricing facilitated by Priceline.com results in price competition. Various organizations such as airlines can decide whether or not to accept customers' bids. When a buyer uses Priceline.com, the major consideration is price. The product is being purchased as a commodity.

The third question asks what are the advantages and disadvantages of Priceline.com's pricing approach for buyers and sellers. For buyers, a major advantage is purchasing a product at a price below marketers' published prices. The disadvantage for buyers is that they must be flexible on the type of product that they will obtain through this approach. The advantage for marketers is that they are able to sell excess products in product categories that are highly perishable, such as services. A clear disadvantage for marketers is that the amount of revenue received from these discounted sales is reduced. Another disadvantage for marketers is that they lose the opportunity to deal directly with customers which, in turn, means that they have a reduced opportunity to build long-term customer relationships.

CHAPTER 22

Setting Prices

TEACHING RESOURCES QUICK REFERENCE GUIDE

Resource	Location
Purpose and Perspective	IRM, p. 415
Guide for Using Color Transparencies	IRM, p. 416
Lecture Outline	IRM, p. 416
Notes for Class Exercises, Debate Issue, and Chapter Quiz	IRM, p. 421
Class Exercise 1	IRM, p. 423
Class Exercise 2	IRM, p. 424
Debate Issue	IRM, p. 425
Chapter Quiz	IRM, p. 426
Answers to Discussion and Review Questions	IRM, p. 427
Comments on the Cases	IRM, p. 428
Case 22.1	IRM, p. 428
Video	Tape 2/DVD 2, Segment 22
Video Information	IRM, p. 429
Multiple-Choice Questions About the Video	IRM, p. 429
Case 22.2	IRM, p. 430
Transparency Acetates	Transparency package
Examination Questions: Essay	TB, p. 641
Examination Questions: Multiple-Choice	TB, p. 642
Examination Questions: True-False	TB, p. 662
Author-Selected Multiple-Choice Test Items	TB, p. 672
HMClassPrep Presentation Resources	CD-ROM
PowerPoint Slides	Instructor's website

Note: Additional resources are updated periodically and may be found on the accompanying student and instructor websites at http://www.prideferrell.com/.

PURPOSE AND PERSPECTIVE

In this chapter, we describe the six-stage price-setting process: 1) Developing pricing objectives; 2) Assessing the target market's evaluation of price and its ability to purchase; 3) Evaluating competitors' prices; 4) Selecting a basis for pricing; 5) Selecting a pricing strategy; and 6) Determining a specific price. We point out that marketers do not always take all of these steps. Rather, these steps should be viewed as guidelines that provide a logical sequence for establishing prices. In some situations, some stages should be included in the price setting process, while in others, some of these stages may not be required.

GUIDE FOR USING COLOR TRANSPARENCIES

There are two groups of color transparencies. The transparencies identified by a double number are the same as the figures and tables in the text. The transparencies labeled with a number and a letter are illustrations that do not appear in the text, but they can be used as additional examples of concepts discussed.

LECTURE OUTLINE

(Transparency Figure 22A: Chapter Outline)

The price-setting process involves six steps that provide a logical way to analyze the effectiveness of price in the marketing mix and the contributions of price to the organization's objectives.

(Transparency Figure 22.1)

I. **Development of Pricing Objectives**
    A. *Pricing objectives* are goals that describe what a firm wants to achieve through pricing efforts.

(Transparency Table 22.1)

        1. Developing pricing objectives is an important task because pricing objectives form the basis for decisions about other stages of pricing.
        2. Pricing objectives must be consistent with organizational and marketing objectives.
        3. Pricing objectives influence decisions in many functional areas, including finance, accounting, and production.
        4. A marketer can use both short- and long-term pricing objectives and can employ one or more multiple pricing objectives.
    B. **Survival**
        A fundamental pricing objective is survival.

        1. Most organizations will tolerate short-run losses, internal upheaval, and many other difficulties if these conditions are necessary for survival.
        2. Because price is such a flexible and convenient variable to adjust, it sometimes is used to increase sales volume to levels that match the organization's expenses.
    C. **Profit**
        1. The objective of profit maximization is rarely operational because it is difficult to measure its achievement.
        2. Specific profit objectives may be stated in terms of actual dollar amounts or in terms of a percentage of sales revenues.

    D.   **Return on Investment**
         1.   Pricing to attain a specified return on the company's investment is also a profit-related pricing objective.
         2.   Unfortunately, most pricing objectives based on return on investment are achieved by trial and error because not all cost and revenue data needed to project the return on investment are available when prices are set.
    E.   **Market Share**
         1.   Many firms establish pricing objectives to maintain or increase market share—a product's sales in relation to total industry sales—in part because they recognize that high relative market share often translates into higher profits.
         2.   Maintaining or increasing market share need not depend on growth or industry sales.
             a)   An organization's sales volume may increase while its market share within the industry decreases, if the overall market is growing.
             b)   However, an organization's market share can also increase even when sales for the industry are decreasing.
    F.   **Cash Flow**
    Some organizations set prices to recover cash as quickly as possible.

         1.   Financial managers are interested in quickly recovering capital that has been spent to develop products.
         2.   A possible disadvantage of this pricing objective is high prices, which might enable competitors with lower prices to gain a large share of the market.
    G.   **Status Quo**
    In some instances, an organization may be in a favorable position and therefore set an objective of status quo.

         1.   Status quo objectives can focus on several dimensions, including maintaining a certain market share, meeting competitors' prices, achieving price stability, or maintaining a favorable public image.
         2.   A status quo pricing objective can reduce a firm's risks by helping stabilize demand for its products.
         3.   The use of status quo pricing objectives sometimes minimizes price as a competitive tool, which can lead to a climate of nonprice competition within an industry.
    H.   **Product Quality**
    An objective of product quality leadership in the market normally results in charging a high price to cover the high product quality and, perhaps, the high cost of research and development.

II.   **Assessment of the Target Market's Evaluation of Price**
    A.   The importance of price depends on the type of product, the type of target market, and the purchase situation.
    B.   Value combines a product's price and quality attributes, which are used by customers to differentiate competing brands.

                          (Transparency Figure 22F)

    C.   Understanding the importance of a product to customers, as well as their expectations of quality and value, helps a marketer correctly assess the target market's evaluation of price.
III.   **Evaluation of Competitors' Prices**
    A.   Learning competitors' prices may be a regular function of marketing research.
    B.   Marketers in an industry in which price competition prevails need competitive price information to ensure that their organization's prices are the same, or lower than, their competitors' prices.

C.   An organization may set its prices slightly above the competition to give its products an exclusive image, or it may use price as a competitive tool and price its products below those of competitors.

IV.   **Selection of a Basis for Pricing**

The three major dimensions on which prices can be based are cost, demand, and competition. The selection of the basis to be used is affected by the type of product, the market structure of the industry, the brand's market share position relative to competing brands, and customer characteristics.

(Transparency Figure 22B)

A.   **Cost-Based Pricing**

When using *cost-based pricing*, a firm determines price by adding a dollar amount or a percentage to the cost of the product. Cost-based pricing is straightforward and easy to implement.

(Transparency Figure 22C)

1.   **Cost-Plus Pricing.** *Cost-plus pricing* is a method whereby the seller's costs are determined, and then a specified dollar amount or percentage of the cost is added to the seller's cost to establish the price.
   a)   This is appropriate when production costs are unpredictable or a long production period is needed.
   b)   One pitfall for the buyer is that the seller may increase costs to establish a larger profit base.
   c)   For industries in which cost-plus pricing is common and sellers have similar costs, price competition may not be especially intense.

2.   **Markup Pricing.** Through *markup pricing*, a product's price is derived by adding a predetermined percentage of the cost, called markup, to the cost of the product.
   a)   Markups can be stated as a percentage of the cost or as a percentage of the selling price.
   b)   Markups usually reflect expectations about operating costs, risks, and stock turnovers.
   c)   To the extent that retailers use similar markups for the same product category, price competition is reduced.

B.   **Demand-Based Pricing**

With *demand-based pricing*, customers pay a higher price when demand for the product is strong and a lower price when demand is weak.

(Transparency Figure 22C)

1.   To use demand-based pricing, a marketer must be able to estimate the amounts of a product consumers will demand at different prices; effectiveness depends on the marketer's ability to estimate demand accurately.

(Building Customer Relationships: Wireless Companies Ring up Competitive Pricing Strategies)

2.   Compared with cost-based pricing, demand-based pricing places a firm in a better position to reach higher profit levels assuming that buyers value the product at levels sufficiently above the product's cost.

C.   **Competition-Based Pricing**

Competition-based pricing is pricing that is influenced primarily by competitors' prices.

(Transparency Figure 22C)

1. The importance of this method increases when competing products are relatively homogeneous and the organization is serving markets in which price is a key purchase consideration.
2. This pricing technique can help attain the pricing objective of increasing sales or market share.

V. **Selection of a Pricing Strategy**

A pricing strategy is an approach or a course of action designed to achieve pricing and marketing objectives. Generally, pricing strategies help marketers solve the practical problems of establishing prices.

(Transparency Table 22.2)

A. **Differential Pricing**
1. An important issue in pricing is whether to use a single price or multiple prices for the same product.
    a) Using a single price has several benefits, including that it is easily understood and it reduces the chance of an adversarial relationship developing between marketer and customer.
    b) A single price also creates some challenges: if a single price is too high, some customers may not be able to afford the product; if it is too low, the firm loses revenue from customers who would have paid more had the price been higher.
2. *Differential pricing* is charging different prices to different buyers for the same quality and quantity of product. The market must consist of multiple segments with different price sensitivities, and the pricing method should be used in a way that avoids confusing or antagonizing customers.
    a) **Negotiated Pricing.** *Negotiated pricing* is establishing a final price through bargaining between the seller and customer. Even when there is a predetermined stated price or a price list, negotiated pricing may still be used to establish the final sales price.
    b) **Secondary-Market Pricing.** *Secondary-market pricing* involves setting a price for use in another market that is different from the price charged in the primary target market. Often, the price charged in the secondary market is a lower price. However, when the costs of serving a secondary market are higher than normal, secondary-market customers may have to pay a higher price.
    c) **Periodic Discounting.** *Periodic discounting* is the temporary reduction of prices on a patterned or systematic basis. Seasonal changes, model year changes, or holidays may be reasons for the systematic price reductions.
    d) **Random Discounting.** *Random discounting* is temporarily reducing a regular-priced product using an unsystematic time schedule. This is done to attract new customers and reduce predictability of price reductions by current customers.
    e) Retailers often employ "tensile pricing," which is using a broad statement about a price reduction as opposed to detailing specific price amounts.

B. **New-Product Pricing**

Setting the base price for a new product is a necessary part of formulating a marketing strategy and is one of the most fundamental decisions in the marketing mix.

1. **Price Skimming.** *Price skimming* is charging the highest possible price that buyers who most desire the product will pay. Price skimming
    a) Can generate much-needed initial cash flows to help offset sizable development costs.
    b) Protects the marketer from problems that arise when the price is set too low to cover costs.

c) Can help keep demand consistent with a firm's production capabilities.
2. **Penetration Pricing.** *Penetration pricing* is setting the price lower than competing brands to penetrate a market and gain a significant market share quickly. Penetration pricing
   a) Puts the marketer in a less flexible position because it is more difficult to raise a penetration price than to lower or discount a skimming price.
   b) Can be especially beneficial when a marketer suspects that competitors could enter the market easily.

C. **Product-Line Pricing**
Product-line pricing is establishing and adjusting prices of multiple products within a product line. A marketer's goal here is to maximize profits for an entire product line rather than to focus on the profitability of an individual product.

1. **Captive Pricing.** *Captive pricing* involves pricing the basic product in a product line low, but pricing related items at a higher level.
2. **Premium Pricing.** *Premium pricing* entails pricing higher quality or more versatile products higher than other models in the product line.
3. **Bait Pricing.** *Bait pricing* occurs when a marketer prices an item in the product line low with the intention of selling a higher-priced item in the line. The lower-priced item will attract customers into the store, while the marketer hopes that once in the store, the customer will purchase the higher-priced one.
4. **Price Lining.** With *price lining*, the organization sets a limited number of prices for selected groups or lines of merchandise. The basic assumption in price lining is that demand is inelastic for various groups or sets of products.

(Transparency Figure 22.2)

D. **Psychological Pricing**
Psychological pricing attempts to influence a customer's perception of price to make the product's price more attractive.

1. **Reference Pricing.** *Reference pricing* is pricing a product at a moderate level and positioning it next to a more expensive model or brand. Reference pricing is based on the "isolation effect," which says that an alternative is less attractive when it appears by itself compared to when it appears with other alternatives.
2. **Bundle Pricing.** *Bundle pricing* is the packaging together of two or more usually complementary products to be sold for a single price. The customer often values the convenience of purchasing a combination of bundled products.
3. **Multiple-Unit Pricing.** *Multiple-unit pricing* occurs when two or more of the same product are packaged together and sold for a single price. A company uses multiple-unit pricing to attract new customers to its brand and, in some instances, to increase consumption of its brands.
4. **Everyday Low Prices (EDLP).** *Everyday low prices* requires setting a low price for products on a consistent basis.
   a) Generally, prices are set far enough below competitors' prices to make customers confident they are receiving a fair price.

(Building Customer Relationships: Family Dollar Stores' Strategy Is Driven by Everyday Low Prices)

   b) A major problem with ELDP is that customers have mixed responses to it: customers seem to have been "trained" to seek and to expect deeply discounted prices.

(Transparency Figure 22D)

5.   **Odd-Even Pricing.** *Odd-even pricing* influences the buyers' perceptions of the price or the product by ending the price with certain numbers. Odd-even pricing assumes that more of a product will be sold at $99.95 than at $100 because customers will think the product is a bargain.

   a)   There are no substantial research findings to support the notion that odd prices produce greater sales.

   b)   An even price supposedly will influence a customer to view the product as being a high-quality, premium brand.

6.   **Customary Pricing.** With *customary pricing*, certain goods are priced primarily on the basis of tradition.

7.   **Prestige Pricing.** With *prestige pricing*, prices are set artificially high to convey a prestige or quality image.

(Transparency Figure 22E)

E.   **Professional Pricing**

Professional pricing includes fees set by people who have great skill or experience in a particular field or activity.

1.   Professionals who provide certain services or products believe their fees should not relate directly to the time and effort spent in specific cases; they charge a standard fee regardless of the problems involved in performing the job.

2.   The concept of professional pricing carries with it the idea that professionals have an ethical responsibility not to overcharge customers.

F.   **Promotional Pricing**

Price, as an ingredient in the marketing mix, is often coordinated with promotion. The two variables sometimes are so interrelated that the pricing policy is promotion-oriented.

1.   **Price Leaders.** Products priced below the usual markup, near cost, or below cost are *price leaders*; management hopes that sales of regularly priced merchandise will more than offset the reduced revenues from the price leaders.

2.   **Special-Event Pricing.** With *special-event pricing*, advertised sales or price cutting is used to increase sales volume and is linked to a holiday, season, or special event.

3.   **Comparison Discounting.** *Comparison discounting* is the pricing of a product at a specific level and comparing it to a higher price. The Federal Trade Commission has established guidelines for comparison pricing in order to dissuade deceptive pricing practices.

VI.   **Determination of a Specific Price**

A.   A pricing strategy will yield a certain price; however, this price may need refinement to make it consistent with pricing practices in a particular market or industry.

B.   Pricing remains a flexible and convenient way to adjust the marketing mix.

NOTES FOR CLASS EXERCISES, DEBATE ISSUE, AND CHAPTER QUIZ

On the following pages, you will find two class exercises, a debate issue, and a chapter quiz. These are formatted in large-size type so that you can use them as class handouts or for making transparencies. Below are the authors' comments on the class exercises, the debate topic for this chapter, and the answers to the chapter quiz.

Comments on Class Exercise 1

The purpose of this exercise is to demonstrate how different situations affect one's range of price acceptability. Although subjective, possible answers are as follows:

1. A 12-oz. soft drink at a

vending machine	$0.60
movie theater	$2.00
supermarket	$0.25

2. A steak dinner at a(n)

cafeteria-style restaurant	$8.00
elegant restaurant	$24.00
charity benefit dinner	$100.00

3. A flat-tire repair

on a lonely stretch of highway	$30.00
in a town where efficient public transportation is available	$15.00
when schools and stores are within walking distance	$10.00

4. A duplicate key

just to have an extra key around	$1.25
at night in a mall parking lot when your keys are locked in your trunk	$30.00
when your nonrefundable airline ticket is in your locked car, your flight leaves in 30 minutes, and your car keys are lost	$60.00

Comments on Class Exercise 2

The objective of this exercise is to help students become more familiar with different pricing strategies by analyzing how they are applied to specific products. Answers:

1. penetration

2. odd/even

3. professional

4. special-event

5. customary

6. price leaders

7. professional

DEBATE ISSUE

Is differential pricing ethical?

CHAPTER QUIZ

Answers to Chapter Quiz 1. e; 2. b; 3. a; 4. a.

Class Exercise 1

WHAT IS YOUR RANGE OF PRICE ACCEPTABILITY? EXPLAIN THE BREADTH IN YOUR RANGE OF PRICE ACCEPTABILITY.

1. How much would you pay for a 12-ounce soft drink at a
   - vending machine?
   - movie theater?
   - supermarket?

2. How much would you pay for a steak dinner at a(n)
   - cafeteria-style restaurant?
   - elegant restaurant?
   - charity benefit dinner?

3. How much would you pay to have a flat tire repaired
   - on a lonely stretch of highway?
   - in a town where efficient public transportation is available?
   - when schools and stores are within walking distance?

4. How much would you pay for a duplicate car key
   - just to have an extra key around?
   - at night in a mall parking lot when your keys are locked in your car?
   - when your nonrefundable airline ticket is in your locked car, your flight leaves in 30 minutes, and your car keys are lost?

Class Exercise 2

WHAT TYPE OF PRICING STRATEGY DOES EACH OF THE FOLLOWING DESCRIBE?

1. Hyundai prices its newest model lower than the price of competing brands.

2. A premium men's shirt has a suggested retail price of $50 instead of $49.95.

3. A doctor charges $65 for a routine office visit.

4. A restaurant lowers the price of its corned beef and cabbage plate during the week before St. Patrick's Day.

5. For years the price of a candy bar was 5 cents, and rarely did a manufacturer charge more.

6. A supermarket prices its eggs, bread, and milk below cost.

7. An attorney advertises a $199 fee for a divorce.

Debate Issue

IS DIFFERENTIAL PRICING ETHICAL?

YES

- Supply and demand dictate prices.

- The type of customer, distribution channel, and time of purchase allow for pricing differences.

- Customers are willing to pay different prices for the same product under different conditions.

NO

- There is no difference in a product just because it's purchased in bulk, at a certain time, or by a customer in a specific market segment.

- Marketer prejudice is difficult to control but does not justify its use.

- It simply is not fair for one person to pay more for a flight or hotel room than another person when both are receiving the same service at the same time.

Chapter Quiz

1. A market share pricing objective
   a. is not recommended when sales for the total industry are declining.
   b. is not especially useful when sales for the total industry are increasing.
   c. is not especially useful when sales for the total industry are flat.
   d. is useful primarily in an industry where total sales are increasing.
   e. can be used effectively whether total industry sales are rising or falling.

2. Companies that focus on particular product categories and rely on everyday low pricing to acquire a large market share though aggressive and competitive pricing strategies are often referred to as
   a. pioneers.
   b. category killers.
   c. comparison discounters.
   d. price leaders.
   e. category leaders.

3. Which of the following pricing approaches is used *most* often by retailers?
   a. Markup pricing
   b. Price discrimination
   c. Multiple-unit pricing
   d. Return on investment
   e. Price skimming

4. The pricing strategy that assumes that demand is relatively inelastic over certain price ranges is called
   a. price lining.
   b. odd-even pricing.
   c. price skimming.
   d. prestige pricing.
   e. customary pricing.

ANSWERS TO DISCUSSION AND REVIEW QUESTIONS

1. **Identify the six stages involved in the process of establishing prices.**

   Stage 1 is developing a pricing objective that dovetails with the organization's overall objectives. Typical pricing objectives include survival, profit, return on investment, market share, cash flow, and maintaining the status quo. Stage 2 is identifying the target market's evaluation of price. Stage 3, evaluating competitors' prices, is helpful in determining the role of price in the marketing strategy. Stage 4 is selecting a pricing strategy to serve as a guiding philosophy designed to influence and determine pricing decisions. Among the most common pricing strategies are differential pricing, new-product pricing, product-line pricing, psychological pricing, professional pricing, and promotional pricing. Stage 5 is choosing a method for calculating the price charged to customers. Three pricing methods are cost-based pricing (which includes cost-plus pricing and markup pricing), demand-based pricing, and competition-based pricing. Stage 6 is determining the final price.

2. **How does a return on investment pricing objective differ from an objective of increasing market share?**

   A return on investment pricing objective is a profit-related objective, and a market share objective is not. Market share pricing objectives will likely lead to higher profits but may result in reduced profits.

3. **Why must marketing objectives and pricing objectives be considered when making pricing decisions?**

   It is important that consumers consider the firm consistent. The marketing objectives are set in conjunction with the organizational objectives that dictate the firm's course of action. To tie pricing decisions into this framework helps facilitate the continuity of the firm and contribute to ease of coordination.

4. **Why should a marketer be aware of competitors' prices?**

   A marketer needs to be aware of competitors' prices to set its own price slightly above, equal to, or below those prices.

5. **What are the benefits of cost-based pricing?**

   Cost-based pricing is simple to calculate and easy to implement.

6. **Under what conditions is cost-plus pricing most appropriate?**

   Cost-plus pricing is most appropriate when actual production costs are difficult to estimate before the product is made.

7. **A retailer purchases a can of soup for 24 cents and sells it for 36 cents. Calculate the markup as percentage of cost and as percentage of selling price.**

   The markup is 50 percent of cost and 33.3 percent of selling price.

8. **What is differential pricing? In what ways can it be achieved?**

   Differential pricing is the charging of different prices to different buyers for the same quality and quantity of product. It can be achieved when the market consists of multiple segments that have different price sensitivities and thus respond differently to price differentials. Differential pricing can occur in several ways, including negotiated pricing, secondary-market discounting, periodic discounting, and random discounting.

9. **For what type of products would price skimming be most appropriate? For what type of products would penetration pricing be more effective?**

   Price skimming would be most appropriate for products that have associated research and developmental costs, for example, cameras, computers, calculators, and many technical products. Products introduced with penetration pricing usually have few differentiated advantages. Market penetration is more typical for lower-cost items such as food products and small household items.

10. **Describe bundle pricing and give three examples using different industries.**

    Bundle pricing is the packaging together of two or more usually complementary products to be sold for a single price. Bundle pricing is commonly found in a number of product categories, including banking, travel, computers, and automobiles with option packages.

11. **What are the advantages and disadvantages of using everyday low prices?**

    An advantage is that it reduces or eliminates the use of frequent short-term price reductions, thus allowing a company to benefit from reduced promotional costs. Another advantage is that of reduced losses from frequent markdowns. A company also experiences more stability in its sales.

    A disadvantage of this pricing strategy is the effect of mixed responses on the part of customers. Some people perceive value in a product when they see slashed prices. They may not trust that this everyday low price is really lower than the rest. Other customers simply feel that everyday low prices are a marketing gimmick.

12. **Why do customers associate price with quality? When should prestige pricing be used?**

    Consumers associate price with quality because of experience and because they have been socialized to believe that the higher the price, the higher the quality. Symbolic pricing should be used when the marketer can determine that a higher price is consistent with buyers' attitudes toward the expected cost of a product.

13. **Are price leaders a realistic approach to pricing? Explain your answer.**

    Price leaders should be used when competitive conditions and consumers' actions indicate that they are appropriate. In the long run, a firm must price at a level to achieve some degree of profit or at least to cover costs in the short run.

COMMENTS ON THE CASES

CASE 22.1 PRICING FOR NEW BALANCE

This case examines how one firm sets prices for its well-known footware products. You might begin the class discussion by asking how many students own a pair of New Balance athletic shoes or asking the class for their opinions of the quality and value of New Balance shoes compared to other leading shoe marketers.

Question 1 asks what pricing objectives New Balance seems to be employing. Based on the facts presented in the case, New Balance seems to be using market share and product quality as primary pricing objectives.

Question 2 asks students to identify the type of pricing strategy employed by New Balance. Based on the facts presented in the case, New Balance seems to be using premium pricing and price lining as pricing strategies. When New Balance shoes are sold in retail stores, some retailers may make use of additional pricing strategies, such as reference pricing, odd-even pricing, and special-event pricing to move New Balance shoes.

Question 3 asks students about other pricing tools employed by New Balance. Based on the facts presented in the case, it would seem that New Balance employs cost-base pricing as its basis for choosing prices. Although not specified in the case, it is possible that New Balance occasionally employs some time of periodic or random discounting to encourage retailers to carry its shoes, and it probably employs other pricing discounts to businesses that were described in Chapter 21.

Video Information

Company:	New Balance
Location:	Tape 2/DVD 2, Segment 22
Length:	10:56

Video Overview: New Balance athletic shoes are known for quality, superior fit, and technological innovation. Many factors must be considered during the product development and pricing process, including material costs, labor costs, and overhead costs. In order to maintain product quality while managing product cost, New Balance has developed an integrated costing and pricing system.

MULTIPLE-CHOICE QUESTIONS ABOUT THE VIDEO

1. New Balance is a brand of athletic shoes that focuses on
    a. lowest price possible.
    b. fit and performance.
    c. endorsements by celebrities.
    d. lowest production cost in Southeast Asian sweatshops.
    e. high fashion.
2. The bulk of manufacturing operations for New Balance are located in
    a. Canada.
    b. Vietnam.
    c. United States.
    d. Germany.
    e. Mexico.
3. New Balance prices its products
    a. at different price points for various market segments.
    b. with one price for all market segments.
    c. based on the gender of the consumer.
    d. based on fashion acceptance.
    e. based on the highest price that the market will bear.

ANSWERS TO MULTIPLE-CHOICE QUESTIONS ABOUT THE VIDEO

1. b
2. c
3. a

CASE 22.2 GENERAL MOTORS TRIES TO REDUCE RELIANCE ON REBATES

This case focuses on how one major automaker is trying to reduce its use of consumer discounts, a task made rather difficult by consumers' growing expectation of rebates and incentives all the time. The case should help students better understand the complexities involved in pricing automobiles, especially with intense competition and high fixed costs. You might begin the discussion by asking whether any students have purchased a new vehicle recently and whether they did so because of a rebate or other incentive offer (such as zero-percent financing). Ask those who have made such purchases whether they would have bought a new vehicle without such incentives.

Question 1 asks what pricing objectives General Motors seems to be using and how these help dictate the firm's use of periodic and random discounts and incentives. Based on information in the case, GM appears to have profit and market share as primary pricing objectives.

Question 2 asks students to identify the type of pricing strategy GM seems to be using. As specified in the case, rebates and incentives are best described as random discounting or even periodic discounting given that consumers have come to expect them all the time. Although not made explicit in the case, most students will recognize that GM also uses product-line pricing with different brands targeted at different markets partly due to pricing (e.g., Chevrolet for entry-level buyers and Cadillac for upscale buyers).

Question 3 asks students to consider the risks that Volkswagen faces in going against the industry and avoiding price incentives. Students' responses will vary, but the question should challenge them to recognize the importance of price in a marketing mix, particularly in a highly competitive industry with a great number of product choices available. Many students will logically argue that Volkswagen will have to emphasize product features that set its models apart in order to avoid using price competition and incentives, which may be difficult given the number of competing choices that are available with some sort of incentive.

APPENDIX A

Case Comments on Strategic Part-Ending Cases

STRATEGIC CASE 1

USA TODAY: *THE NATION'S NEWSPAPER*

The first strategic case gives students a unique opportunity to explore the decisions involved in developing and implementing the strategic plans for a real-world product in a complex and dynamic marketing environment. *USA Today*, now entering its third decade of operation, has been very successful, but Gannett Company continues to upgrade and adapt the newspaper in response to changing customer needs and desires as well as new technology.

The first question asks students to define Gannett's target market for *USA Today* and to describe how the firm's marketing strategy appealed to this market. Gannett initially defined the target market for *USA Today* as "achievement-oriented men in professional and managerial positions who are heavy newspaper readers and frequent travelers." Eventually, the definition was broadened to include all "young, well-educated Americans who are on the move and care about what is going on in the world." The latter definition proved closer to the typical reader of *USA Today*: a well-educated, 40-year-old professional, usually a manager, with an average annual income of about $60,000, To appeal to this market, Allen Neuharth, the paper's founder, sought to make the newspaper enlightening, enjoyable, and easy to process through its extensive use of briefs, secondary headlines, at-a-glance boxes, and colorful graphics. Over the years, the firm has modified the marketing mix somewhat—the newspaper's format and features, as well as its distribution, promotion, and price remain in tune to its target market.

The second question asks about the forces in the marketing environment that created opportunities and challenges for a national daily newspaper. Neuharth recognized that two sociocultural trends, the increasingly short attention span of the generation raised on television and a growing public hunger for more information, represented opportunities that Gannett could address with a new national daily newspaper. Morever, the only serious competitors (*The Wall Street Journal* and *The New York Times*) targeted different audiences. Much later, the company capitalized on the opportunities offered by the growth of the Internet to launch an online version of the newspaper. After the successful launch of *USA Today*, Gannett faced increasing competition from local daily newspapers that sought to emulate *USA Today*'s unique style. The company must continue to respond to changes in the marketing environment, especially competitive, legal and regulatory, technological, and sociocultural forces.

The final question asks students to evaluate *USA Today*'s decision to enter the online news market and whether this decision requires changes to the marketing strategy for the print version of the paper. Students' responses to the first question will vary, but it should help them recognize the importance of keeping up with changes in marketing environment forces in order to remain competitive and continue to satisfy the target market. Introducing a web-based version of *USA Today* does not necessarily require changes to the marketing strategy for the print version of the paper, but students should be able to recognize that the two versions should complement one another and therefore their strategies should be coordinated so that each enhances the other and helps the company achieve its business goals.

STRATEGIC CASE 2

MATTEL TAKES ON GLOBAL CHALLENGES

The purpose of this strategic case is to help students see how a real-world firm has responded to social responsibility concerns and global challenges to maintain and expand its well-known brands. Students are likely to be quite familiar with Mattel and its products, so they should be interested in how to relate what they have learned from the text to a company they know well.

In the first question, students are asked to describe Mattel's target market for Barbie and Hot Wheels and to explain how Mattel's marketing strategy appeals to these markets. Clearly, Mattel's target market for these brands includes children as well as the parents and grandparents who buy toys for them. To appeal to these markets, the company has regularly updated the products and added accessory products to enhance children's (and occasionally adults') enjoyment of them. Barbie, in particular, has undergone numerous makeovers to reflect changes in social attitudes, fashion, and technology, as well as cultural differences when marketed in other countries. The company has also employed promotion to make consumers aware of these changes and to communicate with consumers about the products. Although not specifically addressed in the case, students should also recognize that price and distribution are important components of any marketing strategy. To help them address these two areas, you might prompt them to recall the types of stores where they have seen Barbie and Hot Wheel products and their own perception of the value of these products.

Question 2 asks students to describe how Mattel has tried to be socially responsible in its numerous world markets. According to the case, Mattel has taken steps to strengthen its commitment to business ethics, social responsibility, and the concerns of stakeholders worldwide. It is particularly sensitive to ethical issues associated with marketing to children. One way it has addressed this issue is by providing information about children's Internet safety on its websites, which it encourages parents to read and follow. The company has also worked to address ethical and social issues created by the international environment and technology.

Question 3 asks students to consider the environmental forces that have created challenges for Mattel as it continues to expand into foreign markets. Students' responses will vary but should demonstrate an understanding of the environmental forces described in Chapters 3 and 5. Most will recognize that economic forces, legal and regulatory forces, technology, and particularly sociocultural forces will have a great impact when Mattel introduces Barbie, Hot Wheels, and other products into new foreign markets. Barbie, for example, has been somewhat controversial in some countries and has even been subject to efforts to ban the doll either because she does not resemble desired ethnic features or satisfy local cultural mores about dress and behavior.

The second part of Question 3 asks students to identify markets that have created opportunities for Mattel. Responses will vary, but should demonstrate an understanding that environmental forces create both challenges and opportunities for marketers as they move into new markets. Many students will cite Mattel's purchase or The Learning Company and Fisher-Price as efforts to capitalize on market opportunities with new products. Although the Learning Company acquisition did not work out, Mattel has since worked on integrating technological advances into its marketing strategy as evidenced by websites for Barbie and Hot Wheels.

STRATEGIC CASE 3

FEDEX CORPORATION

As with Strategic Case 1, this case gives students an opportunity to explore the decisions involved in developing and implementing the strategic plans for a well-known service in a complex and dynamic marketing environment. You may wish to remind students that the idea for FedEx was first expressed in a college paper (which earned just a 'C'), and that many well-known companies and products today grew from similar innovative visions by entrepreneurs. A good vision does not guarantee success, however.

The first question asks students to evaluate the methods used by FedEx to grow, both domestically and internationally. Based on the case, FedEx seems to have grown through acquisitions (e.g., Kinko's), expansion, and collaborative alliances with other firms (e.g., the U.S. Postal Service). Students' assessment of these efforts will vary but should demonstrate an understanding of corporate and marketing strategy and how they help guide a firm's growth and success.

The second question asks students to imagine a world without FedEx and how the world and their lives might differ. Students' responses will vary considerably, but most should be able to agree that life without overnight express services, whether offered by FedEx or a rival, would be more challenging in today's fast-paced world, especially when consumers and businesses both expect products delivered "yesterday." If students are having trouble with the question, try asking them if they've ever ordered a product from Amazon.com, eBay, or some other online vendor and how they received their merchandise. Was it fast enough?

The third question asks about the role of information technology and customer relationship management in the success of FedEx. Students should easily recognize that both have played a significant role in the company's success. FedEx was a pioneer in using the Internet to communicate with customers about the status of their packages and to facilitate managing their accounts. The company has experimented with and exploited every available computer technology to make its service as efficient as possible and its demanding customers as satisfied as possible.

STRATEGIC CASE 4

REEBOK RACES INTO THE URBAN MARKET

The goal of this strategic case is to show students how a company combines market segmentation and an understanding of consumer buying behavior to compete very effectively in a dynamic and pressured environment. Students should know the Reebok name and be familiar with many of its competitors (such as Nike, Adidas, and New Balance). You may want to suggest that students research Reebok's Rbk brand and its marketing activities in China before discussing the case in class.

The first question asks students to identify the segmentation variables that Reebok is using for its products and explain why they are appropriate. The company is using geographic variables such as country and urban/rural distinctions. It is also using the psychographic variable of lifestyle, particularly customers' interest or participation in certain sports. In addition, it is using the psychographic variable of motives, including personal appearance, status, and affiliation with admired celebrities or groups. In addition, Reebok is using the behavioristic variable of benefit segmentation, specifically the benefit of high performance (in sports) and the benefit of high fashion. Students may be able to identify other variables in use, as well.

The second question asks which of the three targeting strategies Reebok is applying. Students should be able to recognize that the company is using neither an undifferentiated strategy nor a concentrated strategy. Therefore the company is using a differentiated strategy of directing its marketing efforts at multiple segments with a separate marketing mix for each. One segment consists of people who want to wear the latest urban fashions. For this segment, Reebok's marketing mix includes the Rbk brand, stylish stores, and hip-hop endorsers. Another segment consists of young men in China who are basketball enthusiasts. Reebok's marketing mix for this segment includes Yao's House basketball courts and advertisements featuring NBA star Yao Ming.

The third question asks students to identify the influences on the consumer buying decision process that appear to have the most impact on Reebok's customers' purchase decisions. Students should recognize that psychological influences and social influences are the most important in this situation. The psychological influences of perception, motives, self-concept, attitudes, and lifestyles have a major impact. The social influences of reference groups, opinion leaders, and culture and subculture have a major impact. This is a good opportunity for students to compare their own experiences as buyers of athletic shoes and related products with the buying-decision influences that are affecting Reebok's customers.

The fourth question asks students to explain, in terms of segmentation and buying behavior, this statement by a Reebok executive: "The trends are made in the urban areas and on street basketball courts, just like in the United States." The executive is suggesting that despite geographic differences, the buying behavior of fashion-conscious non-U.S. customers is strongly influenced by reference groups and opinion leaders, just as the behavior of fashion-conscious U.S. customers is affected by those influences. The latest styles worn by young people in urban areas and the apparel worn by street basketball players touch off fashion trends for others and stimulate demand for the clothing and footwear. Seeing a new fashion in an urban setting or on the court may cause a buyer to recognize the problem of not having the most up-to-date apparel. It may also become one of the criteria by which a buyer evaluates products in the consideration set. As a result, the executive is confirming the importance of using psychographic and behavioristic variables to segment the market for Reebok's products.

STRATEGIC CASE 5

RADIO GOES SKY-HIGH AT XM SATELLITE RADIO

This strategic case examines the product decisions made by XM Satellite Radio, a pioneer in digital radio, and the environmental forces affecting the company's marketing. To introduce the case, you might ask how many students are aware of or subscribe to digital radio (as indicated by a show of hands). You may also want to assign students to research a brief update to this case, because the market is developing quite rapidly and XM's situation may have changed.

Question 1 asks how XM Satellite Radio is differentiating its product from that of Sirius Satellite Radio. According to the case, one important point of differentiation is the mix of radio stations and program content XM has created to meet the target market's listening tastes. Another key point of differentiation is XM's pricing, which is lower on a per-month basis than that of Sirius.

The second question concerns the role that quality has played in XM's product development and management. Students should recognize that XM must provide a high level of quality (free from static, for example) to convince customers to switch to digital radio. The quality must also be consistently high regardless of where a customer takes the XM radio (driving in the car or in a room at home). High quality allows XM to charge a monthly subscription fee and attract customers who would otherwise rely on free AM and FM radio broadcasts.

The third question asks students to identify the stage of the product life cycle that satellite radio is in and explain how the rate of adoption is affecting the product's progression through the life cycle. Some students may say it is in the introduction stage, because the product is new and represents a revolutionary innovation. Sales started slowly and buyers must be informed of satellite radio's advantages. Some students may say it is in the growth stage, because XM is acquiring customers at a fast pace and Sirius has entered the market as competition for XM. As competitors enter this market and more customers sign up for satellite radio, the product moves from introduction to growth. You may want to ask students to support their responses to this question through research.

The fourth question asks students to evaluate the brand names of XM Satellite Radio and Sirius Satellite Radio, including the strengths and weaknesses of each and which they consider to be a better brand name. Students' answers will vary. Some may notice that XM is similar to AM and FM, reinforcing the idea that this product is an advanced version of radio. XM may also be seen as an intriguing, forward-looking brand name. Both companies include the words "satellite radio" in their brand names for explanatory purposes. The Sirius brand may remind students of "serious" radio. Sirius is also the name of a bright star, suggesting that the product is also a bright star. Ask students to assess the strengths and weaknesses of each brand name, based on the associations they have with each. What criteria will they use to judge which brand name is better?

STRATEGIC CASE 6

THE HOME DEPOT REINFORCES ITS STRONG CHANNEL STRATEGY

This case offers students an opportunity to examine several aspects of the distribution element of the marketing mix. You may want to ask how many students (through a show of hands) have visited a Home Depot store and how many have visited an Expo store. If some students have visited both, consider having them share their impressions of the similarities and differences between the two types of stores.

Question 1 asks about the roles that physical distribution efforts play in Home Depot's retail success. Physical distribution activities are vital because they enable Home Depot to acquire, transport, store, and inventory for its retail locations and its Internet operations. Efficient order processing, inventory management, materials handling, warehousing, and transportation allow Home Depot to keep costs under control so it can pass savings along to customers in the form of low prices. In particular, Home Depot's use of regional distribution centers and public warehouse space ensures that it has sufficient inventory ready to restock stores quickly, even in peak seasonal selling periods.

In question 2, students are asked to identify some advantages and disadvantages of using public warehouses for seasonal inventory. Two advantages are: (1) the company can rent only as much space as it needs to hold seasonal merchandise, minimizing costs compared with the ongoing costs of a private warehouse or distribution center; (2) the company can rent the warehouse for limited periods, such as prior to and during a peak selling season, to minimize warehousing costs. Two disadvantages are: (1) lack of complete control over the security and physical premises of a public warehouse; and (2) possibility that insufficient storage space will be available in the future if nearby public warehouses are completely rented to other companies.

Question 3 asks about the major strategic dimensions through which Home Depot competes and grows. As a retailer, Home Depot must select appropriate locations (in urban and non-urban markets, for example) and tailor its atmospherics and merchandise assortments to the needs of the targeted customer groups in each market. Therefore, the company has developed a smaller type of Home Depot store for city locations and edited its product mix to fit the needs of city dwellers. It is also opening specialty stores to sell only landscaping products in areas where demand for such items is high. Its Expo stores have more sophisticated decor and merchandise than the Home Depot outlets, because Expo appeals to more affluent customers.

The fourth question asks how the positioning of the Expo store differs from the positioning of the regular Home Depot store. The case indicates that Expo targets fairly affluent consumers, and it carries high-end products for use in remodeling or redecorating homes. In contrast, Home Depot is targeting the broader market of do-it-yourself consumers and builders (business customers), for which it stocks a wider range of less-expensive products. Home Depot also separates products for builders so these customers can find what they want and check out quickly.

STRATEGIC CASE 7

BASS PRO SHOPS REELS THEM IN WITH SALES PROMOTION

This case gives students an opportunity to examine the sales promotion tools used by a unique retailing operation to help them understand the importance of the 'P' in the marketing mix. You may wish to ask whether any students have visited an Outdoor World store; if there are any affirmative responses, ask these students to share their impressions of the store with the class. Other students may be familiar with Bass Pro Shops through its catalog operation.

The first question asks students to give some examples of Bass Pro Shops' use of sales promotion tools. Sales promotion is any activity or material that acts as a direct inducement to purchase by offering added value or incentive for the product, and Bass Pro uses a variety of these tools. Examples students are likely to offer include special events to attract customers to visit the stores, mounted wildlife displays and living creatures to highlight merchandise in-store, and informational brochures that contain a selling message. There are often coupons available in the catalog and in-store, as well. Fishing contests—such as one offering winners a free boat and motor or perhaps a day of fishing with a top fishing pro—and special events like the Spring Fishing Classic keep customers interested in what is happening at Outdoor World stores. In some cases, it is possible to "sample" the merchandise before purchase as in firing a rifle on the indoor firing range.

The second question asks how Bass Pro's use of sales promotion tools makes shopping a better experience for customers. Responses may vary, but most students will recognize that displays help customers find specific products in the giant stores, which may also have a special price or be difficult to obtain elsewhere if they are highlighted in this way. Brochures may provide customers not only with selling messages, but also additional information that can help them select the proper item for their needs and understand how to use the item to obtain the best possible results. Special events that bring well-known experts to the store allow customers to interact with pros and celebrities and to learn how to better enjoy their products from the pros' experience. The customers themselves may even be able to have their photo taken with the famous pro, and perhaps collect his or her autograph as well for display at home.

The third question asks what other elements of the promotion mix are used at Bass Pro. The promotion mix tends to emphasize sales promotion to support personal selling, in part because of the difficulty of reaching such a specialized target market nationwide with radio, television, and newspaper advertising. Personal selling, both in the catalog telemarketing operation and in the retail stores, is crucial to provide information to potential customers beyond what can be reasonably expressed in a catalog. Catalogs can be directed specifically to Bass Pro's highly specialized and somewhat geographically dispersed target market. Radio, television, and newspaper advertising would be far more expensive and far more difficult to direct efficiently to this target market. However, Bass Pro Shops does produce and use some radio and television programs. Bass Pro also uses public relations and publicity tools to maintain its image in its Springfield home and as a way to build excitement at new store openings. These have been used to generate considerable media coverage associated with new store openings and rumors of new store openings. A key to Bass Pro's success is that very personalized attention from highly-trained salespeople helps customers satisfy their special needs. Salespeople also provide product information (including maintenance information) that leads to appropriate product expectations and subsequent customer satisfaction.

STRATEGIC CASE 8

NAPSTER 2.0: THE CAT IS BACK

Students will likely be very interested in this case, which profiles the history, legal issues, and evolving strategy of this pioneer of online music sharing. To introduce the case, you may wish to ask how many students have ever downloaded music from the Internet and from the new Napster specifically. Ask those with an opinion to share their impressions with the classmates, especially with regards to pricing issues in the music industry.

The first question asks students about the factors that have the greatest influence on Napster's pricing decisions. Napster seems to be employing price competition to exploit the fact that consumers, especially younger ones, are growing more discontent with the prices of CDs in stores, as evidenced by the continuing decline in CD sales. In addition, many consumers don't like having to buy an entire CD for just one or two songs; Napster allows them to mix their own CDs with their favorite tunes at a competitive price.

The second question asks students to consider Napster's pricing objectives. The case does not specify the firm's pricing objectives, but students should be able to suggest specific pricing objectives and defend their choices. Most will suggest that the firm's pricing objectives probably include market share, return on investment, and/or survival in an increasingly competitive industry.

The third question asks students to assess the level of price competition in the music industry as a whole and within the online music industry specifically. As evidenced by declining music sales, consumers are apparently becoming more value- and price-conscious when it comes to music, particularly now that options for obtaining releases are growing. Although some major record labels slashed wholesale prices in recent years, it has not stemmed the decline, and more and more consumers are apparently turning not only to the Internet but also to commercial-free satellite radio for their listening pleasure. Within the online music industry, price is rapidly becoming one of the most important factors with the entry of new competitors, including Wal-Mart's 88-cent service. However, the size and quality of each service's catalog is likely to remain an important factor as well, and students are likely to point out that Wal-Mart won't necessarily be the best source for the latest, coolest releases.

The final question asks specifically about Napster's current 99-cent strategy and to suggest circumstances under which the firm should consider changing that strategy. Students' responses will vary but should demonstrate strategic thinking with regard to price in an increasingly cutthroat industry. Many will argue that Napster's price is appropriate given its huge catalog (and the quality of the offerings in that catalog) in comparison to its competitors'. As competitors increase their own catalogs, however, this advantage may no longer hold unless Napster can continue to secure the latest releases from the most sought-after artists before other online services can add them as well. As to the circumstances under which Napster might adjust its current pricing policy, students should recognize that rising costs could force Napster (as well as potentially its competitors) to raise prices in order to remain profitable. Increasing competition might spur the company to reduce its price in order to maintain sales volume or market share. Finding a non-price basis on which to compete, e.g., forming an exclusive alliance with a specific, desirable artist, might allow the firm to raise prices at least on some items. Students may be able to offer additional creative responses based on their own unique understanding of this young market.

APPENDIX B

Financial Analysis in Marketing: Answers to Discussion and Review Questions

1. **How does a manufacturer's income statement differ from a retailer's income statement?**

   A manufacturer's income statement contains a "cost of goods manufactured" entry in the Cost of Goods Sold column, instead of the "purchases" entry used by retailers.

2. **Use the following information to answer questions a through c:**

   Company TEA
   Fiscal year ended June 30, 2005

Net sales	$500,000
Cost of goods sold	300,000
Net income	50,000
Average inventory at cost	100,000
Total assets (total investment)	200,000

   a. **What is the inventory turnover rate for TEA Company? From what sources will the marketing manager determine the significance of the inventory turnover rate?**

   $$\text{Inventory} = \frac{\text{Cost of goods sold}}{\text{Average inventory at cost}}$$

   $$= \frac{\$300,000}{\$100,000}$$

   $$= 3 \text{ times}$$

   The marketing manager must compare the inventory turnover rate with historical turnover rates and industry turnover rates.

   b. **What is the capital turnover ratio? What is the net income ratio? What is the return on investment (ROI)?**

   $$\text{Capital turnover rate} = \frac{\text{Net sales}}{\text{Total investment}}$$

   $$= \frac{\$500,000}{\$200,000}$$

   $$= 2.5 \text{ times}$$

$$\text{Net income ratio} = \frac{\text{Net income}}{\text{Net sales}}$$

$$= \frac{\$50,000}{\$500,000}$$

$$= \text{.1 or } 10\%$$

$$\begin{array}{l}\text{Return on investment} \\ \text{(ROI)}\end{array} = \frac{\text{Net income}}{\text{Total investment}}$$

$$= \frac{\$50,000}{\$200,000}$$

$$= \text{.25 or } 25\%$$

c.   **How many dollars of sales did each dollar of investment produce for TEA Company?**

$$\text{Capital turnover rate} = \frac{\text{Net sales}}{\text{Total investment}}$$

$$= \frac{\$500,000}{\$200,000}$$

$$= \$2.50 \text{ of sales for each dollar invested}$$

3.   **Product A has a markup percentage on cost of 40 percent. What is the markup percentage on selling price?**

$$\begin{array}{l}\text{Markup percentage} \\ \text{on selling price}\end{array} = \frac{\text{Markup percentage on cost}}{100\% + \text{markup \% on cost}}$$

$$= \frac{40}{100 + 40}$$

$$= \text{.286 or } 28.6\%$$

4.   **Product B has a markup percentage on selling price of 30 percent. What is the markup percentage on cost?**

$$\begin{array}{l}\text{Markup percentage} \\ \text{on cost}\end{array} = \frac{\text{Markup percentage on selling price}}{100\% + \text{markup \% on cost}}$$

$$= \frac{30}{100 + 30}$$

$$= \text{.429 or } 42.9\%$$

5. **Product C has a cost of $60 and a usual markup percentage of 25 percent on selling price. What price should be placed on this item?**

$$100\% = 25\% \text{ of selling price} + \text{cost}$$
$$75\% \text{ of selling price} = \text{cost}$$
$$X = \text{price}$$
$$.75X = \$60$$
$$X = \$80$$

6. **Apex Appliance Company sells 20 units of product Q for $100 each and 10 units for $80 each. What is the markdown percentage for product Q?**

$$\text{Markdown percentage} = \frac{\text{Dollar markdowns}}{\text{Net sales in dollars}}$$

$$= \frac{10 \text{ units } (\$20)}{20(\$100) + 10(\$80)}$$

$$= \frac{200}{\$2000 + \$800}$$

$$= .071 \text{ or } 7.1\%$$

APPENDIX C

Role-Play Exercises

WHY USE ROLE-PLAY EXERCISES?

The role-play exercise, or simulation, is an activity in which the class is divided into teams of five to six students each. The students read a very short case situation and are then assigned roles in the simulated organization. They are provided with varying levels of information about the scenario. The teams then interact to provide recommended courses of action representing short-term, mid-term, and long-term consideration. Each team experiences the group dynamics and tension that can occur between different departments and individuals seeking to protect their own interests.

The role-play exercise is a teaching tool that provides students with a realistic experience in a simulated organizational setting. This tool can help students recognize important issues that companies, managers, and employees may face on a daily basis. Beyond a case analysis approach, these exercises simulate the complexities of relationships and incomplete information that are pervasive in an organizational setting. Also, the exercises seek to enhance inherent conflicts between certain departments within the organization. Additionally, the exercises provided include an ethical component to help students recognize the ethical, legal, and social dimensions of decision making in marketing organizations. Therefore, a key goal is to improve individual awareness of the complexities involved in making marketing decisions. Finally, we hope to gain students' absolute involvement and participation in class. By participating in simulation exercises, students can develop their leadership skills and engage in problem solving activities directly related to marketing issues.

INSTRUCTIONS FOR CLASSROOM USE

The role-play exercise complements and enhances traditional approaches to marketing learning experiences because it:

1. Gives students the opportunity to practice making decisions that have marketing consequences

2. Simulates the power, pressures, and information sharing that affects decision making at upper levels in an organization

3. Provides students with a team-based experience enriching their skills and understanding of group processes and dynamics

4. Uses a debriefing and feedback period to allow for the exploration of complex and controversial issues in marketing decision making

These exercises can be used in classes of any size, as the instructor can run independent role-play case teams to fit the class size. A sample implementation process is provided below.

IMPLEMENTATION IN A 50-75 MINUTE CLASS PERIOD

1. Develop teams of five members (depending on roles used). If only three to four participants are available per team, the roles that appear most important and complex should be selected for members of the team.

2. Have each person read the role-play exercise background page as an introduction to the exercise.

3. Assign each person a role to play and give him or her the specific role description to review. Ask each person (role) to present his or her feedback and interaction with the group based on the role description assigned.

4. Indicate the desired outcome of the process (for example, press conference, written and/or oral presentation of short-term, mid-range, and long-term plan recommendations to address the issues, etc.).

5. Allow the teams to proceed without interruption for at least 45 minutes, depending on the outcome specified above. The instructor may visit teams to answer questions and stimulate discussion on key issues.

6. Create a classroom situation appropriate for teams to share their insights, decisions, or recommendations. The instructor may require each team to turn in a written report.

7. Link exercise issues, process, and outcomes, to experiences in the course and learning objectives. Debrief the class about the alternatives, team perspectives, and potential implications. Discuss issues that emerge commonly and appear to provide significant insights in helping the organization deal with the issues.

TEACHING OVERVIEW ON NATIONAL FARM AND GARDEN EXERCISE

The National Farm and Garden role-play exercise was designed with the goal of giving students the opportunity to use their knowledge and skills in solving a dilemma related to a product defect. The simulation centers around a garden tiller that has a safety protection guard that is difficult to reattach after cleaning. There have been incidents of injuries to animals and children when the tiller is run without the guard. Various functional members of the organization have to be prepared for a meeting and to make recommendations for dealing with the negative publicity and possible legal liability associated with damages related to product use. The class should be looking not only at the right thing to do, but also at how to implement the decision.

The students' recommendations should consider product recalls and classes to properly address cleaning and reinstallation of the guard. Relabeling the instructions to clarify the reattachment process for the guard should also be addressed. For the longer term, the company should consider a product redesign to provide a more foolproof mechanism for attaching the guard. Also, there is a need to evaluate the public relations damage and legal liability associated with product injury cases.

ROLE-PLAY EXERCISE ONE

National Farm and Garden, Inc.*

Background

(everyone reads)

National Farm and Garden, Inc. (NFG) was incorporated in Nebraska in 1935 and has been a leading supplier of farming equipment for more than 60 years. Over the last five years, however, demand for NFG' s flagship product, the Ultra Tiller, has been declining. To make matters worse, NFG' s market lead was overtaken by the competition for the first time two years ago.

Last year, NFG expanded its product line with the "Turbo Tiller," a highly advertised and much anticipated upgrade to the Ultra Tiller. The product launch was timed to coincide with last year's fall tilling season. Due to the timing of the release, the research and development process was shortened, and the manufacturing department was pressed to produce high numbers to meet anticipated demand. All responsible divisions approved the product launch and schedule. In order to release the product as scheduled, however, the manufacturing department was forced to employ the safety shield design from the Ultra Tiller. When attached, the shield protects the user from the tilling blades; however, it is necessary to remove the shield in order to clean the product. Because of differences between the Ultra and Turbo models, the Turbo's shield is very difficult to reattach after cleaning and the process requires specialized tools. Owners can have the supplier make modifications on site or at the sales location, or leave the shielding off and continue operation. All product documentation warns against operating the tiller without the shielding, and the product itself has three distinct warning labels on it. Modifications are now available that allow for the shield to be removed and replaced quite easily, and these modifications are covered by the factory warranty. However, most owners have elected to operate the Turbo Tiller without the safety shielding after its first cleaning.

Over the last year, a number of farm animals (chickens, cats, a dog, and two goats) have been killed by Turbo Tillers being operated without the guard. Two weeks ago, a 7-year-old Nebraska boy riding on the back of an unshielded tiller fell off. When the tiller caught the sleeve of his shirt, his arm was permanently mangled, requiring amputation. One of the child's parents owns the local newspaper, which ran a story about the accident on the front page of the local paper the next day. NFG's CEO has called an emergency meeting with the company's divisional vice president, director of product development, director of manufacturing, director of sales, and vice president of public relations to discuss the situation and develop a plan of action.

---

* All rights reserved. Copyright by O.C. Ferrell and Linda Ferrell. The research and conceptual assistance of Larry Gonzales, Pat Hansen, Heidi Hollenbeck, Marilynn Hill, Michael Mitchell, Craig Hurst, Bill Haskins, and Dana Schubert is gratefully acknowledged.

Divisional Vice President

(only the student assigned to this role reads this page)

You are the divisional V.P. and have been with the company for many years. Historically, you have not been a pushy individual and generally prefer to stay in the background. When there are major decisions to be made or crises to address, you are frequently not available. The CEO recently put you on a 60-day "action plan" to improve your division's output; failure to achieve this plan will result in your termination, even though you are just a few years shy of retirement. Therefore, you now find it necessary to satisfy not only your own objectives, but the CEO's very high expectations as well. This has caused great turmoil within all divisions as you place increasing pressure on your subordinates.

As the divisional V.P., you are focused on coordinating all departments. You are responsible for output from the sales, manufacturing, and field service engineering departments. The R&D department, which must sign off on all new products before they are approved for production, is not under your supervision.

Recently, you received a memorandum from the director of R&D outlining some potential problems with the development and testing of the Turbo Tiller. The memo was copied to you, the director of manufacturing, and the director of sales. You agreed with the director of manufacturing not to share the contents of the memo with your CEO because you felt that bringing this small concern to his attention would cause unnecessary problems for each division. Moreover, the CEO is known for his abrasive personality and has a history of yelling at bearers of bad news.

The CEO has called an all-hands emergency meeting at 7:00 a.m. tomorrow. You are expected to bring all knowledge of this situation with you for discussion and creation of a comprehensive action plan.

Director of Product Development

(only the student assigned to this role reads this page)

You are the director of product development. Although you have a master's degree in mechanical engineering from Stanford University, you are originally from the inner cities of Chicago, where you grew up in the school of "hard knocks." From previous experience, you tend to be rather uncompromising about products that are engineered within your organization. Your engineering team has been very successful in the past, and you are quite proud of the many new successful products your department has developed.

You originally fast tracked the Turbo Tiller product due to constant pressure, particularly from the director of sales. However, upon further investigation, you have become concerned about the implementation of the product's safety shield. Consequently, you recently sent a memorandum to the director of manufacturing, director of sales, and the divisional vice president outlining the fact that consumers could sue National Farm and Garden under the state's *strict liability doctrine*, which holds manufacturers, distributors, wholesalers, retailers, and others in the chain of distribution of a defective product liable for the damages caused by the defect regardless of fault. Moreover, plaintiffs could cite the state's *concept of defect of manufacture* when the manufacturer fails to (1) properly assemble a product, (2) properly test a product, and (3) adequately check the quality of the product's component parts or materials used in manufacturing. You now believe that NFG has violated all of these "defects of manufacture."

Having received no response to this memo, you are contemplating whether to escalate the issue by going to the CEO. The only reason you have not already done so is the CEO's historic temper when confronted with negative situations.

The CEO has called an all-hands emergency meeting at 7:00 a.m. tomorrow. You are expected to bring all knowledge of this situation with you for discussion and creation of a comprehensive action plan.

Director of Manufacturing

(only the student assigned to this role reads this page)

You are the director of manufacturing. A graduate from the University of Alabama with a bachelor of science degree in industrial manufacturing, you have worked for NFG for twenty years. You are required to provide reports to top management on a weekly, monthly, and quarterly basis. Top management creates the exact measures of performance that you provide; although you have a say in what these reports focus on, you often disagree with their exact focus. Your overall performance is evaluated based more on numbers of units produced than on quality. Despite this, you enjoy working for the company. You consider the group like family, and especially appreciate the effort the CEO has made to make you feel valued and supported.

You are aware of the difficulties the Ultra Tiller guard poses when used on the Turbo Tiller. Due to the Turbo Tiller's larger size, the guard is nearly impossible to replace after removal. Reattachment of the shield requires a professional machine shop and additional assistance. However, with your knowledge of statistics, you know that, even without the shield in place, the chances of an animal or a person being injured by the Turbo Tiller are small. Thus, you agreed with the divisional V.P. to bury a memo sent by the director of R&D stating related concerns. You both felt that the risks were small enough and that raising these concerns to your superiors would only cause headaches and paperwork. Furthermore, you need to stay on schedule in order to reach your volume goals if you are to earn your bonus.

You have also received several e-mails from the manager of the field service engineering department about reports of farmers operating the Turbo Tiller without the guard. When you requested statistical data regarding the number and location of occurrences and any related accidents, the field service engineering manager replied with field data indicating that more than 85 percent of all Turbo Tillers are eventually operated without the guard.

The CEO has called an all-hands emergency meeting at 7:00 a.m. tomorrow. You are expected to bring all knowledge of this situation with you for discussion and creation of a comprehensive action plan.

Director of Sales

(only the student assigned to this role reads this page)

You are the director of sales and have been with NFG for more than ten years. You were recruited from a competing firm and have more than 25 years of sales experience in the industry. Because of sagging sales, you face extreme pressure from above to meet your numbers. However, you feel that sales forecasts have been set unrealistically. Furthermore, these aggressive forecasts create churning within your department as your sales staff consistently complain that their quotas are unrealistic. Although you are adamant that declining sales are industry and product offering issues, you are reluctant to raise these concerns to the CEO because of his history of ripping the heads off messengers bearing bad news. You have witnessed this phenomenon firsthand as the CEO literally screamed at a coworker who brought a problem to his attention. On the other hand, the CEO has promised you a new Dodge Ram if your department reaches its numbers this year. Of course, you enthusiastically promised to achieve these results and quickly ran from the room.

The Turbo Tiller has been a much-anticipated addition to your stagnant product portfolio, but you were concerned that it would be delayed due to red tape and wrote daily e-mails to the R&D manager about getting it to market on a timely basis. You have received a memo from the R&D manager about some legal concerns over the Turbo Tiller. However, you feel that these concerns are manufacturing's problem, not your department's. Furthermore, because the director of manufacturing received a carbon copy of the memo, you are sure that the concerns will be addressed appropriately.

You have organized training on this product for your sales staff that included proper operating procedures and the dangers of standing within five feet of the tilling blades. Independent of these training sessions, you arranged a separate class on how to address and downplay these concerns with customers.

The CEO has called an all-hands emergency meeting at 7:00 a.m. tomorrow. You are expected to bring all knowledge of this situation with you for discussion and creation of a comprehensive action plan.

Vice President of Public Relations

(only the student assigned to this role reads this page)

You are the most recent addition to the management staff at NFG, having been with the company for just three years. You obtained a bachelor's degree in human resources from Ohio State University, and a master's degree in communications from Florida State University. Prior to working with NFG, you handled public relations at a nonprofit organization for five years. You took this job because you thought it would be a personal challenge to represent a larger for-profit business. Besides, you were raised in Nebraska, and are a farmer at heart.

Nearly six months ago, you learned that the company had developed and released a product that has some safety concerns. Most department heads were not concerned about the problem because of a lack of solid evidence that a danger existed. You have been monitoring the situation, although it has not been your highest priority due to recent union negotiations. Recently, the CEO informed you that a corporate meeting is eminent. As the V.P. of Public Relations, it is your responsibility to gain information about public opinion to present to the CEO. As you begin to collect this information, you find disturbing news. Many consumers don't trust NFG because of its handling of a chemical spill five years ago. Additionally, many rumors are circulating about NFG's hiring practices.

You know that a single negative event can wipe out a company's reputation and destroy favorable customer attitudes established through years of expensive advertising campaigns and other promotional efforts. In this situation you need to minimize the negative publicity, yet still address the media. You suddenly wish the company had developed a crisis plan before this happened.

The CEO has called an all-hands emergency meeting at 7:00 a.m. tomorrow. You are expected to bring all knowledge of this situation with you for discussion and creation of a comprehensive action plan.

TEACHING OVERVIEW ON VIDEOPOLIS EXERCISE

This role-play exercise features a technology company that facilitates information transfers between different organizations and among different divisions of the same organizations. Videopolis manages the electronic transfer of videos, training materials, and other electronic content. Two major issues exist for the company relating to facilitating the transfer of copyrighted materials and how employees are being treated within the organization (promises have been broken with respect to compensation and other issues). The president of Videopolis does not like to hear bad news and gets angry very easily. Various functional members of the organization have been asked to meet and make recommendations to address these two major issues.

Some important concerns in this exercise relate to marketing strategy and implementation (Chapter 2), and intellectual property issues (Chapter 6). The Napster case at the end of Part Eight may also provide a helpful background before students attempt the Videopolis role-play. A solution to the current situation should involve developing checks and balances within the organization to receive copyright releases, legal oversight, and ethical directives associated with the use of copyrighted materials. A key issue is that students will often think that it is acceptable to do something as long as you will not be caught or no one will ever know. This case provides for lengthy discussion of these issues.

ROLE-PLAY EXERCISE TWO

Videopolis[**]

Background

(everyone reads)

Videopolis was founded as VideoNow in 1993 by two former employees of RCA, where they had learned television broadcasting, electrical engineering, satellite downlinking, and telephone networking applications. Today, Videopolis is a communications company that specializes in connecting videoconferencing equipment over digital telephone lines to cities around the world. The company does not produce meetings, conferences, or programs, but instead facilitates the videoconference process. Videopolis' most profitable product, the "Broadcast Service," involves storing and playing prerecorded programs on its VCRs and broadcasting them through its computer equipment to clients' meeting rooms around the world. If a remote site is not immediately available to view a meeting or program from Videopolis, the client can record the program by connecting a VCR to a television monitor. Videopolis does not explicitly state that recording programs is forbidden. Company policy is that all viewing sites must obtain their own permissions from the owners of the content to record any copyrighted materials. There are some concerns that this policy may be facilitating the copying and distribution of copyrighted material.

VideoNow became Videopolis after it was acquired by TeleWide Corp. fifteen months ago. When VideoNow was started, the founders had a clear vision for growth, hiring only the best employees and purchasing the best equipment in more than sufficient quantities to ensure a high level of service and plenty of reserves for growth. Many of VideoNow's original employees joined the firm with high hopes of stock options, promotions, and bonuses based on future growth prospects. Many employees had purchased expensive homes and cars in anticipation of these bonuses and promotions. Unfortunately, the founding partners sold out directly to TeleWide before granting any options or bonuses to VideoNow employees. After the merger, TeleWide immediately instituted a hiring and equipment-purchasing freeze and virtually froze all salaries. The new corporate parent also set aggressive sales and growth goals for Videopolis and developed a highly incentive-based pay structure for upper managers who achieved their goals. This resulted in a considerable amount of turnover as those employees who could afford to leave promptly did so, placing tremendous stress on those who stayed and had to take up the slack. Many of the employees who remained after the buy out believe that promises have been broken and that they were misled about advancement opportunities.

Videopolis' chief legal counsel has sent an e-mail message to arrange a meeting with the CEO, vice president of operations, vice president of human resources, and the vice president of marketing and sales to discuss a number of legal and ethical issues concerning potential legal issues at the company.

[**] All rights reserved. Copyright by O.C. Ferrell and Linda Ferrell. The research and conceptual assistance of Dana Schubert, Brian Hayes, Carrieann McDonough, Jeff Sawyer, and Jon Mullen is gratefully acknowledged.

Bryce Kerwin, Vice President of Marketing and Sales

(only the student assigned to this role reads this page)

Bryce Kerwin is the vice president of sales and marketing for Videopolis. One of the first employees hired by the VideoNow founders, Bryce was among the core group of employees who were promised stock options and promotions if the company ever went public. Bryce is middle-aged, divorced, and has two children. Bryce drives an old beat-up car and has used all the family's financial resources to get into a new, larger house. Relying on the promised stock options, raises, and bonuses, Bryce is now stretched to the limit and is beginning to deeply resent the company because the promised money may never materialize. Alex Rockwell, Videopolis' CEO, has told Bryce that the marketing and sales department can make the difference in helping the company achieve its objectives. Rockwell has implemented a very attractive bonus plan for Bryce if the department achieves its objectives, but the numbers are so aggressive that Bryce feels they are unattainable.

Bryce has been concerned recently by reports that operations can't handle the current workload and rumors that Videopolis has lost its edge. Bryce wonders if this is indeed the case and whether the company can grow at all, let alone by 100 percent, the target number set by the new CEO. Bryce's sales force is also young, inexperienced, and not very familiar with the company's products. Bryce has been driving the sales force very hard in an effort to reach the company's goals (and because Alex has made several threats referring to Bryce's "lack of motivation"). Bryce senses the tension in employee morale, but doesn't know how to address the issues. Bryce was a pivotal employee who helped make the company successful through hard work and wonders why, instead of rewards and recognition, the new management delivers orders to work even harder.

In response to Bryce's incessant pushing, the sales reps are stretching the truth and making promises that the company can't keep in order to book sales. Although Bryce personally hates this practice, it does bring in customers who later learn what Videopolis can actually do and they usually stay (once Bryce meets with them to do "damage control" and pacify them). Videopolis has also started doing business with unfamiliar companies that have high demands for secrecy and privacy. Unfortunately, promises to satisfy their demands remain unfulfilled due to limitations in current technology. Videopolis' most profitable product is the "Broadcast Series," which involves playing feature-length videotapes and broadcasting the signal around the world. Unlike many of the company's other products, the Broadcast Series is not interactive, so aside from equipment costs, it's virtually pure profit for Videopolis.

Yesterday Bryce received an e-mail from M.J. Marshall, the company's chief legal counsel, indicating that there may be intellectual copyright infringement issues with the Broadcast Series and some of the firm's contracts with customers. The attorney has called a meeting with all of Videopolis' upper managers tomorrow to discuss the issues. The CEO has indicated that the vice president of human resources also wants to address some employee issues at the meeting. Bryce hopes that the meeting does not relate to the sales force's tendency to stretch the truth to customers because Bryce has really stretched company policy and personal morals in order to achieve the high goals. Bryce is not looking forward to the meeting.

Alex Rockwell, CEO

(only the student assigned to this role reads this page)

Alex Rockwell was brought in by TeleWide as the CEO of Videopolis at the time of the VideoNow buy out. Alex is a young executive whose entire seven-year professional career has been with TeleWide. Upon graduation from the University of New Hampshire with a B.S. in Marketing and an MBA, Alex began working in TeleWide's marketing department and quickly worked up within the organization.

Prior to taking the reins at Videopolis, Alex had a successful two-year stint as the CEO of a small voice messaging company that had also been acquired by TeleWide. After making some cuts and refocusing the staff, Alex was able to turn a mediocre company into a very profitable one. Because of the cuts, some of the voice messaging company's employees began to refer to Alex as "Hacksaw," which gave Alex a strange sense of pride because it suggested that Alex had the guts required to make unpopular but necessary decisions to make the company profitable.

Alex believes that this appointment to Videopolis will be the final stage of professional grooming prior to landing a corporate vice presidency at TeleWide itself, with its greater responsibility and prestige. After observing other successful executives being appointed to posh TeleWide corporate positions, Alex believes that two to three successful years at Videopolis will guarantee Alex's own appointment to one of these coveted positions.

Alex is a loyal TeleWide employee to the bone. When a corporate mandate came down to increase revenue by a minimum of 50 percent, Alex confidently replied that anything less than 100 percent would be unacceptable. Alex claimed to have studied Videopolis' bottom line and determined that it just was not being run efficiently. In reality, Alex had made this assessment by gut feeling, without taking the time to actually sort though the figures to identify areas for improvement and savings. Alex gauged the average company employee to have little sense of urgency and observed many unnecessary (in Alex's opinion) tasks being performed. Thinking a fear tactic would be the best method to achieve results, Alex has been on a fifteen-month rampage to get the desired bottom-line numbers. The word around Videopolis is, "it's Alex's way or the highway." Through terminations and employee turnover, more than half of the current staff has tenure of less than one year. Now it seems that Alex has a problem with the firm's chief legal counsel, M.J. Marshall. Alex feels that M.J. is too young and lacks the drive to do what it takes to get things done the Alex Rockwell way; perhaps M.J. should be the next one to be "'Hacksawed."

Alex is quite excited about Videopolis' new Broadcast Series of programming. The product involves an employee putting a feature-length tape into a VCR (at the request of a client) and, with a few mouse clicks, broadcasting the requested program to various videoconferencing facilities throughout the country. The margins on this service are very high, and Alex believes that expanding the service could greatly assist the company achieve its goal of a 100 percent increase in revenue. Unfortunately, he questioned the legality of the service from its inception.

Alex recently received a vague e-mail from M.J. Marshall, Videopolis' chief legal counsel, requesting a meeting to discuss potential legal problems that could be brewing within the company. Upon learning of the meeting, Sam Arnold, the company's vice president of human resources, asked that employee issues be placed on the agenda as well. Alex is deeply concerned because potential lawsuits of any magnitude or employee dissatisfaction could dramatically affect the bottom-line numbers and Alex's chances for a corporate V.P. position at TeleWide.

J. Marshall, Chief Legal Counsel

(only the student assigned to this role reads this page)

M.J. Marshall is the bright young attorney hired by VideoNow's founding partners to act as their chief counsel just before the TeleWide buy out. M.J. is single and has been practicing law for just a few years. Before coming to work at VideoNow, M.J. was on the fast track to a partnership in a firm that specialized in intellectual property and copyright protection. M.J. jumped at the opportunity to be chief counsel at an interesting high-tech company that offered better than average pay and the potential for stock options. Soon after being hired by VideoNow, M.J. purchased a new sports car and a loft in a renovated warehouse in the trendy downtown area. When VideoNow was bought out by TeleWide, M.J. was one of the few employees who retained their original salary and received stock options in Videopolis. Being the chief counsel, M.J. was concerned about making a good impression on the new owners, not to mention the much needed salary to cover a large student loan, mortgage, and car payments.

Things have finally settled down after the merger, and M.J. is just now reviewing the contracts signed by VideoNow's founders in order to identify problems. Many of the old VideoNow deals were open ended, based on a handshake, and some had strange provisions especially concerning copyright violations. M.J. has identified some specific concerns about the company's Broadcast Series. M.J. has received complaints from some of the employees regarding the tapes that are being broadcast over company lines. Being familiar with the laws surrounding intellectual property and copyright protection, M.J. suddenly realizes that Videopolis could be liable for copyright infringement if the copyright owners view the broadcasts and recognize their programs as unauthorized copies. M.J. also knows that the federal government has been threatening to crack down on Internet companies for violations of copyright laws. M.J. learned a great deal about intellectual property issues and laws at the law firm and knows that intellectual property losses in the United States total more than $11 billion a year in lost revenue from illegal copying. In order to protect against such losses, the U.S. has enacted copyright laws, including the Digital Millennium Copyright Act, to protect original works in text form, pictures, movies, computer software, multimedia, and audiovisual formats. Although M.J. recognizes that these issues must be dealt with, M.J. also knows that the Broadcast Series is the CEO's baby and that Alex will be very sensitive to any changes in the profitable program. Nonetheless, these issues could potentially be time consuming and very costly to Videopolis.

To add to the pressures M.J. faces, the CEO has hinted to M.J. that if the situation is not managed satisfactorily, TeleWide will bring in a new legal counsel who can satisfy the company's needs. Recognizing the need to get a handle on the situation, M.J. has decided it is time to call a meeting with the top executives. M.J. dreads the meeting, knowing it could affect a number of employees, but believes that these issues must be brought out in the open.

Jerry Abacarian, Vice President of Operations

(only the student assigned to this role reads this page)

Jerry Abacarian, another holdover from the old VideoNow days, is the vice president of operations for Videopolis. Jerry came to the United States from the Middle East in search of riches and cherishes the newfound successful American lifestyle. Jerry has come a long way from humble beginnings as the child of a goat farmer. Jerry is married and has two teenagers. The girls attend the most prestigious private school in the community. Jerry hopes that the investment in their primary education will pay off because the family has not saved enough money to send both girls to college. Jerry spares no expense for the family, buying the best quality merchandise. A recent acquisition is a Mercedes 560 SC, bought on credit through a financing company. Jerry's family is never seen in anything that could be considered middle class and looks down upon people who do not meet their social standards. Now approaching middle age, Jerry worries about what the future holds for a person who has really not done an effective job of saving for the future or retirement.

As an upper manager at VideoNow, Jerry was promised future benefits such as stock options and a dramatically increased salary. Jerry feels betrayed by the founders, believing they sold VideoNow employees out for a fast buck and left them stuck with inadequate salaries and minimal chances for attaining a higher financial status. Thus, Jerry's loyalty to the new company is in question, and Jerry is looking for any way to obtain the promised compensation. The only means for Jerry to reach the expected compensation level is to achieve the new objectives and, hopefully, receive the huge promised bonus.

Since the merger, Jerry's job has become increasingly demanding as the pressure of the day-to-day operations has increased dramatically. In Jerry's opinion, the company is attempting to book too many sales, creating unrealistic daily and quarterly objectives, and forcing the staff to work harder than ever. Many key subordinates and lower level employees have already left the company for more stable and rewarding work environments. With the loss of these individuals, the operations department is having trouble retaining competent employees. The high turnover and generally lower level of knowledge among the remaining work force mean that many of the repetitive and simple tasks, which were always taken for granted in the past, are no longer getting done. For example, employees are being told just to put the tapes in the correct slot without previewing them for copyrighted material as was standard practice at VideoNow. Employees are just supposed to follow orders, because, according to top management, they will never understand what they are supposed to do anyway.

Before leaving for home, late as usual, Jerry received an e-mail from M.J. Marshall, the chief legal counsel, asking Jerry to attend a meeting with the executive staff. The e-mail did not specify the meeting's agenda but hinted about some potential legal liabilities Videopolis may face. Jerry isn't aware of any possible legal problems but welcomes the opportunity to meet with the executive staff. Sam Arnold apparently also wants to talk about employee issues at the meeting, and Jerry hopes this means the end of the hiring freeze so that Jerry can bring in some more qualified people and give his overworked staff some relief. Things simply cannot continue as they have for much longer.

Sam Arnold, Vice President of Human Resources

(only the student assigned to this role reads this page)

Sam Arnold was hired in 1997 as the new vice president of human resources after the previous V.P. quit when the corporation failed to address the promised pay raises and stock options after the merger. This management position was the only one to be filled after the hiring freeze went into effect. However, CEO Alex Rockwell hired the inexperienced Arnold instead of a seasoned HR manager in an effort to reduce costs.

Sam graduated from Ohio State University in 1995. After two years at a pharmaceutical firm, Sam was ready for a change. Sam was familiar with the company after using its services, and was strongly interested in working for a high-tech firm. Sam was not promised the same stock options, raises, and bonuses that other employees were, but Sam had other motives for taking the position. Sam felt that Videopolis represented an excellent opportunity to learn about and ease into the high-technology industry. After two years with this corporation, Sam plans to enroll in the Computer Information Systems Masters program at Colorado State University.

A month into the new job, Sam began to understand why the former V.P. quit. Recently, Sam has been completing several employee termination packets every month. Most are former VideoNow employees who cite broken promises as their reason for quitting. It seems to Sam that Videopolis is hemorrhaging employees and the business is really starting to suffer from the high turnover. The company simply cannot continue at this rate without lifting the hiring freeze.

In addition to the high turnover, Sam recognizes that many employees are disenchanted, demoralized, and ready to quit. The climate at Videopolis has become negative, and many people dread coming to work. Employees often speak of questionable management practices, possible copyright infringement, and a nearly desperate need for better compensation. Most of these complaints have come from employees in Marketing and Sales and the Operations divisions. As the vice president of human resources, Sam hears their complaints and understands the situation better than anyone.

Recently, M.J. Marshall, the company's chief legal counsel, sent out e-mails to all top managers calling a meeting to discuss possible copyright infringement issues. Unfortunately, Sam feels that Videopolis' problems aren't that simple. Accordingly, Sam has contacted the CEO, Alex Rockwell, to add human resources issues to the meeting agenda. Although the copyright issues are important, Sam feels that the people issues warrant greater attention because, without satisfied employees, nothing will get accomplished.

TEACHING OVERVIEW ON REDRIVERSHOPS.COM EXERCISE

The RedRiverShops.com role-play exercise was designed to provide a challenging decision-making experience highlighting strategic marketing and e-marketing issues. The dot-com fall-out should make this an interesting and timely exercise. The exercise centers around the compatibility of a dot-com and a traditional "brick-and-mortar" retail establishment. The simulation creates a dilemma as to whether RedRiverShops.com should merge with American Shopping Mall Properties, a national chain of shopping centers. Student teams are asked to make a single decision as to whether these two firms should merge based on marketing compatibility as well as all the other relevant functional areas of business.

The student teams should make a decision either to merge or not to merge and defend their rationale. Students may find it helpful to list the pros and cons of each decision for RedRiverShops.com. The results of using this simulation in the classroom suggest that the decision is split (50/50) as to which alternative is best. Although there is no right or wrong answer to this exercise, it provides an excellent opportunity to discuss marketing strategy (Chapter 2) and e-marketing issues (Chapter 6). It might be interesting to note that Jeff Bezos, who founded Amazon.com, was confronted with a similar dilemma and quickly indicated that Amazon was not interested in merging with a traditional retail company.

ROLE-PLAY EXERCISE THREE

Redrivershops.com***

Background

(everyone reads)

RedRiverShops.com (RRS.com) is a leading online retailer. This e-commerce firm has more than 10 million customer accounts in twenty countries with sales of (US) $900 million. The company offers products in various categories including computers, software, music, movies, electronics, and sports equipment. For example, RRS.com is the leading online retailer of golf and fishing equipment. The firm has 2 million feet of warehouse and distribution space to store and deliver merchandise to customers. RRS.com is organized into three segments: allied electronics, integrated sports, and business-to-consumer auctions. The business-to-consumer auctions enable registered and approved businesses to offer a wide variety of products in an auction format, similar to eBay's online auctions.

RedRiverShops.com has yet to show a profit due to the high costs of building a distribution system, designing a website, implementing customer transaction and service processes, and creating brand awareness through advertising. Although the company currently has $500 million in cash available for operations, it is losing about $50 million a quarter. Because acquiring additional financing has become increasingly difficult, RRS.com needs to break even in the next two and a half years. As a publicly held corporation, the firm has been criticized for operating in the "red" for too long, and a number of investment firms recently downgraded RRS.com's stock from a "buy" to a "hold."

The board of directors is meeting to consider a proposal from the highly visible chief executive officer, president, and founder of RRS.com. The CEO has been able to develop an opportunity for a possible merger with a major developer of traditional shopping malls. Although not yet sure the merger is the best strategy for RRS.com, the CEO views the meeting with the board of directors as the most important aspect in the decision-making process. The CEO respects the board's ability to make the right recommendation because the members attending the next meeting are company executives with much experience and knowledge in their respective areas of business.

The proposal to be discussed at the board meeting is a merger of RRS.com with American Shopping Mall Properties (ASMP), a Houston-based real estate firm that owns 95 shopping malls in 28 states. ASMP is very profitable with $600 million in rental income yielding a bottom-line profit of $200 million last year. Merging a popular e-commerce portal with a successful shopping mall operator could create the ultimate "clicks-and-bricks" marriage. RRS.com could provide website exposure for shopping mall tenants who, in many cases, have well-established national brands. A joint venture with a mall tenant that markets heavy, durable products, such as washing machines and dryers, could provide an opportunity for RRS.com to market products that could be delivered and serviced by the mall store. ASMP malls could even be co-branded as RRS.com malls, creating a seamless flow between online buying and receiving and returning products in the mall.

It is time for the RRS.com board of directors to meet, discuss, and then approve or disapprove the proposed merger. You, as a member of the board of directors, have been assigned a functional role with unique information that can be used in the discussion.

*** All rights reserved. Copyright by O.C. Ferrell, Linda Ferrell, and Debbie Thorne McAlister.

Vice President and Chief Information Officer

(only the student assigned to this role reads this page)

You have helped RRS.com become the proven technology leader. Because of your leadership, the company has developed an easy-to-use search engine and the most secure payment features available in e-commerce. In addition to the U.S. website, the company operates three internationally focused websites for Japan, the European Union, and China. With the most innovative technology in the industry, RRS.com has the Internet platform to expand into new product lines through relationships with strategic partners. The vast computer technology and information systems developed by RRS.com have already allowed the company to sell products through co-branded (both RRS.com and a retailer or product manufacturer brand name) sections on the RRS.com website.

As the chief information officer, you are concerned about the integrity of the system and the need to add additional software and hardware to upgrade the network infrastructure to accommodate increased traffic from a merger. Without these upgrades, the system could face interruptions, slower response time, and delays. Because all the firm's equipment is at one leased facility in Houston, floods, fire, or similar events could destroy the system. Possibly of greater risk are computer viruses, electronic break-ins, and other events that could prevent servicing customers. Advancing technology and the resources needed to maintain and upgrade the websites represent a significant concern.

In addition, you are concerned about RedRiverShop's image and its possible dilution as a result of the merger with the "bricks-and-mortar" shopping center. You have gone to great lengths to promote RRS.com as an online-only entity and you continually reinforce this commitment both internally and with investors.

President, Chief Executive Officer, and Founder

(only the student assigned to this role reads this page)

Along with your role as president and CEO, you have been chairman of the board since you founded RedRiverShops in 1995. You have been successful in developing a leading e-commerce company that has the resources to pursue opportunities for forming new relationships. Through your leadership, the market value of RRS.com stock has reached $12 billion. Because the market value of ASMP is $2.5 billion, RRS.com could acquire ASMP through a stock-for-stock trade. This would result in a 21 percent dilution in RRS.com's stock shares. The company would also acquire almost $3 billion in ASMP debt because most shopping mall real estate is financed and therefore carries a heavy debt. The bottom line is that it is financially feasible for RRS.com to merge with ASMP without any cash requirements. Perhaps the greater concern is the long-run success of the merger.

A number of disadvantages could result from the proposed merger. The new company could be profitable and some cash requirements for building warehouses and developing inventory could be reduced. RRS.com could increase traffic through websites developed for the mall stores. It could charge a fee for sales at the site, and it might have its name and logo on mall stores to increase its customer visibility. On the other hand, the CEO will lose some control over the management of the company and RRS.com will be less focused as an e-commerce company. Managers will have to spread their time over traditional as well as e-commerce operations. Taking on an additional $3 billion in debt is also a key concern. You are also concerned about investors' perceptions of this move. Through the issuance of new stock, you see this as a possible way in which to raise additional capital. But, you must first convince current and potential investors of the company's commitment and faith in this extension of branding, distribution, and image. One other opportunity that you have been pondering is the possibility of opening RRS branded stores that carry the same merchandise and utilize the same pricing strategy as the online operation.

Vice President of Operations and General Manager

(only the student assigned to this role reads this page)

You have been with the company for one year and were hired to streamline costs. Although RRS.com does not own any real estate, the company has been effective in leasing office facilities in Houston as well as leasing 2 million square feet of warehousing and fulfillment operations space for the company's products. In addition, infrastructure has been established to handle customer orders, supplier relationships, inventory management, and efficient shipment of products based on ordering criteria. There has been uninterrupted operation of the websites and transaction processing systems. On the other hand, continued growth will place a significant strain on management, operational, and human resource systems.

Currently, there are challenges in understanding customer demand and purchase patterns and meeting faster product life cycles. Significant risks are associated with product seasonality, accurately predicting sales, and the ability to negotiate terms with manufacturers, distributors, and other vendors. The ability to expand leased distribution operations and to maintain flexibility in the distribution of logistics systems is difficult due to the inability to predict sales increases. In fact, distribution centers are currently underutilized and operating at 60 percent of capacity. Finally, competition with online and traditional stores is projected to intensify. Internet technologies foster quick comparison of prices and could reduce operating margins. Traditional retail stores may become more aggressive competitors with their own websites and strategic partnerships. But you know that the most successful web operators maintain a "bricks-and-mortar" presence.

Vice President of Marketing

(only the student assigned to this role reads this page)

As vice president of marketing, you helped establish RRS.com as the number one online store for sports and fishing equipment. *Customer Reports*, the most recognized source on rating e-commerce, has rated RRS.com as the best online store for sports, fishing, and consumer electronics. Customers around the world are choosing RRS.com for online business-to-consumer auctions for a variety of products. RRS.com has maintained low competitive prices through low product gross margins.

Through centralized distribution warehouses, RRS.com can physically stock all products the company needs in its inventory. Through joint agreements with UPS, FedEx, and the U.S. Postal Service, efficient delivery of products is maintained. Through advertising, RRS.com has established a brand name that has considerable value on the Internet. Overall, the company has an excellent marketing program driven by marketing research and a focus on customer value. The marketing strategy is focused on strengthening the brand name, increasing website hits, and building customer loyalty and repeat purchases.

In addition, you realize that your RRS.com credit card program has been responsible for increasing sales. The average purchase on an RRS.com credit card is 25 percent higher than the average for all other major credit cards. You are concerned about extending credit terms with the additional stores through the potential mall alliance. One other area you have been contemplating is how to relate your pricing strategy to that of the other stores you would become involved within the malls. Do you utilize a low margin, high volume pricing strategy? If so, how do you improve the overall profitability of the company and generate positive cash flow?

Chief Financial Officer

(only the student assigned to this role reads this page)

RRS.com has not made a profit and has incurred significant losses since it started doing business in 1995. As of July 31, 2001, RRS.com has accumulated losses of $643 million. Losses may be significantly higher in the next year because RRS.com must continue to invest in marketing, information technology, and operating infrastructure. Aggressive pricing, including meeting competitors' advertised online prices, has resulted in low gross margins on products. Current growth and pricing strategies will result in proportionately higher losses as sales increases. In addition, RRS.com has incurred significant debt totaling approximately $1.35 billion. If the company is unable to acquire additional funds through financial or stock markets, it could face serious liquidity problems. If cash flow is inadequate to meet service debt obligations, a major financial crisis and drop in stock value could occur. In addition, RRS.com cannot accurately forecast revenues and may experience significant fluctuations in operating costs.

Acquiring profitable ASMP shopping malls could decrease losses and help develop a more stable financial condition. However, even traditional shopping malls are subject to seasonality, business cycles, and increased competition. In addition, RRS.com would increase its debt from $1.35 billion to $4.35 billion in the merger. The newly merged organization would be under considerable financial pressure to service debt obligations. Any problems meeting these payments could result in default. Additional concerns relate to the fact that some of the malls are in less desirable locations within their metro markets. Trends in "urban sprawl' mean that outlying malls tend to be newer and larger than those found in downtown areas.